The Linguistic Typology of Templates

This book represents the first comprehensive examination of templatic constructions – i.e., linguistic structures involving unexpected linear stipulation – in both morphology and syntax from a typological perspective. It provides a state-of-the-art overview of the previous literature, develops a new typology for categorizing templatic constructions across grammatical domains, and examines their cross-linguistic variation by employing cutting-edge computational methods. It will be of interest to descriptive linguists seeking to gain a better sense of the diversity of the world's templatic constructions, theoretical linguists developing restrictive models of possible templates, and typologists interested in the attested range of patterns of linear stipulation and the application of new kinds of multivariate methods to cross-linguistic data. The new typological framework is illustrated in detail via a number of case studies involving languages of Africa, Europe, Asia, and the Americas, and numerous other templatic constructions are also considered over the course of the book.

JEFF GOOD is Associate Professor of Linguistics at the University at Buffalo. He is currently co-editor of *Language Dynamics and Change* and co-editor-in-chief of *Linguistics Vanguard*.

The Linguistic Typology
of Templates

Jeff Good

CAMBRIDGE
UNIVERSITY PRESS

University Printing House, Cambridge CB2 8BS, United Kingdom

One Liberty Plaza, 20th Floor, New York, NY 10006, USA

477 Williamstown Road, Port Melbourne, VIC 3207, Australia

314-321, 3rd Floor, Plot 3, Splendor Forum, Jasola District Centre, New Delhi - 110025, India

79 Anson Road, #06-04/06, Singapore 079906

Cambridge University Press is part of the University of Cambridge.

It furthers the University's mission by disseminating knowledge in the pursuit of education, learning and research at the highest international levels of excellence.

www.cambridge.org
Information on this title: www.cambridge.org/9781108707732

© Jeff Good 2016

This publication is in copyright. Subject to statutory exception
and to the provisions of relevant collective licensing agreements,
no reproduction of any part may take place without the written
permission of Cambridge University Press.

First published 2016
First paperback edition 2019

A catalogue record for this publication is available from the British Library

Library of Congress Cataloging in Publication data
Good, Jeff, author.
The linguistic typology of templates / Jeff Good.
    pages   cm
ISBN 978-1-107-01502-9 (hardback)
1. Linguistic change.   2. Typology (Linguistics)   3. Linguistic analysis (Linguistics)
I. Title.
P204.G66   2016
415.01–dc23
2015019143

ISBN   978-1-107-01502-9   Hardback
ISBN   978-1-108-70773-2   Paperback

Cambridge University Press has no responsibility for the persistence or
accuracy of URLs for external or third-party internet websites referred to in
this publication, and does not guarantee that any content on such websites is,
or will remain, accurate or appropriate.

Contents

List of figures		*page* vii
List of tables		x
Acknowledgments		xii
Glossing abbreviations		xiv
1	**Defining** *template*	1
	1.1 Templates: often invoked, but undertheorized	1
	1.2 Theoretical context of this study	4
	1.3 Templates as unexpected linearity	6
	1.4 An initial survey of template types	7
	1.5 Templates: a twice incoherent class of phenomena	22
	1.6 Wastebaskets as a tool for theory refinement	27
	1.7 Templates as analyses not "grammar"	31
	1.8 Previous work on template typology	34
	1.9 Typologizing templates	38
2	**A typological description language for templates**	40
	2.1 The language of linear stipulation	40
	2.2 Overview of the classificatory scheme	46
	2.3 Components	53
	2.4 Desmemes	65
	2.5 Additional templatic complexities	87
	2.6 Typed feature structures and templatic descriptions	92
	2.7 The nature of typologization in the present study	97
	2.8 What kind of typological results might we expect?	98
	2.9 Implementing the description language in a database	100
3	**Typologizing templates: case studies**	104
	3.1 Introduction to the case studies	104
	3.2 Turkish stems	106
	3.3 Chintang prefixes	109
	3.4 Nimboran verbs	117

vi   Contents

3.5	Four templates found in Bantu verb stems	130
3.6	Chechen Preverbal *'a*	168
3.7	Serbo-Croatian *je*	184
3.8	Serbo-Croatian topicalization	190
3.9	Aghem clauses	191
3.10	Mande clauses	197
3.11	Meskwaki clauses	203
3.12	German clauses	207
3.13	Two non-templatic desmemes in English	211
3.14	Summary of the case studies	214

4   Typologizing templates: comparison   216

4.1	Comparing templatic descriptions	216
4.2	From graphs to a similarity metric	220
4.3	Detecting similar subparts of templates	233
4.4	Exploiting the database to detect typological universals	251
4.5	The feasibility of graph-based typology	257

5   Moving forward   259

5.1	Next steps in the study of templatic constructions	259
5.2	Extending the present study	259
5.3	Explaining templates	266

Appendix   **Specification of template description language**   272

References	283
Author index	310
Language index	316
Term index	318

Figures

2.1	Overview of description language for templatic constructions	*page* 49
2.2	Overview of description language for components of templates	50
2.3	German *vc* component	61
2.4	German *mf* component	61
2.5	Graph representation of the German *mf* component	61
2.6	Bantu Applicative component	64
2.7	Graph representation of the Bantu Applicative component	64
2.8	Schematization of a span foundation	77
2.9	Schematization of an arch foundation	77
2.10	Bantu Causative–Applicative template	81
2.11	Graph representation of the Bantu Causative–Applicative template	83
2.12	Schematization of the Bantu Causative–Applicative template	84
2.13	Serbo-Croatian topicalization template	85
2.14	Graph representation of the Serbo-Croatian topicalization template	86
2.15	Schematization of the Serbo-Croatian topicalization template	87
3.1	Turkish disyllabic minimal size restriction template for nouns	108
3.2	Turkish disyllabic minimal size restriction template for verbs	109
3.3	Chintang verbal prefix template	115
3.4	A graph representation of the Chintang verbal prefix template	116
3.5	Schematization of the Chintang verbal prefix template	117
3.6	Schematization of the Nimboran verbal system following Inkelas (1993)	119
3.7	Nimboran verb template	127

viii   List of figures

3.8	Nimboran verb template restkomponenten	128
3.9	Schematization of the Nimboran verb template	129
3.10	Bantu Causative–Transitive template	137
3.11	Bantu Transitive final-positioning template	138
3.12	Schematization of the Bantu Causative–Transitive template	139
3.13	Bantu Causative–Applicative template	145
3.14	Ndebele variant of Causative–Applicative template	149
3.15	Chichewa Applicative–Reciprocal template	153
3.16	Tiene derived verb stem prosodic template	158
3.17	Tiene verb stem segmental template	161
3.18	Schematization of the two Tiene templates	162
3.19	Chechen preverbal *'a* template	182
3.20	Schematization of the Chechen Preverbal *'a* template	184
3.21	Serbo-Croatian second-position clitic template	189
3.22	Schematization of the Serbo-Croatian second-position clitic template	190
3.23	Serbo-Croatian topicalization template	192
3.24	Schematization of the Serbo-Croatian topicalization template	192
3.25	Aghem clausal template	198
3.26	Schematization of the Aghem clausal template	199
3.27	Mande clausal template	201
3.28	Schematization of the Mande clausal template	202
3.29	Meskwaki clausal structure following Dahlstrom (1993: 13)	203
3.30	Meskwaki clausal template	206
3.31	Schematization of the Meskwaki clausal template	207
3.32	German clausal template	209
3.33	Schematization of the German clausal template	211
3.34	English plural suffix as a desmeme	213
3.35	English verb phrase as a desmeme	214
4.1	German clausal template	218
4.2	Turkish disyllabic minimal size restriction template for nouns	219
4.3	A graph representation of the Tiene derived verb stem prosodic template	222
4.4	Schematic graphs for illustrating simUI graph comparison method	224
4.5	Split graph for similarity among templates, including components	229

	List of figures	ix

4.6	Split graph for similarity among templates, excluding components	232
4.7	First schematic graph to illustrate pairwise connectivity	235
4.8	Second schematic graph to illustrate pairwise connectivity	235
4.9	Pairwise connectivity graph for the graphs in Figures 4.7 and 4.8	237
4.10	Transformation of the pairwise connectivity graph in Figure 4.9 for flooding	239
4.11	The Chechen template in Figure 3.19 as a graph	245
4.12	The Mande template in Figure 3.27 as a graph	246
4.13	The Aghem template in Figure 3.25 as a graph	248

Tables

1.1	A pan-Athabaskan verbal template (Hoijer 1971: 125)	*page* 2
1.2	A Japanese nickname template (Poser 1990)	2
1.3	CV templates in Sierra Miwok (Freeland 1951: 94)	10
1.4	German topological fields (Kathol 2000: 78)	18
1.5	Layered vs. templatic morphology adapted from Simpson & Withgott (1986: 156)	36
2.1	Causative verb forms in Tiene (Hyman 2010a: 147–148)	42
2.2	German topological fields (Kathol 2000: 78)	60
2.3	CV templates in Sierra Miwok (Freeland 1951: 94)	67
2.4	Causative verb forms in Tiene (Hyman 2010a: 147–148)	67
2.5	Turkish stem minimality and ineffability	70
2.6	Ndebele stem minimality and insertion repair	72
3.1	Turkish stem minimality	107
3.2	Causative verb forms in Tiene	155
3.3	Applicative verb forms in Tiene	156
3.4	Stative verb forms in Tiene	156
3.5	Alternation in the realization of the Chechen Copy Infinitive (Conathan & Good 2001: 54)	176
4.1	Pairwise distances among examined templates, including component nodes	226
4.2	Pairwise distances among examined templates, excluding component nodes	231
4.3	Application of four iterations of similarity flooding procedure	241
4.4	Similarity scores for the Chechen (Figure 4.11) and Mande (Figure 4.12) templates	244
4.5	Similarity scores for the Aghem (Figure 4.13) and Mande (Figure 4.12) templates	249
4.6	Extraction of select features across the templates in the database	252

4.7	Predictability scores across different templatic features	254
4.8	Predictability scores across different templatic features without potential artifacts	255
A.1	Conventions used to describe the database ontology	272

Acknowledgments

The ideas leading up to this work have been developing for well over a decade, making it difficult to properly acknowledge the full range of individuals and funding sources that have made it possible. Its origins lie in my 2003 University of California, Berkeley, Ph.D. dissertation, "Strong linearity: Three case studies towards a theory of morphosyntactic templatic constructions," where I first attempted to grapple with the issues raised by devising a typology of templatic constructions that was not limited to morphological domains. Therefore, all who were acknowledged in that work deserve acknowledgment here as well, and, rather than repeat that list, I will simply single out my committee members, Larry Hyman, Johanna Nichols, and Andrew Garrett. The influence of each can be felt here in a wide range of ways.

The specific direction this book has taken was profoundly impacted by my time in the Department of Linguistics at the Max Planck Institute for Evolutionary Anthropology in Leipzig. It was there that I was able to become familiar with cutting-edge developments in linguistic typology, and I would like to single out, in particular, Balthasar Bickel (then based at the University of Leipzig), Michael Cysouw, and Martin Haspelmath for discussions which greatly informed the approach adopted here. Bernard Comrie also deserves special thanks for his role in creating such a congenial department, where new ideas about typology could be nurtured and more fully developed. During part of this same period, I also worked for the Rosetta Project (run by the Long Now Foundation) on efforts to migrate its database from a table-based format to an RDF one, and many of the skills I obtained in doing that work were put to direct use in developing the database discussed in the pages below. Those activities were funded by US National Science Foundation Award no. 0333727.

In addition, aspects of this research were developed during two graduate seminars at the University at Buffalo, and I received useful feedback from talks presented at various venues, especially at the Association for Linguistic Typology conferences in Berkeley in 2009 and Leipzig in 2013. Additional useful feedback has come from Sebastian Nordhoff as well as a number of anonymous reviewers. The majority of the text of this book was written during a sabbatical leave sponsored by the University at Buffalo in 2013. Finally, I am not sure this book ever would have seen the light of day without the encouragement of Helen Barton at Cambridge University Press.

Glossing abbreviations

Language and family names are included for glossing categories whose interpretation is especially language dependent. Where possible, glossing conventions follow the Leipzig Glossing Rules (Bickel et al. 2008).

&	preverbal conjunctive enclitic (Chechen)
>	(person) on (person)
1–10 (not followed by s/p)	noun class (Bantu)
1, 2, 3 (followed by s/p)	first, second, third person
3'	third person obviative (Meskwaki)
A	agent (Mohawk)
	actor (Chintang)
	"A" nominal form (Aghem)
ACC	accusative
ADV	adverbial suffix
AOR	aorist
APPL	applicative
AUX	auxiliary verb
B	gender category (Chechen)
	"B" nominal form (Aghem)
CAUS	causative
CLF	classifier (Ahtna)
COND	conditional
CVANT	anterior converb (Chechen)
CVSIM	simultaneous converb (Chechen)
CVTEMP	temporal converb (Chechen)
D	gender category (Chechen)
DAT	dative
	dative case
DIM	diminutive
DPST	distant past

Glossing abbreviations

DS	dummy subject (Aghem)
DU	dual
DUALIC	dualic (Mohawk)
DUR	durative
DX	deictic prefix (Chechen)
ERG	ergative
FEM	feminine
FOC	focus marker
FUT	future
FV	final vowel (Bantu)
GEN	genitive
INAN	inanimate
INCL	inclusive
INDP	independent conjugation (Meskwaki)
INF	infinitive
IPFV	imperfective
IRR	irrealis converb (Chechen)
ITER	iterative
J	gender category (Chechen)
LAT	lative case (Chechen)
LOC	locative
M	masculine
NEG	negative
NEG1	negative affix (Ahtna)
NEG2	negative affix (Ahtna)
NEG3	negative affix (Ahtna)
NOM	nominative case
NS	non-singular
NZ	nominalizer
O2	second object (Meskwaki)
OBJ	object
OBV	obviative
OPT	optative
PCL	proclitic (Meskwaki)
PFV	perfective
PFX	prefix
PM	predicate marker (Mande)
POSS	possessive
POSTP	postposition
PROG	progressive
PRS	present
PRT	particle

xvi   Glossing abbreviations

PST   past
PTCP   participle
QUAL   qualifier (Ahtna)
RECP   reciprocal
REFL   reflexive
RPT   repetitive
RR   relative root (Meskwaki)
S   "S" perfective-negative (Ahtna)
SBJ   subject
SM   subject marker (Aghem)
SONG   defective root with form *song* (Kinande)
STAT   stative
THM   thematic prefix (Ahtna)
TRANS   transitive (Bantu)
V   gender category (Chechen)
VSF1   verbal suffix (Ahtna)
VSF2   verbal suffix (Ahtna)
WP   witnessed past (Chechen)
YI   stabilizing prefix with form *yi* (Ndebele)

1 Defining *template*

1.1 Templates: often invoked, but undertheorized

The notion of a *template* has been used in a number of linguistic domains to refer to grammatical patterns where the form of some linguistic constituent appears to be well conceptualized as consisting of a fixed linear structure, whether in terms of the arrangement of its subconstituents or its overall length.[1] To take two examples, consider Table 1.1, which schematizes the ordering of morphemes in verbs across the Athabaskan family, and Table 1.2, which gives data illustrating the application of a particular nickname formation strategy in Japanese where the resulting nicknames must be bimoraic in length.

The pan-Athabaskan template described in Table 1.1 characterizes verbs in this family as consisting of a series of "slots" into which morphemes of different grammatically defined classes appear. Hoijer (1971) did not explicitly use the word *template* to characterize his analysis, though this term is often found in the Athabaskanist literature to describe the verbal system (see, e.g., Rice (2000: 9)). Section 1.3 will discuss, in detail, the issue of how we might rigorously define *template*, but at this point, it will be sufficient to say that the crucial feature of Hoijer's analysis which prompts the application of the label is that the linear order of these verbal morphemes is treated as grammatically stipulated rather than deriving from some general principle. As such, the use of the term seems to be an extension of its informal use as referring to a device which sets a pattern on the basis of which objects of a given kind can be constructed.

Poser (1990: 81) does explicitly use the word *template* to describe the pattern exemplified in Table 1.2, wherein a full name participating in this nickname construction in Japanese must be realized as bimoraic either via truncation of a longer name (e.g., *hanako* → *hana-*) or lengthening of a shorter name (e.g., *ti* → *tii-*), among other possibilities (see Mester (1990) for additional discussion of the templatic properties of Japanese nicknames). What makes this pattern templatic is the fact that a particular morphological constituent must be of a specific length regardless of what its length would be expected

---

[1] Good (2011) gives an overview of the typology of templates which summarizes some of the key points made in this chapter, as well as other parts of this book.

2   Defining *template*

Table 1.1 *A pan-Athabaskan verbal template (Hoijer 1971: 125)*

SLOT	DESCRIPTION
1	Zero, one or more adverbial prefixes.
2	The prefix for the iterative paradigm.
3	A pluralizing prefix.
4	An object pronoun prefix.
5	A deictic subject prefix.
6	Zero, one or two adverbial prefixes.
7	A prefix marking mode, tense, or aspect.
8	A subject pronoun prefix.
9	A classifier prefix.
10	A stem.

Table 1.2 *A Japanese nickname template (Poser 1990)*

NAME	NICKNAME
hanako	*hana-tyan*
yukiko	*yuki-tyan*
akira	*aki-tyan*
taroo	*taro-tyan*
yooko	*yoo-tyan*
kazuhiko	*kazu-tyan*
ti	*tii-tyan*
tiemi	*tii-tyan*

to be on the basis of its lexical segmental specification. Again, the use of the term is an extension of the informal sense of template to refer to a general "foundational" pattern, though, in this case, the relevant pattern is a restriction on length rather than order, as seen in Table 1.1.

At first glance, the juxtaposition of the data in Tables 1.1 and 1.2, each exemplifying apparently quite different kinds of grammatical phenomena, might be taken to suggest that the word *template* has been applied to such a heterogenous range of patterns as to make a detailed exploration of what it means to be a "template" a questionable enterprise. After all, a morphophonological size restriction does not obviously have very much in common with a morphosyntactic ordering restriction. Nevertheless, a leading idea of this book is that there is a common thread linking a wide number of apparently disparate kinds of templates that makes examining them together an exercise of clear typological and theoretical significance. In particular, we will see that a detailed

1.1 Templates: often invoked, but undertheorized 3

exploration of "templates" can give us important insights into the nature of linearization in language and can reveal important gaps in our models of how linguistic units come to form linearly ordered and bounded constituents.

Even if some readers ultimately reject the idea that it is sensible to treat the wide range of patterns to be examined here in one place, this book will nevertheless offer a more detailed basis on which to make these arguments since, to the best of my knowledge, the present work is novel in even attempting to examine the extent to which "templates" may represent a unified phenomenon.[2] If nothing else, therefore, the discussion here can be construed as a detailed exploration of a linguistic concept that descriptive linguists have long found valuable despite widespread ambivalence about its status in linguistic theory.

However, my intention is for this book to represent quite a bit more. As will be made clear over subsequent chapters, consideration of "templates" forces us to confront broader questions of the typology of linear stipulation in grammars. This, in turn, will require the construction of new ways of classifying linguistic constructions, and these will themselves require consideration of methods of comparison for characterizations of structural descriptions that have yet to be used within linguistics. Thus, what begins with a juxtaposition of curiosities like those exemplified in Tables 1.1 and 1.2 will develop into something which I hope will be of interest for a wide range of reasons and even to readers who might not be particularly interested in templates in and of themselves.

This chapter will begin by focusing on how we might rigorously define the term *template*, drawing on phonological, morphophonological, morphosyntactic, and syntactic analyses of "templatic" phenomena. The definition that will be ultimately arrived at is first anticipated in Section 1.3, which will be followed by a survey of existing work on templatic patterns in Section 1.4. An examination of various conceptual and practical issues surrounding the study of templates will then be taken up in the remaining sections of the chapter.

This will then set the stage for subsequent chapters of the book which will offer a new kind of typological description language for patterns of linear stipulation of the sort associated with morphophonological, morphosyntactic, and syntactic templates (Chapter 2), a number of case studies illustrating the application of the description language (Chapter 3), and a demonstration of how the framework developed here can permit rigorous typological comparison of templatic constructions (Chapter 4). The book will then conclude with an outline of how this work could be expanded into a large-scale typological comparison of intricate patterns of linearization. This will include brief consideration of theoretical issues relating to templates which are clearly of interest but outside the focus of the main discussion (Chapter 5).

---

[2] Good (2003b, 2007b, 2011) also takes a similar approach.

4   Defining *template*

Before moving onto any these topics, however, it will first be important to clarify the theoretical context that will inform the discussion throughout, which is the subject of the next section.

1.2   Theoretical context of this study

The grammatical subject matter of this book is a very special kind of linguistic form, the linearization template, and the analytical approach to be introduced in Chapter 2 will be "formal" in the sense that it will introduce a formalism for describing different kinds of linear stipulation in a relatively precise way. However, the term *formal* has taken on a range of uses in theoretical linguistics. It is therefore important to make clear that this work is not an instance of "formal linguistics" in its commonly employed sense to refer to linguistic work adopting a theoretical orientation that emphasizes, among other things, the delineation of a universal grammar and the encoding of analyses in a formal model based directly on that delineation (see, e.g., Newmeyer (1998: 7–9), Dryer (2006: 223), Nichols (2007b), and ten Hacken (2007: 217) for relevant discussion).

At the same time, the overall theoretical perspective adopted in this book is one that could be labeled *typological*, but this term, too, must be appropriately qualified. No universals will be proposed, and no systematic genealogically balanced survey has been undertaken. In short, this work will not – and is not designed to – develop a set of typological "results" that can become the basis for new theoretical models of grammar. Instead, the primary concern of this book is devising the methodological foundations through which we might systematically discover the range and nature of variation in templatic (and related) constructions. Indeed, one of its central claims is that designing a rigorous means to compare templatic constructions is far from trivial and can only be successfully achieved by enhancing existing methods in multivariate typology (see Bickel (2010)), a kind of methodology which itself has only recently been properly developed (see Section 2.7 for further discussion).

This orientation may be disappointing, and even confusing, to some readers, especially those more accustomed to generative approaches to the analysis of linguistic phenomena. This is because *explanation*, in particular, is not a key concern of this book. Rather, it is focused on the development of a system of explicit *description* and rigorous *comparison*. In the ideal case, the means used to create the relevant descriptions and the methods used for comparison will further allow for the creation of replicable results (see Chappell (2006) for relevant discussion in a typological context). This approach is taken here not because explanation is considered to be unimportant, but, rather, because, in this context, attempts at explanation would seem to be premature (though Chapter 5 will contain some speculation in this regard). There has, to this point,

1.2 Theoretical context of this study

only been something approaching systematic investigation of templates in one grammatical domain, morphophonology (see Section 1.8.2). It would, therefore, seem ill-advised to try to theorize on the general properties of templates before we even have a common language to talk about them. The discussion in Chapter 2 will hopefully make clearer why this work takes an apparent step "backwards" in its goals in focusing more on a "taxonomic, data processing approach" (Chomsky 1965: 52) than on one which promises to be more "explanatory" (see also Joos (1958: v)).[3]

For those readers who are more familiar with the showcase results of typological investigation, for example, the establishment of the famous "Greenbergian" patterns of word order (see, e.g., Dryer (2007)), as opposed to the methods of typology, as practiced by "typologists," Bickel (2007) and Nichols (2007b) contain discussion that should make the general approach assumed in this book clearer. In particular, this work should be understood as exploring the problem of templates at the "hypothesis-raising" stage, starting with a "convenience sample," rather than the "hypothesis-testing" stage (Nichols 2007b: 234), and it attempts to achieve this goal by "developing sets of variables" rather than serving as another "method used in U[niversal] G[rammar] research" (Bickel 2007: 242). This approach can be contrasted with that advocated by Baker & McCloskey (2007), which is more concerned with how certain kinds of cross-linguistic investigation that are sometimes given the label "typological" can provide important data for refining universalist-oriented theories.

Adopting such an orientation means that this work may appear to be more clearly aligned with "functional" approaches to linguistics rather than more "formal" approaches (at least in the caricatured senses of the terms described by Newmeyer (1998: 1–5)). However, this distinction, is not, in fact, clearly relevant at the level of investigation of templates found here. This is because our understanding of templates, across phonology, morphology, and syntax, is, in my view, not even at the point where the oppositions between such approaches even matter. We do not yet know how to coherently talk about templates, let alone know how to determine if their properties support one broad theoretical stance over another.

Indeed, while future work on this topic may argue for the adoption of one or the other of these perspectives in the analysis of templates, the present book, while far from atheoretical (as will be clear in Chapter 2), is intended to be

---

[3] Anonymous reviews of the work leading up to this book have, at times, been sharply divided: For some reviewers, the need for the approach assumed in this work seems immediately obvious. Different reviewers seem to think of it as essentially misguided. I believe that this opposition is most likely the result of some linguists, especially those identifying as "typologists," seeing more value in work which aims for "mere" descriptive adequacy, while others believe that it is more important to focus, from the outset, on explanatory adequacy.

6   Defining *template*

agnostic on most of those issues which animate debates between proponents of major linguistic theories today. This follows from my own conviction that quite a lot of theoretical groundwork needs to be laid before more "interesting" debates about templates, and other forms of linear stipulation, can be usefully conducted.

Before moving on, there is another issue regarding the broad theoretical context of this study that is worth remarking on, since it is also likely to be somewhat novel to many readers. A key feature of the analytical point of view adopted in here is that grammatical patterns of linear stipulation may involve richly articulated structures of interacting elements which can be categorized across a number of distinctive dimensions. Indeed, the structures that will be proposed here to characterize linear stipulation (see, e.g., Chapters 2 and 3), in many respects, have a degree of complexity more typically seen in the representation of syntactic constructions. Linearization patterns, by contrast, are too often treated as representable in the simple form of strings which are primarily manipulated by a single operation, namely concatenation. Suffice it to say that, here, the representational device of the string is considered inadequate for properly capturing patterns of linear stipulation, and the case studies in Chapter 3, in particular, can be considered an implicit argument for this position. Of course, the idea that there is more to linear stipulation than the assemblage of strings is not especially innovative, as it has long been a mainstay of phonological theory (see, e.g., Section 1.8.2 for relevant discussion in the present context). However, the syntactic literature, in particular, often seems to adopt the view (whether implicitly or explicitly) that strings, representing words and concatenations of words, are a more or less adequate means for representing the surface linearization patterns of grammatical structures, a view which is seen as overly simplistic here (see also Section 5.3.1).

1.3   Templates as unexpected linearity

The term *template* has been applied to phenomena in a number of distinct grammatical domains (e.g., phonology, morphology, and syntax) in the linguistics literature and has also been used informally in fairly distinct ways. This is, at least partly, due to the fact that the word has a non-technical sense that has allowed it to be extended to a wide range of phenomena, some of which clearly have little in common with each other. Here, I delimit the possible range of phenomena to be examined to descriptive or formal schemes primarily employed to characterize constraints on linear realization, whether in terms of order (as in Table 1.1), length (as in Table 1.2), or some combination of the two (as in Table 1.3, to be further discussed in Section 1.4.2).[4] This

---

[4] The opposition between templatic restrictions involving ordering or length developed here is anticipated by Mester's (1990) distinction between "mapping" and "delimiting" templates.

delimitation is based on a consideration of the term as found in diverse sources, including Simpson & Withgott (1986), Itô (1989), Kari (1989), Zec & Inkelas (1990), Inkelas (1993), Stump (1997), Van Valin & LaPolla (1997), Rice (2000), and Downing (2006). It has, therefore, been arrived at via a descriptive examination rather than intending to be a prescriptive statement, which will have consequences for the development of a formal model of templatic restrictions in Chapter 2. An important point for later discussion is that, having arrived at this informal delineation, this study will also examine phenomena that fall within it even if the word *template* has not been specifically used to describe them (see, e.g., Section 1.4.5 for a clear example).

I give the actual definition of *template* that will be assumed in this work in (1). Much of the rest of this chapter will be devoted to its justification.

(1) **Template:** An analytical device used to characterize the linear realization of a linguistic constituent whose linear stipulations are unexpected from the point of view of a given linguist's approach to linguistic analysis.

This definition highlights two key features of templates (i) that they involve linear stipulation and (ii) that they can only be understood with respect to what kinds of linear stipulation are considered "normal" within a given approach to linguistic analysis. It should immediately be clear that, if one assumes a definition like that in (1), the apparent subjectivity of linking the term to a given linguist's expectations regarding linearity makes it problematic as a basis on which to conduct a rigorous investigation. I will come back to this issue in Section 1.5.

A final aspect of the definition worth noting is that a template is treated here not as a feature of the grammar of a given language but, rather, as a device used to analyze a given set of grammatical patterns. This is because we cannot easily speak of templates without referring to a given linguist's analysis of the linearization of a grammatical constituent. This issue will be discussed in detail in Section 1.7.

1.4 An initial survey of template types

1.4.1 Templates in phonology, morphology, and syntax

The focus of this section is consideration of representative examples of work on templates across morphophonology (Section 1.4.2), morphosyntax (Section 1.4.3), phonology (Section 1.4.4), and syntax (Section 1.4.5). Section 1.4.5 will also discuss the possibility of templates in the domain of phonosyntax. I begin with the two types of morphological templates since they have

8   Defining *template*

played a more prominent role in the literature than the other two types to be considered. In Section 1.4.6, there will be brief discussions of cases where the word template has been used in the linguistic literature to refer to phenomena which are not of primary interest here and which deviate from the more common use of the term to refer to structures involving apparent linear stipulation. In some cases, the works to be discussed below do not explicitly use the word template to describe their analyses of the relevant phenomena. Nevertheless, the conceptual relationship between patterns frequently labeled templatic and these other patterns is clear enough to make it important to examine them here as well.

As will be seen, the overview of template types makes use of qualifications of the term, describing, for example, a given template as *morphophonological* or *phonological*. These terms are adopted here for expository convenience, rather than reflecting a particular analytical tradition, and the senses of these terms, as developed below, should not be expected to automatically carry over into other literature on templates. A good example of this can be found in Vihman & Croft (2007) who apply the term template to patterns which they characterize as phonological but which, here, would be better characterized as morphophonological, since the relevant constraints apply at the level of the word, rather than a purely phonological unit.

One of the distinguishing features of this study, as opposed to previous work on templates, is its attention to apparently templatic phenomena across grammatical domains in order to see what, if anything, they may have in common. Such "cross-domain" studies of grammatical patterns are not typical to the field, especially in work which conceptualizes grammar in terms of "modules" and "interfaces" (see Ramchand & Reiss (2007) for overview discussion). However, this is necessitated here for two reasons. First, templates themselves have been invoked across domains. It may be that this is due to infelicitous conceptual conflation, but we will not be able to determine if this is the case without first trying to see if these different "templates" may have something in common (and, as we will see in Section 1.5, they do appear to). Second, analytical invocations of templates are invariably bound to the problem of how to account for the linearization patterns of grammatical constituents, which itself is clearly a cross-domain issue insofar as accounting for patterns of linearization is a central concern of phonology, morphology, and syntax.

Moreover, even if problems of "linearization" are not usually modeled as belonging to a single "component" or "module" (though see Sadock (2012: 111–146)), there is clearly something component-like to linearization's interaction with other domains of grammatical generalization insofar as there are common features of linear ordering relations in phonology, morphology and syntax. The "primacy" of linearization, in this regard, is not frequently emphasized in my experience, though this observation is not particularly novel.

1.4 An initial survey of template types

For instance, immediately after introducing his famous first principle regarding the arbitrary nature of the linguistic sign, Saussure gives a second principle regarding the "linear nature of the signifier", stating that, while it "is obvious, apparently linguists have always neglected to state it, doubtless because they found it too simple; nevertheless, it is fundamental, and its consequences are incalculable. Its importance equals that of Principle I; the whole mechanism of language depends upon it..." (Saussure 1916/1959: 70).

Before moving on, it is important to stress here an issue that will be returned to at various points below: the characterization of a given pattern as templatic is the product of a particular linguistic analysis. Therefore, analytical disagreements can easily lead to one work treating a given pattern as being best explained by a template, while another would reject the need for a template, or at least a highly elaborated one. Perhaps the clearest example of this in the literature involves contrasting analyses of the Athabaskan verbal system as exemplified by Kari (1989, 1992) and Rice (2000) (see also Hargus & Tuttle (2003)), wherein the former adheres to the sort of templatic approach schematized in Table 1.1, while the latter devises an alternative analysis that attempts to avoid the use of templates for languages of this family (see Section 1.4.3 for further discussion). I will return to the significance of this general issue in Section 1.7, and it will also play a role in the discussion in Chapters 2 and 3.

1.4.2   Morphophonological templates

By *morphophonological template*, I refer to templatic analyses where the linear realization of the components of a morphological construction is described in terms of constraints involving phonological categories. The most famous templatic constructions of this type are almost certainly so-called CV "skeleton" templates (Halle & Vergnaud 1980: 84), familiar in particular from Semitic morphology, where the order of consonants and vowels in a given morphological category apparently needs to be stated separately from the order of the consonants and vowels of its constituent lexical items. Work done by McCarthy (1979, 1981) is generally considered foundational for the contemporary analysis of these patterns, though earlier treatments can also be found (see Ussishkin (2000: 5)). (See Broselow (1995: 180–182) for an overview in the context of generative phonology.)

An example of this type of template can be seen in Table 1.3, which gives data from Sierra Miwok, a Penutian language of California, adapted from Freeland (1951: 94). Smith (1985) gives an early application of a CV-skeleton analysis to Sierra Miwok, based on the descriptions of Broadbent (1964) and Freeland (1951) (see also Goldsmith (1990: 83–95).

The data in Table 1.3 exemplifies the four stem shapes associated with verbs of a particular inflectional class (Freeland's "type I") in Sierra Miwok. The

10 Defining *template*

Table 1.3 *CV templates in Sierra Miwok (Freeland 1951: 94)*

PRIMARY	SECOND	THIRD	FOURTH	GLOSS
tuyá:ŋ	tuyáŋ:	túy:aŋ	túyŋa	'jump'
polá:ŋ	poláŋ:	pól:aŋ	pólŋa	'fall'
ṭopó:n	ṭopón:	ṭóp:on	ṭópno	'wrap'
huṭé:l	huṭél:	húṭ:el	húṭle	'roll'
telé:y	teléy:	tél:ey	télye	'hear'
CVCV:C	CVCVC:	CVC:VC	CVCCV	

alternations among these stem forms are governed by the suffix (e.g., a tense suffix) which immediately follows the stem (Freeland 1951: 96). As indicated in the bottom of row of the table, these alternations can be schematized via patterns of consonants and vowels (including indication of length). The forms of the stems across each stem class make use of the same consonant and vowels, in the same relative order respectively, but the lengths of the consonants and vowels change and the positioning of the consonants and vowels with respect to each other can change (as can be seen by contrasting the Fourth stem with the other three stems). Freeland (1951) does not explicitly give the CV patterns indicated in Table 1.3, though these are easily derived from her description. In the present context, it is noteworthy, that, while the templates illustrated above in Section 1.1 primarily exemplified restrictions involving order (Table 1.1) *or* length (Table 1.2), the Sierra Miwok CV template describes restrictions of both order and length. The two classes of restrictions are not, in principle, mutually exclusive, and I will return to this issue in Sections 2.4.4 and 2.5.

What prompts the use of the label *template* (see, e.g., McCarthy (1981: 387)) for a pattern like the one exemplified in Table 1.3 is the fact that a word's CV-patterning is generally expected to be derivative of a fixed linear specification of its morphemes' segmental patterns. For example, in an English word like *cat*, the fact that it shows a CVC shape can be straightforwardly treated as an epiphenomenon of fact that it has a segmental specification /kæt/, which simply happens to consist of a consonant followed by a vowel.followed by another consonant. Accounting for a pattern like that seen in Table 1.3, by contrast, requires an additional analytical device – in this case a morphophonological template. What makes this template *morphophonological*, in the sense of the term as understood here, is that the morphological construction of the stem is subject to constraints characterized in terms of phonological categories, namely consonants and vowels.

Table 1.2, discussed in Section 1.1, offers another example of a morphophonological template, in that case one involving a restriction solely in terms

1.4 An initial survey of template types

of phonological size. Specifically, roots in a particular morphological construction are obligatorily bimoraic, forcing either truncation or lengthening of the root as compared to its lexical form. Comparable phenomena are frequently found in partial reduplication constructions, which have also been given templatic analyses (see, e.g., Hayes & Abad (1989), McCarthy & Prince (1996), and Hendricks (1999: 15–29)). Further cases of morphophonological templates will be discussed in Chapters 2 and 3.

Morphophonological templates have seen much more attention in the theoretical linguistic literature than any of the other classes of templates discussed here, in particular in the context of research into "prosodic morphology" within generative phonology (see, e.g., McCarthy & Prince (1995, 1996) and Downing (2006), among many others), and they have been employed not only as tools for synchronic analysis but also for modelling language change (Davis & Napoli 1994). In the present context, a particularly interesting aspect of this line of research is the fact that, in addition to producing detailed analyses of a number of apparently templatic phenomena, it has also been associated with a restrictive theory of templatic form making strong typological predictions, as will be discussed in Section 1.8.2.

An important feature of the theoretical linguistic literature on morphophonological templates is the fact that, at least for quite some time, templates were considered valid – and even, to some extent, explanatory – analytical devices and additionally played a prominent role in refining phonological theory generally, in particular within generative phonology (see, e.g., Urbanczyk (1996: 1–20) and Ussishkin (2005: 169–173)). While recent theoretical work has offered non-templatic analyses for phenomena that had been previously analyzed by means of morphophonological templates (see, e.g., Hendricks (1999: 39–59), Urbanczyk (2006: 182), and Ussishkin (2005: 172)), at least some of these developments can be cast as following a "positive" analytical progression wherein a more detailed understanding of the relevant cross-linguistic patterns permitted less stipulative analyses over time (Downing 2006: 134) (though see Rose (2003: 92) for a contrasting viewpoint partly responding to this trend). Because of this, for the most part, such work is quite useful in revealing a range of interesting templatic patterns regardless of one's theoretical orientation. Indeed, it would seem reasonable to say that some of the best typological work on templatic constructions done to date emanates from the generative phonological tradition, and many of its insights will be adapted here to the extent possible given the very different theoretical context assumed in this work (see Section 1.2). As will be discussed in Section 1.4.3, the use of templates as an analytical device in theoretical work analyzing morphosyntactic phenomena has not seen the same acceptance as within morphophonology, a point that will be returned to in Section 1.6.

12   Defining *template*

Because of both a lack of research and a lack of expertise, templatic phenomena in sign languages will not receive treatment in this book, though given that templates are intimately linked to the modality-dependent problem of linearization, it is clear that, even if our only goal was to understand the typology of templates in spoken languages, such efforts would be greatly enhanced by the availability of extensive detailed analyses of template-like phenomena in sign languages for comparative purposes. The literature on sign languages does contain some discussion of how templates can be used to analyze linearization patterns found within them, applying, in particular, insights from work in morphophonology of the sort just described in order to account for restrictions on the realization of morphological signs that can be characterized in phonological terms (see, e.g., Perlmutter (1992: 436), Corina & Sandler (1993: 187), Brentari (2005), and Sandler & Lillo-Martin (2006: 51–60, 139–143)). I am not aware of work on templates in sign languages in further grammatical domains other than research employing so-called syllable templates in the analysis of sign language phenomena (see Section 1.4.4) and, possibly, research on "templated" representations as well (see Section 1.4.6).

1.4.3   Morphosyntactic templates

By *morphosyntactic template*, I refer to analyses of templates where the linear realization of a morphological construction's components is described in terms of stipulated constraints on elements characterized via morphosyntactic or morphosemantic categories like *agreement* or *tense* affix. Languages making use of elaborate morphosyntactic templates are sometimes treated as making use of *position classes* (see, e.g., Anderson (1992: 131), Stump (1993, 2001: 138–139), Mel'čuk (1997: 159)) or *slot-filler* morphology (see, e.g., McDonough (2000a: 157–160)). Such templates have been placed into the class of *significantia artificialiter* by Simpson & Withgott (1986: 173) – that is, a kind of constructive signifier – following the use of the term by Jakobson & Waugh (1979: 30) (which they, in turn, attribute to Thomas Aquinas) to characterize phonemes, a class of grammatical elements which lack associations with meaning in their own right, but allow for the construction of signifiers. In the context of morphosyntactic templates, they characterize the structure of these *significantia artificialiter* as "members of a species whose meaning is conveyed with the grammatical device of relative, oppositive, and potentially empty slots" (Simpson & Withgott 1986: 173).[5]

On the basis of Simpson & Withgott (1986) (discussed in Section 1.8.3 further below), it has been common to propose an opposition between layered

---

[5] The tagmemic approach to linguistic analysis associated with Pike (1967) also employs the notion of *slot* in a comparable way, though not restricting it to morphology (see, e.g., Pike (1967: 218–222)). As Russell G. Schuh has pointed out to me, this approach can be considered

1.4 An initial survey of template types

morphology (associated with hierarchical structure) and template morphology (associated with a "flat" structure) in morphosyntax. (See Stump (2006) for a recent summary overview, Stump (1997) for a more critical appraisal, and Manova & Aronoff (2010) and Rice (2011) for recent surveys on principles of affix ordering, an issue of relevance to establishing the presence or absence of articulated morphological structure.) Inkelas (1993: 560) gives a concise characterization of these kinds of templates as involving cases where "morphemes or morpheme classes are organized into a total linear ordering that has no apparent connection to syntactic, semantic, or even phonological representation." Templates of this kind are usually labeled *morphological* rather than *morphosyntactic*, reflecting the fact that they involve restrictions on word structure. The choice of label used here is intended to clarify the way in which templates of this kind are distinct from morphophonological templates as discussed in Section 1.4.2.

Two examples of structures that have been taken to exemplify morphosyntactic templates are given in (2) and (3). The example in (2) gives the templatic analysis assigned to an Ahtna (Athabaskan) verb by Kari (1989). The examples in (3) support a templatic analysis offered by Hyman (2003c) (see also Good (2005)) of the order of a pair of valency-changing suffixes in Chichewa (Bantu). These two examples are meant to be illustrative of the more complex end of proposed morphosyntactic templates (2) and the less complex end (3).

(2) na_{10A}-gh_{4A}-i_{3D}-z_{3D}-i_2-$ł_1$-$niik_{ROOT}$-$\emptyset_{VSF1}$-e_{VSF2} → *naghiziłniige*
THM-QUAL-IPFV.NEG1-S-2s-CLF-feel-IPFV.NEG2-IPFV.NEG3
"you have not yet found a fabric-like object"   (Kari 1989: 441)

(3)   a. *Alenjé   a-ku-líl-íts-il-a*   *mwaná ndodo.*
          2.hunter 2-PROG-cry-CAUS-APPL-FV 1.child 10.sticks
          "The hunters are [making [the child cry] with sticks]."
      b. *Alenjé   a-ku-tákás-its-il-a*   *mkází   mthíko.*
          2.hunter 2-PROG-stir-CAUS-APPL-FV 1.woman 9.spoon
          "The hunters are [making [the woman stir with a spoon]]."
          (Hyman 2003c: 248)

The example in (2) gives a morphological analysis of an Ahtna verb wherein it is treated as consisting of nine morphemes, each assigned a specific position class (indicated with a subscript label) in the highly elaborated template described in detail in Kari (1989, 1990). The template is derived from the same analytical tradition as that seen in Table 1.1, though it contains many more

the most templatic general theory of grammar that has been developed. Its relative marginalization in the structurally oriented linguistic tradition, however, makes it hard to assess its relationship to other work on templates.

14   Defining *template*

positions (around thirty) and also adopts a right-to-left numbering convention beginning with the verb root, reflecting the fact that most of the morphology is prefixal (though the root is also followed by several suffixal positions). What makes the analysis in (2) templatic is the fact that these position classes are treated as basic units of analysis that are, moreover, discovered by examining constraints on morpheme linearization (Kari 1989: 434–437), rather than, say, semantic function. While there are potential complications (such as the presence of positions possibly allowing more than one "filler" element, as seen in Table 1.1), the canonical position class in this type of analysis is one that can only be filled by a single element, resulting in a complementarity of appearance of the morphemes associated with that position, even if their co-occurrence would otherwise be expected to be semantically or morphosyntactically compatible. In other words, the template, in effect, overrides the surfacing of expressions that would otherwise be thought to be present. A more detailed example of this type of templatic system will be presented in Section 3.4.

The data in (3) illustrates a much simpler morphosyntactic template which can be reduced to constraints on the relative order of morphemes when they happen to co-occur. In this case, the morphemes of interest are the Causative and Applicative in Chichewa, each of which increases the valency of a verb. The Causative adds causative semantics to the verb, including the introduction of an agent of the caused action, and the Applicative allows the verb to be realized with a second object argument without the need for adpositional marking. In the examples in (3), the additional object arguments are the instruments *ndodo* 'sticks' and *mthíko* 'spoon.' The important descriptive generalization illustrated by the data in (3) is that, despite the fact that (3a) and (3b) show different scopal interpretations for causativization with respect to applicativization, each meaning is expressed with the same Causative–Applicative morpheme order. In (3a), applicativization has scope over causativization, giving a reading where the introduced instrument is used by the causer *alenjé* 'hunters,' while, in (3b), causativization has scope over applicativization, giving a reading where the instrument is used by the causee *mkází* 'woman.' As discussed in detail in Hyman (2003c), what makes this pattern templatic is the fact that the order of the suffixes is apparently fixed by the morphology rather than being determined by some more general principle. More detailed examination of this and related templatic patterns in Bantu languages will be presented in Section 3.5.

Morphosyntactic templates have been a widely employed device in descriptive work for decades, especially for North American languages. Further examples can be found in: Lounsbury (1953: 18–20, 45, 71, 73, 89) for Oneida (Iroquoian), Bloomfield (1962: 101–111) for Menomini (Algonquian), McLendon (1975: 77–78) for Eastern Pomo (Hokan), Kimball (1991: 113)

1.4 An initial survey of template types

for Koasati (Muskogean), Stanley (1969: 31–33) and Young (2000: 17–26) for Navajo (Athabaskan), Leer (1991: 91) for Tlingit (Na-Dene), Melnar (2004: 10–20) for Caddo (Caddoan), McFarland (2009: 245) for Filomeno Mata Totonac (Totonac-Tepehua), and, outside North America, Maganga & Schadeberg (1992: 97–98) for Kinyamwezi prefixes (Bantu) and Vajda (2004: 44–45) for Ket (Yeniseic). This list is hardly exhaustive.[6] Morphosyntactic templates are also, at times, employed as informal descriptive devices even in very formally oriented work (see, e.g., Stump & Finkel (2013: 347)). An additional phenomenon that has played an important role in contemporary approaches to morphosyntactic templates are so-called clitic clusters, elements which, regardless of their overall syntactic placement in a clause, have been treated as having templatic internal structure (Simpson & Withgott 1986, Halpern 1995: 191–193, Spencer & Luís 2012b: 112–126).[7]

Unlike the formal literature on morphophonological templates (see Section 1.4.2), much of the formal literature on morphosyntactic templates has been oriented toward the reanalysis of apparent instances of morphosyntactic templates as unrecognized instances of layered morphology, rather than developing specific "templatic" formal devices. In some cases, this is done by appealing to abstract phonological analyses (even making use of morphophonological templates) (see, e.g., Barrett-Keach (1986), Myers (1987: 14–40), McDonough (1990, 2000a,b), Speas (1984, 1987, 1990: 247–275), Rose (1996), Rice (2000), Hale (2001), and, in a somewhat different vein, Noyer

---

[6] Discussions of verbal templatic structure are unusually rich in the literature on Athabaskan languages, as typified in work like that of Kari (1989, 1992). Especially striking is the use of evocative metaphors to describe such systems as requiring discontinuous sets of morphemes to "intermesh" (Kari 1989: 435), as involving "interdigitation" (Kari 1992: 109), or resulting from a process akin to the "superimposition of transparency diagrams" (Axelrod 1993: 22). The earliest term of this kind appears to be "interrupted synthesis" (Kari 1989: 428), used by Edward Sapir and Benjamin Lee Whorf (see, e.g., Whorf (1956: 133)). Tlingit, a relative of the Athabaskan languages, also prompted the proposal of the *Principle of Templatic Attraction*, whereby morphemes of similar phonological shape are suggested to be "attracted" to one another in the sense that they tend to appear in the same templatic position or in adjacent ones (Leer 1991: 92) (see also Tuttle & Hargus (2004: 94–95)). This is an intriguing hypothesis that seems worthy of systematic investigation, but this is beyond the scope of the present work. Hymes (1956) also bears mentioning here as an attempt to use templatic patterns in Na-Dene (the higher-level family to which Athabaskan belongs) as evidence for the unity of the family, which required the development of a means for comparing templatic positions across languages of the group.

[7] Perhaps the most well-known cases of "clitic clusters" in the literature are those associated with person marking in Romance languages (see, among others, Perlmutter (1968, 1970, 1971), Bonet (1991, 1995), Crysmann (2000, 2002), Heggie & Ordóñez (2005), and Bonami & Boyé (2007)). A key difficulty in their analysis, which has clear consequences for their treatment as templatic phenomena or not, is the extent to which the relevant elements are better considered as a set of "affixes" or "clitics." The title of Miller & Sag (1997) clearly signals the problem. Nevertheless, it is noteworthy in this context that, at least from early generative analyses onward (see, e.g., Perlmutter (1968: 157)), treatments of them have frequently invoked templatic mechanisms.

16   Defining *template*

(2001), which is based on the description of Heath (1984: 347–375)). Spencer (2003) offers an informative review of many of the key issues (see also Spencer (1991: 208–214)), and Nordlinger (2010) defends the need for a templatic approach to some morphosyntactic patterns which takes into account arguments made in work like Rice (2000) (see also Tuttle & Hargus (2004)).

The different degree of acceptance of templates in formal work on morphophonology versus morphosyntax will be returned to in Section 1.6. The most notable exception to this pattern that I am aware of is found in work adopting the model of Head-driven Phrase Structure Grammar (HPSG). Not only are some of the most explicitly templatic formal analyses of syntactic constructions found within the HPSG tradition (see Section 1.4.5), but morphological analyses making use of slots, or comparable types of linear specification, have also been proposed, and have not been signaled as inherently problematic. This is found, for instance, in Miller & Sag (1997: 594) (building on the work of Stump (1993)) as well as Crysmann (2002: 172–197) (see also Crysmann (1999)).

1.4.4   *Phonological templates*

Following the structure of the definitions of morphophonological and morphosyntactic templates given in Sections 1.4.2 and 1.4.3, a *phonological template* can understood to refer to analyses where the linear realization of the components of a phonological construction is described in terms of constraints involving phonological categories.

Probably the most prominent type of template in this regard is the so-called syllable structure template, a device which treats a language's syllabification patterns as analyzable by means of a general well-formedness condition (see Itô (1986: 4); published as Itô (1988)) describing allowable combinations of segments in the syllables of a given language (see also Itô (1989)). Syllabification is then understood, at least partly, as a process of mapping segmental material onto a syllable template as specified in the grammar of a given language. In the generative literature, such templatic approaches can be set against rule-based approaches to syllabification (see, e.g., Blevins (1995: 222)), though, for the purposes of the discussion here, the choice of formal analytical device is less important than determining the extent to which a given analysis treats some linearization pattern as resulting from an external stipulation or whether it treats it as resulting from more general considerations (see also Section 1.7). Illustrative examples of analyses of specific languages employing syllable structure templates include Cairns & Feinstein (1982) and Bagemihl (1991). Gordon (1999) (published as Gordon (2006)) contains discussion of the interaction between syllable templates and weight, demonstrating their continued utility as analytical devices for phonological patterns,

1.4 An initial survey of template types

and Brentari (1993) argues for their applicability to the study of sign language phenomena.

Crowhurst (1991) applies essentially the same approach to the problem of metrical footing, proposing that it, too, involves mapping to templatic structures. Something similar is found for the inventories of foot templates adopted by Hayes (1995).

An important feature of such work is that, on the whole, it proposes that available phonological templates are either drawn from a universal inventory (see, e.g., Crowhurst (1991: 54)) or are highly constrained by universal phonological principles, for instance, in the case of syllables, a sonority sequencing requirement (see, e.g., Itô (1989: 221–227)). This is largely connected to the fact that this line of research has been conducted within the generative tradition and is closely connected to other generative work done in the context of prosodic morphology (see Sections 1.4.2 and 1.8.2), which adopts similar assumptions.

As will become clear from the discussion to be provided in Section 1.5, the "universal" nature of these approaches means that the phonological templates that I am aware of having been discussed in the literature fall outside the scope of the core range of phenomena which will be examined in detail here, which are taken to include only cases of "unexpected" linear stipulation. However, this is not a logical necessity deriving from the general notion of a phonological template but, rather, seems to merely reflect the nature of the phonological templates that have been proposed in the literature.

1.4.5 Syntactic templates

By *syntactic template*, I refer to templatic analyses where the linear realization of the components of a syntactic construction is described in terms of stipulated constraints on elements characterized in syntactic or semantic terms such as *subject phrase* or *pronoun*. The word template is not nearly as commonly employed for linearization restrictions in syntax as it is for morphosyntax. Nevertheless, one can find syntactic analyses of linearization which are sufficiently parallel to morphosyntactic analyses explicitly invoking templates to make it clear that the two sets can sensibly be considered together, at least in informal terms.

One of the clearest examples of a class of analyses involving a syntactic template comes from the so-called topological fields approach to German syntax (see, for example, Höhle (1986) and van Riemsdijk (2002: 146–148)).[8]

---

[8] These analyses are sometimes understood as being based on the idea that two kinds of syntactic structure, phenogrammatical and tectogrammatical, should be separated from each other, with the former kind of structure being that associated with linear ordering. See Mihalicek (2012: 8–11) and Section 2.1.

18 Defining *template*

Table 1.4 *German topological
fields (Kathol 2000: 78)*

LABEL	CHARACTERIZATION
vf	First Position
cf	Second Position
mf	Middlefield
vc	Verb Cluster
nf	Postverbal Field

Essentially the same approach has been applied to Dutch syntax (Shannon 2000: fn. 1), and a quite comparable approach has been developed for Danish and has been extended to other Scandinavian languages (see Bjerre et al. (2008: 135–142) and Sobkowiak (2011: 308–309)).[9]

In Kathol's (2000) formal treatment employing this model, developed within the framework of Head-driven Phrase Structure Grammar, the German clause is treated as being comprised of five positions, given in Table 1.4, which are strictly ordered following the linear specification in (4), where "$<$" should be interpreted as "precedes." The characterizations of the positions in Table 1.4 are simplified for purposes of presentation here, and some positions (e.g., *mf*) can contain more than one element. The abbreviation labels are not intended to be readily interpretable, and are, thus, logically comparable to the number-based system for referring to position classes exemplified in (2) in Section 1.4.3. The term *field* is used instead of *slot* in this approach to signal the fact that the relevant "slots" may contain more than one element, and I will use the word field here informally at times to characterize such "expandable" slots (see also Section 2.3.3).

(4) vf $<$ cf $<$ mf $<$ vc $<$ nf   (Kathol 2000: 79)

A key motivation behind the characterization of clauses in a language like German via a series of position classes of the sort given in Table 1.4 is that their linearization patterns do not appear to be straightforwardly analyzable in terms of linear ordering constraints on "natural" syntactic classes like subject but, rather, require the use of "unnatural" categories like *either* finite verb or complementizer, which is the case with the *cf* position. This is illustrated in the examples in (5), adapted from Kathol (2000: 80).

[9] While not restricted to syntax, the tagmemic approach of Pike (see, e.g., Pike (1967: 218)) can also be understood to employ something like syntactic templates.

1.4 An initial survey of template types

(5) a. [*Die*   *Blume*]$_{vf}$ [*sieht*]$_{cf}$ [*Lisa*]$_{mf}$.
     the.FEM.ACC flower   see.PRS.3s   Lisa
     "Lisa sees the flower."

   b. ... [*daß*]$_{cf}$ [*Lisa*]$_{mf}$ [*die*   *Blume*]$_{mf}$ [*sieht*]$_{vc}$.
     ... that   Lisa   the.FEM.ACC flower   see.PRS.3s
     "... that Lisa sees the flower."

The sentences in (5) schematize Kathol's (2000) field-based analysis of the German clause via subscripts corresponding to the abbreviations in Table 1.4. In (5a) a finite verb is assigned to the *cf* position, but in (5b) a complementizer is assigned to this position. Furthermore, in (5a) the object is assigned to the *vf* position, but in (5b) it is assigned to an *mf* position. The analysis of the clause into strictly ordered clausal positions which cannot be straightforwardly characterized in more usual syntactic terms like "subjects precede the verb" is what makes Kathol's (2000) treatment quite comparable to templatic analyses of morphosyntactic patterns.

As is well known, alternative analyses have been provided for important aspects of the sentential syntax of German (and related languages) not involving positional classes. The classic work of den Besten (1983: 60), in the transformationalist tradition, for example, treats the appearance of finite verbs either in the *vc* or the *cf* position as being determined by whether or not the verb has moved from an underlying position in a constituency tree where it is at the end of the head-final verb phrase to a position that is prototypically occupied by complementizers (see Sapp (2006: 266–284, 2011: 167–179) for further discussion of this and other transformationalist approaches to German syntax). Even within Head-driven Phrase Structure Grammar (see Sag et al. (2003)), the formal approach adopted by Kathol (2000), whose analysis was just discussed above, alternative approaches have been proposed without invoking position-class-like analytical devices (see Wetta (2011: 253–254) for an overview). I will discuss this issue of "competing" analyses, and how they impact this study, in Section 1.7.

While Kathol (2000) does not use the word "template" to characterize his analysis, as mentioned above, a comparable sort of syntactic analysis is found in Dik (1997: 70–71) (see also Connolly (1983, 1991: 50–55)), as part of a general model of constituent ordering, and, in this case, the word template is specifically employed. Something similar is found in Sadock (2012: 111–122). Dahlstrom's (1993, 1995) approach to Meskwaki (Algonquian) clausal syntax also employs the term (and will be discussed in detail in Section 3.11), as does Awóyalé (1988) (see also Ekundayo & Akinnaso (1983: 123–126)) whose "semantic templates," here, would be classified as syntactic templates. The use of the term template can also be found in descriptive work as a means to

20   Defining *template*

characterize the basic word order patterns of a given constituent type (see, e.g., Blackings & Fabb (2003: 259), Enfield (2006: 312), and Epps (2008: 284)).

In addition to syntactic templates like those just discussed that show clear parallels to morphosyntactic templates (see Section 1.4.3), there is a somewhat different phenomenon which has also been given analyses making use of syntactic templates: this is the second-position clitic (see, e.g., Zwicky (1977: 18–20), Anderson (1993, 1996, 2000, 2005: 108–114), and Halpern (1995: 13–76)). Second-position clitics have received a wide range of analyses, not all of which are clearly templatic, and the word *template* itself is not regularly applied even to templatic analyses of the phenomenon (though see Revithiadou (2006: 80)). Nevertheless, they represent another possible kind of, fairly restricted, syntactic template.

While they do not use the word template, Zec & Inkelas (1990: 369) notably analyze aspects of second-position clitics in Serbo-Croatian by means of an explicit prosodic "subcategorization frame" associated with the clitic that specifies it must be preceded by a phonological word. Their analysis bears clear similarities to cases of morphophonological templates that are also described in terms of phonological constituents (see Section 1.4.2). In the classificatory system developed here, such a template would be best termed *phonosyntactic* rather than syntactic. Such templates do not seem to have been frequently proposed, though there are at least a few other examples (e.g., Zec & Inkelas (1990: 372–377), Inkelas & Zec (1995: 545–546), and Good (2003b: 360)). The Serbo-Croatian template associated with second-position clitics will be analyzed in more detail in Section 3.7, and another phonosyntactic template in Serbo-Croatian will be examined in Section 3.8.

Work in constructional approaches to syntax (see, e.g., Goldberg & Suttle (2010) and Michaelis (2010)) may sometimes informally characterize a given syntactic construction in terms that make it appear to be templatic in nature. However, whether or not a template is part of the structure of a given construction can only be determined on the basis of a specific analysis of its patterns of linearization. For example, Kay & Fillmore (1999) refer to a specific English pattern as the *What's X doing Y?* construction, suggesting the presence of two open "slots" in a templatic structure. However, they ultimately argue that the construction's syntactic linearization is derivable from more general syntactic properties of English (Kay & Fillmore 1999: 30), implying that it is not, in fact, templatic. Of course, the fact that constructional approaches to syntax typically pay more attention to idiosyncratic aspects of a language's syntax than patterns that are generalizable to a language's major word classes – which are sometimes considered to "project" syntactic structure in a highly systematic way (see, e.g., Hale & Keyser (1993), Geuder & Butt (1998)) – means that they are not unlikely to end up targeting templatic aspects of a language's syntax. However, this is not at all a logical necessity.

1.4 An initial survey of template types   21

1.4.6   *Other uses of the word* template

The word *template* has uses in the linguistics literature beyond the sense restricted to patterns of linearization adopted here, reflecting the fact that the word is popularly used to refer to any construct that describes a general pattern (in linguistics and far beyond). I briefly discuss a few examples of other uses of the term in this section to help clarify the phenomena of focus here.

Van Valin & LaPolla's (1997) approach to syntax, Role and Reference Grammar makes use of the notion of the *constructional template*, which is a label for a grammatical object that combines "a specific set of morphosyntactic, semantic and pragmatic properties, which may be combined with other templates to form more complex structures" (Van Valin & LaPolla 1997: 73).[10] It is clear that these constructional templates can include specification of linearization constraints, as seen, for instance, in the invocation of a "precore slot" template to account for the presence of *wh*-words towards the beginning of the sentence in content questions in English (Van Valin & LaPolla 1997: 434). However, in the sense of the term template adopted here, Van Valin & LaPolla's (1997) constructional templates would not be considered "templates" since their primary function is not to characterize constraints on linearization patterns. At the same time, it is possible that, in addition to other things, they may include descriptions of linearization templates, but this can only be determined by factoring out the descriptive parts of the device relating to linearity from those relating to other aspects of grammatical specification. A comparable use of the term template can be found in recent work in construction morphology (see Booij 2010a: 550, 2010b: 18).

Rappaport Hovav & Levin (1998: 106–111) develop the device of an *event structure template* to model recurrent aspects of meaning typically associated with predicate classes such as activities, states, accomplishments, etc. Unlike Van Valin & LaPolla's (1997) constructional templates, which can, in some cases, be used to characterize constraints on linear realization, these templates do not directly encode constraints on linearization at all. Rather, as characterizations of verbal meaning, they would, at most, only be related to linearization indirectly, for instance, if one adopted a model of syntax whereby verbal semantic representations are taken to map onto syntactic form in a predictable way. (See also Wunderlich (2006: 6) for an apparently similar use of the term.)

In a very different domain, the term *templated* has been used in the literature on sign languages to refer to cases where signs can be related to

---

[10] As Van Valin & LaPolla (1997: 73) develop the theory of Role and Reference Grammar, they explicitly characterize constructional approaches to syntax as also making use of such templates. See Section 1.4.5 for comments on the role of "templates" in constructional approaches.

22   Defining *template*

visual perception, but only in highly schematic ways (Cogill-Koez 2000). From this, a notion of template is developed that refers to signs that can be combined together to express certain kinds of meaning, for instance a sign classifying an upright person (via an index finger pointing upwards) and a sign involving linear movement for motion towards a goal (Engberg-Pedersen 2010: 256–258). As with the constructional templates just discussed, these sorts of templates may involve specification of linear realization, but they are not limited to this. Of course, if one were to expand the study here to sign languages, it is not completely clear that the relevant sense of template should only involve linearization restrictions, as opposed to restrictions in spatial configuration, especially since one of the dominant metaphors for morphosyntactic templates, the slot-filler model, is partly spatial in nature. Thus, restrictions on the possible combination of sign language schematic "templates," in the sense of (Cogill-Koez 2000) – as well as other kinds of signs – may turn out to be quite relevant for understanding linearization templates. However, in this particular case, the two templates seem to clearly be of different types since linearization templates involve constraints applying to classes of signs rather than the schematic features of individual signs.

These three sample cases of other kinds of "templates" are simply intended to be illustrative, not exhaustive. Moreover, it seems clear that the dominant sense of the term in the linguistics literature centers around the characterization of constraints on linearization. This does not mean the term is straightforward to define, however, as will be discussed in the next section.

1.5   Templates: a twice incoherent class of phenomena

Having surveyed various kinds of templatic analyses across grammatical domains, we are now in a position to return to the definition of *template* that will be used in this book in order to situate templatic patterns within the larger picture of patterns of linearization in grammar. The definition, repeated from (1), is given in (6).

(6) **Template:** An analytical device used to characterize the linear realization of a linguistic constituent whose linear stipulations are unexpected from the point of view of a given linguist's approach to linguistic analysis.

As the most widely used term for the broad class of phenomena of interest to the present study, the word *template* will continue to play a prominent role in the following discussion, but it should be emphasized that the definition in (6) is meant to be descriptive, not prescriptive, and, clearly, it cannot form the

1.5 Templates: a twice incoherent class of phenomena 23

basis of a rigorous study due to its reliance on the notion of "unexpected" stipulation. When greater terminological precision is required, a different term, *desmeme*, emphasizing merely linear stipulation, without the associated sense of "unexpectedness," will sometimes be employed, as discussed in Section 2.1.

The closest parallel to the above definition in previous work on templates is probably that of Simpson & Withgott (1986: 173), who use the term *significantia artificialiter* in their discussion of morphosyntactic templates (see Section 1.4.3), simultaneously emphasizing their status as arbitrary (and, thereby, stipulated) signifiers that, unlike canonical signifiers, do not directly convey meaning but rather are a kind of "meta-device" which allows meaning-bearing signifiers to be constructed.

Even though the definition in (6), due to its descriptive nature, does not immediately "solve" the problems associated with understanding what templates are, it is useful insofar as it immediately prompts a question that is central to linguistic analysis, even if only rarely explicitly addressed: what kinds of linear stipulations are expected and what kinds are unexpected? This is a difficult question because our expectations for linear stipulation vary considerably across different domains of grammar. For instance, within lexical items, fairly elaborated linear stipulation can be deemed entirely unexceptional. The English lexicon is filled with "minimal" sets which seemingly require analyses involving linear stipulation of segmental ordering in one way or another. For instance, the words *cat*, *tack*, and *act* are all based on the same three segments arranged in different ways. Principles of English syllabification and other aspects of its phonotactics mean that it is not strictly necessary to state an explicit ordering among all three segments for each word in a lexical description of English, but some sort of ordering specification – for instance, which consonant (if any) is found in the onset of the single syllable of each word – is clearly necessary.

However, it is not a logical necessity in general that lexical items include specification of the order of the phonological elements which comprise them. Yip's (1989) analysis of Cantonese, for example, building on ideas found in Prince (1987: 499) and McCarthy (1989), suggests it can be analyzed as a language where specification of the relative order of consonants and vowels in a lexical item is not required due to the language's phonotactic restrictions. Because Cantonese does allow CVC syllables, some specification of linear order of consonants in lexical specifications seems unavoidable. However, it is quite straightforward to imagine historical change in a language like Cantonese resulting in it having only CV syllables, without problematic loss of contrast due to the availability of a rich system of tonal contrasts. The end stage would be a language which requires no specification of linear ordering among segments in its lexical items. Therefore, the idea that a language of this

24   Defining *template*

type might exist seems plausible, if not attested to the best of my knowledge (see also McCarthy (1989: 90–92)).[11]

The plausibility of such a language suggests that linear stipulation of segment orderings is not a strict necessity in languages, making it unclear why this is not considered templatic as, for instance, the ordering of morphemes in a slot-filler morphological system often is (see Section 1.4.3). Indeed, there does not appear to be any reason not to consider stipulation of segment ordering in lexical items templatic except for the fact that it is the "normal" (i.e., most common) state of affairs. In other words, linear stipulation that is expected – as is the case for segments in a lexical item – is, by virtue of those expectations, not considered to be remarkable enough to be given a special label and "template" is reserved for those cases of linearization patterns deemed (for whatever reason) to be unusual.

To take an example from a different domain, while stipulated order among sets of affixes can typically be deemed templatic, there is another key aspect of affix linearization which is not usually considered to be templatic – that is, whether or not an affix appears in a fixed position before or after its host – as attested by the ubiquitous and unremarked use of the terms *prefix* and *suffix*. That an affix must be lexically or grammatically specified as either prefixing or suffixing is not a logical necessity, and cases have been proposed of affixes lacking such stipulation and whose appearance can be (at least partly) predicted based on other considerations (Noyer 1994, Kim 2010). However, such instances of "mobile" affixes are considered the unusual case, and, indeed, it has even been suggested that "mobile affixation does not really exist" but only appears to as the result of the misanalysis of the relevant patterns (Paster 2009: 36). Mobile affixes further offer challenges to conventional definitions of a word as (among other things) being composed of elements that must occur in a fixed order (see, e.g., Dixon & Aikhenvald (2002: 19)). Again, we see a clear instance where a kind of linear stipulation, far from requiring a special label such as templatic, is actually considered to represent the "normal" situation.

As a final example, while there are some analyses of patterns of syntactic linear stipulation which can clearly be seen as templatic (see Section 1.4.5), there are, again, instances where such stipulation is not associated with that label, with the most well-known case being patterns of basic word order, such as whether a language is best categorized as SVO, SOV, etc. (see Dryer (2007) for a general overview of word order typology). There have been attempts to reduce the degree of specification required to account for syntactic word

---

[11] In describing such a language, I should make clear that, throughout this work, I am quite emphatically not interested in mental representations but, rather, available logical descriptions. I, therefore, view whether or not one can describe a language's lexical representations without specifying linear order among segments as a completely distinct issue from whether or not this is how they may be cognitively represented. See Section 1.2 for further relevant discussion.

1.5 Templates: a twice incoherent class of phenomena

order patterns, most notably in the context of proposals regarding the presence of grammatical "parameters" which are taken govern them (see, e.g., Baker (2010) for a recent overview from a generative and typological perspective). This suggests that various analysts believe that syntactic linearization, in some sense, should only be minimally "stipulative," and, when only a relatively limited degree of stipulation remains in a given analysis, it is generally not labeled templatic. This seems to be because some level of linear stipulation, for instance regarding the ordering of an object and its verb, is simply considered "normal," even though languages with flexible word order are, of course, well attested (see Dryer (2013b)), clearly showing that stipulated order of syntactic elements is not only not a logical necessity but also is an apparent grammatical possibility.

Linear stipulation, therefore, in and of itself, is only a necessary, but not a sufficient, condition for some grammatical construction to be considered templatic. An additional condition must also be met: the nature of the stipulation must, in some way, be considered to deviate from expectations. Unfortunately, on the whole, such expectations are merely implicit, and linguistics lacks anything resembling a generalized theory (or even descriptive model) of what kinds of linear stipulation are "normal" for a given class of linguistic elements. It is even hard to find explicit statements regarding basic generalizations that would almost certainly be uncontroversial: for example, that smaller domains (such as words) allow for a more elaborated degree of linear stipulation than larger domains (such as sentences) or that phonology's somehow more "intimate" connection to grammatical linearization when set against, for instance, syntax means that we should see a general correlation between the degree of a construction's phonological specifications and linear ones (see also Good (2003b: 508) and Sadock (2012: 207)). Instead, one finds such ideas expressed more often in indirect guises, for instance via notions like juncture strength (see, e.g., Anderson (1992: 227–249) for overview discussion of boundary elements as well as Aronoff (1998: 413) and Hockett (1950)). Something similar is found in well-known treatments of phonological constituency involving the role of a prosodic hierarchy in structuring the application of phonological rules from smaller to larger domains (see, e.g., Nespor & Vogel (1986)).

Thus, even though I believe the claim that linearization restrictions are expected to be greater in smaller domains than larger ones would be uncontroversial (if not necessarily correct), one usually has to demonstrate this via inference. For instance, one might note that morphophonological templates have, in general, been much more widely accepted as possible grammatical structures in the theoretical literature than syntactic ones (see Good (2011: 740–741)) or point to the influence of work in syntax like that of Kayne (1994), which attempts to show that a certain kind of abstract syntactic analysis

26 Defining *template*

allows one to characterize constituency structure without the need for traditional word order parameters and, therefore, employs essentially no linear stipulation.

We are left then with a definition of the term *template* which makes them a kind of "double" wastebasket class. On the one hand, they involve stipulation, something which, by its very nature is deemed to be unexplainable. On the other hand, they involve constructions with an *unexpected* kind of stipulation – that is, they are a wastebasket within a wastebasket, a twice incoherent class of phenomena. This raises an immediate question: Why investigate a set of patterns as though they are a coherent class if, by definition, they are incoherent? I take up this issue below in Section 1.6.

Before moving on, I would like to briefly address another potentially problematic aspect of relying on the definition in (6) in this book: the risk of circularity in delineating the objects to be analyzed. As discussed in Section 1.4.6, the term *template* has been used in various ways in the linguistics literature beyond the notion of a linearization template. Moreover, as made clear in Section 1.4, I will also consider some phenomena that have not been explicitly labeled "templatic" but which appear to me to be close enough to other kinds of templates that it would seem inadvisable to exclude them merely because a given analyst did not happen to use the word. This leaves this work potentially open to the criticism that my real understanding of template is "whatever I want to label one."

In some ways, this criticism is valid, but, ultimately, of little practical significance in the wider descriptive and theoretical context in which this study is embedded. There are various reasons for this. First, as will be made clear in Chapter 2, I will not base the formal and typological investigation on a vague notion of *template* but, rather, on the more concrete notion of linear stipulation. The discussion of "templates" in this chapter should be understood not to embody a set of theoretical claims but, rather, as a summary of previous research that I deem to be highly relevant for the more rigorous examination to follow. Linguists, after all, have been talking about linearization templates for decades often without it being clear precisely what they mean by this term, and, before attempting to improve upon this state of affairs, it seems advisable to first have a clear understanding of the "state of the art," as it were, even if it is not a particularly satisfactory one. We can, therefore, understand the definition in (6) to be one derived from largely ostensive examination, which is intended to prepare us for the construction of a set of terms which can be defined intensionally and, therefore, serve as a stronger foundation for future investigation (see Gupta (2012) for discussion of different classes of definitions).

Another reason why this criticism is weaker than it might first appear is somewhat more subjective: this study is based on more than a decade of research on patterns of linear stipulation. What this means is that, while the various case studies to be examined in Chapter 3 were not chosen "scientifically," they were also not chosen lightly. They are intended to both present distinct problems and to help us see similarities among seemingly disparate constructions that might otherwise be obscured. Accordingly, while, undoubtedly, there are linearization constructions out there which will not be adequately covered in the framework to be developed here, I am reasonably confident that it will be sufficient as a starting point for further typological refinement and that, whatever its deficiencies, it represents a significant improvement over what has been previously available.

Finally, in understanding the nature of the definition proposed above in (6), we must acknowledge that the research here is fundamentally confronted with a "chicken or the egg" dilemma: many linguists have clearly had an intuition that templates can play an important role in structuring grammatical objects (even if others are skeptical, as will be discussed in Section 1.6), but no widely accepted general definition of them exists. At the same time, if we want to come to a better understanding of what makes a template a template, we need to find a way to delimit our initial investigations, requiring some sort of definition. The definition in (6) is ultimately designed to help break through this difficult circularity not by "solving" the problem but, rather, by serving as a heuristic device to guide us through the initial stages of investigation.

1.6   Wastebaskets as a tool for theory refinement

Assuming the definition of *template* offered in (6), a possible conclusion one might reach – even though this work will take the opposite approach – is that the incoherency of the class of phenomena which we might label templatic makes them unsuitable as a general object of study. This conclusion may even be considered to be unavoidable if one were to assume that the primary goal of linguistics is to uncover regularity in language (see, e.g., Pesetsky (2009) for a recent defense of this position, though in a somewhat different context). Indeed, in choosing to study templates here, I do not mean to suggest that they should be considered coherent, and I will not attempt, for instance, to detect an underlying abstract unity underpinning their surface diversity. Rather, I believe the primary justification for studying them is precisely because they represent cases where our analytical tools have failed to yield evidence of clear holistic patterns (though see Section 1.8.2 for patterns detected within one grammatical subdomain). They, therefore, are a valuable tool for making visible a set of problems relating to how we describe and interpret the nature of linearization in grammars.[12] To make an analogy with another type of "uncategorizable"

---

[12] It is perhaps noteworthy in this context that an informal examination of *Das Grammatische Raritätenkabinett* ("The Grammatical Rarities Cabinet") (Plank 2006), a collection of grammatical rarities, reveals that around thirty of 147 (around 20 percent) listed rara appear to be

28   Defining *template*

grammatical category, they are, in some ways, reminiscent of clitics whose liminal status – neither clearly words nor affixes – has made them an interesting proving ground for models of morphology and syntax, despite the fact that it is hard to pin down a set of criteria that effectively cover the class of elements that linguists tend to think of as belonging to the category (see Spencer & Luís (2012a, 2012b: 321–328)).

Put another way, templates can be understood as a kind of grammatical pathology, adapting the sense of *pathological* as found in mathematics (Bottazzini 1986: 200).[13] There is a class of "well-behaved" grammatical constructions, from the perspective of their linearization patterns, for example an affix which only behaves as a prefix or a suffix (see Section 1.5), and a class which deviates from our expectations in varying degrees and ways. The assumption that guides this work is that if we can isolate the specific characteristics of such pathological constructions that make them pathological, we will not only have a better understanding of the pathologies themselves but also of non-pathological constructions. Corbett (2007), conducted in the canonical approach to typology, explores a similar intuition, namely that a typologically "extreme" phenomenon, like suppletion, challenges us to develop new tools for exploring linguistic diversity.

Of course, as will be discussed in Section 1.7, templates do not simply "exist" in the world but, rather, are the result of a particular analysis of the linearization patterns of a given linguistic element. Therefore, we must, in principle, be open to the idea that some templatic "pathologies" are, in effect, misdiagnosed. However, as the case studies in Chapter 3 should make abundantly clear, the range of templatic patterns that have been described strongly suggests that they cannot, across the board, be attributed to infelicitous analysis.

In this context, it is worth highlighting a fact, discussed above in Sections 1.4.2 and 1.4.3, that there is, indeed, a significant line of work on ordering relations in morphosyntax which does suggest that templatic analyses of morphosyntactic structure do generally represent just such misdiagnoses. This is in clear contrast to work on morphophonological linearization, where templates have seen greater acceptance. Part of the explanation almost certainly lies with the fact that the linearization of linguistic constituents is often understood not to result from "logical necessity" but, rather, constraints inherent to the use of the auditory-vocal modality in spoken language (see, e.g., Wojdak (2008: 7) for

---

connected to patterns of linear stipulation, which adds further potential value in exploring templatic phenomena, since this might help us better understand why a large class of possible grammatical patterns is so poorly attested.

[13] See Aronoff (1998: 413) for another instance where it has been suggested a "disease" metaphor may be an apt way to understand a class of grammatical phenomena.

1.6 Wastebaskets as a tool for theory refinement

recent discussion in the context of a non-templatic analysis of affix ordering). If linearization is thought of as an accidental "by-product" of the form that spoken languages happen to take, then it should not be surprising that work focused on a domain more closely linked to form (morphophonology) should find it more natural to employ a device involving stipulation of linear order than work focused on a domain less closely linked to form (morphosyntax) and that work on the domain under consideration here with the weakest connection to form (syntax), does not have nearly as extensive a literature devoted to "templates" as the other two. Comparable ideas have been expressed in work on sign languages as well. Morphophonological templates have been proposed to account for aspects of linear realization in the visual-gestural modality (see Section 1.4.2), while, at the same time, it has been suggested that the effects of modality should be relatively constrained in sign language syntax (Lillo-Martin 2002: 242–244)).

It is, however, worth bearing in mind that a full analysis of any language seems unimaginable without some amount of linear stipulation, if only in the specification of the order of segments in lexical items, for example. We could perhaps construct a logically possible language where no linear stipulation is required, but, even so, no such language has been attested. Therefore, what is at stake is not *whether* language allows linear stipulation but *where* it is allowed. In this sense, work in morphosyntax that has tried to avoid templatic analyses can be well understood as making a claim that, since many aspects of linear ordering in morphosyntax can be analyzed without the need for the sort elaborated linear stipulation embodied by templates, it is reasonable to assume that this is because morphosyntax, in some sense, "allows" for nothing but the most basic kinds of linear stipulation (e.g., whether an affix is prefixing or suffixing). As a result, one finds proposals like the Mirror Principle (Baker 1985: 375) (see also Baker (1988)), which suggest that syntactic principles, in fact, explain principles of ordering within not only syntactic constituents but also morphosyntactic ones – thus explicitly attempting to delink morphosyntax from the accidents of form.

Work in morphophonology has recently seen some attempts to replace templatic analyses of certain phenomena, especially those involving length restrictions, with non-templatic ones – though this was only after the possibilities for templatic analyses had been explored in detail, as discussed in Section 2.2. Moreover, phonologically oriented work on affix ordering does not appear to view as a viable option the possibility that phonological principles alone may explain affix order, except, perhaps, in relatively unusual cases (see, e.g., Hyman (2010b) and Paster (2006, 2009: 29–33)). It, therefore, seems reasonable to consider that the difficulties in explaining key aspects of their linearization in purely phonological terms, coupled with the relative importance of linear order in phonological representations (especially when set

30   Defining *template*

against syntactic representations), has led scholars analyzing morphophonological patterns to be relatively more comfortable with the idea that grammatical phenomena may be regulated by templates, at least on the whole.

At the same time, it must be admitted that the discrepancy in the relative acceptance morphophonological templates as opposed to morphosyntactic ones is probably not purely about the nature of the phenomena being studied but also is somewhat "cultural," insofar as much of the work looking at linearization phenomena from a more syntactic perspective simply appears to place a high value on approaches that avoid linear stipulation even when this runs counter to (surface) empirical observations. This is seen quite strikingly, for example, in the influential work of Kayne (1994) (within generative syntax) that proposes that syntactic structures, in fact, only allow underlying specifier-head-complement order (e.g., SVO for transitive clauses) with other surfacing orders (e.g., SOV) somehow derived from this configuration (Kayne 1994: 35), thus permitting the removal of "directionality parameters" from models of syntax (Kayne 1994: 49–50). This proposal has been made despite the fact that worldwide surveys suggest that SOV word order may be universally preferred to SVO, or, at the very least, is not obviously subordinate to it (see Dryer (1989: 269–270, 2013b) and Nichols (1992: 93–95)).[14]

In fact, in surveying the literature on "templatic" restrictions across grammatical domains, it is hard not to conclude that the question of whether or not a "template" may be the best way to analyze a given pattern is potentially misleading. The crucial issue is the following: given some analytical treatment of a linguistic constituent, which of its linear patterns must be treated as stipulated, and to what extent do those stipulations seem to be in line with stipulations seen in other analyses of comparable phenomena? On this view, one way to read Rice (2000), for example, is not as an argument against the use of linear stipulation in any form in the analysis of the Athabaskan verb, but, rather, as an argument against the highly elaborated template that typifies much descriptive work on the family (see, e.g., Rice (2000: 395) and also Noyer (1991: 199) and Good (2003b: 104) for relevant points). A key difficulty in generalizing on this insight, however, is that the field lacks an accepted framework for characterizing patterns of linearization independent from the factors – whether semantic, syntactic, or phonological – taken to partly condition those patterns. This can make it quite difficult to compare how different analyses "parcel out" predicted patterns of linearization from stipulated ones.

To take one example, Bošković (2001: 84) argues for a treatment of second-position clitics in Serbo-Croatian (see Section 1.4.5) involving a "filter" which

---

[14] From the typological perspective adopted here, of course, there is nothing to gain by adopting an approach like that of Kayne (1994). An abstract analysis which renders SVO and SOV languages the "same" at some level of representation does not alter the fact that they represent significantly distinct patterns of linearization, which is precisely what is of interest here.

blocks sentences which do not allow for fulfillment of the clitics' templatic requirements over one involving phonologically motivated "movement." While this distinction is of crucial importance within the transformationalist framework he adopts, determining the precise ways in which a "filtering" analysis of predictable versus "templatic" linearity differs from a "movement" one, which is a prerequisite for comparing them in more general typological terms, is not at all obvious.

One issue that has been raised in work which seeks to justify analyzing "templatic" systems without templates is the apparently ad hoc nature of templatic stipulations (see, e.g., McDonough (2003: 18)). It is notable, therefore, that the definition of templates given in (6) more or less requires that any device used to analyze them will have to be ad hoc – in the sense that it will have be designed to capture stipulations which could not be explained through other theoretical devices that are readily available. While the term *ad hoc* is often used pejoratively in linguistics – and beyond (see Laudan (1977: 114–118)) – following McCawley (1998: xii), I do not regard ad hocness to be inherently problematic in grammatical analysis (see also Dryer (2006: 223–224)). Quite the contrary, probably one of the few things that is universally true of languages is that, "All grammars leak" (Sapir 1921: 39), and I take it as a given that, quite frequently, the best analysis of such "leaks" will involve an ad hoc stipulation. In other words, if a grammatical construction is genuinely not regular, there is no reason to avoid an analysis which implies that this is the case.

As understood here, the challenge of research into an inherently ad hoc class of grammatical constructions is not to show they are not ad hoc at all. Rather, we need to make sure our analyses are only as ad hoc as absolutely necessary. That is, they should not devolve into becoming "*gratuitously* ad hoc" (McCawley 1998: xii), and it may very well be the case that some proposed templates cross that line, which is why we must always be aware that templates are the products of specific analyses and, in a study like this one, must focus on those analyses where the proposed linear stipulations are most likely to be found, in one form or another, in most (if not all) possible alternative analyses. This issue is the subject of the next section.

1.7   Templates as analyses not "grammar"

Templates derive from particular analyses of linguistic phenomena, making them, first and foremost, linguists' objects as opposed to objects with "true" grammatical reality. This book will deal with this issue by remaining agnostic on the extent to which templates are grammatically "real" and, instead, focus on specific templatic *analyses* of representative phenomena. While it is clear that such an approach is, in some sense, less satisfying than focusing on constructions which all might agree could be considered templates,

32   Defining *template*

it is taken here so that the properties of a wide range of phenomena can be explored without prematurely disregarding controversial instances of templates which, even if ultimately analyzable in a non-templatic way, might still lend important insights to the development of a set of typological categories to describe templatic restrictions. (However, the Athabaskan case will not be subject to detailed investigation precisely because of the difficulties surrounding its analysis – see Section 3.1.)

To pick an example, in languages where content question words are displaced from canonical positions (e.g., to a position towards the beginning of the clause), should such ordering be considered templatic? The analysis that Van Valin & LaPolla (1997: 434) offer employing a precore slot (see Section 1.4.6) suggests a templatic analysis is possible for such surface patterns. However, the standard transformationalist treatment for such phenomena involves so-called *wh*-movement (or, more generally, "operator" movement) (see, e.g., Radford (1997: 267–271) for textbook discussion).

Would this linearization pattern be considered templatic under a transformationalist approach? First, we would have to decide if the movement should be predictable or stipulated, with the answer being probably being "both": that is, some of its properties derive from general considerations and others derive from language-specific grammatical patterns, which, at an extreme, may be reducible to a single parameter which is primarily aimed at capturing surface linearization facts. This is found in, for instance, the influential proposal of Huang (1982: 254) that question words are abstractly displaced in all languages but only the syntax of some languages, such as English, is associated with a restriction that this abstract displacement should generally be associated with linear displacement in a sentence's surfacing form. If we accept that this counts as a kind of linear stipulation (which is not obvious since the relevant restriction in such approaches is treated as one involving movement rather than a targeted position), we then have to consider whether it should be considered an "unexpected" stipulation. The answer is not straightforward, but, in the end, it probably should not be. This difference among languages has been taken to reflect a kind of syntactic parameterization (see, e.g, Huang (2003: 276)) that is not specifically tied to linear ordering and, as such, the linearization patterns associated with it could be taken to derive from more basic considerations.

At the same time, it is important to bear in mind that there may be cases of unexpected linear stipulation that are obscured by a particular analysis, creating the possibility of "false negatives" alongside the potential "false positives." Bošković's (2001) treatment of Serbo-Croatian second-position clitics, discussed above in Section 1.6, potentially falls into this category: conceptualizing their second-position linearization restriction as connected to a filter preventing them from appearing in the "wrong" position, rather than using a more positively oriented generalization explicitly invoking second position, obscures the fact that their linear behavior is both stipulated and unexpected under either approach. Of course, there may be some reason to favor the filtering approach, even in templatic terms, but, in order to know this is the case, we must still find the potential template that is "hiding" within it.

The present work adopts several measures to help mitigate problems that arise from the fact that whether or not something is a "template" is dependent on the analysis given to it. First and foremost, as stated above, it defines the primary object of its typological investigation to be linear stipulation (see Chapter 2) rather than "templates," per se. The extent to which a given construction may involve linear stipulation may be controversial, but this approach allows the overall patterns of stipulation to be broken down into subpatterns, meaning that more controversial aspects of the analyzed stipulation can be separated from less controversial ones, in principle. Second, this work adopts a case study approach (see Chapter 3), allowing its analytical framework to be applied to a range of grammatical phenomena, at least some of which involve relatively uncontroversial cases of stipulation. While this does not directly address issues arising from cases where its presence may be controversial, it does mean the framework can be illustrated using analyses that the majority of linguists would be expected to find reasonable.

Finally, as already indicated in Section 1.2, and will be reiterated at many points below, this work is primarily designed to lay the methodological foundations for more comprehensive investigations of linear stipulation. This weakens the potential negative impact of adopting the "wrong" analysis of a construction since the present goal is not to conclusively answer a question like, *How much linear stipulation is possible in languages?* but, rather one like, *How can we construct a database that will allow us to determine how much linear stipulation is possible in languages?* If a templatic analysis of a given construction turns out to be anomalous or even "wrong," one of the uses of such a database will be to allow us to detect this. Therefore, designing it to describe "incorrect" patterns is not inherently problematic. This falls out directly from the fact that the model for linear stipulation that will be developed here is not meant to be explanatory (see Section 1.2) but rather descriptive, though, importantly, it will be a formal descriptive model rather than an informal one (see Dryer (2006: 223)). While such an approach is quite distinctive from what is the norm in the Chomskyan tradition, where developing theories that are intended to be simultaneously descriptive and explanatory is especially valued (Dryer 2006: 207–208), it is not unique here, and can be found in more "formally" oriented work on diverse aspects of grammar (see, e.g., Inkelas &

34   Defining *template*

Zoll (2007: 163–166) for something comparable for phonology and Culicover (1999: 42) for syntax).

It might be useful, therefore, to compare the current investigations (from a methodological perspective) to early explorations of basic word order in the world's languages. Seminal work like that of Greenberg (1963) established that certain basic word orders (e.g., OSV) were clearly much rarer than others. Such broad typological work could not conclusively establish whether or not certain basic word orders could or could not be a possible "underlying" word order in language, but it did make clear that descriptive claims that a given language showed one of the rare word orders merited careful scrutiny regarding their evidentiary basis (see, for example, Dryer (1995) and Whitman (2008)). Even in the absence of a comprehensive theory of some phenomenon (whether it be word order, templates, or something else), it is clear that exploring characterizations as presented in existing descriptions can be a crucial step forward.

Thus, the approach adopted here, while not itself imposing strong theoretical constraints on the patterns to be examined and described, should be of value even to those who would adopt a restrictive theory of templatic restrictions. It will establish a more consistent mode of description for templates cross-linguistically and cross-constructionally, and the elements of its descriptive model can then be related to relevant constructs in a given theory in order to explore the extent to which the phenomena examined may be consistent with that theory – much as, for example, typological work like that found in Haspelmath et al. (2005) can be of use to linguists from a wide range of theoretical backgrounds, even though it is not strongly theoretical on the whole. In other words, the present work, despite its somewhat atypical approach, is intended to complement work within various linguistic theories rather than being opposed or irrelevant to them.

1.8   Previous work on template typology

1.8.1   *Two previous lines of research on the typology of templates*

There are at least two previous lines of research relevant to the broad question of the nature of variation found in templatic structures. One of these is the Prosodic Morphology Hypothesis, which will be briefly discussed in Section 1.8.2 and which makes very specific claims regarding the possible shapes of a specific subclass of templates. The other is the approach to morphosyntactic templates outlined in Simpson & Withgott (1986), which, while not associated with nearly the same level of theoretical development as the Prosodic Morphology Hypothesis, could be viewed as making a very specific and testable typological claim which the work described here could play a role in verifying. It will be discussed in Section 1.8.3.

1.8 Previous work on template typology

1.8.2 The Prosodic Morphology Hypothesis

In one grammatical domain – that of morphophonology (see Section 1.4.2) – a proposal known as the Prosodic Morphology Hypothesis (McCarthy & Prince 1995: 318, 1996) regarding the possible shape of templates has received a fair degree of interest (see Downing (2006: 5–16)). It deserves mention here due to the fact that it is almost certainly the most well-developed and influential theory of templatic constructions that has been developed to date. At its core, it suggests that there is a close relationship between prosodic structure and morphophonological templates, specifically claiming that such templates will always be describable in terms of a universal set of prosodic constituents. (See Nespor & Vogel (1986) for a classic reference on prosodic constituency and Bickel et al. (2009) and Schiering et al. (2010) for recent typologically oriented discussion.) This would predict, for example, that a morphophonological template with the shape of a syllable could be attested but not one consisting merely of a single consonant, since the latter is not a prosodic constituent (Hendricks 1999: 35–36).

While it was developed in a way quite distinct methodologically than is the norm within work coming out of typology as a subfield, the Prosodic Morphology Hypothesis's claim of a link between prosodic constituency and templates is clearly of interest (and paralleled by ideas developed in Good (2003b, 2007b)). However, it is not, in and of itself, an adequate framework for constructing a rigorous descriptive typology of templates (morphophonological or otherwise) because of its methodological stance wherein description and explanation of a given phenomena are brought together into a single framework using universal categories (see Dryer (2006: 223–224) for relevant discussion). This runs counter to significant ideas within current typological practice both in terms of overall approach (Nichols 2007b: 231–232) and in the understanding of grammatical categories as language-specific phenomena, at least partly, rather than being universal in nature (see, e.g., Dryer (1997a), Croft (2001), Haspelmath (2007), Cristofaro (2009)). Of course, the goals of work done in the context of the Prosodic Morphology Hypothesis are quite different from those of contemporary typology. So, this discrepancy is hardly surprising and should not be construed as indicative of any inherent problem with this line of research in general.

Another aspect of the Prosodic Morphology Hypothesis which needs to be emphasized here is that it only encompasses a subset of the templatic restrictions connected to the morphophonological patterns taken to be of interest here. This can be seen, for example, in the case study of the Tiene verb, to be presented in Section 3.5.5, which involves the imposition of two templates, only one of which can be understood as falling within the rubric of this hypothesis (see specifically Figure 3.16 and also Section 5.3.1).

36 Defining *template*

Table 1.5 *Layered vs. templatic morphology adapted from Simpson & Withgott (1986: 156)*

PROPERTY	LAYERED	TEMPLATIC
Subject to lexical phonological rules	✓	✓
Structure based on one root	✓	—
Uncoded morphological derivation	✓	—
Maximum of one argument indexed on a verb	✓	—
Significative absence	—	✓
Non-canonical morphological dependencies	—	✓

1.8.3 Templatic morphology and layered morphology

While it has not been subject to the same level of theoretical scrutiny or development as the Prosodic Morphology Hypothesis, Simpson & Withgott's (1986) discussion of templatic morphology has been influential in providing a foundation for discussion of morphosyntactic templates, even in work which attempts to argue that they are not needed to analyze morphosyntactic linearization phenomena (see, e.g., Spencer (1991: 212), Rice (2000: 11)). They propose a two-way distinction between "layered" and "templatic" morphology. Table 1.5 adapts the morphological properties they consider in proposing this distinction.

Simpson & Withgott (1986) detail the sorts of morphological patterns associated with each of the characteristics given in Table 1.5, and I will only briefly discuss them here (see also Stump (1997: 218–222)). The first feature given in Table 1.5, whether or not a given domain is associated with so-called "lexical" phonological rules, refers to rules that are, roughly speaking, sensitive to morphological structure (see Kiparsky (1982a,b) for an early theoretical treatment that strongly informs the understanding of the term as used by Simpson & Withgott (1986)). This feature is not of particular interest here since it is common to both layered and templatic morphology.

The three following features are all proposed to be specific to layered morphology. The first is that the structure of a word is, in some sense, built up from a root to which affixes are conceptualized as being added in a kind of one-by-one fashion, giving rise to an articulated internal structure. The next is what is often referred to as "zero-derivation" or "conversion" (see Bauer & Valera (2005) for a general overview and Štekauer et al. (2012: 213–218) for cross-linguistically informed discussion), where a word associated with one word class (e.g., a noun) becomes used in another word class (e.g., as a verb) without a surface morphological change as part of a language's processes of word formation (as seen, for instance, in the English word *bus*, which has primarily nominal, but also verbal, function). Finally, Simpson & Withgott (1986: 158)

1.8 Previous work on template typology 37

suggest that layered morphology tends to be associated with verbal systems where only one argument (e.g., the subject) can be indexed on the verb as opposed to multiple arguments (e.g., subject and object).

The final two features in Table 1.5 are taken to be specific to templatic morphology. The first of these is the presence of significative absence (see Stump (1997: 219)), where absence of a morpheme is taken to be in paradigmatic opposition with a non-zero morpheme in a given templatic "slot" (Simpson & Withgott 1986: 157). (This is in opposition to the notion of "zero-derivation" just discussed above.) Such analyses are usually described as involving so-called zero morphemes (most typically represented along the lines of $\emptyset$).[15] There are, of course, difficult theoretical issues surrounding the notion of zero-morphemes and how they pertain to the identification of "slots" in position class analyses. On the whole, this issue will not be directly explored here with the focus instead on simply classifying cases where a position must be filled on the surface and cases where it does not need to be (see Section 2.3.3).

The second feature that is taken to be specific to templatic morphology is the existence of non-canonical morphological dependencies – a term that I use to subsume two properties discussed by Simpson & Withgott (1986), an "adjacency" constraint and a "no lookahead" constraint. These two properties are embedded in a morphological model where the "usual" state of affairs is taken to be one where affixes are added to stems without being sensitive to the specific morphological composition of those stems or to the possible appearance of morphemes that might be added "after" them in a word. Taken together, these are constraints against the appearance of non-adjacent morphemes being sensitive to one another with the adjacency constraint concerned with "inward" sensitivity and the no lookahead constraint being concerned with "outward" sensitivity (Stump 1997: 222). I will not have much to say directly about the issue of "lookahead" here since it is not clear how to apply a notion that is metaphorically embedded in a generative model of word formation into a typological study like this one (see also Rice (2000: 14)). The issue of adjacency, being sensitive to surface configuration, is amenable to typological investigation, however, and I will return to it under the rubric of discontinuous dependencies in Section 2.3.4.

A notable feature of Simpson & Withgott (1986) is that they appear to view the distinction between layered and templatic morphology as an either/or opposition – that is, a morphological system will either be layered *or* templatic, rather than, for instance, exhibiting different degrees of templaticity (see also

---

[15] I avoid reliance on the term zero morpheme here due to possible ambiguity between analyses involving zero morphemes as members of a paradigm in direct opposition to non-zero morphemes (i.e., significative absence) and analyses involving zero morphemes employed primarily as placeholders in articulated syntactic structures, i.e., so-called "empty categories" (see Bender (2000: 26–40) for critical discussion).

38   Defining *template*

Spencer (1991: 208–214) for a similar treatment). To the best of my knowledge such a proposition has never been seriously explored typologically, and I think it must remain an open question whether or not the claims embodied in Table 1.5 are typologically valid (though I would be surprised if they held up as more than tendencies, at best, given Simpson & Withgott's (1986) quite limited dataset of examination).[16] Instead, emphasis in the theoretical literature has either been on modelling cases where templatic structure is assumed to exist (e.g., Stump (1993)) or showing how a non-templatic analysis for apparently templatic data is available (see Section 1.4.3). (Tuttle & Hargus (2004) is a notable exception to this pattern.) Moreover, there are well-described cases of morphological patterns in the literature that do not comfortably fit into such an opposition – i.e., whose behavior appears to be determined both by templatic and by "layered" principles (see, e.g., Hyman (2003c) for detailed examination of just such a system, as well as Section 3.5).

The present work, not specifically focused on morphology, is not able to address this issue generally, but the framework for classifying linear stipulation to be developed below could be used as the foundation for rigorous study of this question. However, it should be noted that conducting such a study would be complicated by the need to ensure cross-linguistically rigorous ways of working with sometimes slippery notions like "root" or "derivation."

1.9   Typologizing templates

The previous sections have attempted to summarize the present state of our knowledge with respect to linearization templates, and, whatever one's views regarding the existence and nature of such templates, it seems clear that our understanding is quite lacking. It seems relatively unlikely that we are dealing with a unified set of phenomena. Our ability to even understand when an instance of linear stipulation is templatic or not appears to be uncomfortably bound to a mostly implicit set of expectations that linguists have regarding linearity. And, perhaps most strikingly, the field, to this point, has not developed a generalized way to discuss linearization patterns that do not conflate them with other aspects of morphophonology and morphosyntax, as will be emphasized in Section 2.1.

The rest of this book, therefore, attempts to chart a path forward via three informing questions: (i) Given the apparent "wastebasket" status of the category *template*, what generally applicable typological categories can we devise to describe constructions labeled "templatic", bearing in mind that any system

---

[16] This is not meant to be a strong criticism as the focus of Simpson & Withgott (1986) is not templatic morphology in general but, rather, the properties of clitic clusters (see Section 1.4.3).

1.9 Typologizing templates

to be developed should ideally apply equally well to templatic and non-templatic stipulation for purposes of comparison (Chapter 2)? (ii) How can we describe specific templatic constructions using those categories, keeping in mind that templates may be structurally fairly complex (Chapter 3)? And, (iii) what methodologies are required to compare these descriptions once they are constructed (Chapter 4)?

While the grammatical subject matter of this book is templatic constructions, it will become apparent in Chapter 2 that the problems posed by comparing templatic constructions will require us to develop new methods for typological classification and comparison. Accordingly, the remainder of this book is not intended solely to help us better understand templates but also to expand our ability to perform rigorous typological comparison across grammatical constructions which are too heterogenous for the methods of "classical holistic typology" (Bickel 2007: 245) to apply.

It will also become clear, over the course of the discussion, that templates quickly become a kind of "Pandora's box" for linguistic analysis. One cannot really understand their diversity without tackling a number of distinct problems together. As a result, the rest of this study is intended to be primarily foundational in nature. That is, it focuses on establishing a general framework through which templates specifically, and patterns of linear stipulation more broadly, can be rigorously examined and compared, rather than attempting to provide a definitive, "final" typology of templatic constructions. Arriving at this final typology is an ultimate goal, as is understanding the nature of linear stipulation in grammar more generally, but getting there will take some time. What follows are just the first steps.

2 A typological description language for templates

2.1 The language of linear stipulation

Descriptive linguistics has long relied on categories like *prefix*, *enclitic*, *verb second* or *head final* to refer to grammatical categories combining linear ordering restrictions with other morphophonological or morphosyntactic properties.[1] For example, a prefix is conventionally understood as an element that is both morphologically dependent on a stem and which appears before the stem in a linear sequence. This is opposed to the more generic term *affix*, and the existence of so-called mobile affixes (see Section 1.5) suggests that, even if there is a strong tendency for morphological dependency and fixed order between dependent and host, this is not an absolute necessity. Similarly, a category like *head final* references a linearly defined generalization over classes of phrases in a given language delimited by the fact that they contain a syntactic head.

From the perspective of the present study, hybrid categories like these cannot be considered "basic" but rather are a kind of grammatical "chimera," and I will refer to them as *chimerics* here in order to emphasize the non-necessary nature of the pairing of a linear specification with other, logically independent grammatical properties.[2] The ubiquity of such categories appears to have obscured an important gap in the conceptual and terminological foundations

[1] While not directly adaptable to the present study because of its focus on morphological phenomena, Igor Mel'čuk's five-volume *Cours de morphologie générale* (Mel'čuk 1993, 1994, 1996, 1997, 2000; see also Mel'čuk (2006) for an abbreviated English presentation) should be singled out for the degree of terminological rigor it applies to the study of all aspects of morphology, including explicit consideration of various aspects of linearization not usually emphasized in discussions of morphology, for instance, in its proposal of the term *confix* to encompass those affixes which neither interrupt the root they attached to nor are interrupted by that root (Mel'čuk 2000: 414).

[2] An emphasis on the separability of linear aspects of "grammar" from other aspects is also found in work in syntax that develops a distinction between relations of linear ordering and other sorts of combinatorial relations (e.g., those connected to argument structure) under the headings of *phenogrammar* (for linear relations) and *tectogrammar* (for the other sort). See Mihalicek (2012: 8–11) for a recent overview and Section 1.4.5 for discussion of specific templatic analyses that fall roughly within this tradition. These specific terms can be attributed to Curry (1961).

2.1 The language of linear stipulation

of linguistic description: the lack of a truly generalized vocabulary to categorize patterns of linear stipulation independent of other grammatical features. To continue with the two examples of chimerics just discussed, in the present context, it is important to keep track of the fact that the terms *prefix* and *head final* both imply the existence of a linguistic constituent where an element taken to be more dependent (whether this is an affix or a non-head syntactic constituent) precedes an element taken to be less dependent (whether this is a stem or a syntactic constituent serving as a head). Each category may belong to quite distinct grammatical domains in traditional terms, but they share a significant aspect of what one might call their "linear grammar."

Chimeric categories are so deeply embedded in the way linguists analyze grammatical patterns that it may not be immediately obvious why a generalized vocabulary for linear stipulation is needed, or what it would even look like, without a concrete example.[3] I will therefore anticipate some of the discussion that will be the focus of Chapter 3 by introducing a pair of constructions which are quite distinctive in morphosyntactic terms but show potentially interesting similarities in linearization terms. These are the Mande clause and the Tiene verb, which are discussed in more detail in Sections 3.10 and 3.5.5 respectively. Relevant data is given in (7), with examples drawn from the Mande language Bambara, and Table 2.1, which gives a number of verb forms from Tiene.

(7) a. *sékù bɛ́ mǎdú kálán tùbàbùkán ꜜná*
     Sekou PM Madou teach French   POSTP
     "Sekou is teaching French to Madou."

   b. *ù bɛ́nà fántà dí à mà   mùsó ꜛyé*
     3p PM Fanta give 3s POSTP wife POSTP
     "They will give him Fanta as a wife."   (Creissels 2006: 37)

The syntax of transitive clauses in Mande languages has been characterized as adhering closely to a template consisting of: a subject, a predicative marker expressing various categories (e.g., tense, aspect, polarity) typically associated with auxiliary verbs, a single additional verbal argument, the verb itself, and then any other arguments. Thus, in (7a), one sees a word order that can be informally labeled as S-Aux-IO-V-DO, while in (7b) the order is along the lines of S-Aux-IO-V-DO-X (where IO and DO stand for indirect object and direct object respectively). This template can be generalized to S-Aux-OVX.

The data in Table 2.1, on the surface, exemplifies what appears to be a very different phenomenon in Tiene: a morphophonological template where affixation patterns are sensitive to place of articulation. The paired verbs seen in the

---

[3] Indeed, a striking example of this is the sense of *morphological* as not referring merely to form, as would be etymologically expected but, rather, the formation of words, which are specifically elements pairing form and meaning (see also Aronoff (1994: 1–2)).

42   A typological description language for templates

Table 2.1 *Causative verb forms in Tiene (Hyman 2010a: 147–148)*

INFINITIVE	CAUSATIVE	GLOSS
-lɛ	-léesɛ	'eat'
-laba	-lasaba	'walk'
-lóka	-lósekɛ	'vomit'
-mata	-maasa	'go away'
-pala	-paasa	'arrive'
-píína	-píísɛ	'be black'

table are of non-causative and causativized stems, where causativized verbs appear with a Causative affix that can be associated with an underlying form along the lines of *-es-*.[4] This can be seen most easily in the first verb pair in the table *-lɛ/-léesɛ* 'eat.' However, there is an unusual set of restrictions on the shape of verb stems in Tiene which, among other things, disallows coronals as the third consonant. In causativized stems based on forms which end in labials, this restriction is satisfied by having the *s* of the Causative appear as the second consonant, seemingly behaving as a kind of infix, thus resulting in pairs like *-laba/-lasaba* 'walk.' In causativized stems based on forms which end in coronals, the restriction is fulfilled by having the *s* of the Causative effectively replace the coronal that would otherwise be expected to appear, thus resulting in pairs like *-pala/-paasa* 'arrive.' (The other changes seen in the verb pairs are discussed in Section 3.5.5.) These patterns can be roughly characterized via a template along the lines of CVTVK where T is used for any coronal consonant and K for a non-coronal. (The final vowel seen in the forms in Table 2.1 is left out of the template since its appearance can be attributed to independent aspects of the morphological structure of the verb.)

If our attention is focused on how the linear patterns of each of these templates relates to other aspects of grammar, it is hard to contemplate how they could possibly be directly compared to each other. The Mande data appears to fall within a domain of grammar of interest to syntacticians, and the Tiene data within a domain of interest to phonologists. However, if we look at these patterns not in their chimerical form as "constructions" but, rather, focus solely on their patterns of linearization, there are clear similarities between them. For instance, both can be characterized as consisting of five "slots" (though the final analysis to be presented in Section 3.5.5 will not fully adhere to this aspect

---

[4] Following Comrie (1976: 10), I will attempt to adhere to a convention in this book wherein language-specific categories are indicated with an initial capital letter while general linguistic categories will be given in all lower-case letters. See Haspelmath (2010: 674) for discussion.

2.1 The language of linear stipulation

of this informal surface analysis). Both of these templates are also restrictions on the ordering of their components rather than their length. At the same time, there are also clear differences in the linearization patterns of these two templates, with a striking one being that the Mande final "X" slot can contain multiple elements while all of the Tiene slots are restricted to a single element.

Of course, just because this process of linear abstraction allows us to compare the patterns of linearization in Mande and Tiene does not necessarily mean that we *should* do so. However, this sort of comparison has never been systematically attempted to the best of my knowledge. So, we simply do not know what kinds of insights it will yield, and both of the logically possible extreme results would be of unambiguous interest. On the one hand, if we found that templatic constructions across grammatical domains showed remarkable similarities in their possible structures, that would allow us to discover significant new universals. On the other hand, if we found that they were quite distinctive in different domains – that is, that some chimerical combinations of form and meaning are much more common than others – that would bolster the justification for traditional distinctions such as the one between morphological and syntactic phenomena. As such, at least some investigation along these abstract lines seems warranted.

Even though truly generalized comparisons of linear stipulation have not been conducted, there is precedent for comparing cross-domain patterns of linearization in more limited ways. For instance, there is a well-established line of research trying to find correlations between morphosyntactic and syntactic ordering patterns, within both functionalist and formalist traditions (see, e.g., Givón (1971), Baker (1985: 375, 1988), and Bybee (1985: 13), among others). Similarly, Yu (2007: 206–218) draws connections between the linear properties of infixes and endoclitics and Anderson (1993) argues that second-position clitics and verb-second word order can be treated as unified phenomena. Finally, while not specifically geared towards linearization patterns, the proposal of Carstairs-McCarthy (1999: 143–144) to view similarities between syllable structure and sentential structure as something other than a coincidence also bears mentioning in this regard.

Nevertheless, while significant in their own terms, such accounts fail to provide – nor were they intended to provide – a general terminological and conceptual framework for classifying patterns of linear stipulation, which is the focus of the present chapter. While this framework will be relatively elaborated, it must be understood as an initial proposal rather than a final statement. Following the general orientation of this book (see Section 1.6), it has been developed via an examination of proposed templatic constructions rather than "better-behaved" cases of linear stipulation, under the assumption that any system that can handle the most complex patterns of linear stipulation proposed will also be sufficient for handling the less complex ones.

44   A typological description language for templates

The typology is built around three core concepts (as well as several other concepts less specifically tied to the modeling of templates): STRICTURE (Section 2.4.4), FOUNDATION (Section 2.4.5), and COMPONENT (Section 2.3), each capable of describing different aspects of a given templatic construction. A key feature of this typology is that it is designed to characterize templatic constructions at a relatively high degree of precision, not only placing them into high-level categories but also indicating how their subconstituents (here COMPONENTS) interrelate. As will be seen, the ultimate form of the typological classifications will more closely resemble the kinds of objects associated with language-specific syntactic descriptions in formal models of grammar making use of feature structures, rather than using more familiar "holistic" categories such as "basic SOV word order." Head-driven Phrase Structure Grammar (HPSG) (Sag et al. 2003) has been particularly influential with respect to the formal approach developed here.

Since there is, to the best of my knowledge, no existing grammatical term encompassing the category of "pattern of linear stipulation," it will be useful to devise two terms that will help to characterize this category. The first of these is *lineate*, which will be used as a noun to characterize any kind of linguistic element where ordering enters into its representation, whether or not this pattern is "surprising," "templatic," or used to convey "special" meaning in one way or another. The word, therefore, can be understood as a term for a broad class of chimerics, in the sense just developed above, i.e., those that are chimerical at least by virtue of combining a linear order stipulation with stipulation of some other linguistic properties.[5] While, in principle, one could avoid the use of this term simply by referring to a given lineate using some other descriptive label (e.g., *morpheme*), it is used here in contexts when the focus is on the linearization properties of the relevant element. The second term, *desmeme*, will be employed to refer to the stipulated linearization patterns that are analyzed directly as being part of the construction of some meaningful sign, as opposed to appearing merely incidentally as the result of more general principles, except in cases where linear stipulation consists merely of a specification of the ordering of segments and suprasegments in the specification of a canonical lexical item. The word is based on a Greek term, δεσμός (*desmos*), meaning 'band' or 'chain.' A canonical case of a desmeme, in the existing literature on templates, are morphosyntactic templates, which have been explicitly treated as analogous to phonemes (see Section 1.4.3). I will, at points, use desmeme as a quasi-synonym for template with the caveat that template, as discussed in Chapter 1, is understood as an informal term here, while desmeme is intended

---

[5] While many chimerical categories (e.g., *prefix*, *enclitic*, etc.), will be lineates, there are others which may not necessarily be, such as *morpheme*, which refers to a pairing of form and meaning but does not entail that the form must involve a specification linear stipulation of any kind, even if this is predominantly the case.

2.1 The language of linear stipulation 45

to be more precise (though still, of course, dependent on a specific analysis of a linearization pattern – see Section 1.7).[6] To make the sense of the term clearer, it can be usefully understood as that aspect of a linguistic form used to convey meaning solely connected to linearization, as opposed to aspects of form involving, for example, the presence of specific phonological segments.

In order to make clear the difference between more usual methods of typological classification and the one adopted here, I refer to the model that will be developed below to characterize linearization restrictions as a *description language*, to emphasize that it is intended not to simply enumerate properties that apply to a given templatic construction as a whole but also to specify how the different components of a templatic construction relate to each other. I borrow this term from work done in the area of technical specifications in domains such as data encoding standards for the Web (see, e.g., Brickley & Guha (2004)). The next section gives an overview of this description language, with subsequent sections providing an account of its various features in detail.

A warning to the reader is probably advisable at this stage: there is an inherent tension when developing a relatively complex new coding scheme between ensuring that the scheme itself is thoroughly presented and inspectable in a single place while also providing sufficient exemplification of the objects being coded so that the more abstract aspects of the scheme will be intelligible. This chapter skews towards giving a more systematic overview of the description language and is, as a consequence, relatively abstract in its discussion. In Chapter 3, the discussion is much more concrete in nature: it applies the description language to a number of exemplary case studies of templatic constructions. At the same time, the particularity of each case to be examined in Chapter 3 makes it inherently difficult to discuss the entire description language in systematic fashion there. Some readers may find it more effective to look at Chapter 3 before the present chapter or to move back and forth between the chapters, perhaps focusing at first on case studies considering language data they are already familiar with to serve as a basis for how generalizations they have already encountered are recoded in the description language used here.

---

[6] It is important to note that, here, the notion of desmeme is employed as a comparative concept, in the sense of Haspelmath (2010), to facilitate cross-linguistic examination of patterns of linearity. Thus, it should not be treated as a proxy for a word-formation device of the sort associated with, for instance, so-called Item-and-Arrangement, Item-and-Process, or Word-and-Paradigm approaches to morphological analysis (see Hockett (1958), Matthews (1991: 21–22), Anderson (1992: 72), and Stump (2001: 1–3)). If the concept were adapted for use in the synchronic description of the grammars of different languages, it would fit most comfortably in an Item-and-Arrangement-style approach, where the desmeme simply becomes another "item" comprising part of a word (or some larger or smaller unit). However, nothing in the present study hinges on adopting any specific approach to the analysis of synchronic grammars (see Section 1.7), and the use of the comparatively "static" notion of the desmeme is made here primarily to facilitate comparison of templatic constructions by virtue of its being readily expressible using a formalism interpretable as a graph (see Chapter 4).

46   A typological description language for templates

2.2   Overview of the classificatory scheme

The typological description language to be developed here is intended to be used to used to conduct constructional typology, rather than holistic or generalizing typology (see Croft (1995: 92–95)). As such, it is designed to be able to apply to any construction involving linear stipulation in a given language and across languages, rather than trying to assign an overall linear stipulation "type" for a language (though, in principle, it could be useful for such typologizing as well, much as Nichols & Bickel (2013) combine two construction-based typologies to derive a whole language one). While my impression is that constructional typology is not as strongly associated with typology as a subdiscipline as is whole-language typology, it is not at all uncommon in general with some other examples being Stassen (2000) on noun phrase conjunction, Evans (2008) on reciprocal constructions, Bickel et al. (2009) on phonological word domains, Bickel (2010) on clause linking, and Malchukov et al. (2010) on ditransitive constructions, among many others.

Engaging in such typological investigation requires setting up a system of descriptive variables that can, in principle, be applied in a uniform manner to each of the language-specific constructions being described. When dealing with a phenomenon like the linearization template, which has a history of being used informally, work like that of Keenan (1976), breaking down the traditional notion of subject, or Hopper & Thompson (1980), on transitivity, provides a useful example of how to proceed – as does more recent work adopting the *canonical* approach to typology (see, e.g., Corbett (2005, 2007), Brown & Chumakina (2012)). The challenge is to try to deconstruct a category in a way which allows for rigorous investigation but is also consistent with the underlying intuitions that prompted it to be employed in the first place. In the present context, this requires first and foremost a way for us to characterize patterns of linear stipulation. The focus of this chapter could, therefore, be understood as an instance of "typologically biased metalinguistics," in the sense of (Mel'čuk 2006: 6). Furthermore, like Mel'čuk (1993, 1994, 1996, 1997, 2000), I am especially concerned with devising a model that is conceptually rigorous. It is, therefore, tested later in the book first by applying it to a range of specific templatic constructions (Chapter 3). I then examine the instantiation of descriptions employing it in a database designed to enforce adherence to the model as described and use that database to conduct initial typological comparison (Chapter 4).

The core concepts that form the basis of the typological description language developed here are meant to capture key features of three aspects of linear stipulation, which will be discussed in more detail in the following sections: the nature of the linear restriction (whether in terms of ordering or length), the nature of the organization of a template's subconstituents, and the internal

2.2 Overview of the classificatory scheme

properties of the subconstituents themselves. The term *stricture* will be used to refer to the high-level nature of the restrictions. The term *foundation* will be used to categorize different types of constituent organization. The notion of *component* will be employed as a cover term for any constituent (phonological, morphological, or syntactic) whose external linear realization is (at least partly) specified by a given templatic construction. There is more to the typology than just these concepts, as will be seen, but they are the most central to understanding how templates are modeled here.

The terms used in the description language have been deliberately chosen so as not to overlap with existing terminology in order to avoid accidental conceptual conflation of distinct categories, though, as will be seen, some of them will have clear parallels to more familiar notions. For example, the notion of *keystone*, to be developed in Section 2.4.5, is roughly analogous to the syntactic notion of *head*, and it would not be unreasonable to consider a keystone to be the head of a certain class of templates. Nevertheless, the potential value of such terminological conflation is simply too unclear at this point to make it advisable to construct a terminologically reductive description language.

These three conceptual tools of stricture, foundation, and component can be usefully understood as establishing, in effect, the basis of a syntax for templatic description. While the terms that underlie this description language could presumably be used to refer to language-specific categories, it is crucial to bear in mind that this is not how they are intended to be interpreted here. Rather, they are comparative concepts in the sense of Haspelmath (2010) (see also Corbett (2012: 108–111) and footnote 6 of this chapter).[7]

An overview (with various simplifications) of the elements of the entire typological description language is given in Figures 2.1 and 2.2.[8] A full specification of the features and types used in the database informing this study is given in the Appendix, along with information on how to access digital versions of the database and its specifications. The actual database contains more information than is used for the typological comparison (e.g., it employs a controlled vocabulary for referring to grammatical functions of templates for purposes of reference) and the Appendix reflects this while, in general, the discussion in this chapter and elsewhere abstracts away from the less theoretically and typologically relevant details. The figures below also leave out

---

[7] The notion of *taxonomic* category, as developed by Whorf (1945: 11), would seem to anticipate Haspelmath's (2010) notion of comparative concept.

[8] To give one example of a way of a way in which the diagram in Figure 2.1 is simplified, when compared to the actual data structure in the database used in this study, the feature RESTKOMPONENTEN is technically associated with an intermediate feature of *restkomponentenSet* which points to one or more components, rather than being directly associated with an "unnamed" set. This was done to simplify certain aspects of data processing and is not of particular theoretical significance.

48   A typological description language for templates

some categories that will be introduced in later discussion in order to maintain a degree of presentational simplicity, the most significant of which is the *lexicoConstructional* subtype of the *conditioning* type (see Section 2.4.2).

An important feature of this description language is that it is not intended to merely assign a set of "unordered" values to a given construction across a predetermined range of classificatory features but to also provide a description of the internal structural relations holding among the components of a template. This means that different subtypes of templates may allow for the specification of distinct sets of classificatory features, as consistent with the descriptive properties of those subtypes. In other words, the precise set of properties available to describe a given template may be treated as being logically dependent on the value the template shows for some other property. In addition, the value of a given feature may itself be a complex object consisting of a so-called feature structure, that is a set of feature–value pairings grouped together (see Section 2.6). Each part of the description language will be discussed in detail in subsequent sections, with examples drawn from relevant templatic constructions.

The conventions in Figures 2.1 and 2.2 are somewhat complex, but this merely reflects the comparatively fine-grained nature of the description language when set against, for instance, the conventions adopted in the multivariate study of Bickel (2010), which partly inspires the approach taken here but where clause linking constructions are described essentially as "bags" of unstructured feature–value pairs. The conventions of the description language, on the whole, build on those associated with Head-driven Phrase Structure Grammar (HPSG; see Sag et al. (2003)). The reasons for this will be clarified in Section 2.6, but the most critical one can be stated relatively succinctly: this typological description language is easily modeled using the formal device of a typed feature structure (Sag et al. 2003: 52–58), which is also the primary formal device used within HPSG. Adopting HPSG conventions, therefore, provides a ready-made set of formal tools that is already in use and well-documented within linguistics. While the specific use HPSG conventions for cross-linguistic comparison is, to the best of my knowledge, novel here, the description language can be readily seen as a straightforward extension of existing typological schemes aimed at fine-grained comparison such as those associated with the AUTOTYP project (Bickel & Nichols 2002) or Canonical Typology (Brown & Chumakina 2012). The most significant way in which the current description language differs from these similar approaches is in the way it allows structural relations to be described via nested feature structures (to be discussed shortly below) and via "reentrancy" (see Section 2.6).

In the rest of this section, I give an overview of how to interpret Figures 2.1 and 2.2 in a general way and then discuss the specific sense of the terms used in the figures in Sections 2.3 and 2.4 below – that is, I will begin by focusing

2.2 Overview of the classificatory scheme

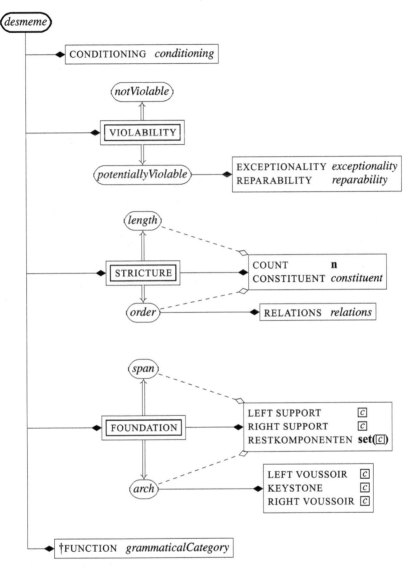

Figure 2.1 Overview of description language for templatic constructions

on the basic structural traits of the description language before clarifying the nature of the templatic patterns it is intended to describe.

Italicized terms in the figures (e.g., *desmeme* or *arch* in Figure 2.1) represent labels for abstract types of linguistic objects, where a given type label should

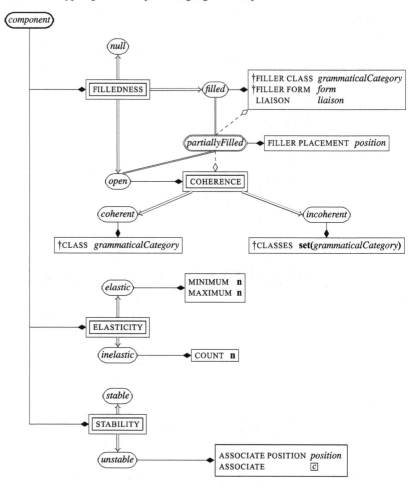

Figure 2.2 Overview of description language for components of templates

be construed as indexing a comparative concept. The *desmeme* and *component* types are surrounded by thick-bordered rounded boxes to indicate that they are the foundational types around which the description language is built. These types are, in turn, associated with feature–value pairs deemed relevant to their description (see Section 2.7 for further discussion). As will be clarified below, many of the type labels in Figures 2.1 and 2.2 represent the labels for supertypes of sets of types that can serve as the value for the relevant feature. This is the case for all the types that are directly to the right of a feature within the same box (e.g., *exceptionality*, *reparability*, *relations*, *position*, etc.). Thus,

2.2 Overview of the classificatory scheme 51

in the case of *exceptionality*, for instance, that label refers to the fact that the EXCEPTIONALITY feature will have as its value a concept which is classified as a subtype of *exceptionality*, namely *lexical*, *semantic*, or *noKnownExceptions*. The subtypes currently employed are all listed in the Appendix.[9]

The association of a type with its feature–value pairings is indicated with a diamond-tipped arrow. Feature names are given in small capital letters (e.g., CONDITIONING or STRICTURE). The values of feature–value pairings may themselves be abstract types, which can, in turn, be associated with their own feature–value pairings, thus producing complex descriptions of nested feature–value pairings (though not all types are associated with feature–value pairings). The relevant details will be made clearer in subsequent sections, but the most significant instance of this is where a feature of a desememe points to a component (indicated with a boxed *c*, as in ⓒ, and to be discussed further below). In some cases, a given type may be associated with feature–value pairings via inheritance of a specification for those pairings from some supertype of which it is a subtype. This is seen, for instance, in the case of the two types of stricture (see Figure 2.1), *length* and *order*, where each is associated with the COUNT and CONSTITUENT features, while *order* is associated with one additional type-specific feature of RELATIONS. (Technically, the COUNT and CONSTITUENT features associated with *length* and *order* are associated with a *stricture* supertype, but this is not explicitly depicted for the sake of descriptive brevity.) Inheritance of feature–value pairs is depicted via dashed arrows with "open" diamond tips. Features marked with an initial dagger symbol (i.e., "†") are included in the database but will not factor into typological comparison (see Sections 2.3.2 and 2.4.6 for discussion).

One type in the current description language, *partiallyFilled*, as given in Figure 2.2, is modeled as a subtype of two other types, *open* and *filled*, which means it inherits the features of both types. It is also associated with one feature of its own, FILLER PLACEMENT. This multiple inheritance is signified with a doubled outline and doubled lines connecting *partiallyFilled* to each of its parent types.

In addition to features having types as values, the description language also employs features having an integer as their value (indicated with a boldface **n**) as well as features which have a specific templatic component as their value

---

[9] As can be seen in Figures 2.1 and 2.2, there is a convention of not using spaces in value names built mnemonically using multiple English words but, rather, employing so-called "camel case," where capitals are allowed in the middle of an orthographic word to signal a word boundary. When referring to such categories in prose, I will often make use of normal English writing conventions since I do not expect there to be any difficulties in interpreting the relationship between a formal category such as *noKnownExceptions* and reference to it via a phrase such as "no known exceptions." In addition, in the prose, I will often informally refer to such categories without italicization when I do not anticipate any problems in interpretation and will, for similar reasons, not always refer to features using small capital letters either.

52   A typological description language for templates

(the purpose of which will be made clearer below in Section 2.3). This is indicated with a boxed *c* (i.e., $\boxed{c}$). While the italicized word *component* will be used to refer to an abstract type, the $\boxed{c}$ refers to a specific, described instance of that type.

The final convention found in Figures 2.1 and 2.2 that needs to be discussed is its representation of logical dependencies holding among linguistic types and their associated feature–value pairs. These are indicated by the depiction of some features with double-bordered boxes from which double arrows emanate, encoding that the value of these features is required to be a choice of two or more types, each of which will be associated with its own feature–value pairings. Thus, for example, a template's STRICTURE feature (see Figure 2.1) can have, as its value, either an object of type *length* or *order*. If its value is *length*, its associated features are only those generally associated with stricture. If its value is *order*, it is associated with an additional feature–value pairing involving the RELATIONS feature. The use of "typed" feature structures to encode such logical dependencies on the association between linguistic types and feature–value pairings, while presented differently in visual terms above, is more or less the same as what is found in HPSG (Sag et al. 2003) (see Section 2.6).

This discussion has not defined all the terms used in Figures 2.1 and 2.2, but these will be clarified in subsequent sections of this chapter.

It should be fairly clear that the typological description language adopted here is much more powerful, in terms of descriptive precision in particular, than more traditional typological approaches either involving a limited set of "atomic" category labels (such as SOV, SVO, etc.) of the sort associated with basic word order typology (see, e.g., Dryer (2007)) or an unstructured list of feature–value pairs (as found in, for instance, Bickel (2010)). The closest existing typological description system to the description language developed here is probably that associated with Canonical Typology (Brown & Chumakina 2012), though even its more complex system for describing categories does not allow for the expression of logical dependencies, to the best of my knowledge. An immediate drawback of the approach taken here is that the comparison of constructions becomes more difficult since it is not a simple matter of seeing if they are of the "same" type or if they partially match across different variables. I will return to this issue in Section 2.7 and Chapter 4. Another drawback is that the added complexity of the descriptions makes coding a given construction relatively time consuming and also makes achieving consistency in coding criteria much more difficult (see Sections 5.2.1 and 5.2.2).

In the immediately following sections, I will discuss the description language in more detail and exemplify its application to the typological categorization of specific templatic phenomena. The discussion will begin with an overview of the internal properties that can be assigned to templatic

2.3 Components 53

components (Section 2.3), and then move to properties characterizing templates themselves (Section 2.4). This discussion will also introduce various conventions for presenting formal descriptions of templatic phenomena that will play a prominent role in Chapter 3. The remaining sections of this chapter situate the description language with respect to other work, with Section 2.6 describing in more detail how it builds on research making use of typed feature structures in the analysis of syntactic phenomena, Section 2.7 discussing the procedure through which the description language was developed and placing it in the broader picture of typological modeling, Section 2.8 considering the sorts of typological results one could discover on the basis of a database using the descriptive scheme developed here, and Section 2.9 giving an overview of how the description language is expressed in a machine-readable format for the purposes of database construction.

In all of the discussion to follow, it is important to bear in mind that the typological description language devised here is not conceptualized as a "fixed" or "complete" entity. In the most well-known types of typological investigation, such as studies of basic word order typology, the logical possibilities for variants of a given functional class (e.g., the simple clause) are often taken to exhaust the space of typological possibility, perhaps with the addition of an "unclassified" type, such as *no dominant word order* (see Dryer (1997b, 2013a) for critical discussion). The present study, however, explores a domain where the space of logical possibilities is incredibly large and not yet well understood. One needs to start somewhere – which is why a typology is developed here – but, at the same time, the application of a typology to a relatively unexplored area inevitably leads to the discovery that the typology is in need of refinement (see also Bickel & Nichols (2002)). What is offered here, therefore, should be understood as a "snapshot" of the typology, arrived at via an initial convenience sample, which is mature enough to serve as the basis of foundational investigation but by no means conceptualized as "finished." While not often explicitly discussed, presenting a study at such a stage of investigation appears to be quite normal within typological investigation (Nichols 2007b: 233–234; see also Section 2.7). It is perhaps unusual for it to be the focus of a book-length investigation, though, as will become clear, the problems of interest here are sufficiently complex to require quite a bit of space to properly explore.

2.3 Components

2.3.1 Three high-level component features

Templates here are modeled as a kind of grammatical entity with their own internal constituency, and the term *component* is used here as a label for the immediate subconstituents of a given templatic construction. (See

Section 2.5.5 for an indication as to why the qualification *immediate* is used here.) As with more familiar kinds of subconstituents (e.g., words and phrases), components can be categorized both with respect to the role they play in a larger templatic structure and with respect to their own internal properties, and it is the latter topic that is the focus of the present section. Moreover, as will be discussed in Section 2.4.5, individual components may play more than one structural role in a given template, further necessitating that their internal properties are described independently of the higher-level features of a template, so that a single component can be referred to more than once in a template's structural description.

The closest analog to the notion of component found in the previous literature on templates is that of the "slot" in a slot-filler structure (see Section 1.4.3). That is, a component should not be understood as a specific morpheme, syllable, or phrase, but, rather, as a structural position that has the potential to be filled with a "concrete" grammatical entity. This aspect of components is most clearly seen in the fact that most of them here will be treated as being "open" – that is, they may be filled with an entire class of elements rather than a specific one.

As schematized in Figure 2.2, components are associated with three high-level features. These are FILLEDNESS, ELASTICITY, and STABILITY. Each of these is briefly described in turn in (8), with more elaborated discussion in Sections 2.3.2, 2.3.3, and 2.3.4 immediately below. In Section 2.3.5, some sample descriptions of components that will be discussed in more detail in Chapter 3 are given, in order to make the discussion less abstract and to clarify the application of the description language.

(8) a. FILLEDNESS: A feature for characterizing the nature of the class of elements that is found within a given component, for instance whether it can be occupied by only one morpheme or an entire class of morphemes.

b. ELASTICITY: A feature for characterizing the overall size of a component, including whether or not its size is fixed or variable.

c. STABILITY: A feature for characterizing a component's dependencies, in particular for cases where the nature of the content of one component can somehow be dependent on what is found in another component.

The discussion below focuses on those aspects of the typological description language for components relevant to the typological comparison presented in Chapter 4. A full specification of the features and values associated with components, including those which do not factor into the typological comparison, is given in the Appendix.

2.3 Components

2.3.2 Filledness

As indicated in Figure 2.2 there are explicit specifications in the description language regarding the values of the features in (8), with those for FILLEDNESS being the most complex. However, before elaborating the technical details of the notion of filledness, as understood here, it may be worthwhile to informally relate it to more familiar notions in other domains of grammar. Filledness fulfills a role comparable to, say, the specification of a morphosyntactic category in part of a syntactic construction. A given position in a syntactic construction might, in principle be open to any element of the right lexical class (e.g., a noun), or it might be highly restricted, only allowing a specific morpheme, as is the case for the productive formation strategy for plurals in English, which always involves *s*. Similarly, in this model for characterizing templates, a given component may be fillable with an entire class of elements (e.g., syllables or tense affixes) or be restricted to containing just a single element associated with its own idiosyncratic templatic restrictions.

Components with the former property are referred to via the type *open* here, while those with the latter are referred to via the type *filled*.[10] As can be seen in Figure 2.2, there are additional types of *partiallyFilled* and a kind of "bookkeeping" type, *null*, for cases where specific structural classes of slots (see Section 2.4.5) are not found in a given template. As the name indicates, *partiallyFilled* is used to characterize components containing both an "open" portion and a "filled" portion. For discussion of cases where this type appears to be of value in the description of templates see Sections 3.6 and 3.7.

With the exception of the type *null* (see Figure 2.2), the various types of FILLEDNESS have additional features associated with them. For instance, *unfilled* and *partiallyFilled* components can also be specified for COHERENCE, which is intended to capture whether the elements that can appear in a given component comprise a *coherent* grammatical class (e.g., person markers or heavy syllables) or whether they form an apparently arbitrary *incoherent* set of classes. If they form a coherent group, then a further specification is given for a type label for the specification of the class of elements that can fill that component. If they do not form a coherent group, then a list of classes can be given. These classes are referred to using the label *grammaticalCategory*, which should be construed broadly to cover phonological, morphosyntactic, and semantic elements. Obviously, describing this aspect of templatic structure, in principle, raises a set of difficult conceptual questions: what constitutes

---

[10] These notions show a rough parallel to the distinction between *schematic* and *substantive* constructions, as developed by Croft (see, e.g, Croft 2000: 203, 2001: 15), with the caveat that these can be applied to the modeling of patterns of form and meaning, while the present study is focused on formal patterns alone. Croft's development of this distinction builds directly on its application to the analysis of idioms in Fillmore et al. (1988: 505), who also make use of the terms of *filled* and *open*.

56 A typological description language for templates

a given "category"? How do we deal with cases where a given class is largely coherent but certain members of the class are not allowed in a component (e.g., most person markers, but not all)? From what sources do we derive our categories for grammatical types?[11] Etc.

For the most part, these questions are sidestepped here since, while the components of the templates to be examined in Chapter 3 are specified for their associated grammatical categories in the database, these labels are not considered in the comparative typological analysis of Chapter 4 and, therefore, will not appear in the formal templatic descriptions to be presented. Rather, all that is considered is whether or not a given component is or is not coherent and what its filledness value is, with the specific grammatical categories for coherence indicated, at this stage, as a mere documentary convenience. The determination of whether or not a given component is open or coherent is then done by following the lead of the original descriptions to the extent possible, in accordance with the general orientation of this study to work from existing analyses (see Section 1.7). Adopting this approach is not meant to forestall the idea that examination of the correlation between formal types of components and their associated classes of fillers would offer useful insights into the structure of templates. Rather, it is simply viewed as being beyond the scope of the present study. Section 2.7 offers further discussion of this issue.

For the two types of filledness involving some concrete filler (whether the component is partially filled or completely filled), additional indication can be given for the form of the filler, which, like the inclusion of grammatical categories, just discussed, is included for documentary purposes but is not factored into the typological comparison to be done in Chapter 4. For cases where the component is *filled*, there is an additional specification of the grammatical type of the filler (again included, here, solely for documentary purposes) and whether the filler shows a phonological dependency such as what is usual for an affix or a clitic, specified via LIAISON. This specification will be considered in the later comparison. Components that are partially filled are also associated with a feature specifying the filler position (e.g., whether it is *initial* or *final*) in the component and additionally inherit all the features associated with open components, in which case those features are understood to apply to that part of the component not occupied by the filler.

2.3.3   Elasticity

A component is referred to as *elastic* if the number of elements that can be contained within it can vary (with an optional component being one that is allowed

---

[11] Regarding this last question, in the database used for this study (see Section 2.9), where possible, the categories are drawn from the General Ontology for Linguistic Description (GOLD) (Farrar & Langendoen 2003, 2009, Farrar & Lewis 2007).

2.3 Components

to have zero elements) and *inelastic* if it must be obligatorily filled with a certain number of elements. In the templatic descriptions that I am familiar with, inelastic components tend to have a size of one (see also Section 5.3.2), and none are treated otherwise here. It might be possible to treat certain kinds of length restrictions as involving components which must be filled by two elements (e.g., restrictions comparable to those seen in Section 3.2 or 3.8), and, in general, it may be that inelastic components of size greater than one would be hard to detect since they would generally be open to reanalysis as consisting of multiple adjacent inelastic components or as comprising a single component of a special type.[12] Inelastic components requiring one element are the prototypical "slot" of slot-filler morphology (see Section 1.4.3). The most well-known example of what would here be treated as an elastic component is the German middlefield (see Section 1.4.5).

As indicated in Figure 2.2, a component's ELASTICITY feature is specified, as relevant, for a maximum and minimum length or a fixed length count.

2.3.4 Stability

In the morphosyntactic literature, one of the special properties of position-class style templates that has been cited is the presence of so-called discontinuous dependencies (see, e.g., Rice (2000: 11–12) and Mithun (2000: 237)) where one element must co-occur with another element even if the two are not adjacent (see also Section 1.8.3).[13] In the syntactic domain, English verb-particle pairs have the potential to create such discontinuous dependencies when a noun phrase or pronoun intervenes between the verb and particle (as in, for example, *do him in* in the sense of 'kill him'). In the morphological domain, one sees similar patterns where, for instance, a verb root must always appear with a specific affix even if the semantic contribution of that affix is not clear and the affix may be very distant from the root, as in example (9) from Mohawk.

---

[12] For an example of the latter type, see Inkelas & Zec (1995: 543–544) for discussion of how a notion of "branchingness," related to syntactic constituency, can be reinterpreted along the lines of "heaviness." The former characterization could be associated with multiple components, while the latter treats the special property of the relevant constituent via a subdivision of a class of single components into different categories.

[13] The term *discontinuous dependency* does not appear to be fully standardized in the literature. In the present context, I use it to refer to cases where co-occurrence restrictions on non-adjacent elements appear to be lexicalized, in a broad sense, as opposed to connected to more general constructions. Thus, for instance, I do not mean to include so-called *long-distance dependencies* (see Sag et al. (2003: 427–452)) of the sort commonly associated with "movement" constructions such as those involved in the formation of content questions in a language like English. Discontinuous dependencies appear to be conceptually similar to the phenomena of multiple exponence or discontinuous exponence (Caballero & Harris 2012, Campbell 2012) to the extent that both seem to involve the encoding of what is conceptualized as a single meaning via instances of linguistic form found in more than one linear position.

(9) *taųsahsaterʌnóːtʌ*
   t-aų-sa-hs-ate-rʌn-ot-ʌ-'
   DUALIC-OPT-RPT-2s.A-REFL-song-stand-CAUS-PFV
   "You should sing again." (Mithun 2000: 237)

In the example in (9), the Dualic prefix *t-* is reported as obligatorily appearing with the verb stem based on the elements glossed as 'song' and 'stand.' There is, thus, a dependency holding between the Dualic and verbal elements separated from it by four other affixes. In order to capture the possibility of such dependencies, the present typology makes use of the feature STABILITY, which is a property of individual components. Components that are analyzed as never having a dependency with another component are classified as *stable*, while those which can have a dependency with another component (regardless as to whether or not they might exhibit a dependency in a specific construction) are classified as *unstable*.

Components that are *unstable* are in turn specified for the ASSOCIATE feature which indicates which component they have an unpredictable relationship with, as well as an ASSOCIATE POSITION feature, which specifies whether their associated component precedes or follows them using values like *left* or *right*. In some cases, these sorts of dependencies can be treated as asymmetric because there is reason to believe that the appearance of one element conditions the appearance of the other, rather than the other way around (see, e.g., Section 3.4). In other cases there may not be clear evidence, at least in terms of templatic restrictions, for such an asymmetric relationship, in which case each element is treated as having the other as an associate (see, e.g., Section 3.12). The typology does not specifically enforce that such dependencies must be discontinuous, though the cases of such dependencies to be examined in Chapter 3 happen to be of this form (see Sections 3.11 and 3.12).

A way in which the typology might need to be revised in this domain is in its restriction that a given dependent component will only have a single associate component. It is logically possible for a component to have multiple associates, and there are attested patterns that might even be instances of this (though detailed analysis would be required to make the nature of their potential dependencies clear). For instance, Leer (1991: 208) describes the coding of the Future in the (templatic) Tlingit verb as requiring the presence of three adjacent morphemes, suggesting potential multi-way dependencies of some kind. Furthermore, descriptions of Athabaskan languages discuss the presence of verb "themes," treated as complex stem-like verbal lexical entries, consisting of multiple discontinuous morphemes, potentially involving more than just a pair of elements (see, e.g., Kari (1992: 114) and Hargus (2007: 331)), again suggesting the possibility of multi-way dependence.

2.3 Components

Finally, the typological specification that a given component is unstable here would, perhaps, be better labeled as *potentially unstable*. That is, it is used when a component is reported as possibly being dependent on another component, rather than obligatorily. In fact, I am not aware of any generally obligatory dependency of this kind that must be analyzed as templatic. Rather, the dependencies appear to be specific to certain pairings of component fillers, as is the case, for instance, with the Mohawk dependency exemplified in (9), where the presence of the dependent element, the Dualic, is linked only to specific stems.

2.3.5 Specific examples of component descriptions

The discussion to this point has been relatively abstract, largely in anticipation of the detailed case studies to be offered in Chapter 3. However, it will be helpful at this stage to give some concrete examples of descriptions of specific templatic components within the typological framework developed here. Examples will be drawn from two cases to be examined in Chapter 3, the German clause (see Section 3.12) and a class of Bantu verbal suffixes known as extensions (see Section 3.5.3) so that the full analyses can also be referenced by interested readers. Following general practice here, the typological descriptions will only include those features that will factor into the typological comparison in Chapter 4. This means, in effect, features marked with a dagger in Figure 2.2 are not discussed or presented here (see Section 2.3.2 for relevant discussion). This section makes use of formal devices as part of the more general exposition, such as typed feature structures and graph-based representations of data, which may not be familiar to all readers. These are discussed in detail Sections 2.6 and 2.9.

The analysis of German clausal components to be explored here adopts the topological field approach to German syntax introduced in Section 1.4.5, with a specific emphasis on the analysis of Kathol (2000). In Table 2.2, the various position classes associated with this analysis are listed, and the examples in (10) (adapted from Kathol (2000: 58, 80)) provide an analysis of two sentences breaking down their subconstituents across these position classes to the extent they are present.

(10) a. [*Peter*]$_{vf}$ [*ruft*]$_{cf}$ [*Paul*]$_{mf}$ [*an*]$_{vc}$.
          Peter   call.PRS.3s Paul   PRT
          "Peter calls Paul up."

      b. ... [*daß*]$_{cf}$ [*Lisa*]$_{mf}$ [*die*   *Blume*]$_{mf}$ [*sieht*]$_{vc}$.
          ...that   Lisa   the.FEM.ACC flower   see.PRS.3s
          "...that Lisa sees the flower."

60   A typological description language for templates

Table 2.2 *German topological fields (Kathol 2000: 78)*

LABEL	CHARACTERIZATION
vf	First Position
cf	Second Position
mf	Middlefield
vc	Verb Cluster
nf	Postverbal Field

Two of the position classes, *vc* and *mf*, will be typologically classified using the description language for templatic components just developed. The *vc* position is chosen because it is an example of an *unstable* component, having, in some cases, a discontinuous dependency with elements that can occupy *cf* position. This is seen in (10a), where the combination of *an*, a verbal particle homophonous with a German preposition, and *rufen*, a verb meaning 'to call,' appear together in a verb–particle combination encoding a meaning along the lines of 'to telephone.' In some contexts, such as the citation form, the particle precedes the verb (and is written without a space), as in a form like *anrufen*. In others, such as root clauses where *anrufen* is the finite verb, the verbal portion of the construction appears in *cf* position, and the particle appears in *vc* position. As will be discussed in Section 3.12, I treat this as a symmetric discontinuous dependency where the *vc* position is potentially dependent on the *cf* position and vice versa.

The *mf* position is chosen as an example of a simpler component. Like the *vc* position, it allows more than one element of the relevant type to appear within it, though the elements may be of quite different types. This is seen in (10b) where two constituents, *Lisa* and *die Blume* are found within the *mf* "slot," which is found, in this case between the complementizer and the final finite verb. Fuller justification of the feature–value pairings for these two components is given in Section 3.12.

Depending on what is being emphasized at a given point in the discussion, two different representational systems will be used to present component (and template) descriptions. More frequently, typed feature structures will be presented, as in Figures 2.3 and 2.4, and this will be their dominant mode of representation in Chapter 3. In some cases (especially in Chapter 4), it will be more useful to present the descriptions in the form of graphs, as in Figure 2.5, which corresponds to Figure 2.4, representing precisely the same information in a different way. See Sections 2.6 and 2.9 for further general discussion on typed feature structures and the graph-based representations as used here.

2.3 Components

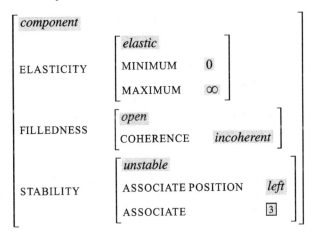

Figure 2.3 German *vc* component

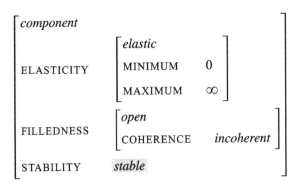

Figure 2.4 German *mf* component

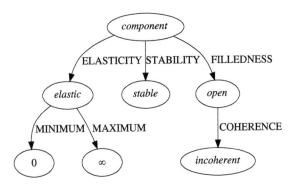

Figure 2.5 Graph representation of the German *mf* component

62   A typological description language for templates

As will be described in more detail in Section 2.6, in the feature structure representations in Figures 2.3 and 2.4, italicized terms represent abstract linguistic types, with the types seen here specifically being comparative concepts in the sense of Haspelmath (2010).[14] In some cases a type has no associated features and is therefore simply given as a stand-alone label. When a type is associated with features, it appears in the upper right corner a feature structure, with the associated features of that type appearing under it in small capital letters and, in turn, having as their values other linguistic types (which may, themselves, also be associated with feature structures).

Thus, for instance, looking at Figure 2.3, we have a description of a templatic *component* whose ELASTICITY feature is specified as *elastic*, meaning the number of elements appearing within it is flexible in nature. The *elasticity* type is additionally associated with features indicating that the component is optionally filled (since its minimum size is zero) but that it can also be filled with multiple elements whose number is constrained not by the templatic restrictions but, rather, other grammatical factors pertaining to the structure of the German verbal complex. This descriptive scenario here is coded via a maximum of "infinity," which should simply be understood as a notational shorthand for "not restricted by the template itself." For ease of readability, the feature structure is shaded in a number of places in line with the characteristics just discussed (and this practice will be repeated at various points below), but these shadings have no formal status in the description language.

This component is further specified for a FILLEDNESS of *open*, meaning it can be filled by a class of elements rather than a specific one, and treated as *incoherent* because those elements are not all characterizable in terms of a single grammatical class. The component's STABILITY feature includes a complex specification of the fact that it is treated as having a dependency with another component (the *cf* component in Table 2.2) which appears to the *left* of this component and is, here, represented only as a reference to another component via a boxed integer. This convention is discussed in more detail in Section 2.4.7.

The *mf* component depicted in Figure 2.4 is simpler in structure, since it is not associated with a dependency and is, therefore, simply *stable* without any additional featural specification required for that type. Its elasticity is the same as that for the *vc* component, and its coherence is similarly treated as *incoherent* since the elements that can occupy the *mf* position are not functionally coherent in any clear way. As mentioned above, justification for these

---

[14] The feature structures employed here are specifically represented as attribute–value matrices (see Sag et al. (2003: 193) for formal discussion). I will generally refer to them simply as feature structures, conflating the conceptual object and the visual representation, except in cases where the distinction is of specific interest.

2.3 Components
63

analyses of German clausal positions will be provided in Section 3.12, with the discussion here being exemplary in nature.

As already mentioned, the representation in Figure 2.5 simply restates the information in Figure 2.4 in the format of a (directed) graph (see Sections 2.6 and 2.9 for further discussion of graph-based formalisms), where types are represented as nodes and features as arrows connecting nodes to their values, which may themselves be nodes for other types. The feature structure representations will be used more often here than the graph representations since the former are already widely used in linguistic analysis. However, as will be discussed in Chapter 4, graph representations have the advantage of being well explored in disciplines outside of linguistics, meaning that tools and methods for their comparison are independently available, which will turn out to be of value here.

Moving on to a different example, one of the components of a template associated with the verbal extension system in Bantu languages will be introduced here as an illustration of a filled component. Relevant data, repeated from Section 1.4.3, is given in (11) from Chichewa.

(11) a. *Alenjé   a-ku-líl-íts-il-a*   *mwaná ndodo.*
       2.hunter 2-PROG-cry-CAUS-APPL-FV 1.child 10.sticks
       "The hunters are [making [the child cry] with sticks]."
    b. *Alenjé   a-ku-tákás-its-il-a*   *mkází   mthíko.*
       2.hunter 2-PROG-stir-CAUS-APPL-FV 1.woman 9.spoon
       "The hunters are [making [the woman stir with a spoon]]."
       (Hyman 2003c: 248)

In Chichewa, Causative and Applicative morphemes must occur in the order Causative–Applicative regardless of their semantic contribution to the verb. This is part of a more general Bantu pattern (see Hyman & Mchombo (1992), Hyman (2003c) and Good (2005)). In (11a), the semantic scope of applicativization with respect to causativization is what would be expected under approaches to morphological ordering adopting something like the Mirror Principle (Baker 1985: 375) since the "outer" Applicative introduces an instrumental argument which is used to initiate the caused action coded by the "inner" Causative. In (11b), however, the same morpheme order codes the "wrong" scope, since the outer Applicative suffix introduces an instrumental argument that is used in the caused action coded by the inner Causative.

This "illogical" ordering is due to a templatic restriction that requires the Causative to proceed the Applicative when both are present. It is, therefore, specific to these morphemes (though, as will be seen in Chapter 3, other verbal suffixes are implicated in similar patterns in Bantu languages), though it involves components that are optional as far as the template is concerned,

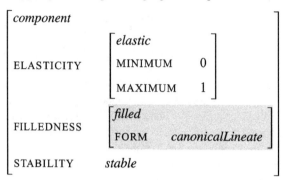

Figure 2.6 Bantu Applicative component

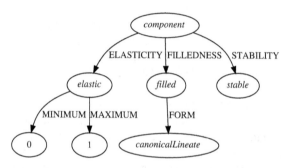

Figure 2.7 Graph representation of the Bantu Applicative component

since the appearance of these morphemes is dictated by syntactic or semantic principles, not the template itself.

The feature structure in Figure 2.6 gives a typological description of the component that the Applicative suffix occupies in this template and Figure 2.7 presents it in the informationally equivalent graph form introduced in Figure 2.5 just above. Like the German *vc* and *mf* components, this component is *elastic*. Unlike them, however, its size can only be zero or one, meaning that it is optionally filled but, if it is filled, only one element can be found within it. Its FILLEDNESS feature further specifies that it is *filled*, meaning only one element can appear within it, namely the Applicative suffix. There is an additional specification that the FORM of the filler is a *canonicalLineate*, stating, in effect, that it is a lexical item of the usual sort involving a pairing of a substantive linguistic form with some meaning. For ease of readability, the filledness specification of this component is shaded in Figure 2.6.

In the templates to be examined here, most of the fillers will be of the *canonicalLineate* type, but, in order to capture all kinds of templates, we need to also admit the possibility that a templatic component may itself consist of another

2.4 Desmemes

template creating a kind of templatic embedding. This possibility will be discussed in more detail in Section 2.5.5. Finally, the Bantu Applicative component has no dependencies with other components and is, therefore, stable.

An important point about the typological description language that comes through fairly clearly in an example like Figure 2.6 is the fact that these descriptions are of cross-linguistic types, not language-specific constructions. If we were trying to produce a language-specific description, then the FORM feature would presumably have a value somewhere along the lines of *-ir-* to represent the actual Applicative form. However, since this description is intended to facilitate cross-linguistic comparison, this level of detail is not included in the typological description (though it is indicated in the database for purposes of reference) (see also Section 2.7).

Having introduced the system adopted here for typological classification of templatic components, we can now turn to the system for the properties of the templates themselves in the next section.

2.4 Desmemes

2.4.1 Five high-level desmeme features

The term *desmeme* was introduced in Section 2.1 to refer to linear patterns analyzed as being directly part of the construction of meaningful signs, as opposed to appearing merely incidentally as the result of a more general pattern, except for cases where linear stipulation consists only of the ordering of segments and suprasegments in the specification of a canonical lexical item. In other words, *desmeme* is informally comparable to the term *template*, as understood here (the term which will be used more frequently), but does not, for instance, take on the various other senses of template that exist in the literature (see Section 1.4.6). Desmemes are treated here as characterizable in terms of five features, some of which may have complex values. These five features are summarized in (12). The features of STRICTURE and FOUNDATION are most central to the characterization of templates, as distinct from other kinds of grammatical objects, while the other features are more general in nature.

(12) a. CONDITIONING: A feature for characterizing the type of grammatical environment where a template is found, for instance, whether it appears in a specific morphosyntactic context or morphophonological one.

   b. VIOLABILITY: A feature for characterizing whether or not the linearization restrictions of a given template can be violated or not and what repair strategies may be activated in cases of potential violation.

66 A typological description language for templates

    c. STRICTURE: A feature giving a high-level classification of the nature of the linearization specifications associated with a given template, in particular whether they involve restrictions on the length of a constituent or the order of its components.

    d. FOUNDATION: A feature that classifies the nature of the relationships among a template's components, including partial indication of their relative order and what sorts of dependencies might hold among them.

    e. FUNCTION: A feature that indicates the general grammatical function of a given template. This feature does not enter into the typological comparison at present but is included due its usefulness for purposes of reference and potential interest for future studies.

Each of the features in (12) is discussed respectively in the following sections. Examples of desmeme descriptions, parallel to what was found in Section 2.3.5, are then provided in Section 2.4.7. The discussion here does not exhaustively list all of the types associated with each of these features, since a number of them will be discussed in detail in Chapter 3. A full list of the current features and values used in the typology is given in the Appendix, and Section 2.7 discusses the methodology used to determine which values are included in the present typology.

2.4.2   Conditioning

As discussed in Section 1.4, templates can be found in a range of grammatical environments, with morphophonological and morphosyntactic templates having had an especially prominent place in the literature. This diversity of environments means that the conditioning factors which may trigger the appearance of a given template are also potentially quite diverse. For instance, a template may be treated as being a crucial device in the construction of all elements categorized as verbs in a language. Or, a template may be activated in a particular syntactic construction only; and this is, in principle, independent of whether or not a given template imposes ordering or length constraints. Consider, for instance, the templates affecting the forms given in Table 2.3 (repeated from Table 1.3), containing verbs from Sierra Miwok, and Table 2.4 (repeated from Table 2.1), containing verbs from Tiene.

The templatic constraints exemplified in Tables 2.3 and 2.4 are both morphophonological in nature, and both affect the realization of verbs. However, the Sierra Miwok verb alternations are analyzed as being tied to particular patterns of verbal conjugation (Freeland 1951: 93), while the Tiene alternations are analyzed as being driven by phonological constraints on licit stem shapes (Hyman 2010a: 152–153). Specifically, Tiene exhibits evidence for severe restrictions

2.4 Desmemes

Table 2.3 *CV templates in Sierra Miwok (Freeland 1951: 94)*

PRIMARY	SECOND	THIRD	FOURTH	GLOSS
tuyá:ŋ	*tuyáŋ:*	*túy:aŋ*	*túyŋa*	'jump'
polá:ŋ	*poláŋ:*	*pól:aŋ*	*pólŋa*	'fall'
ṭopó:n	*ṭopón:*	*ṭóp:on*	*ṭópno*	'wrap'
huṭé:l	*huṭél:*	*húṭ:el*	*húṭle*	'roll'
telé:y	*teléy:*	*tél:ey*	*télye*	'hear'
CVCV:C	CVCVC:	CVC:VC	CVCCV	

Table 2.4 *Causative verb forms in Tiene (Hyman 2010a: 147–148)*

INFINITIVE	CAUSATIVE	GLOSS
-lɛ	*-léesɛ*	'eat'
-laba	*-lasaba*	'walk'
-lóka	*-lósekɛ*	'vomit'
-mata	*-maasa*	'go away'
-pala	*-paasa*	'arrive'
-píína	*-píísɛ*	'be black'

on the second and third consonants of stems, where only one coronal and one non-coronal are allowed in those positions and, if both are filled, then the coronal must precede the non-coronal. This restriction triggers the irregular patterns of causative formation seen in Table 2.4 (see Sections 2.1 and 3.5.5 for more detailed discussion). The templatic restrictions seen in Tiene stems are only readily visible in verbs since nouns tend to be too short to demonstrate them (Hyman 2010a: 155).

Therefore, unlike the Sierra Miwok case, the Tiene template's apparent restriction to verbs can be treated as incidental in nature, rather than being fundamental to the template itself. We can, thus, say that the conditioning factor for the Tiene template is, broadly speaking, phonological in nature, while the conditioning factor for the Sierra Miwok template is morphosyntactic in nature. Of course, the Tiene template also has some degree of morphosyntactic conditioning to the extent that it is stem-bound, but, unlike the Sierra Miwok template, it is primarily driven by constraints on licit phonological patterns in the language rather than morphological ones.

The typological description language used here includes specification of a high-level conditioning type for each template. Obviously, one can imagine various fine-grained ways of classifying such conditions, but, at this

68   A typological description language for templates

stage of database construction, given the database's relatively small size (see Chapter 4), the various templates are only classified across three types *constructionalConditioning*, which covers both morphological and syntactic conditioning where phonological considerations do not appear to be a significant factor, *lexicoconstructionalConditioning*, which is comparable to constructional conditioning but with the additional specification that a specific canonical lexical item or set of canonical lexical items appears to be part of the triggering environment for the template, and *prosodicConditioning*, where prosodic phonological structure is the primary conditioning factor for the template. With respect to the examples just discussed, the Sierra Miwok template would be an example of constructional conditioning, and the Tiene case an example of prosodic conditioning.

The *lexicoconstructionalConditioning* type is more complex than the other two because it is associated with its own features (not depicted in Figure 2.1). The first is FILLER POSITION, and the second is FILLED COMPONENTS. Each relates to the lexical item that plays a role in triggering the appearance of the template. The FILLER POSITION feature specifies a general position of the filler with respect to the overall template (e.g., that it occupies the *final* position in the structure), and the FILLED COMPONENTS feature gives a list which serves to indicate which templatic components contain the lexical items associated with the conditioning. (Section 2.4.5 goes into more detail about features which are used to "point" to components in this way.)

An example of a template with lexico-constructional conditioning was already seen in Section 2.3.5: This is the Bantu template involving an ordering restriction of the Causative with respect to the Applicative. For reasons to be discussed in Section 3.5.3, the Applicative will be treated as the component triggering the appearance of this templatic restriction. (With the evidence presented to this stage, either the Causative or the Applicative would seem like reasonable candidates.) Since the Applicative appears at the right edge of the relevant constituent (the verb stem), this would mean the FILLER POSITION is *final*, and the component containing the Applicative (which will be termed the *right support*) (see Section 2.4.5) would be the FILLER COMPONENT. (See Section 2.4.7 for a more detailed formalization.)

Of course, a notion like "conditioning" is potentially slippery, and it may not always be obvious how to choose a category and where to draw the line between them. For the case studies to be considered in Chapter 3, however, the distinctions seem relatively straightforward, though a larger database would almost certainly result in unanticipated complications, and this aspect of the typology should probably be considered relatively underdeveloped at this stage. Nevertheless, it seems important to include it on some level because, ultimately, it will be of interest to test whether there are significant patterns holding between kinds of conditioning factors and other templatic properties,

2.4 Desmemes

which means the typologization of conditioning should be begun at an early stage of investigation (see also Section 2.7).

2.4.3 Violability

The feature VIOLABILITY encompasses related, but potentially distinct, notions of "violation" of a template. On the one hand, under certain conditions, a given templatic constraint may simply fail to apply where it might otherwise be expected to. For instance, a language may generally impose a minimal size constraint on stems, which may be violated by a small set of lexical items even if there is grammatical evidence that the restriction is, in some sense, "active." On the other hand, one can consider whether or not the grammar of a language allows for a template to be potentially violated. If so, one can then examine whether potential violations are realized as actual violations (as in the case of lexical violations just mentioned) or whether some repair strategy is instantiated.

While these are aspects of the general notion of violability are partly independent, if a given templatic construction is not embedded in a grammar allowing the second kind of violability, then, logically, it will also not exhibit the first kind of violability. This logical dependency is why the two notions are treated together under a common feature here. The VIOLABILITY feature, specifically, has two subtypes. The simpler one is *notViolable*, which is associated with no further features, and is used for templates where one not only never sees surface violations but also where the grammar of a language does not even provide environments where there could be violations that are, somehow, repaired. The more complex type is *potentiallyViolable* for cases where the grammar does offer potential violations. This type is associated with two additional features, EXCEPTIONALITY, where it is possible to specify the nature of the contexts where any surface exceptions are found (e.g., *lexical* exceptionality if specific lexical items are exceptional), and REPARABILITY, describing how potential exceptions may be repaired. One possibility is that potential violations cannot be repaired, in which case the violation is treated as *irreparable*. Certain expected expressions in a language would then be ineffable (i.e., "unsayable") (see Fanselow & Féry (2002) for general discussion of ineffability as it relates to Optimality Theory). In other cases, the lack of a repair strategy may simply result in a surface exception (see Sections 3.2 and 3.9 for contrasting cases). As with conditioning, just discussed in Section 2.4.2, it is easy to imagine expanding the typology of violability in various ways, though the present size of the database has not necessitated this.

Data from Turkish will serve to illustrate some of the patterns of violability just described. It involves the presence of a disyllabic templatic length restriction whose effects can be seen in Table 2.5. The specific forms are adapted

70   A typological description language for templates

Table 2.5 *Turkish stem minimality and ineffability*

WORD	GLOSS
*fa-m	'F.note-1s.POSS
*fa-n	'F.note-2s.POSS'
*be-n	'B.letter-2s.POSS'
*ye-n	'eat-PASS'
kafa-m	'head-1s.POSS'
sol-üm	'G.note-1s.POSS'
fa-mız	'F.note-1p.POSS'
iç-il	'drink-PASS'
ye-di	'eat-PST'
ye-n-il	'eat-PASS-PASS'

from Inkelas & Orgun (1995: 769–773) (see also Itô & Hankamer (1989)). This templatic restriction will be taken up in detail in Section 3.2.

Some varieties of Istanbul Turkish exhibit a grammatical pattern wherein monosyllabic roots which can stand on their own in certain contexts (e.g., in bare citation forms for nouns or uninflected imperative forms for verbs) cannot appear in morphologically complex environments unless the resulting words are at least disyllabic – i.e., unless they satisfy a specific length template. (McCarthy & Prince (1993: 45–48) present a general discussion of such minimality constraints.) The forms in the first part of the table illustrate the application of the template. They are attempts to construct expected paradigmatic forms of short roots corresponding to the name of a musical note, a letter of the alphabet, and the root meaning 'eat.' In all cases, the forms are not allowed since they do not meet the disyllabic minimality requirement. For nouns, the relevant meanings cannot be expressed morphologically, creating a morphological gap (see Sims (2006: 1–19) for general discussion of gaps).

The attested forms in Table 2.5, given in the second table division, serve to demonstrate that the unavailability of forms like *fam, *fan, *ben, or *yen cannot be accounted for due to restrictions on segmental patterning or semantics. The form kafam meaning 'my head' is perfectly acceptable even though it contains the same sequence as *fam. The form solüm 'my G note' is acceptable by virtue of the fact that a consonant final root takes an allomorph of the first-person singular possessive suffix consisting of a -Vm shape, rather than the shorter -m form associated with vowel-final roots (see Lewis (1967: 38–40)). (Second-person singular possessive forms ending in a vowel also take a single-consonant suffix, with shape -n.) This makes the first-person possessive form of sol "naturally" disyllabic and, therefore, permissible, even though its semantics are all but the same as those that would be expected for *fam.

2.4 Desmemes

Similarly, the form *fa-mız* 'our F note' is allowed, because the first-person plural possessive suffix consists of a full syllable, allowing the entire word to be two syllables in length.

As indicated, in the cases of the nouns in the first section of Table 2.5, there is apparently no way to express their intended meanings purely morphologically for speakers of the relevant varieties.[15] In the typology here, then, the templatic restriction for nouns is first considered *potentiallyViolable* since there are contexts where it could be violated. At the same time, it is then considered *irreparable* since there is no dedicated repair strategy in the language. Its exceptionality is classified as *noKnownException* since no actual surface violations are found. (See Figure 3.1 in Chapter 3 for the full formalization.)

For the verb, however, there is an available repair strategy, as indicated in Table 2.5. The disallowed form uses the allomorph of the Passive suffix that is expected on verbs ending in a vowel, consisting of an *-n* (see Lewis (1967: 149–150)). This form is not allowed, but not for semantic reasons, as indicated by the allowed form *yenil-*. This form appears with two Passive suffixes, the second of which, *-il*, is the expected form after a verb stem ending in certain consonants. This suffix contains a vowel, thus making the stem disyllabic and allowing it to match the templatic restriction. In the case of verbs, therefore, the template is reparable, and this type of reparability is specifically classified as *morphosyntacticInsertion* since the repair involves the appearance of an otherwise unexpected morphosyntactic element. Beyond this, the templatic restriction for verbs shares all of its features with the one imposed on nouns.[16] (See Figure 3.2 in Chapter 3 for the full formalization.)

Another, more straightforward, instance of insertion being used as a repair strategy can be found in Ndebele, a Bantu language. The vast majority of verb roots in the language are of shape -CVC- or longer – that is, they consist of at least a single syllable. However, there is also a small number of roots with a shape consisting merely of -C-. Sibanda (2004: 16) reports that twenty-three such roots were found in a database of 1,432 verb roots. As with the Turkish case, when such roots are used in larger morphological constructions, their small size results in potential templatic violations, for instance that a word should be minimally disyllabic. The data in Table 2.6, drawn from Hyman et al. (2009: 283), gives a number of Imperative forms for both -C-

---

[15] One speaker I consulted about this suggested a way to build the possessives of such forms would be to use a compound along the lines of the English *fa note*, for example. Thus, the meaning is, in some sense, expressible, but one must leave the confines of the language's regular paradigmatic system.

[16] This Turkish pattern raises a question: Are we dealing with one template with two context-sensitive variants of reparability or two very similar templates? I will briefly address this issue in Section 2.5.4.

72   A typological description language for templates

Table 2.6 *Ndebele stem minimality and insertion repair*

IMPERATIVE	GLOSS	TRANSLATION
lim-a	'cultivate-FV'	'cultivate!'
bamb-a	'catch-FV'	'catch!'
thum-a (H)	'send-FV'	'send!'
nambith-a (H)	'taste-FV'	'taste!'
yi-dl-a (H) (**dl-a*)	'YI-eat-FV'	'eat!'
yi-lw-a (H/L) (**lw-a*)	'YI-fight-FV'	'fight!'
yi-m-a (H) (**m-a*)	'YI-stand-FV'	'stand!'
yi-z-a (H/L) (**z-a*)	'YI-come-FV'	'come!'

roots and larger ones.[17] The Imperative regularly consists of the verb root followed by an inflectional Final Vowel (of form *a* in Table 2.6). In -CVC- (or longer) roots, this strategy automatically results in a surfacing word of at least two syllables, as seen in the data in the first half of the table. This is not the case for the -C- roots in the second half of the table, however, which, with a form like *Ca*, would be only monosyllabic. One of the available repair strategies for forming imperatives of such verbs is seen in Table 2.6, where a formative of shape *yi-*, which does not contribute to verbal semantics, is prefixed to the stem (see Sibanda (2004: 113–114) for discussion of other repair strategies and Gowlett (1984) for general discussion of "stabilizers" of this sort in Bantu languages).[18]

The Ndebele data is also useful for illustrating the other feature (in addition to REPARABILITY) associated with templatic violability, EXCEPTIONALITY. Verb roots of shape -C- constitute a very small portion of the Ndebele lexicon and their exceptionality is often implied in descriptive analyses in cases where -C- roots are explicitly given the label "subminimal" (see, e.g., Hyman (2009: 191)). If we were to accept this analysis, they would constitute instances of *lexical* exceptionality for a minimal root template of some kind. Another type of exceptionality employed in this study is *semantic* exceptionality. This is found in a Chichewa template discussed in Section 3.5.4, for example.

The discussion of violability to this point has focused on cases where there is potential violability of a template since those are the cases where further descriptive specification is required. As discussed at the beginning of

---

[17] The abbreviations "H" and "L" in Table 2.6 indicate the tone class of the verbs they follow (Hyman et al. 2009: 308).

[18] In the wider Bantu context, the Ndebele case is not an isolated one, and comparable patterns are seen in other languages (see Downing (2006: 54–55, 144–151) for discussion of further examples).

2.4 Desmemes 73

this section, however, some templates are associated with a violability type (*notViolable*) that indicates that, given other aspects of a language's grammar, there do not appear to be contexts where a templatic restriction could be violated. An example of such a template is that associated with the German clause (see Sections 2.3.5 and 3.12). This template is understood to simply apply to all German declarative clauses, in some sense "defining" them, and is, therefore, considered not violable here. Of course, we can imagine a language very much like German where such a template could be violated, for instance if there were a small class of verbs associated with exceptional word ordering.[19]

Assessment of violability is somewhat complex, since it can only be done with respect to aspects of a language's grammar beyond the template itself. Moreover, there has clearly been a bias, especially in the literature on morphophonological templates (see Section 1.4.2), to focus on the analysis of templates which are violable, since this then opens up consideration of the interesting question of repair strategies such as the one exemplified in Table 2.6 for Ndebele. If Ndebele, for example, completely lacked a category of -C-stems, then its minimal size restrictions would remain somewhat "invisible" in the sense that they would consist solely of exceptionless patterns of surface realization without any paradigmatic irregularity, making them a less interesting subject for linguistic analysis. In fact, in general, since one of the most clear-cut ways to demonstrate that a template is grammatically active is to show that it triggers a repair strategy or disallows the appearance of otherwise expected forms (as seen in Table 2.5 for Turkish), templates which are not violable are almost certainly severely underreported, an issue I will return to briefly in Section 5.2.3.

2.4.4 Stricture

Three of the five high-level features of desmemes (conditioning, violability, and function) relate to general linguistic notions that could also be applied (if not strictly in the way developed here) to other types of linguistic objects. The other two, STRICTURE and FOUNDATION, are understood to be specific to desmemes, and are, therefore, the key features for modeling the special properties of templates. Specifically, the notion of stricture is used to describe the overall nature of the linear restriction imposed by a given template, while the notion of foundation is used to describe the relationships holding among a

---

[19] I am not aware of a language where specific verbs are associated with different word order patterns where semantic or pragmatic factors are not considered to be the primary determinant of these alternations (see, e.g., Hansen (2011: 232–260) for discussion). However, cases of apparent lexical exceptions to more general patterns of adposition order are found, such as instances of postpositions in German, which go against the dominant pattern in the language where adpositions are prepositional (see Di Meola (2003)).

74   A typological description language for templates

template's components. This section focuses on stricture, and foundation will be discussed immediately below in Section 2.4.5.

Two types of stricture are assumed here, *length* and *order*, each corresponding to the two major kinds of restrictions that have been observed in templates, as treated in earlier work (see Chapter 1). A canonical instance of a *length* template would be a minimal size restriction on words or stems of the sort just discussed in Section 2.4.3.[20] A canonical instance of an order template would be verbal systems describable in terms of position classes (see Section 1.4.3). This two-way distinction implies that a template cannot simultaneously involve both length and order restrictions, though one does find grammatical patterns where both kinds of restrictions appear to be active at the same time, as is the case for the Sierra Miwok data discussed in Section 1.4.2. In that case, templates involving restrictions on consonant and vowel occurrences in verbs both stipulated relative ordering constraints on segments and imposed overall length restrictions. The current typology requires treating such templates as involving a conjunction of two desmemes, one specifying distinctive ordering restrictions and another specifying length restrictions. (This will also be the case for one of the case studies covered in Chapter 3, as will be seen in Section 3.5.5.) The issue of multiple templates converging on the same domain like this is discussed below in Section 2.5.2.

Both *length* and *order* templates are associated with the features COUNT and CONSTITUENT, though the interpretation of these features is slightly different for each type. For a length template, the CONSTITUENT feature refers to what the relevant kind of constituent is that the length restriction is calculated with respect to (e.g., a mora or a syllable), while COUNT indicates the number of those units that the length restriction requires to be present (e.g., two syllables).[21] For an order template, CONSTITUENT specifies the general class of constituents involved in the ordering restriction (e.g., a segment or a morpheme), while COUNT indicates how many "slots" (here, *components*) are found in the template.

---

[20] The term *length* here is comparable to the notion of *weight* as often used in the phonological domain in the context of work on prosodic phonology. I have chosen to refer to this notion as *length*, however, to reflect the fact that, logically speaking, a length restriction may or may not be defined in terms of phonological units, though, in practice, I do not know of a clearcut case of a length template not describable in prosodic terms, as evidenced by the summary of the high-level features of the templates examined in detail here that will be presented in Table 4.6.

[21] For all the templatic restrictions that will be examined in the case studies in Chapter 3, the specification of COUNT for stricture is, in fact, redundant, since it could be derived by counting the components of a given template. This is because these descriptions include descriptions of all a template's components for the purposes of illustration. However, since it is conceivable that a given study may not choose to describe all of a template's components in a given typological characterization, the COUNT feature provides a way of explicitly indicating how many components are in a given template, whether or not they are formally described.

2.4 Desmemes

Order templates are specified for the additional feature RELATIONS which indicates whether or not the various templatic components are grouped into categories in a way that produces taxonomic relationships among them. Most order templates appear to exhibit only *simple* relations, meaning that the only way the various components are taxonomically related is by virtue of being elements of the same template. There are cases of templatic analyses, however, where components are subdivided into distinctive groups on the basis of observed interactions among the elements that can fill them.

An example of this is found in Kathol's (2000) analysis of the German clause, already discussed at various points (see, e.g., Section 2.3.5), and which will be fully examined in Section 3.12. Two non-adjacent positions in its template (see Table 2.2), *vf* and *vc*, are associated with a higher-level category *verbal*, which specifies that each is a position that can be filled by a verb (Kathol 2000: 83). The other positions are expected to be filled by different kinds of syntactic elements. One of the other case studies will also involve an order template with taxonomic relationships among its components, namely that of the Nimboran verb (see Section 3.4). The notion of a verbal *zone* developed by Kari (1989) indicates that there may be taxonomic relationships within the components of Athabaskan verbs, though, in this case, the zones represent specific groups of adjacent components unlike, for instance, the German case (see also Hymes (1955: 16–17) for an early, comparable suggestion for Athabaskan languages).[22] Whether or not taxonomic relationships among adjacent components versus non-adjacent ones may be interestingly distinct will have to await further research.

2.4.5 Foundation

In conjunction with stricture, FOUNDATION is the second key feature of the typological description language that is understood to be specific to desmemes. It is used to characterize how a template's components are organized into an overall templatic form. A template's foundation is associated, in particular, with a number of features that specify a role for a template's components in the larger templatic structure. For instance, all templates are associated with two positions, LEFT SUPPORT and RIGHT SUPPORT, which refer to those components occupying the leftmost and rightmost positions of the template respectively.

The term *support*, in this context, is meant to evoke a metaphor where a template is treated as a kind physical structure wherein various "blocks" have been arranged together to form a stable whole, and two other terms

---

[22] Hymes (1955: 17) also uses the word *taxonomic* (following Whorf (1945)) in a way comparable to how it is used here.

76   A typological description language for templates

for foundation positions are drawn directly from vocabulary for referring to different parts of arches, namely *keystone* and *voussoir* (see Cain (1893: 11–14)). The former term refers to the topmost stone in an arch and, in the present context, is reserved for a component that is, in some sense, the "head" of a template, as will be discussed further below. The latter term is used for the components directly adjacent to the keystone, if they are present in the template, and the typology specifically employs the features LEFT VOUS-SOIR and RIGHT VOUSSOIR in parallel with LEFT SUPPORT and RIGHT SUPPORT.

Template foundations themselves are classified into two types, again using architectural metaphors, *span* and *arch*. The former class of templates are those that lack a keystone component and associated voussoir positions (since voussoirs are defined in relation to the keystone). A given template may, of course, have more components than those found in the predefined positions given above, and there is, therefore, an additional feature of RESTKOMPO-NENTEN, which is formed from German elements to mean something like 'remaining components.' This features allows for the specification of a list of all the templatic components that do not occupy the predefined positions in a given template.[23]

The choice here to single out the positions at the edge of a template, a possible "headlike" position (i.e., the keystone), as well as the two positions adjacent to the keystone, is made largely intuitively. Having examined a large number of templates, my impression is that these specific positions may have distinctive properties from other positions. Fully testing this idea, however, will have to await future study. The most important point to bear in mind, at this stage, is that the description language is designed to be powerful enough to assign components roles in a templatic structure, to the extent this is deemed to be of potential typological interest. Since the "internal" properties of components can also be described using feature–value pairings at a comparatively high degree of precision, this means that components can have properties as elements in an overall templatic structure while also each having features sensitive to the particular "role" they play within it, making them analogous to grammatical relations as characterized by Bickel (2011: 402) in terms of being sensitive both to an argument's function in a larger construction and to its referential properties.

For purposes of illustration, the structures of span and arch foundations are schematized in Figures 2.8 and 2.9 respectively. The templatic components are depicted as a series of linearly arranged blocks and labeled for their position in the foundation using the terminology just introduced above. These

---

[23] The proximate inspiration for this coinage is the usage of the element *Rest* in an earlier name of the Ghana-Togo Mountain languages, *Togorestsprachen* (Heine 1968).

2.4 Desmemes

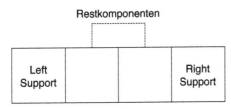

Figure 2.8 Schematization of a span foundation

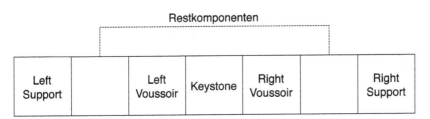

Figure 2.9 Schematization of an arch foundation

schematizations are not taken to describe actual templates, but this graphical representation will be adapted in Section 2.4.7 when two full desmeme descriptions will be given in anticipation of the case studies to be presented in Chapter 3. In Figure 2.8, the span foundation only contains two specially defined positions, the left and right supports, with the remaining components being restkomponenten. In Figure 2.9, the arch foundation contains both supports as well as a keystone and two voussoirs, in addition to two restkomponenten.

The notions of arch and span templates parallel those of headed and nonheaded structures respectively, though the differences are substantial enough that new terminology seems to be warranted. For instance, the notion of head is often used for an element that determines the semantic or syntactic category for a larger constituent, for instance in so-called "headed" (or endocentric) compounds (see Bisetto & Scalise (2005), Aikhenvald (2007: 30–31), Scalise & Bisetto (2009), and Štekauer et al. (2012: 79–82) for general discussion). However, a keystone component is not logically associated with such properties, even if the elements that fill that component may happen to be heads in a semantic sense.

To the extent that the keystone is a component around which other components are understood to be organized, it is probably closer to the phonological sense of head as a "strong" position in a prosodic constituent such as the foot (see, e.g., Prince (1983: 22) and Kenstowicz (1994: 557)) or the nucleus as the head of a syllable (see Goldsmith (2011: 169)), but, even so, the potential

78   A typological description language for templates

for confusion if that term was reused (again) is clear enough to avoid taking that path here. Moreover, clearly separating such notions terminologically will make it more straightforward, in the long run, to explore questions surrounding correlations between the properties of templatic components and other grammatical entities, such as whether morphosyntactic heads are more likely to take on the role of templatic keystones (see Section 2.8).

In terms of formal representation, foundations are the most prominent instance of the use complex feature–value pairings in the description language employed here, since the various foundation features do not simply have atomic values but, rather, their values are entire component descriptions (see Section 2.3.5). Moreover, the description language also allows the same component to fulfill multiple roles. For instance, a single component may simultaneously serve as a keystone and a support, as will be seen in some of the examples to be provided in Section 2.4.7.

2.4.6   Function

The final high-level feature of desmemes found in the present typology is, in some respects, the most straightforward, but also the least developed. This is FUNCTION, which specifies a broad functional category that the desmeme is associated with. In some sense, it could even be understood as a coding of the desmeme's general "meaning." The reason for including such a feature seems relatively clear: ultimately one would want to be able to consider whether or not there are correlations between a template's function and a templates's form. For instance, while a number of templates have been proposed for clausal constructions (see Section 1.4.5), all the cases I am aware of have involved templates whose stricture involves order instead of length.

Thus, while there is good evidence for templates imposing, say, minimal size restrictions on a constituent (see Section 2.4.3) and that these constituents may even be as large as a phrase (see, e.g., Sections 3.6 and 3.8), one does not find templatic constraints on sentence size stipulating that something like a sentence must consist of at least two prosodic words. Instead, when one does see grammatical patterns that, in effect, enforce a restriction like this at the clausal level, they are usually given analyses that do not refer to minimal length. This is the case, for instance, with the appearance of expletives in sentences like *It's raining*. There are various accounts for the appearance of *it* in such sentences. Some of these do not connect it in any obvious way to linearization patterns and treat its conditioning environment as resulting from abstract syntactic conditions (see, e.g., Sag et al. (2003: 346)). Others, though not explicitly invoking templates, suggest that their appearance may be conditioned by factors relating to overall surface linearization and, thereby, are comparable in nature to

2.4 Desmemes 79

templatic constraints as understood here (see, e.g., Bobaljik (2002: 252)).[24] The cases like this that I am aware of, however, never invoke a length restriction but, rather, one comparable to an order restriction, suggesting, for instance that something like a preverbal "slot" must be filled in a declarative sentence. Similarly, Good (2010: 58) develops a templatic analysis for clauses in various Bantoid languages, partly to account for apparent expletive objects, in terms of a set of ordering restrictions, parallel to what has been proposed for German clauses (see Section 3.12), rather than proposing a length restriction (see also Section 3.9).

It may be the case that this apparent correlation between clausal templates and order templates is an accident of sampling, but the current level of evidence suggests that it is at least worth exploring the possibility that something more systematic is at work and looking for other form–function correlations in templates. Doing so requires some degree of typologization of templatic function, which is precisely why a FUNCTION feature is included in the typology. At the same time, the present size of the database would not allow for anything beyond impressionistic examination of this area, and there is an additional concern that investigating it properly would require a relatively carefully worked out model of grammatical "functions," something which is beyond the scope of the present study, as already discussed in Section 2.3.2. Therefore, while the FUNCTION feature is included in the database, and each template is associated with a relevant functional category (in a broad sense), these will not be considered in the formal templatic descriptions below and the feature serves primarily as a placeholder to facilitate future investigation into templatic form–function correspondences. The actual function labels used are drawn, where possible, from the General Ontology for Linguistic Description (GOLD) (Farrar & Langendoen 2003, 2009, Farrar & Lewis 2007) or have been created on an ad hoc basis. They are enumerated in the Appendix.

2.4.7 Specific examples of desmeme descriptions

For the sake of concreteness, here I include two instances of full desmeme descriptions, one for an order template and one for a length template. The first is drawn from Bantu suffix ordering restrictions, continuing the development of

---

[24] The analysis of Bobaljik (2002) is developed within the syntactic approach known as Minimalism (see Hornstein et al. (2005) for an introduction). It is notoriously difficult to interpret analyses cast within this (and earlier Chomskyan frameworks) in more general descriptive terms (see, e.g., Nichols (2007b: 232)) Nevertheless, Bobaljik's (2002) unambiguous treatment of (at least some) expletives as involving constraints on surface form clearly gives it some similarity to analyses involving templates. In particular, he invokes the so-called Extended Projection Principle (see Baker (1988: 38–39) for an accessible introduction), which, in effect, imposes a formal, rather than semantic, requirement that sentences should have a preverbal "subject."

80   A typological description language for templates

the formal description of the template introduced in Section 2.3.5 (and which will be fully developed in Section 3.5.3). The second is for a constraint on the length of constituents in a Serbo-Croatian topicalization construction, which will be fully developed in Section 3.8.

As already seen in Section 2.4.7, there is a general Bantu pattern wherein a Causative suffix must precede an Applicative suffix when both are present, regardless of the semantics of their combination. While the Bantu verb can consist of a large number of prefixes and suffixes, this particular restriction is centered on the verb stem alone, which consists of the root and suffixes only (see Hyman (1993)). This template can, therefore, be understood as involving three components: the verb root, the Causative suffix, and the Applicative suffix. Since the template involves restrictions on the expansion of the root, this component is treated as being a privileged component around which the other components are structured. Thus, the root is categorized as a keystone, which, in turn, means that the template has an arch foundation (see Section 2.4.5). Since this same component is also at the left edge of the template, it is additionally categorized as the left support – that is, one component is the value of two foundation features. The Causative is the right voussoir since, when present, it must precede the Applicative and be immediately adjacent to the root, and the Applicative is the right support since, when present, it is at the right edge of the verb stem in this construction. Since this template is sensitive to the presence of two specific suffixes, it is classified as having lexico-constructional conditioning with the Causative and Applicative serving as its two filled components. This analysis is formalized in the feature structure in Figure 2.10.

Many of the conventions, features, values, and types in Figure 2.10 have already been discussed, or should be relatively straightforward to interpret at this stage. One such new type is the shaded *filledComponentSet* type, which serves as a kind of container where filler components can be listed. Further details regarding this formal description will be given in Section 3.5.3, and definitions of all of the features and types are in the Appendix, as discussed above. The most significant convention not yet introduced involves cases where a single component is classified as the value of more than one feature. This is indicated in the feature structure using "tags" represented as boxed numbers (e.g., [1]), following a convention developed for HPSG (see Section 2.6). When a tag precedes a feature structure (as is the case for the [2] tag preceding the value for the shaded KEYSTONE), this means that the following feature structure is the interpretation of the tag. When the tag is seen on its own, this serves as a reference to whatever the full value of the tag is. Thus, when considering the value of the template's LEFT SUPPORT, the shaded [2] can be understood along the lines of, "the value of this feature is the same as that of the feature structure preceded by this tag found elsewhere in the overall

2.4 Desmemes

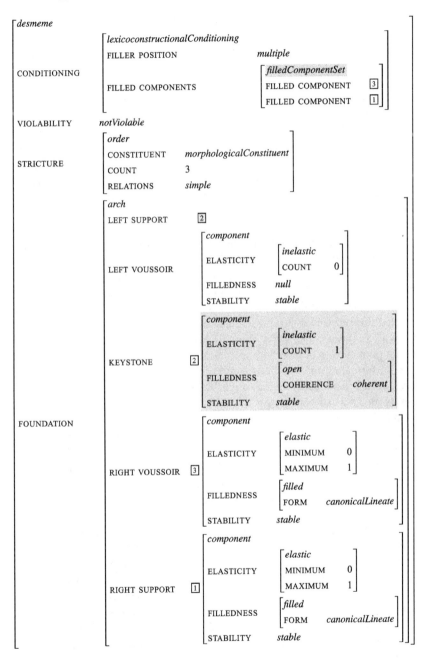

Figure 2.10 Bantu Causative–Applicative template

82   A typological description language for templates

feature structure" (which, in this case, is the feature structure which is the value of the KEYSTONE feature). This formal device is simply a representation of a more abstract notion of "value sharing" or "reentrancy" (see Francez & Winter (2012: 30–31)), which allows for an indication that the same linguistic element may be fulfilling multiple roles in a templatic structure.

A graph-based representation of the template's formal characterization is able to express this sharing relation more intuitively, as seen in Figure 2.11. The crucial features of the graph, in this regard, are the fact that three of the components have two arrows pointing to them, rather than just one, indicating shared values. Despite the fact that the graph-based representation is visually more intuitive in some respects, it will be used less often than the matrix-based representation due to matters of space on the page and the fact that matrix-based representations are more commonly used in linguistic work.

Finally, for purposes of presentation, a simplified graphical presentation of the desmemic description for the Bantu Causative–Applicative template is provided in Figure 2.12. This presentation builds on the schematization of an arch foundation given in Figure 2.9 and depicts the template as a series of block-like components. The non-existent left voussoir is given as a crossed-out component, and the left support and keystone occupy a single (vertically elongated) component to represent that one component takes on both of those roles in this case. The right voussoir and right support are represented as being optional (or *elastic* with a minimum size of zero and a maximum of one, in formal terms) via the zigzag horizontal lines, and they have a shaded background to indicate that they are filled components. The components themselves are also associated with labels underneath them indicating which parts of the Bantu verb stem they are associated with. Because of the fact that it is not straightforward to include all dimensions of templatic variation in a visual schema like the one in Figure 2.12 and the fact that visually oriented descriptions cannot be straightforwardly compared to each other in a rigorous fashion, such schematizations will not be presented systematically in Chapter 3 even if they do constitute a somewhat intuitive means to convey templatic descriptions.

The second example of a formal templatic description to be given in this section is for a simple length template found in Serbo-Croatian, whose templatic analysis will be fully introduced in Section 3.8. Serbo-Croatian exhibits a topicalization construction which requires that (in addition to whatever syntactic constraints might be present) the topicalized constituent consist of a phonological phrase that is at least two phonological words in length. Relevant data, drawn from Inkelas & Zec (1995: 545–546), is given in (13). The symbol "ω" in the examples in (13) stands for a phonological word, and the symbol "ϕ" stands for a phonological phrase.

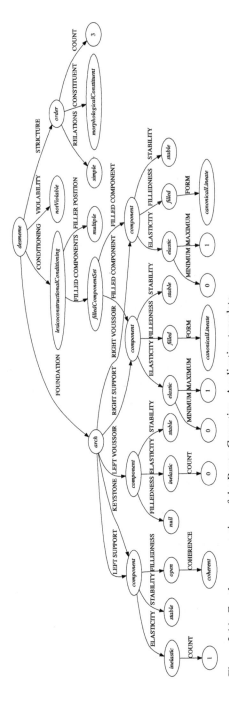

Figure 2.11 Graph representation of the Bantu Causative–Applicative template

84   A typological description language for templates

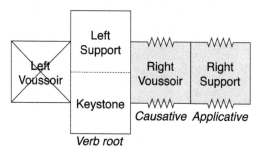

Figure 2.12 Schematization of the Bantu Causative–Applicative template

(13) a. [[*Taj*]_ω [*čovek*]_ω]_φ *voleo=je Mariju.*
    that   man.NOM loved=AUX Mary.ACC
    'That man loved Mary.'
  b.*[[*Petar*]_ω]_φ *voleo=je Mariju.*
    Peter.NOM loved-AUX Mary.ACC
    'Peter loved Mary.'
  c. [[*Petar*]_ω   [*Petrović*]_ω]_φ *voleo=je Mariju.*
    Peter.NOM Petrovic.NOM loved=AUX Mary.ACC
    'Peter Petrovic loved Mary.'

The critical distinction in (13) is that between the unallowable (13b) and the allowable (13c). In syntactic and semantic terms, the sentences are virtually identical. In phonological terms, however, (13b) is an attempt to topicalize a one-word proper name, while (13c) involves topicalization of a two-word proper name, which appears to be a crucial factor in allowing the construction to be used. Serbo-Croatian can, therefore, be analyzed as employing a length template in this construction, containing two obligatory components, each consisting of a phonological word. A feature-structure representation of the template, in the specific form of an attribute-value matrix, is given in Figure 2.13, and a graph-based representation is also provided in Figure 2.14, for purposes of illustration. Neither of these components appears to have a particular privileged status over the other, which makes this a span template, rather than an arch one, giving it a simpler foundation than what was seen in Figure 2.10.

The key conventions in Figure 2.13 have already been introduced, and the main point of interest at present is the fact that its stricture is indicated as being of type *length* (highlighted with shading) and its foundation consists of just two components, each of which serves as a support in the template's foundation. An additional point of note is that the two-word minimum is characterized via a specification that each of the components must have a length of at least

2.4 Desmemes

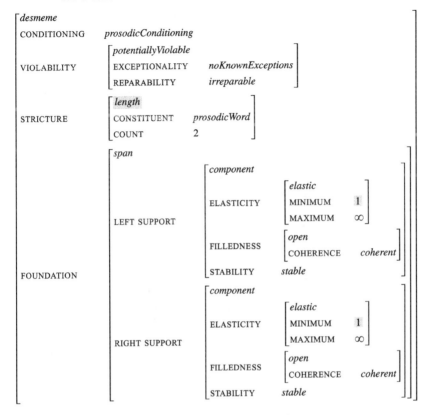

Figure 2.13 Serbo-Croatian topicalization template

one prosodic word (indicated by the shaded values of the MINIMUM features), though the components can also be longer. (A similar convention is adopted in Section 3.2, where a Turkish templatic restriction is considered.)

In Figure 2.15, a visual representation of the above desmemic description is presented, following the earlier example of a span foundation in Figure 2.8 and the representation of the Bantu Causative–Applicative template given in Figure 2.12. Here, the two components of the template are indicated as elastic via zigzag horizontal lines, and the fact that they can contain more than one constituent of the relevant kind is indicated by the fact the blocks representing the two components are horizontally elongated, as compared to the components seen in earlier schematizations.

As discussed in Chapter 1, a key motivation for the present study is to be able to conduct rigorous typological comparison of templatic constructions. The relatively elaborate featural descriptions of templates developed here, and just

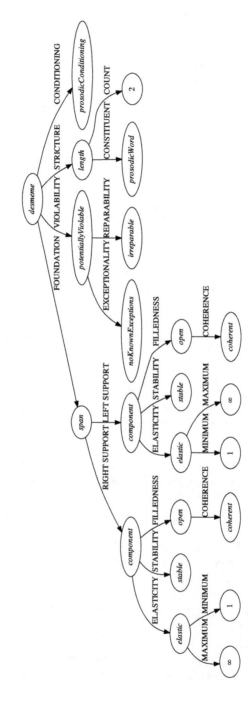

Figure 2.14 Graph representation of the Serbo-Croatian topicalization template

2.5 Additional templatic complexities

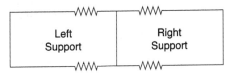

Figure 2.15 Schematization of the Serbo-Croatian topicalization template

exemplified above in Figures 2.10 and 2.13, can be justified in terms of how they allow a fine-grained characterization of the similarities and differences among the example templates (though, in the case of this pair, the differences seemingly outweigh the similarities). However, at the same time, it is clear that systematically comparing descriptions of this type is not a trivial task. The issue of how to do this is explored in detail in Chapter 4.

Now that the template description language employed here has been introduced, the remaining sections explore some additional conceptual and technical issues regarding the typologization of templates as understood here.

2.5 Additional templatic complexities

2.5.1 Four additional issues in templatic description

The presentation of the template description language to this point has made various oversimplifying assumptions or left clear issues of interest unexplored, at least in descriptive terms. These are briefly considered in this section, along with discussion of how they could be addressed in future work. The points to be covered in this section are: (i) the implicit claim that any given templatic construction will only exhibit behaviors consistent with one of the various value choices for a given feature (Section 2.5.2); (ii) the potential for seeing templatic constructions in a given language as potentially being related to each other in taxonomic fashion (Section 2.5.4); (iii) cases of convergence of multiple templatic constraints within the same grammatical domain (Section 2.5.3); and (iv) the possibility of the filler of a component in a given template consisting of another template rather than a canonical lineate (Section 2.5.5).

2.5.2 Multiple templatic types targeting a single constituent

An implicit assumption that has guided the development of the description language here is that any given templatic construction can only exhibit behaviors consistent with one of the various value choices for a given feature. For instance, a template must be specified as either being a length or an order template, but cannot be both. Such an assumption is relatively easily

88   A typological description language for templates

counterexemplified in surface terms. The Sierra Miwok data introduced in Section 1.4.2 (see also Section 2.4.2 in this chapter) involves both length and ordering restrictions. In terms of typologization, there is a tension between the fact that there are logical dependencies on the sorts of descriptive properties that are sensibly associated with different types of templates and the fact that "real" templates may not segregate themselves neatly into the types implied by those dependencies.

While it will not be carefully developed here, the initial solution to this problem in the present framework seems relatively straightforward: one can simply treat a given class of constituents as being subject to the constraints of multiple templates of different types. A given theoretical treatment may treat those types as fundamentally interconnected in some way, but in terms of typological description, the idea that certain kinds of logically distinct classes of templates might co-occur at greater than chance frequency is something to discover. So, an inability to describe such correspondences directly is not a problem in and of itself. Indeed, this method of classification could presumably help serve as verification of independently developed theoretical approaches, such as the Prosodic Morphology Hypothesis (see Section 1.8.2), which claims that morphophonological templates should be largely describable in terms of a universal set of prosodic constituents, suggesting, in effect, that restrictions on length may be driving other aspects of templatic structure – in particular segmental ordering – in a given morphological constituent (see, e.g., McCarthy & Prince (1990)). If, for instance, one finds an implication that the presence of an ordering template in the segmental domain is associated with a length template, but not the other way around, this would serve as verification of the Prosodic Morphology Hypothesis's claim that prosody drives templatic patterns at the word level.

In Section 3.5.5, an analysis will be developed of templatic restrictions in Tiene stems (see Table 2.1) where they are treated as being subject to two sets of templatic restrictions involving length and order so that the approach just outlined can be exemplified. Because only the Tiene case exemplifies this complication in the database, no specific coding system has been developed at this point to "link" multiple desmemic descriptions as part of the same template. However, the nature of the database would make this a relatively trivial addition for future work (see Section 2.9).

2.5.3   Multiple templates converging on a single domain

An under-recognized problem in the analysis of templates is the fact that many apparent "templates" are open to two different classes of interpretation regarding the relationships holding among the templatic constraints they are associated with. On the one hand, one could adopt a "splitting" approach which

2.5 Additional templatic complexities

would maximally dissociate each templatic constraint into its own "minimal" template. On the other hand, one could adopt a "lumping" approach where any set of constraints affecting the same constituent are treated as part of one template barring strong evidence to the contrary. For instance, is each pair of position classes in a given slot-filler template (see Section 1.4.3) a "miniature" template in its own right or is there one template that describes a "total linear ordering" (Inkelas 1993: 560)? This problem is similar, in some ways, to cases where multiple templates target a single constituent, as just discussed in Section 2.5.2, except that, in those cases, one is dealing with instances of templates that are distinct due to the logic of the description language, while the phenomena focused on in this section involve cases where the problems are not a byproduct of the descriptive framework devised here.

Whether one should be a templatic lumper or splitter is not a question that can be answered generally but, rather, depends on the specific facts of each language. In many cases, however, either a lumping or a splitting analysis may be equally plausible. Thus, for instance, Hyman (2003c) develops an analysis of a Bantu verbal suffix ordering constraints of the sort exemplified above in Section 2.3.5, and which will be explored in more detail in Chapter 3, involving a "CARP" constraint that enforces a template stipulating that the Causative, Applicative, Reciprocal, and Passive suffixes, if present, must occur in that order. At the same time, he suggests that breaking down this constraint into a series of pairwise constraints (e.g., Causative must precede Applicative, Applicative must precede Reciprocal, etc.) is also a possible analysis (Hyman 2003c: 276, fn.8).

The three case studies of Bantu verbal suffix ordering in Chapter 3 will adopt a more "splitting" approach for reasons to be given in the relevant sections, and that discussion will help serve as an example regarding the factors that may cause one to decide between one analysis and another in such cases (see, specifically, Section 3.5.6). Nevertheless, the default stance here will be to adopt a splitting approach over a lumping one for a largely metatheoretical reason: To the extent that templatic patterns do exist, it seems reasonable to assume that they truly are unusual given linguists' perception over decades that they are not the "normal" way that patterns of linearization are structured (see Section 1.5). This conventional wisdom may very well be wrong, but it seems reasonable to follow it at this stage, and it would lead, in general, to positing that templatic restrictions are simpler rather than more complex, all things being equal, which favors a splitting approach. Even putting conventional wisdom aside, this stance is consistent with the general typological approach adopted here which favors the splitting of typological distinctions over the lumping of them.

At the same time, the database is structured in a way that allows for cases of "converging" templates, where different constraints apparently target the same

90   A typological description language for templates

constituent, to be explicitly coded for where and how the values of their features overlap in terms of actual linguistic instances, rather than simply types (see Section 2.9). This aspect of data coding is not represented in the analyses here because it does not strongly factor in the present study, and presentations like those seen in Section 2.4.7 abstract away from this. However, in effect, many of the values in the database, for instance those relating to specific components, are associated with a unique identifier that allows them, when considered analytically desirable, to be "reused" across templates. This is most prominently used for the templates described in Section 3.5, where various restrictions related to the Bantu verb stem will be examined in detail, and components that are shared across the various templatic descriptions, such as the one containing the verb root, are defined only once but referred to in whichever templates they are found within the database.

What this means, in effect, is that, even though a "splitting" stance is adopted here, it is straightforward to discover a large class of cases where it might be reasonable to combine various sets of templatic restrictions into a larger structure. One can simply look for instances of templates with overlapping "pieces" to see how their restrictions can be merged. While this cannot be done fully automatically, the implementation of the database, at least when compared to other kinds of databases used in typological study, makes it comparatively easy to do.

2.5.4   *Language-specific subgrouping of templates*

This study's focus on typological comparison of templatic constructions means that another important area of their modeling, how they pattern together within the grammar of a specific language, will not be explored. Nevertheless, it seems important to at least observe that, as with other kinds of grammatical constructions, it appears to be the case that a language's templatic constructions can show taxonomic relationships of the sort that can be modeled via inheritance hierarchies wherein a set of templatic constructions are treated as subtypes of an abstract supertype by virtue of sharing a common set of characteristics which they are understood as "inheriting" from the supertype. They would then additionally be specified for those characteristics which are specific to their subtype (see Sag et al. (2003: 52) and Michaelis (2010: 141) for further discussion of such hierarchies).

A case where such a hierarchy would almost certainly be of value can be found in the Turkish disyllabic minimal size restriction exemplified in Table 2.5. As discussed in Section 2.4.3, while nouns and verbs are both subject to this restriction, there are different possibilities for repair of potential violations. For nouns, forms violating the restriction are *irreparable* in the sense that

2.5 Additional templatic complexities

there's no dedicated grammatical strategy to allow morpheme combinations that one would otherwise expect to be allowed to surface. By contrast, for Passive verbs, at least, there is a dedicated repair strategy involving the "doubling" of Passive morphology. In the current descriptive framework, the templatic restrictions on nouns and verbs are completely the same except for their REPARABILITY feature. It would be counterintuitive to treat them as completely distinct constructions in a synchronic description of Turkish (and work on this aspect of the language has treated them as connected to each other for this reason).

If we understood both sets of restrictions to be subtypes of a higher-level templatic supertype which was unspecified for reparability, then it would be straightforward to encode the close relationship among these two sets of restrictions. Moreover, the formalism developed here is straightforwardly compatible with the notion of feature unification (see Blevins (2011: 306–307) and Corbett (2012: 37–40)), which has already been exploited to describe taxonomic relationships like these for the purposes of modeling language-specific constructional relationships (Sag et al. 2003: 83–84). Extending it to describe such relationships here should be perfectly straightforward, even though it will not be pursued since it would shift us too far from the domain of typological comparison towards the encoding of grammars of particular languages.

2.5.5 Templates within templates

Logically speaking, there is no reason to exclude the possibility that a given template may contain a component which itself consists of a template. Moreover, it is not particularly difficult to uncover potential instances of such a phenomenon. For instance, there are various reported cases where second-position elements, whose placement is sometimes considered templatic (see Section 1.4.5), consist of clitic clusters, which have also been given templatic analyses (see Section 1.4.3). Thus, a component of a second-position template may itself potentially contain a template, depending on the details of the analysis. Good candidates for languages exemplifying this pattern are Luiseño and Serbo-Croatian (and perhaps some other South Slavic languages) (see Steele (1976), Akmajian et al. (1979: 2–15), and Steele et al. (1981: 23–59) for discussion of Luiseño, Franks & King (2000) for a detailed survey of the relevant issues in Slavic languages, and Spencer & Luís (2012b: 118–126) for overview discussion).

Similarly, the work of Kathol (1998, 2000:179–251) on the syntax of the German clause analyzes the entire clause via a template (see Section 2.3.5) and also treats aspects of the ordering of elements of one of its components, the *vc* component (see Table 2.2), as showing apparently template-like restrictions

92   A typological description language for templates

among the constituents it can contain, making it another potential case of a template within a template (see also Bouma & van Noord (1998)).[25]

The description language developed here can be readily extended to describe cases of templates within templates. The specification of templatic components already allows for them to be specified as *filled*, and, when the component is itself templatic, the filler can simply be a structural description of another template, i.e., an element of type *desmeme*. The templatic fillers to be seen in the present study will be largely restricted to those that are not desmemes – i.e., that are of type *canonicalLineate*. The one exception to this is the treatment of Serbo-Croatian second-position clitics in Section 3.7, where the second-position element will be classified as an *embeddedDesmeme* which is not further described. These limitations are not connected to any issue surrounding the power of the description language but, rather, the difficulties involved in devising algorithms for rigorous comparison when templates contain embedded templates, for reasons that will be discussed in Section 4.2.2. Clearly, it would be interesting to examine what kinds of templates tend to contain embedded templates. For instance, one might wonder if second-position elements are more likely to be templatic than other kinds of components, and, if so, what kind of templates are found in this position. However, exploring this issue is outside the scope of the present study.

2.6   Typed feature structures and templatic descriptions

The preceding discussion has already introduced various aspects of the use of typed feature structures as a formal means of encoding templatic descriptions. This section will briefly explain the reason for this choice in direct terms, bringing together a number of observations made above and adding a few relevant new points.

The primary reason for adopting this formalism is that it is well suited to capturing the range of variation among templatic constraints that have been identified to this point in a declarative "description-based" way, without relying on additional processual mechanisms such as rules of the sort that relate different structures to each other, which characterize some approaches to the

---

[25] The treatment of the *vc* component as an *embeddedDesmeme* will not be pursued below in Section 3.12 due to the level of analysis and interpretation which would be required to fully establish the position's desmemic status. This would ultimately distract from the templatic analysis of the clause itself, and this issue is, therefore, left open for now, with the *vc* component simply treated as an unfilled elastic component. (See Kathol (1995: 316–411) for detailed discussion of problems surrounding the ordering of elements in the *vc* position.) Another component of the German clause under this analysis also consists of an elastic component, the *mf* component (more generally known as the *Mittelfeld*), but, for that component, principles have been proposed to explain the ordering of multiple elements when they co-occur that do not make reference to linear stipulation (see, e.g., Uszkoreit (1987: 24)).

2.6 Typed feature structures and templatic descriptions 93

analysis of complex linguistic structure (see Blevins (2011: 298)). Since the goal of typological investigation is, in some sense, to compare descriptions, a non-processual descriptive apparatus seems preferable here.

Moreover, there is now a well-developed tradition of analyzing complex linguistic relations by means of feature structures, as seen, for instance, in their use in both Head-driven Phrase Structure Grammar (HPSG) (Sag et al. 2003) and Lexical–Functional Grammar (LFG) (Bresnan 2001) (among other frameworks). This means that it is possible to use previous work making use of feature structures as a guide for the present work and that they will already be familiar to a relatively wide audience. As indicated, the formalism here does not employ "plain" feature structures, but, rather, so-called typed feature structures, which augment the feature–value pairs of a feature structure with an additional label referencing the type of object the feature structure describes. Thus, for instance, the component feature structure descriptions in Figures 2.3 and 2.4 do not merely give feature–value pairs for the component but also include a specific indication that those pairs are describing an object of type *component*. The use of such a "typing" device is part of the introductory discussion of HPSG found in Sag et al. (2003) and is described in more formal detail in Copestake (2002: 32–79). More general discussion can be found in Corbett (2012: 36–37) and Francez & Winter (2012: 84), and Carpenter (1992) also discusses the topic in detail from a formal perspective. Here, I will focus on the value of typing for typological description.

The use of typed feature structures, rather than "plain" ones, here is directly borrowed from HPSG, since adding types to feature structures allows for the properties of a feature structure to be connected to taxonomic relations among different types of objects being described. This is especially useful for cases where two kinds of grammatical objects can be readily modeled as subtypes of a common supertype. For instance, as indicated in Figure 2.1 and discussed in detail in Section 2.4.5, the model for templatic constraints used here employs a two-way distinction in terms of templatic foundations: *span* and *arch*. Each kind of foundation shares a set of associated feature–value pairs (e.g., both have LEFT SUPPORT and RIGHT SUPPORT features), but arch templates have additional features, such as the KEYSTONE feature. If we want to encode that their shared features are not simply a coincidence but, rather, derive from the fact that they are both types of foundations, then we need some mechanism to relate feature structures to different kinds of objects in a way that allows these objects to be embedded in a taxonomy. This is precisely what is permitted by adding type information to feature structures once the additional step is taken of placing the types within an independently specified taxonomy, as is done here (see, in particular, the Appendix).

Taken together, the use of feature structures and types permits us to encode three useful kinds of information. First, as just discussed, types allow us

94   A typological description language for templates

to relate taxonomic classifications of linguistic categories to the kinds of descriptions we would like to associate with those categories, including specification of descriptive features that are shared across subtypes. Second, feature structures themselves can be used to describe part–whole relationships (i.e., partonomic/meronymic relations) of the sort associated with the notion of "constituency," which, in the case of templates, means they allow us to specify relationships among a template's components.[26] Third, in addition to describing part–whole relationships, feature structures can also be used to provide fine-grained typological classification, in particular for kinds of classification that can logically cross-cut different kinds of templates. For instance, there is no reason to reject, from a conceptual standpoint, the idea that any type of templatic violability (see Section 2.4.3) could be associated with any type of templatic stricture (see Section 2.4.4). Therefore, our descriptive system should allow the types associated with these features to freely co-vary.[27]

An additional way that the feature structures used here are augmented beyond being associated with types is that reentrancy is allowed, as already discussed in Section 2.4.7.[28] This, in effect, means that, if it appears that the same object needs to be described for a template in more than one place (e.g., if a component fulfills multiple roles in a foundation), it is actually described only once and the same description is referenced in multiple places (see Blevins (2011: 318) for discussion of the status of reentrancy in linguistic analysis using feature structures). This is desirable in the present instance since, if the same linguistic object is conceptualized as fulfilling multiple roles, describing it twice would fail to make clear that the similarities holding among the values of those features which "share" that object are not merely coincidental. The use of reentrancy in feature structures is again borrowed from HPSG and is, for instance, employed within that framework in the analysis of the shared conceptual subject pattern associated with so-called raising verbs in English such as *seem* (Sag et al. 2003: 367) (see McCawley (1998: 129) for contextualization of the use of the term *raising* for such verbs).

Adopting a formal device such as the typed feature structure does not, of course, directly entail adopting any particular means of representing that device, as already seen in the comparison between Figures 2.4 and 2.5, where a matrix-based and graph-based representation were employed to encode the

---

[26] See Moravcsik (2010: 646) for general conceptual discussion of the role of partonomy and taxonomy in linguistic analysis.

[27] Of course, this is not to say there are no actual restrictions on their attested co-variation to be discovered. Rather, there is no reason to embed any such restrictions in the description language itself (see also Section 1.2).

[28] The use of the term reentrancy for this concept derives from the fact that typed feature structures can be modeled as directed graphs (see Section 2.9) where the pattern of value sharing is represented by two directed paths (graphically seen as arrows) pointing to the same node, as depicted in, for instance, Copestake (2002: 49) and Figure 2.10.

2.6 Typed feature structures and templatic descriptions 95

same feature–value relationships. The actual machine-readable implementation of the database used here will be discussed in Section 2.9. In terms of presentation, these structures are most often represented in a matrix-based format that should be largely familiar to those familiar with HPSG, since practitioners in that framework have already had to consider significant issues, such as how to visually portray feature–value pairings, the type of a feature structure, reentrancy, etc. The key devices include: (i) representation of features using small capital letters (e.g., FOUNDATION); (ii) representation of types via italicization (e.g., *desmeme*); (iii) representation of a feature structure via a listing of feature–value parings, arranged vertically where the order is not significant and which are enclosed in square brackets; (iv) representation of the type of a feature structure via a type label in the upper-right corner of a feature structure; and (v) representation of reentrancy by means of tags consisting of a boxed number (e.g., [1]) where any features whose values are shared will be indicated by use of the same tag and with the full feature structure only appearing once (after a tag) to avoid redundancy. In addition, as already discussed above, the value of a feature can be another feature structure allowing for embedding of feature structures, or it can simply be a reference to a type.

While HPSG generally makes use of attribute–value matrices to represent feature structures, it has also been recognized that its feature structures can be understood as a kind of graph, in the mathematical sense (Kepser & Mönnich 2008: 115) (see Section 2.9 for discussion of this notion). Therefore, alternating between matrix-based representations of templates and graph-based ones is not intended to be any particular sort of innovation and merely results from the fact that different visual representations of the descriptions are more suited for certain expositional goals (see, e.g., Arnold & Linardaki (2007: 4) for an example of similar practice in work within HPSG itself).

However, while the formal devices used to represent typological descriptions of templates here overlap considerably with those used for HPSG, there is a critical distinction in their interpretation, which derives directly from the fact that the goals of HPSG are quite different from those of the present study. In HPSG, feature structures are used to characterize grammatical patterns within a particular language and are not intended to be used directly for cross-linguistic comparison. There are cases where parts of HPSG analyses of one language can be straightforwardly adapted for analyses of other languages (see, e.g., Bender et al. (2002)), but, even then, this is not intended to directly result in the construction of formal objects to support cross-linguistic comparison. Rather, the usual use of feature structures is as part of the analysis of forms that are attestable in a given language.

By contrast, here, while the feature structures are used to describe constructions in particular languages, just as in HPSG, they are not intended to be embedded in a larger grammatical analysis of those languages – and, indeed,

96 A typological description language for templates

important language-specific information may be left out if it is not expected to factor into cross-linguistic comparison. The most concrete difference between the two kinds of feature structures relates to the interpretation of features and types. The features and types of HPSG feature structures are used primarily to represent language-specific grammatical categories, while, for the feature structures employed here, the features and types are intended to represent comparative concepts, to borrow from Haspelmath's (2010) terminology. In other words, the outward form of the feature structure descriptions in both cases to some extent obscures the fact that they are being used to represent quite different kinds of linguistic description.

It does not appear to be the case that typed feature structures have previously played a major role in typological comparison.[29] Typologists do, of course, often depend on the use of features and values in their work (Corbett 2012: 108), and they also look at the interaction of multiple features and values. Bickel (2010), for instance, is a recent, quite explicit example of this that involves a large number of features used to categorize specific linguistic constructions (specifically, clause-combining constructions), making it similar to the present study. Bickel's features, however, are not arranged into feature structures.

Nevertheless, even though feature structures have not yet been employed in typological studies, there are two key reasons to make use of them here. First, as justified in Section 2.3 and Section 2.4, when modeling templates, it is important to consider their internal structure, which requires a feature system that can go beyond characterizing the properties of a construction as a whole but also can characterize its subconstituents and their arrangement. Typologizing the structure of constructions in this way has, to the best of my knowledge, not been undertaken before, which presumably partly explains why typed feature structures have yet to be employed in typological studies. We must also bear in mind that, as will be made clearer in Section 2.9 and Chapter 4, the technological tools that have been used in this study to rigorously compare typological descriptions in the form of typed feature structures have only recently become available. Up until now, a study of the sort done here would have been quite impractical – perhaps even impossible – without

---

[29] Of course, to some extent, this depends on what one means by "typology." The sense I intend here is essentially the sense discussed in Nichols (2007b). However, if one uses the somewhat looser term "typological," which is often employed to characterize studies focusing on analyzing and formally modelling patterns of variation across a handful (or even just two) languages, then Lexical Functional Grammar could be understood as employing feature structures within the context of typological investigation, insofar as its representation of certain types of grammatical information in a dedicated functional-structure (or "f-structure"), which is expressed as a feature structure, can be used to model shared grammatical characteristics of distinct surface structures across languages (Asudeh & Toivonen 2010: 450). See Bresnan & Mchombo (1987) for an exemplary application.

2.7 The nature of typologization in the present study

a research team of a size that is very rare in typological studies. Indeed, the practical difficulties involved in doing typology using typed feature structures may even partly explain why earlier studies have not attempted the kinds of structural comparisons of interest here.

2.7 The nature of typologization in the present study

The discussion to this point has made frequent use of the term *typological*, but the specifics of the approach assumed here to investigating phenomena from a "typological" perspective have yet to be fully clarified. In the most general terms, the typological approach adopted in this work should be identified with that of typology as a subdiscipline rather than merely meaning something like "cross-linguistic." Nichols (2007b: 231) offers useful discussion in this regard giving the following characteristics of typology of this kind: "framework-neutral definitions...emphasis on codability in definitions and in applications of theory, bottom-up or data-driven constructs, and concern with observable phenomena that pattern interestingly in the world's languages." The fact that the present work does not make use of a large sample may make it at first appear to be closer in spirit to the "Middle Way" approach advocated by Baker & McCloskey (2007: 294) which argues for looking at more languages than is typically found in generative approaches to morphosyntactic analysis (which often involve detailed analysis of a single language) but not making use of a particularly large sample. However, as pointed out by Nichols (2007b: 233), most studies falling within the discipline of typology do not make use of particularly large samples, especially in cases of work applying a new kind of typological metric or analysis, as is found here (see also Section 1.2 for further relevant discussion).

If we shift the focus to different approaches within the subfield of typology, I understand the specifics of the current approach to represent a continuation and extension of aspects of "autotypologizing" methods as described by Bickel & Nichols (2002). These are, among other things, based on the idea that, in order to properly describe cross-linguistic variation, it is more effective to allow typological categories to emerge inductively rather than to define a set of possible types beforehand. Moreover, I assume, along the lines of Bickel (2010), that it is not merely the values of features that should emerge inductively, but the features themselves, as well as their logical patterning. Therefore, while the presentation in this chapter began with a "complete" description language, in fact, the systems summarized in Figures 2.1 and 2.2 are actually a representation of the "state of the art" of a developing typology that has been constructed on the basis of the examination of a range of templatic phenomena believed to be representative of templatic diversity, with those in Chapter 3 being the ones that were subject to particular scrutiny. This explains why, for example, some

98 A typological description language for templates

logically possible feature values, say a value like *segmentalConditioning* for the feature CONDITIONING (see the Appendix) are missing from the present version of the description language – they simply have not yet been needed. The present descriptive apparatus, furthermore, tries to move a step beyond Bickel's (2010) multivariate approach in allowing logical relations to emerge among features in addition to new features themselves.

One drawback of the approach taken here, albeit one that is common to work trying to examine a domain that has previously not been subject to rigorous typological scrutiny, is that it is based on an extended "convenience sample" (Nichols 2007b: 234), rather than a "balanced" sample (regardless of the metric we might choose to assess whether or not a sample is balanced in a construction-based typological study – see Section 5.2.1). This limits the kinds of inferences we can make from a comparison of constructions in the database and means that Chapter 4, which focuses on comparison, will be more concerned with possible methods of comparison rather than drawing strong conclusions on the basis of the applications of those methods.

The use of an autotypologizing method of categorization – whether an expanded variant like the one adopted here or a simpler one – still relies significantly, of course, on the analyst to identify just what features are really needed in the typology. The way the specific ones here were chosen followed a principle that, if some aspect of two different templates seemed to be different in descriptive terms, that aspect should be coded differently. While this criterion may seem to be relatively simple on the surface, in practice it is probably the case that there will be disagreement with my assessment of when an apparent difference represented an actual difference. Such issues can only be properly resolved after initial proposals have been made, however, which is an important motivation behind undertaking the present work. Finally, the data that has already been collected suggests ways that the typological description language could be refined beyond what is seen here, as described in Section 2.5. These have not been pursued not because they are deemed irrelevant or uninteresting, but, rather, to ensure this study is of manageable scope.

2.8 What kind of typological results might we expect?

As just discussed in Section 2.7, the nature of the sample used in this study means that, while it can be used to generate hypotheses, it is neither large enough nor based on a sufficiently balanced sampling procedure that would allow it to be used to generate reliable results with respect to detecting linguistically interesting, statistically robust typological correlations. However, given that the complexity of the description language may obscure its potential typological uses, it is worth remarking here on the sorts of questions one might try to investigate if a larger, balanced sample were available.

2.8 What kind of typological results might we expect? 99

On the one hand, one could simply investigate whether there were greater than chance correlations among different sorts of templatic categories, for instance values for stricture and foundation. (Initial investigations in this regard will be presented in Section 4.4.) As discussed in Section 2.4.5, the two categories of foundation are *span* and *arch*, and the two categories of stricture are *length* and *order*, as discussed in Section 2.4.4. My impression based on the templatic descriptions that I have examined (including those not discussed here) is that templates with arch foundations tend to be larger in size than templates with span foundations, perhaps because their head-like element is associated with more complex internal organization in general. At the same time, templates with length stricture tend to involve fewer components than templates with order stricture since, for whatever reason, the size restrictions that are well described often involve two prosodic units, following from an apparent phonological bias towards binarity in prosodic structures (see, e.g., Inkelas & Zec (1995: 544) and Downing (2006: 9)). Therefore, we might suspect that length templates (i.e., templates whose stricture involves length) will tend to also be span templates (i.e., templates whose foundation lacks a foundational keystone) – that is, templates which are smaller due to their stricture will be associated with the kind of foundation that also tends to be associated with smaller templates.

To pick another example, the descriptions I have seen of templates involving unbounded elastic components (more traditionally referred to as "fields") have more often involved syntactic constituents than morphological ones. This is not entirely surprising given that "syntax" is generally understood to be less bounded than "morphology," but, with a larger database, it is nevertheless something that could be rigorously explored.

On the other hand, one could also explore the patterning of templatic constructions, or desmemic constructions more generally (see Section 2.1), within and across languages rather than simply across constructions, in a way comparable to the studies of phonological processes in "word" domains found in Bickel et al. (2009) and Schiering et al. (2010). Such studies would allow one to assess, for instance, whether templatic constructions tend to non-trivially converge onto common domains (see also Section 2.5.2 and Section 2.5.3) or even more abstract concerns such as whether languages tend to exhibit comparable levels of overall "templaticity" when their overall grammars are considered, even if their templaticity within different grammatical domains is clearly quite distinct. Studying such a question would, of course, involve developing new (and potentially complex) kinds of metrics, but one could immediately imagine it being used to help address a long-standing question regarding the relationship between morphology and syntax: the extent to which the elaborate morphology of polysynthetic languages, which often displays templatic properties, is associated with syntax that is more "free" in some

100   A typological description language for templates

sense (see, e.g., Jelinek (1984) and Baker (1996: 9–35), with much of this and related work being inspired by earlier observations of Hale (1983); Koenig & Michelson (2012) offer a recent, somewhat different, though still relevant, approach). There is of course quite a bit more involved in the relationship between morphological and syntactic constructions than linear ordering, but, even so, patterns of linear ordering between constructions of both types within and across languages clearly have bearing on even such basic questions as whether it is reasonable to assume that a two-way distinction between "morphological" and "syntactic" constructions is a useful one for understanding the grammars of all languages.

The sampling required for the various studies of the sort just described above would be somewhat different in nature for each (see also Section 5.2.1). In order to look for correlations of different templatic properties across constructions, the database would have be expanded to include many more constructions regardless of the language they are found in, with relevant parameters presumably centering around having a balance of morphophonological, morphosyntactic, and syntactic constructions in order to ensure that a wide range of grammatical contexts are considered. In order to look for patterns within and across languages, one would presumably want to locate and describe all patterns of linear stipulation found within a given set of languages, in effect producing a kind of "templatic grammar" for them. This latter sort of collection would clearly be time consuming and would only be possible for exceptionally well-described languages, but the required efforts would probably be roughly on the order of the studies of word domains described in Bickel et al. (2009) and Schiering et al. (2010), which suggests that they would be feasible, if not necessarily easy.

2.9   Implementing the description language in a database

Because typological comparison involving feature structure representations is, to the best of my knowledge, novel, some remarks will be made regarding the implementation of the database used in this study. While this section will discuss some of the specific technologies chosen for various aspects of data modeling and encoding, it should be emphasized that what is most crucial is making use of a system designed to characterize formal descriptions with graph-like properties, regardless of the particular tools employed. In using the term *graph*, I follow its technical mathematical sense as used in graph theory (see, e.g., Diestel (1997) for an introductory text), where a graph is understood as a set of *nodes* (also termed *points* or *vertices*) and *arcs* (also termed *edges* or *lines*) connecting those nodes (see, e.g., Diestel (1997: 2)). Nodes and arcs of this kind can be seen in Figures 2.5 and 2.7 above (though see below for a slight qualification regarding how the presentation of these graphs differs from

2.9 Implementing the description language in a database

what one would find in a graph strictly adhering to the usual mathematical sense).

The graphs used to describe templates here have two other significant additional properties from a linguistic and formal perspective. They are *directed*, meaning that, for a given pair of nodes that are connected by an arc, there is an ordering specification which treats one node as initiating the arc and the other as terminating it. (Such directed graphs are sometimes also referred to as *digraphs* (Diestel 1997: 23).) The directed arc relation is indicated in the figures just referenced above with arrows, where the arrowhead points to the terminal node. In addition, the graphs make use of labels on arcs (indicating feature names). (The formal interpretation of the labels on the nodes will be discussed immediately below.) Adding directionality and arc labels to the graphs allows them to effectively represent feature–value pairs where the initiating node is interpreted as being specified for a feature indicated via an arc label, with the terminal node serving as the value of that feature. The addition of these properties means that the graphs employed here deviate from core cases of mathematical graphs, though, as we will see, existing tools make them straightforward to encode in machine-readable form despite this.

From a mathematical perspective, typed feature structures (see Section 2.6) and directed graphs can be treated as more or less equivalent, though typed feature structures have a semi-standardized interpretation in linguistics that graphs do not. Moreover, graphs, in and of themselves, do not make use of a privileged notion of "typing" for subparts of a graph as found in typed feature structures, but this can be straightforwardly modeled by associating any node associated with a type (which includes all nodes of focus for this study except those used to encode integer values) with an additional arc pointing to a node indicating the type of the node initiating the arc. In fact, this is what is found in the database used here, but this arc is in, in effect, collapsed onto its node as a node label in the presentation forms of the graphs in the interests of clarity, given the important role of a node's type in the descriptive model.

The actual implementation of these graph-based descriptions is achieved using technologies developed for the Semantic Web, in particular, the contemporary set of technologies associated with the Linked Data approach to the Semantic Web (see Allemang & Hendler (2011) for a general introduction to the Semantic Web, Bizer et al. (2009a) for a general introduction to Linked Data, and Good & Hendryx-Parker (2006), Good (2012: 4–8), Chiarcos et al. (2012), Moran (2012), and Nordhoff (2012) for discussion in a linguistic context, with the latter two papers oriented towards Linked Data for typological investigation).[30]

---

[30] The current implementation of the database does not have the whole range of characteristics commonly associated with the Linked Data. For instance, there is no attempt to connect the

102   A typological description language for templates

While these technologies are primarily intended to facilitate publication of large, machine-readable datasets on the Web, they are useful in the present context for several reasons not directly connected to this aim. First, since the Web itself is well represented as a kind of graph (see, e.g., Kleinberg et al. (1999)), a number of technologies designed to make data more accessible on the Web are also effective at encoding and processing graph-based representations of information more generally. Second, these technologies allow for a straightforward separation of the encoding of the general model used to characterize specific kinds of data (i.e., what is here called a description language) and the descriptions themselves, which makes documentation of, and adherence to, that model more straightforward (see Farrar (2012: 241–249) for relevant discussion in a typological context). Third, the current role of these technologies in making data more accessible on the Web has generated significant interest, in particular in the domain of tool development, reducing the workload involved in encoding and processing data making use of them. Finally, of course, if one does want to make the contents of a database widely available, there are clear advantages to encoding it using methods designed to facilitate Web-based dissemination from the start.

The most significant Semantic Web technology for the development of the database is the Resource Description Framework (RDF), which can effectively be understood as a machine-readable language for describing arbitrary sets of objects and their properties. It is built around the notion that entities can effectively be described via "triples," three-part statements of the form SUBJECT PREDICATE OBJECT. In these triples, the subjects and objects can additionally be given unique identifiers permitting their participation in more than one triple. This effectively allows one to encode data in the form of graphs where the basic units of the graph are triples with potentially overlapping nodes (corresponding to subjects or objects). RDF has not yet been widely deployed for traditional descriptive linguistics but, as an important means for disseminating Linked Data, its use has been increasing, and it is one of the export formats for typological datasets associated with the *World Atlas of Language Structures* (WALS) (Dryer & Haspelmath 2013), the *World Loanword Database* (Haspelmath & Tadmor 2009), and the *Atlas of Pidgin and Creole Structures* (Michaelis et al. 2013) (see also Forkel (2014)). Further discussion of RDF in a descriptive or typological linguistic context can be found in Simons

contents of the database to important data "hubs" such as DBpedia (see Bizer et al. (2009b)), since the specialized nature of the database's content does not result in significant, clearly valuable points of linkage. Similarly, the various URIs used to identify entities described in the database cannot, at this time, be automatically dereferenced due, again, to the lack of obvious need for this at present given the database's specialized use. Nevertheless, I use the term Linked Data here since it has become a more familiar reference point for linguists for the general implementational approach adopted here than other possible terms as such the Semantic Web or RDF.

2.9 Implementing the description language in a database

(2005), Good & Hendryx-Parker (2006), Cysouw (2007b: 63–65), and Good (2012: 4–8). It has also seen attention in research in computational linguistics (see, e.g., Ide et al. (2003) and McCrae et al. (2011)).

The various descriptions of templates in the database are encoded in RDF, and a machine-readable encoding of the overall description language is encoded in RDF Schema, a means to describe RDF data models using RDF itself (Brickley & Guha 2004). The RDF database was built using the Protégé ontology editor and knowledge-base framework.[31] Processing of the data in the database to create presentation forms of the templatic descriptions (e.g., in the form of graph-based descriptions, such as that seen in Figure 2.5 or feature structures, such as that seen Figure 2.3), and to conduct quantitative comparative investigation (see Chapter 4), was done via various scripts, which relied, in particular, on the RDFLib RDF processing library written for Python.[32]

The database itself, and related materials, such as the scripts employed in this study, are presently available at https://github.com/jcgood/desmeme. The discussion here only considers technical issues at a very broad level under the assumption that those wishing to explore them in more detail can do so by inspecting the online materials (which were not reviewed directly for this book).

Having now presented the description language developed here to conduct a typological comparison of templates in some detail, the next chapter applies that description to a range of exemplary case studies.

---

[31] The current version of Protégé can be found at http://protege.stanford.edu and a historical overview of the tool, including its extension to work with RDF, is given in Gennari et al. (2003). The specific version of Protégé used in this study is the Protégé-Frames variant.

[32] See http://python.org for further information on the Python programming language and https://github.com/RDFLib for information on RDFLib. In more limited instances, Perl scripts and R were used as well to facilitate some of the data processing reported on in Chapter 4 (see Sections 4.3 and 4.4).

3 Typologizing templates: case studies

3.1 Introduction to the case studies

Chapter 2 developed a typological description language for templatic constructions and introduced, for purposes of exemplification, a number of descriptions of templates and template fragments using that description language. In this chapter, these descriptions – which will often be referred to as *formal characterizations* below – are presented more systematically via a number of case studies of specific templatic constructions. These case studies should be understood as constituting a convenience sample, rather than a balanced sample, but, at the same time, they are designed to cover a wide enough range of patterns that it is hoped they will offer a reasonable approximation of the variation that would be found via more systematic collection efforts. A convenience sample is adopted at this stage for two reasons. First, the procedure for collecting a "balanced" sample of templatic constructions is not obvious, and it seems sensible, therefore, to at first make sure the typological space is reasonably well explored in qualitative terms before attempting to address an additional concern such as "balance."[1] Second, in considering a domain that is relatively unexamined typologically, one first needs to, in effect, "test" one's typological models and coding procedures across a diverse array of constructions, which is more efficiently done by using an impressionistic sampling procedure, assembling constructions showing clear surface diversity, than following a more rigid collection procedure. There are, of course, clear drawbacks to adopting such a method, the most important of which being the limited range of typological conclusions one can draw from data sampled in this way but, as Nichols (2007b: 233–234) points out, beginning the investigation of a complex grammatical phenomenon in this way is not unusual in typological studies.

As will be made clear in subsequent sections, several of the templatic constructions to be considered derive from my own work on linearization

---

[1] While significant attention has been paid to issues surrounding typological sampling of languages to control for genealogical and areal effects (see, e.g, Dryer (1989), Bickel (2008), and Dahl (2008)), there does not appear to be a body of work dedicated to achieving balanced samples across other kinds of linguistic objects that are, in effect, sampled in one way or another, such as constructions or grammatical features (see also Section 5.2.1).

3.1 Introduction to the case studies

phenomena. However, most of them are drawn from descriptions developed by other authors. I also include an analysis of two "control" constructions involving linear stipulation so that they can be compared with the templatic constructions. These are the English plural strategy involving suffixal -*s* and the English verb phrase ordering restrictions on unflagged objects (see Haspelmath (2005: 2) and Malchukov et al. (2010: 8) for use of the term *flagging*). These are developed in Section 3.13.

There is an inherent danger involved in any kind of typological investigation that the categorization ultimately assumed by the typologist on the basis of available descriptions may be "incorrect" for any number of reasons. These range from an outright misinterpretation of a description, to a plausible, but ultimately less than ideal, interpretation of a vague description, to a "correct" interpretation of a description that is itself flawed when set against the empirical facts of the language. Given the complexity of the typological descriptions employed here, the chances of errors of one kind or another appearing in the formal characterizations of templates to be presented below due to these, or other, reasons is quite high. Readers are, therefore, encouraged to consult the original sources if they seek to use the results of this study to draw secondary conclusions, especially given that considerations of space will sometimes require the justifications for a given formal templatic characterization to be relatively abbreviated. At the same time, the fine-grained nature of the typological descriptions employed here means that a single error in categorization does not mean an entire template is necessarily miscategorized, as could be the case in more reductionist typologies. (See also Section 5.2.2 for related discussion.)

As will be seen below, the case studies are drawn from a wide range of morphophonological and morphosyntactic patterns, as well as from a wide range of languages and language families. Perhaps the most conspicuous absence will be the lack of an analysis of the template that has been described for the Athabaskan verb (see Section 1.4.3). It is left out because, based on various available descriptions, the canonical Athabaskan verb appears to be a good candidate for an analysis involving multiple templates converging on a single domain (see Section 2.5.3) as well as templates embedded within templates (see Section 2.5.5), or something very much like this (see, e.g., Hargus (2010: 1028–1029) for overview discussion). While the description language developed in Chapter 2 could straightforwardly be extended to describe such complications, they pose problems with respect to making use of algorithms for typological comparison (see Chapter 4). Moreover, from an outside perspective, I have found it difficult to find a specific templatic analysis of an Athabaskan verb to treat as "canonical" given the large number of analyses that have been provided for verb forms in its daughter languages. In the case studies below, the one that seems descriptively most similar to the patterns

106   Typologizing templates: case studies

found in the Athabaskan verb is probably the one focusing on the Nimboran verb in Section 3.4.

Another potentially surprising omission from the case studies below may be the lack of a study exemplifying Semitic CV-skeleton templates (see Section 1.4.2). In broad structural terms, the Tiene (Section 3.5.5) case study covers similar phenomena, providing an example of how the approach adopted here could be used for such patterns. The primary reason that they are not included here is because one of their special areas of interest, the way the various templates organize themselves into paradigms (along the lines of what was seen for Sierra Miwok in Table 1.3) is beyond the scope of the present study. (See Aronoff (1994: 123–164) for detailed discussion of such paradigmatic patterns.)

In the following sections, the various case studies are presented, arranged roughly from smallest to largest constituent size (in terms of phonological length), though with some exceptions to this ordering for ease of exposition (e.g., grouping the discussion of the Tiene verb stem with those of other Bantu languages even though its properties are quite distinct). Readers who have not read Chapter 2 may find aspects of this chapter difficult to follow since much of it assumes at least passive familiarity with the typological description language developed in that chapter. The definitions of the full set concepts used in the description language are given in the Appendix, which may prove a useful reference in interpreting the analyses given below.

3.2   Turkish stems

The first case study to be examined here involves a disyllabic minimal size restriction on Turkish stems that was already discussed in Section 2.4.3 and that will be briefly re-summarized here. As discussed in Section 2.5.4, the Turkish data serves as a useful illustration of the issue of templatic subgrouping.

The analysis here is based on Inkelas & Orgun (1995). Relevant data is given below in Table 3.1, repeated from Table 2.5 (Inkelas & Orgun 1995: 769–773). The template requires any morphologically complex noun or verb stem to be at least two syllables in length. Most stems will fulfill this restriction "naturally" by virtue of the shapes of the root morphemes and any accompanying affix. However, the template becomes visible for roots with shape CV in morphological environments where an accompanying suffix would be expected to be shape C. In such cases, the predicted CV-C stems do not surface due to the templatic restriction. As discussed in Section 2.4.3, this makes certain nominal expressions ineffable, such as those in the first section of Table 3.1. Verbs are also subject to this restriction but, in the morphological environment where the restriction is visible involving the Passive suffix, forms that would

3.2 Turkish stems

Table 3.1 *Turkish stem minimality*

WORD	GLOSS
*fa-m	'F.note-1s.POSS
*fa-n	'F.note-2s.POSS'
*be-n	'B.letter-2s.POSS'
*ye-n	'eat-PASS'
kafa-m	'head-1s.POSS'
sol-üm	'G.note-1s.POSS'
fa-mız	'F.note-1p.POSS'
iç-il	'drink-PASS'
ye-di	'eat-PST'
ye-n-il	'eat-PASS-PASS'

violate the template, rather than being ineffable, can be repaired via addition of a semantically redundant doubled Passive suffix.

As a restriction involving a minimal size restriction stated in terms of prosodic units, this Turkish pattern is, at least from the perspective of template typology, relatively unremarkable. It falls broadly in line with the Prosodic Morphology Hypothesis (see Section 1.8.2), for example, and minimality constraints sensitive to phonological size do not appear to be particularly unusual (see Section 2.4.3 for further discussion). To the extent that there is a complication of note here, it is not in the templatic restriction in and of itself but, rather, with the fact that there are two distinct patterns of violability, as already discussed in Section 2.5.4: one for nouns involving ineffability, which is associated with the value of *irreparable* for the REPARABILITY feature in the present typology, and another for verbs where repair is possible via *morphosyntacticInsertion*. In the description language developed here this means that we must treat each of these patterns as involving separate templates, even though there is significant overlap between them.

The template for nouns is formally characterized in Figure 3.1, and the template for verbs is formally characterized in Figure 3.2.

As can be seen in Figures 3.1 and 3.2, we are dealing with templates whose stricture is clearly of type *length* and whose foundations are of type *span*, since neither of the syllables involved in the length restriction appears to be privileged in any sense. In addition, the overall conditioning environment of the template involves a prosodic restriction, and potential exceptions to the template are lexical in nature involving short roots such as those in Table 3.1. There are two components specified, corresponding to each of the two syllables in a licit minimal word. These both have the same description as consisting of at least one obligatory syllable, but possibly more, to indicate that the templatic

108   Typologizing templates: case studies

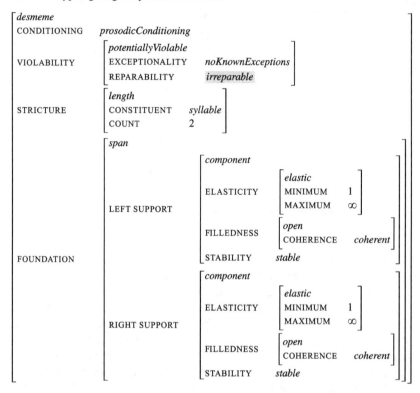

Figure 3.1 Turkish disyllabic minimal size restriction template for nouns

restriction involves a minimality requirement, not a maximality one (see Section 3.5.5 for a contrasting case). The specific convention used to code this is to treat each component as elastic with a minimum value of one and a maximum of "infinity."[2] This latter value is used as a shorthand for a length that is not restricted by the template itself (see also Section 2.3.5). This convention will additionally be found for the analysis of a Serbo-Croatian topicalization template discussed in Section 3.8. These components fill out the left and right support positions of the templates' foundations and are treated as coherent, since their content can be classified in terms of the general class of allowed syllables in the language, and stable, since neither shows evidence for dependency on the other.

---

[2] The restriction could be described in other ways, for instance by making the first component inelastic with a size of one and the second elastic with a minimum size of one. The particular convention employed in Figures 3.1 and 3.2 is chosen due to the fact that there is no evidence for any asymmetry among the two syllables fulfilling the disyllabic minimal size restriction. Therefore, they are described the same way.

3.3 Chintang prefixes

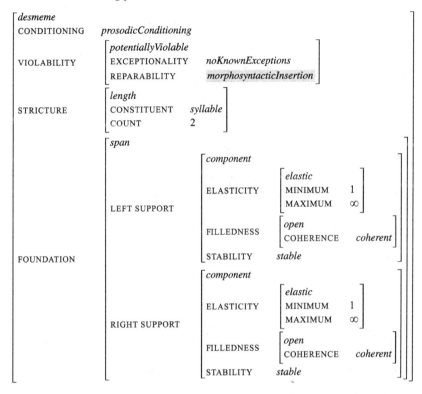

Figure 3.2 Turkish disyllabic minimal size restriction template for verbs

Consistent with the discussion above, the formal characterizations for these two Turkish templates are the same except for their REPARABILITY feature, whose value is shaded across the two examples for ease of reference. The parallels between these Turkish templates and the Serbo-Croatian topicalization template, already introduced in Section 2.4.7, are noteworthy: in desmemic terms, they are more or less the same with the salient surface difference that the Serbo-Croatian template targets a larger prosodic constituent (the prosodic word) than the Turkish templates. Thus, the schematic presentation of the Serbo-Croatian topicalization template presented in Figure 2.15 can also serve as a simplified presentation of these Turkish templates.

3.3 Chintang prefixes

The templatic analysis considered in this section is based on the discussion presented in Bickel et al. (2007), and only the most pertinent details of that

110 Typologizing templates: case studies

analysis are summarized here. Chintang verbal prefixes are subject to a relatively simple templatic restriction wherein they must precede a verbal element that is a prosodic word or more in size. Roughly speaking, a prosodic word must consist of at least a single syllable with an onset consonant (Bickel et al. 2007: 56–57). Strikingly, the nature of this restriction allows for a degree of freedom in prefix ordering in Chintang that is not otherwise attested.

In general cross-linguistically, affixes are linearly specified as prefixes versus suffixes (see Section 1.5), as is the case here. But, they are also usually additionally specified as being subject to morphosyntactically defined ordering restrictions rather than phonologically defined ones. This means, in effect, that their order tends to be "fixed" (see, e.g., Dixon & Aikhenvald (2002: 19) and Bickel & Nichols (2007: 190)), unlike the Chintang case. Moreover, other attested cases of apparent free morpheme order do not treat it as resulting primarily from phonological conditions on order but, rather, as the result morpheme-specific generalizations that happen to permit freedom of permutation (see, e.g., Good & Yu (2005)).

Initial examples from Chintang illustrating phonologically conditioned prefix order are given in (14) (Bickel et al. 2007: 44). The relevant prefixes are a second-person marker *a* and a negative marker *ma*, and each can permute with the other. The examples in (15) illustrate the same basic pattern, but three prefixes are involved, and all six logically possible permutations among them are allowed, as indicated by the examples (Bickel et al. 2007: 44). The relevant prefixes in this case are a third-person marker *u*, a first-person marker *kha*, and the negative marker *mă*, seen also in (14).

(14) a. *a-ma-im-yokt-e*
2-NEG-sleep-NEG-PST

      b. *ma-a-im-yokt-e*
NEG-2-sleep-NEG-PST

      "You didn't sleep."

(15) a. *u-kha-ma-cop-yokt-e*
3NS.A-1NS.P-NEG-see-NEG-PST

      b. *u-ma-kha-cop-yokt-e*
3NS.A-NEG-1NS.P-see-NEG-PST

      c. *kha-u-ma-cop-yokt-e*
1NS.P-3NS.A-NEG-see-NEG-PST

      d. *ma-u-kha-cop-yokt-e*
NEG-3NS.A-1NS.P-see-NEG-PST

3.3 Chintang prefixes

    e. *kha-ma-u-cop-yokt-e*
      1NS.P-NEG-3NS.A-see-NEG-PST

    f. *ma-kha-u-cop-yokt-e*
      NEG-1NS.P-3NS.A-see-NEG-PST

    "They didn't see us."

Bickel et al. (2007) present extensive arguments to support both the analysis of these Chintang elements as prefixes, as opposed to, say, free words, and the analysis of their ordering restrictions (or lack thereof) as being due to a specification that their host consist must consist of a prosodic word, rather than the more usual morphological root or stem. They formalize this restriction via the simple specification in (16) which states that a prefix (PFX) must precede a prosodic word (Bickel et al. 2007: 65). Since a prosodic word may consist only of a single syllable but a morphological word may consist of multiple syllables, this means a given prefix may have a range of possible hosts with which to form an allowable verb structure, depending on the verb's phonological form. Prefixes themselves form prosodic words on their own (Bickel et al. 2007: 58). This allows them to permute with each other as seen in (14) and (15), since each prefix meets the requirements to serve as the host for any other prefix.

(16) PFX-ω

The templatic analysis of Chintang to be developed below is a straight-forward translation of Bickel et al.'s (2007) analysis depicted in (16) to the descriptive model used here. Accordingly, I do not offer a full justification for it below (though, where appropriate, I will justify the specific choices for the typological coding in the formal description given in Figure 3.3). However, for comparative purposes, it will be worthwhile to contrast the analysis of the Chintang verbal prefixes in (16) with that of a more typical kind of affix. Following Bickel et al. (2007: 59–60), I will compare Chintang with the case of suffixes in Turkish which also display ordering variability, but where the variability is not phonologically conditioned. Relevant examples are given in (17) and (18) (Good & Yu 2005: 317–318) (see also Good & Yu (1999) and Yu & Good (2000)).

(17) a. *gör-dü-yse-m*   vs.   *gör-dü-m-se*
         see-PAST-COND-1s   see-PAST-1s-COND
         "if I saw…"

      b. *gör-dü-yse-n*   vs.   *gör-dü-n-se*
         see-PAST-COND-2s   see-PAST-2s-COND
         "if you saw…"

112   Typologizing templates: case studies

c. *gör-dü-yse-k*   vs.   *gör-dü-k-se*
   see-PAST-COND-1p   see-PAST-1p-COND
   "if we saw…"

d. *gör-dü-yse-niz*   vs.   *gör-dü-nüz-se*
   see-PAST-COND-2p   see-PAST-2p-COND
   "if you (plural) saw…"

(18) a. *bul-uyor-muş-sun*
         find-PROG-EVID-2s
         "you are finding"
      b.*bul-uyor-sun-muş*
         find-PROG-2s-EVID

The examples in (17) demonstrate that suffixes marking subject agreement
in Turkish can appear either between a Past and Conditional suffix or after
both of them in a past conditional construction. This variability is not limited
to this one morpheme combination but is allowed when there are two verbal suffixes present that are associated with a particular agreement paradigm.
When this condition does not hold, as in (18), where there are two verbal suffixes each associated with different agreement paradigms (as seen by the fact
that the second singular agreement marker has the form *-sun*, as opposed to
the *-n* seen in (17)), such variability is not allowed. (See Sezer (2001: 21–24)
for an overview of subject agreement patterns in Turkish.) The sensitivity of
this variability to the identity of specific morphemes means that the Turkish
pattern, though involving ordering variability as is the case with Chintang, is
not phonologically conditioned, thus leading Bickel et al. (2007) to propose
an interpretation of its ordering constraints along the lines formalized in (19)
(adapted from proposals in Bickel et al. (2007: 60)).

(19) TNS-AGR

The schematization in (19) abstracts away from the complications connected
to the presence of multiple agreement paradigms in Turkish, and only treats the
patterns seen in (17) (see Good & Yu (2005) for more detailed analysis and formalization). It states that agreement markers follow Tense markers (where the
term Tense markers here is intended to subsume both the Past and Conditional
suffixes). Importantly, it does not specify any further environment, for instance
whether a given Tense marker is final or immediately follows the root. Thus,
any Tense marker is free to serve as a host for the agreement suffix, consistent
with the variability seen in (17).

Morpheme ordering variability not associated with a change in meaning is
generally considered unusual, as mentioned above, but the Turkish case is less

3.3 Chintang prefixes

unusual than the Chintang one because the variability is at least morphosyntactically conditioned, consistent with the fact that morphological ordering is only rarely attested to be primarily driven by phonological considerations, as briefly discussed in Section 1.6 (see also Paster (2006, 2009: 29–33) and Section 3.5.5 below). Chintang represents a double rarity: variable affix ordering and phonologically conditioned affix placement.

There is, in some sense, something quite curious about this rarity, however. This is the simplicity of the system. The formalization in (16) is quite straightforward and by obvious metrics simpler than, for instance, the Turkish case schematized in (19) because of the latter's "normal" sensitivity to specific morphological categories. Nevertheless, the Chintang verbal prefix linearization pattern is clearly unexpected. (If it had been expected, the extended argumentation of Bickel et al. (2007) would hardly have been considered necessary.) This makes it templatic by the definition assumed here (see (6)). Bickel et al. (2007) do not apply this term to their analysis of the verbal prefix ordering, but their formalization in (16) has the important property of primarily characterizing a constraint on linear ordering, in line with what is found in more canonical templates.

The Chintang pattern, therefore, becomes templatic, in some sense, by virtue of its simplicity rather than its complexity, unlike, say, position-class morphological systems, which are generally considered unusually complex (see Section 1.4.3). This is because, as with the ordering restrictions on the form of lexical items (see Section 1.5), it is considered entirely normal for an affix to impose morphosyntactic restrictions on its host, even though this requires more stipulation than what is found in Chintang. Even in the case of infixes, where prosodic conditions on the placement of the infix within its host are the norm (Yu 2007: 67), the phonological aspects of affix placement amount to an additional condition above those imposed by morphosyntactic constraints, unlike the more "purely" phonological Chintang pattern, where the only morphosyntactic restriction on the prefixes is that they appear with a verbal stem of some kind (as opposed to, say, a noun stem) (Bickel et al. 2007: 52).

The fact that an unusually simple pattern will be set against unusually complex ones, as the various case studies are developed below, might seem, on the surface, to present a problem in that it implies that the set of phenomena being examined here are not sufficiently unified to merit common investigation. However, as discussed in detail in Section 1.6, this study is not based on the assumption that templates are, in fact, a coherent phenomenon. Rather, it is the fact that they do not fit comfortably within existing models that makes them interesting as a tool to refine our understanding of linearization patterns in grammar in general. The theoretical question of interest here, then, is not whether all templates are the "same" at some level of representation but, rather, whether there is significant clustering with respect to patterns of

114   Typologizing templates: case studies

templaticity. In the case of the Chintang verbal prefixes, one would want to know, for instance, if the descriptive intuition that it is the simplicity of Chintang that makes it templatic will be somehow visible in a rigorous comparison of templatic constructions. As will be seen in Chapter 4, at least with respect to the templates examined here, this does, in fact, seem to be the case, with the Chintang verbal prefixes patterning relatively closely with the non-templatic control constructions discussed in Section 3.13.

The full formal typological characterization of the Chintang template assumed here is given in Figure 3.3. Its various features are further discussed below. The value of its CONDITIONING and VIOLABILITY features, its foundation type, and the left voussoir component features are shaded, reflecting the fact that they represent aspects of the template typology, as represented by the description language presented in Chapter 2, not yet discussed in this chapter.

The characterization in Figure 3.3 can also be represented in a graph form as in Figure 3.4, which more saliently depicts the fact that each of the template's non-null components takes on two roles within the template's foundation (to be discussed shortly below). This is the only point in this chapter where a graph-based visualization of a template's formal characterization will be presented, and this is merely for purposes of illustration. This type of representation will play a more prominent role in Chapter 4.

As indicated in Figure 3.3, the Chintang template is treated as being conditioned constructionally, which, in effect, means the template is associated with a class of morphemes rather than a specific morpheme. Following the description of Bickel et al. (2007), it does not appear to be the case that it is ever violable because the sorts of verbal structures (based on the verb root) that the verbal prefixes attach to will always consist of at least a prosodic word for independent reasons.[3]

The stricture involved in this construction is analyzed as one involving ordering relations over prosodic words. This is because the prefixes, in addition to their hosts, consist of prosodic words (or, in Bickel et al.'s (2007) terminology, *phonological words*) which can themselves serve as hosts for other prefixes, as mentioned above. Thus, the overall templatic constraint can be analyzed as simply involving a pairing of prosodic words. Since prosodic words are a well-defined class of elements, the two templatic components corresponding to them are treated as open and coherent. These are the components occupying the keystone/left support position and the right voussoir/right support position, discussed further below.

Because this template involves an asymmetry between the prefix and its host wherein the prefix is interpreted as subcategorizing for the host (Bickel et al.

---

[3]   There is another templatic restriction associated with the Chintang verb, where a certain class of verbal elements must be preceded by another verbal element consisting of at least a disyllabic foot. In cases where this restriction might be violated, a repair strategy is employed where a dummy morphological element is inserted into the verbal structure (Bickel et al. 2007: 49–51).

3.3 Chintang prefixes

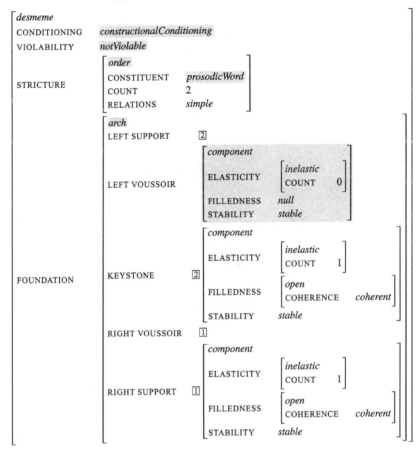

Figure 3.3 Chintang verbal prefix template

2007: 65), it is classified as an arch template here with the prefixal component as the keystone. (In this respect, the "headedness" of the template differs from what headedness would be expected to be, based on other criteria.) While the template only contains two surface components, the typological categorization in Figure 3.3, perhaps counterintuitively, gives three components for the template. The third component, that corresponding to the template's left voussoir, is merely a formal placeholder explicitly coding this position as not present in the templatic structure. (As a placeholder component, rather than a "real" one, a null component does not contribute to a template's count value in its stricture specification.) This is indicated by the component's classification as being inelastic with a size of zero and a filledness of null.

The left voussoir is treated as absent due to the fact that the prefix is treated as not only the keystone but also the left support, as indicated by the [2] tag that

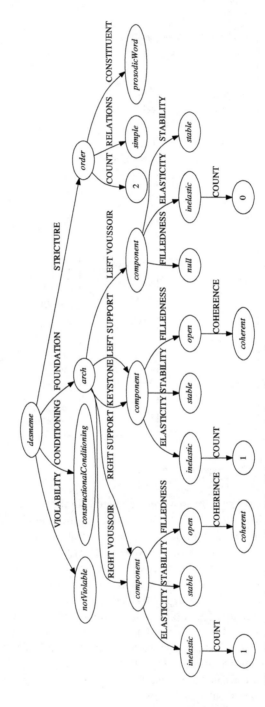

Figure 3.4 A graph representation of the Chintang verbal prefix template

3.4 Nimboran verbs

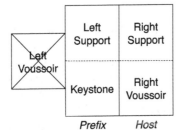

Figure 3.5 Schematization of the Chintang verbal prefix template

precedes the full component description for the keystone feature and serves as the value for the left support feature. Based on the definitions of these two positions, such component "sharing" (see Sections 2.4.7 and 2.6) is possible since the notion of support is defined with respect to the edges of a template, while the notion of keystone is defined independently from linear position (see Section 2.4.5). Voussoirs are defined in linear terms with respect to the keystone, being the components immediately adjacent to the keystone. If a keystone happens to be a support, by definition, there can be no component on one of its sides and one voussoir cannot be occupied. Various imaginable coding choices are possible for these "empty" voussoirs, and the convention seen in Figure 3.3, which will also be found below (see, e.g., Figure 3.10), is simply a specification of the values for the features required for components that is consistent with the "null" status of these absent voussoirs. Components of this type are always readily identifiable by means of their *null* filledness value.

The final aspect of the templatic analysis in Figure 3.3 which should be remarked upon is the status of the prosodic word host for the prefix, which is treated as both the right support, being at the right edge of the template, and the right voussoir, by virtue of being to the immediate right of the keystone. It is fully described in the value for the right support feature, and this full description is referred to using the [1] tag for the value specification of the right voussoir feature.

To make the overall structural analysis clearer, we can adapt the informal template visualization schemes presented in Chapter 2 as in Figure 3.5, where the dual roles of the two templatic components are represented as vertically elongated "stacked" blocks, and the null left voussoir is crossed out. The components are additionally given descriptive labels for purposes of clarity.

3.4 Nimboran verbs

The analysis of morpheme ordering in the Nimboran verb presented in the impressively detailed treatment of Inkelas (1993) involves a very complex

118   Typologizing templates: case studies

morphosyntactic template, both in terms of the number of components involved and in terms of their relationships among each other. The details of the analysis of Inkelas (1993) are not necessarily uncontroversial (see, e.g., Noyer (1998)), though this controversy appears to derive from theoretical concerns about possible morphological structures and the relationship between morphology and syntax, rather than being centered around the overall description of the system (see also Section 1.6).[4] Inkelas's analysis is adopted here due to its relative explicitness, clarity of presentation, and the fact that it attempts to serve as a comprehensive treatment of verbal morpheme ordering restrictions in the language, rather than focusing on only part of the system. At its core, it presents a relatively canonical example of a morphosyntactic position class template (see Section 1.4.3), but with interesting additional complications, and has the advantage of being supported by detailed analysis rather than given (as is quite typical in grammars) merely as a summarizing descriptive statement. The core "templatic" part of the Nimboran verb to be treated here does not include all of the morphemes in the verbal complex and, in particular, excludes the verb root and subject agreement markers, as will be discussed in more detail below. All theoretical, as well as more descriptively oriented work on Nimboran (e.g., Steinhauer (1997) and Baerman (2006)), is ultimately based on Anceaux's (1965) admirably detailed descriptive characterization of the language's verbal system.

In Figure 3.6, the schematization of Nimboran verb structure given by Inkelas (1993: 597) is adapted for presentation here.[5] This represents an overview of her analysis of the complex facts of the Nimboran system, which will be introduced below. The template to be analyzed is enclosed in large square brackets in Figure 3.6, reflecting the fact that Inkelas (1993: 563) treats this unit, which she terms the "modifier" (as opposed to the stem), as comprising a template in its own right separate from the verb stem. This treatment is based

---

[4] Noyer (1998), for instance, works within the framework of Distributed Morphology (see Harley & Noyer (1999)), which is associated with a complex set of assumptions regarding possible interaction among the lexicon, syntax, and morphology, partly mediated through the use of a loosely formalized set of morphosyntactic features. This model does not directly allow for a characterization of morphological patterns in terms of position classes, though it is essentially impossible to determine whether this is a "real" or only apparent distinction where the formal equivalent to position classes in the model is merely recapitulated in different terms. The issue, in this case, lies with the fact that the model is only informally "formalized" hindering rigorous cross-model comparison.

[5] The abbreviations for the position class labels in Figure 3.6 are interpreted as follows (see Inkelas (1993: 561): PL.SBJ, Plural Subject marker; DU.SBJ, Dual Subject marker; PL.OBJ, Plural Object marker; M.OBJ, Masculine Object marker; INC.DU.SBJ, Inclusive Dual Subject marker; LOC, Directional–Locational markers; ITER, Iterative marker; TNS, Tense markers; SBJ.PERS, Subject Person (and gender) markers. Inkelas (1993: 589) is equivocal on the exact assignment of a position class to the Plural Object marker. It is included in Position 2 here for ease of exposition, while available data suggests that either this is the most reasonable analysis or it occupies both Position 2 and Position 3 by virtue of being associated with a super-position defined via the label B–C, whose significance will be discussed further below.

3.4 Nimboran verbs

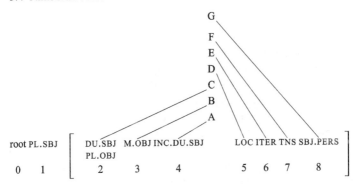

Figure 3.6 Schematization of the Nimboran verbal system following Inkelas (1993)

primarily on phonological considerations and is comparable to analyses of so-called clitic clusters (see Section 1.4.3), which also involve templates whose components do not include the element which might be considered to serve as their head in traditional morphosyntactic terms. The horizontal structuring of the Nimboran verb at the bottom of the figure breaks down its components across a series of position classes, each numbered outward with respect to the stem. Position 1, not included within the template, is occupied by only one morpheme, the Plural Subject marker, which does not have a segmental realization, making its actual morphological position in the position class system, in effect, indeterminable (see Inkelas (1993: 569–570)). Accordingly Position 1, in this scheme, is more of a position by convention rather than an actual linearly defined position.

While the enumeration of position classes, as seen in Figure 3.6, has extensive precedent elsewhere (see Section 1.4.3), the vertically arranged classification of positions via the letters A–G, and associated partitioning of Positions 2–4 from Positions 5–8, is unusual. In effect, it imposes a set of taxonomic relationships on the various position classes. These relationships involve a specification of Positions 2–4 as being prefixal in nature and Positions 5–8 as being suffixal (putting aside, for now, the fact that there is no root for these affixes within the template), and the ordering A–G defines sets of position classes which are considered eligible as potential, "super-positions" where multiple position classes join into a larger position class. Particular morphemes may be specified as associated with these super-position classes, thereby occupying the slots in a way that causes them to "straddle" more than one of the numbered positions.[6] I will come back to this shortly below.

---

[6] Inkelas (1993) analyzes these super-positions in terms of the device of "level-ordering" associated with Lexical Phonology in the generative tradition (see Kiparsky (1982a,b)). I avoid characterizing the Nimboran analysis in terms of this analytical device here due the difficulties involved in performing typological comparison across analyses where some make use of such devices and other do not.

120   Typologizing templates: case studies

The examples in (20) illustrate morphemes occupying each of the eight position classes that Inkelas (1993) analyzes in the Nimboran verbal system.[7] In addition to the complications raised by its templatic ordering constraints, there are also significant morphophonemic alternations that, in some cases, obscure the identity of morphemes across examples. These are not discussed in detail here, as they are covered in Inkelas (1993), but they do raise the issue of whether the co-occurrence of complex morphophonology and complex templatic structure is coincidental or, somehow, connected – an issue that has to be left open for future research, but which is tempting to consider in light of the complex morphophonological patterns also found in Athabaskan languages (see, e.g., Hargus (1988), McDonough (1990), and Rice (1993), among others), which have also been analyzed as exhibiting complex morphosyntactic templates (see Section 1.4.3). The morphological analysis in the examples is drawn from Inkelas (1993), where specific reference to the original source, Anceaux (1965), can be found. Some changes in glossing and transcription conventions have been made, for ease of exposition in the present context, involving, in particular, the addition of labels corresponding to the numbered position classes in Figure 3.6.[8] Acute marks in (20) indicate the position of an accent whose primary surface realization involves pitch (Anceaux 1965: 36–37).

(20) a. *ŋgedóio-^{i}$_1$-d$_7$-u$_8$ →   *ŋgedóidiu*
        draw.PL-PL.SBJ-FUT-1s/p
        "we (more than two) will draw here"   (Inkelas 1993: 568)
      b. *ŋgedóu$_0$-k$_2$-be$_5$-k$_7$-u$_8$ →   *ŋgedóukebekú*
        draw.DU-DU.SBJ-to.above-PST-1s/p
        "we two drew from here to above"   (Inkelas 1993: 563)
      c. *ŋgedúo$_0$-rár$_3$-ŋa$_5$-k$_7$-u$_8$ →   *ŋgedúoreŋáku*
        draw.SG-M.OBJ-below-PST-1s/p
        "I drew him below"   (Inkelas 1993: 570)

---

[7] The element written as ^{i} in (20a) represents a kind of morphological marking that is realized as an apparent inserted front high vowel in certain phonological contexts (Inkelas 1993: 568–570) (see also Anceaux (1965: 92)). The Iterative marker, exemplified in (20e) has a complex morphophonological realization (see Inkelas (1993: 572–573) and Anceaux (1965: 97–103)), and the specific underlying representation given for it in (20e) follows Inkelas (1993), but should not be taken as a definitive analysis. The fact that the surface from of the directional element glossed as 'from below' in (20e) contains an *e* after *b* rather than *a* appears to be a morphophonological irregularity (Anceaux 1965: 99, 102). The complications involved in the realization of the Iterative, possibly involving some sort of infixation (see Inkelas (1993: 572) and Anceaux (1965: 102)), are suggestive of the possibility of a morpheme-specific template being embedded within the general Nimboran verbal template (see Section 2.5.5), though Inkelas (1993: fn. 14) offers a sketch of a fully phonological analysis for its positioning.

[8] Certain verb roots in Nimboran show various, ablaut-like changes in their final syllable that is, at least in part, conditioned by the number of the subject, hence the glossing of verb stems with number information in (20). See Inkelas (1993: 605–608) and Steinhauer (1997: 121) for further discussion.

3.4 Nimboran verbs

121

d. $\eta gu\acute{a}_0\text{-}maN_4\text{-}k_7\text{-}\acute{a}m_8$ $\rightarrow$ $\eta gu\acute{a}ma\eta k\acute{a}m$
bite.DU-INCL.DU.SBJ-PST-INCL
"you (sg.) and I bit (here)"   (Inkelas 1993: 567)

e. $\eta ged\acute{u}o_0\text{-}b\acute{a}N_5\text{-}\eta k\acute{a}t_6\text{-}k_7\text{-}am_8$ $\rightarrow$ $\eta ged\acute{u}obek\acute{a}\eta kam$
draw.SG-from.below-ITER-PST-3s.M
"he drew repeatedly from below to here"   (Inkelas 1993: 572)

As suggested by the examples in (20), within the template, only Position 7 and Position 8, corresponding to tense marking and subject marking, are obligatory. However, Position 7 can only be treated as obligatory if one assumes significative absence (i.e., "zero morphemes") (see Section 1.8.3) as the filler of a component in some verb forms. This seems reasonable, in this case, due to the fact that significative absence appears to be a central part of the language's paradigmatic system of tense marking (Inkelas 1993: 573).[9]

For full justification of the position class of analysis for Nimboran, the reader is referred to Inkelas (1993), though here I would like to present one important kind of evidence relating to semantic interpretation, since it connects well to the arbitrariness of ordering relations in Nimboran that is part of the unexpectedness of the properties of templatic constructions. The first point to note in this regard is that there are cases where two morphemes which, at least by means of the most straightforward analyses, would appear to be semantically compatible, but which cannot co-occur due to purely morphological restrictions. For instance, the Dual Subject marker $-k-$ and the Plural Object marker $-d\acute{a}r-$ are both associated with Position 2, meaning that neither can appear when the other is present. However, there is not a lack of semantic compatibility between these two notions.[10] This can be illustrated by consideration of the data in (21) (Inkelas 1993: 583–584).[11]

---

[9] In fact, more surprising is the fact that, in Nimboran, Position 0 in Figure 3.6 also appears to be associated with significative absence, where "zero roots" can encode a surprising variety of meanings depending on the morphemes appearing in the Nimboran template of focus here (Inkelas 1993: 610–613).

[10] A fact which I am not aware of having been discussed in the literature on position classes is that there is nothing, in principle, that would disallow an analysis that treated each morpheme in a position class as having unusually specific semantics that would make it incompatible with the other morphemes in its slot. For instance, rather than treating the Nimboran Dual Subject marker as meaning something like 'dual subject,' it could be analyzed as having a meaning like 'dual subject and object not specified for number.' Such analyses are, presumably, not proposed because they violate key intuitions regarding the semantic analysis of morphemes, though, ideally, this should emanate from explicitly stated principles. For present purposes, this issue can be attenuated if we simply assume, for the purposes of comparison, that all semantic analyses should make use of a "minimal" semantic specification, which seems to be the case in the existing literature anyway.

[11] See Inkelas (1993: 605–610) and Anceaux (1965: 87) for discussion of the fact that the verb in (21c) shows a Dual stem in the presence of a singular subject in (21a) and (21d).

122   Typologizing templates: case studies

(21) a. *ŋgedúo$_0$-d$_7$-u$_8$*   →   *ŋgedúodu*
        draw.SG-FUT-1s/p
        "I will draw (here)"

      b. *ŋgedóu$_0$-k$_2$-d$_7$-u$_8$*   →   *ŋgedóukedú*
        draw.DU-DU.SBJ-FUT-1s/p
        "we two will draw (here)"

      c. *ŋgedóu$_0$-dár$_2$-d$_7$-u$_8$*   →   *ŋgedóudáru*
        draw.DU-PL.OBJ-FUT-1s/p
        "I will draw them here"

      d. *ŋgedói$_0$-^{i}$_1$-dár$_2$-d$_7$-u$_8$*   →   *ŋgedóidiáru*
        draw.PL-PL.SBJ-PL.OBJ-FUT-1s/p
        "we will draw them here"

The forms in (21a) and (21b) illustrate how the presence of the Dual Subject marker changes the interpretation of the number of the subject in a predictable way. In (21c), the use of the Plural Object marker is illustrated with a singular subject, and there is nothing especially noteworthy about this form in this respect. The example in (21d) illustrates how, in the presence a Plural Object marker, which cannot co-occur with the Dual Subject marker, the verb can be marked for a Plural Subject, but, according to Anceaux (1965: 107), the interpretation of the Plural Subject marker here is different than it is in other contexts. It appears that in verb forms where the Dual Subject marker is not blocked from appearing, a verb with Plural Subject marking does not allow for a dual interpretation, but only has a reading involving subjects whose number is of three or more (Anceaux 1965: 93). Thus, there is not a semantic overlap between the Dual and Plural where the distinction is made (Anceaux 1965: 84). However, in verb forms where the appearance of the Dual Subject marker is blocked due to the appearance of the Plural Object marker, this restriction on semantic interpretation does not hold (Anceaux 1965: 107), and the semantic opposition between dual and plural is neutralized. Thus, an example such as the one in (21d) is vague with respect to a dual or plural interpretation, in contrast with (20a) and (21b), which only have more specific interpretations. These facts suggest that Nimboran is, in some sense, "sensitive" to the way that the arbitrary linearization restrictions of the template have consequences for the possibility for expression of certain kinds of semantic combinations. Moreover, they provide evidence for the position class as an actual grammatical object rather than simply being a convenient analytical device for the linguist. At the same time, it must also be acknowledged that there are instances where the apparent blocking associated with a given position class can be readily explained due to semantic incompatibility, as is the case for the various tense-marking morphemes of Nimboran associated with Position 7. For that position,

3.4 Nimboran verbs

the evidence for the active grammatical status of a position class is clearly less striking.

The discussion to this point has presented a simplified picture of the Nimboran system, since it has assumed that each morpheme is assigned to one of the numbered positions given in Figure 3.6. However, as discussed above, an important characteristic of Inkelas's (1993) analysis is the fact that the properties of position classes are not limited to the sets of morphemes they are associated with and their position in a linear arrangement. They are additionally categorized as to whether they are Prefixing or Suffixing and across a set of categories defining possible super-positions, indicated via letters in Figure 3.6. These categorizations are proposed by Inkelas (1993) in order to deal with patterns of morphological blocking which cannot be straightforwardly accounted for by referencing the numbered position classes alone. Relevant examples are provided in (22).[12] The superscript e appearing with the Durative marker indicates that it is associated with a morphophonological process of vowel fronting (also seen in (20e) above) causing certain vowels to front (see Inkelas (1993: 565–566)).

(22) a. *ŋgedóu$_0$-k$_2$-rár$_3$-k$_7$-u$_8$*   →   *ŋgedóukráku*
        draw.DU-DU.SBJ-M.OBJ-PST-1s/p
        "we two drew him (here)"   (Inkelas 1993: 587)

     b. *ŋgedóu$_0$-k$_2$-t$_7$-u$_8$*   →   *ŋgedóuketú*
        draw.DU-DU.SBJ-PRS-1s/p
        "we two draw (here)"   (Inkelas 1993: 586)

     c. *ŋgedói$_0$-^{i}$_1$-tam^e$_{BC}$-t$_7$-u$_8$*   →   *ŋgedóitiemtɨ*
        draw.PL-PL.SUBJ-DUR-PRS-1s/p
        "we are drawing (here)"   (Inkelas 1993: 586)

     d. *príb$_0$-rár$_3$-be$_5$-d$_7$-u$_8$*   →   *príbrebedú*
        throw-M.OBJ-to.above-FUT-1s/p
        "I will throw him from here to above"   (Inkelas 1993: 584)

     e. *príb$_0$-tam^e$_{BC}$-be$_5$-t$_7$-u$_8$*   →   *príptembetɨ*
        throw-DUR-to.above-PRS-1s/p
        "I am throwing him/Ø from here to above'"   (Inkelas 1993: 585)

The verb form in (22a) illustrates that the Dual Subject marker and the Masculine Object marker can co-occur, justifying an analysis of them as belonging to different position classes (here, Position 2 and Position 3). The form in (22b) simply gives a verb with a Dual Subject marker illustrating that the presence of this affix results in a reading of the subject as dual, as would be expected. In (22c), the Durative blocks the appearance of the Dual Subject marker, and

---

[12] Inkelas (1993: 587) gives the underlying form of the Dual Subject marker in (22b) as *-ke-*, rather than *-k-*. This is normalized here to follow the analysis she gives elsewhere in the paper.

124   Typologizing templates: case studies

this allows the verb to show ambiguity for a dual/plural reading (Anceaux 1965: 108), just as we saw in (21d) above. This would suggest the Durative belongs to Position 2. However, in comparing (22d) with (22e), a different blocking pattern is observed where the Durative does not allow the Masculine Object marker to appear, again leading to an ambiguous form (Anceaux 1965: 109). This would suggest the Durative belongs to Position 3. Inkelas (1993: 587) resolves this apparent paradox by suggesting the Durative simultaneously occupies Position 2 and Position 3. In other words, it is a morpheme that is associated with the super-position defined by B–C in Figure 3.6 (hence the marking of it with a subscript in *BC* in (22c) and (22e)).

If the apparent super-positions found in Nimboran were limited to those definable in terms of linearly adjacent classes, such as the B–C class of the Durative, then there might not be a need for the vertically arranged categories in Figure 3.6. However, there are cases of morphemes where the relevant super-position involves non-adjacent positions. These are morphemes that Inkelas (1993: 574) terms *particles* and Anceaux (1965: 123) refers to as *blockading* categories. The former term will be employed here. These particles combine with certain verb roots in lexically specified combinations. Particles and roots do not need to be adjacent, and they are specified for their own position classes. One verb root that can appear with a particle is *príŋ-*, which, when combined with a particle that Inkelas (1993: 619) analyzes as having the underlying form *-tar^e-*$_{CD}$, means 'fly' in verb forms appearing with the Future and which cannot contain a Position 2 Dual Subject Marker or a Position 5 Directional–Locational marker.[13] As indicated in the representation of

---

[13] It should be noted that Inkelas's (1993) analyses of these particles as being associated with super-positions, in particular involving non-adjacent positions, is difficult to reconstruct on the basis of Anceaux's (1965) description. In the case of the example just cited, the relevant part of Anceaux (1965: 134) seems to be roughly as follows, with discussion specifically of the verb for 'fly': Future forms of the First Position category all have an accent on the subject morpheme, e.g., *príntere̱* 'I will fly (here).' (The transcription, punctuation, and terminological conventions have been changed from Anceaux (1965) to be consistent with the conventions of Inkelas (1993) and for readability.) In order to derive from this that there is a particle of form *-tar^e-* associated with super-position C–D, one must be aware of several non-obvious points. First, Inkelas (1993) assigns the particle the segmental form *-tar-*, while Anceaux (1965: 134) assigns it the form *-te-*, following an analysis where (i) some consonantal alternations associated with it in the Future form suggest it should be associated with a final *r* (see Inkelas (1993: fn. 12)) and (ii) the *e* is seen as due to a process of vowel fronting found in the language that is associated with the category of the *Apophonic* morpheme series of Anceaux (1965: 134), resulting in a treatment of the form as having an underlying *a* and a diacritic fronting marker. Second, the fact that the accent appears on the final vowel coding subject person results in the analysis of the particle as being accentless (see Inkelas (1993: 563–564) for her analysis of the placement of accent) and being opposed to a segmentally very similar particle, with shape *-tár^e-*, found in different forms of the verb, but which is associated with an accent. Finally, the treatment of this particle as blocking Position 5 can only be understood with reference to the fact that Anceaux (1965: 64) uses the term *First Position* to refer to verbs whose action is interpreted as being in the same place as the speaker and which do not appear with an element

3.4 Nimboran verbs

125

the form, Inkelas (1993: 616) analyzes this as being due to the fact that the particle is assigned to a super-position defined by classes C–D. As seen in Figure 3.6 this super-position is defined over two slots that are linearly quite far apart.

The further categorization of the elements of the Nimboran verb as being divided into a Prefixing and Suffixing class (even in the absence of a root around which they are organized in the template itself) is also connected to super-positional patterns. In particular, Position 4 only forms a super-position with Position 2 and Position 3, and never Position 5. Inkelas (1993: 597) chooses to model this as an opposition between "prefixes" and "suffixes" in the template, though for our purposes, this part of her analysis is not particularly significant. Rather, what is important is that it represents an additional layer of classification on top of that surrounding the A–G lettered classification.

As even a cursory examination of Anceaux (1965) will reveal, the linear patterning of morphemes in the Nimboran verb is quite complex. Thus, it is not surprising that Inkelas's (1993) theoretical reinterpretation of the description is also complex. Many of the details of her analysis rely on reconstructing key aspects of the Nimboran system from Anceaux's (1965) description, where the exemplification of the patterns is sparse. It would therefore be surprising if they were to hold up fully if further data were available and, in particular, it would seem to be likely to be the case that some of the analyses of the positional restrictions of particles are open to various kinds of reinterpretation. Moreover, only a small set of possible super-positions appear to be attested (see Inkelas (1993: 604)), suggesting that a refinement to the analysis of the super-position categories may be advisable, at least from a typological perspective. At the same time, for the purposes of the system of typological classification developed here, these complications are not so problematic. For instance, while the existence of super-positions involving non-adjacent elements may involve fairly complex reanalysis of the original description (see footnote 13), less striking instances of super-positions, such as those exemplified in (22), fall out more straightforwardly from the data.

From the present perspective, this strongly suggests that these Nimboran template positions should be considered to exhibit taxonomic relationships of some kind. Moreover, since the description language used here only employs two types of *relations* at present, *simple* and *taxonomic* (as discussed in Section 2.4.4), the categorization choice here is clear. Of course, a label like

in Position 5 (and which, for Inkelas's (1993) treatment to hold, must not be treated as a significative absence). Inkelas (1993: 591) gives only sparse information on how to arrive at the positional analyses and underlying forms of the particles, making it hard for me to replicate the logic behind all of them. This issue will be briefly returned to below. These comments are not intended as a criticism of Inkelas (1993), however, since it would scarcely have been possible for the full logic of her analyses to have been presented in the space allotted a journal article, and her discussion is already exceptionally thorough.

126   Typologizing templates: case studies

taxonomic obscures the fact there could be many different kinds of taxonomic relations. However, at this stage, I have only encountered two other templatic analyses clearly making use of such relations. One of these is associated with the topological fields analysis of the German clause, to be discussed in Section 3.12, and the other relates to the notion of zones in the Athabaskan verb (see Section 2.4.4). With so few examples it is not yet clear what kinds of subdivisions of the category might be useful for comparative investigation, and this is an area left open for further research at this point. If this aspect of the template typology becomes further elaborated, the analytical complications of the Nimboran system may need to be revisited, but, for now, it seems that this can be avoided.

Having given an overview of the Nimboran verb template schematized in Figure 3.6, it is now possible to give its formal typological characterization, which is presented in Figures 3.7 and 3.8. Many aspects of its classification should be relatively familiar by now. One potential exception, however, is the feature RESTKOMPONENTEN, which serves as a container for templatic positions not belonging to a dedicated structural position in a foundation. Another is the ASSOCIATE feature for coding discontinuous dependencies (see Section 2.3.4). Due to the large number of components associated with this template, its formal representation cannot be effectively presented in a single figure, and Figure 3.8 gives the expansion of the RESTKOMPONENTEN from Figure 3.7, represented as a partial description of a *span* foundation. First, the analysis at the level of the template will be discussed, followed by discussion of the various components. The value of the template's RELATIONS feature and the restkomponenten list (not given in detail in Figure 3.7) are shaded to indicate that they are features of particular interest in the analysis of the Nimboran verb template at this point in the discussion.

Points to note about the templatic description in Figure 3.7 not already explicitly discussed are as follows: it is treated as constructionally conditioned, being sensitive to the presence of a particular type of morphosyntactic constituent (i.e., the verb). Inkelas (1993) does not report that it can be violated on the surface. In cases where it might be, such as where two morphemes that are semantically compatible are templatically blocked, we saw in (21) that the result is a verb form that becomes unexpectedly ambiguous, meaning the template appears to be potentially violable with an available repair strategy involving homophony. In addition, the template is, of course, an order template (since the role of position classes is to specify ordering relations), and the ordering involves seven positions within a morphological constituent. The template further has a span foundation under Inkelas's (1993) analysis since, within the template itself, there is no privileged element. The usual candidate for a keystone for a verb, the verb root, falls outside the template itself, and

3.4 Nimboran verbs

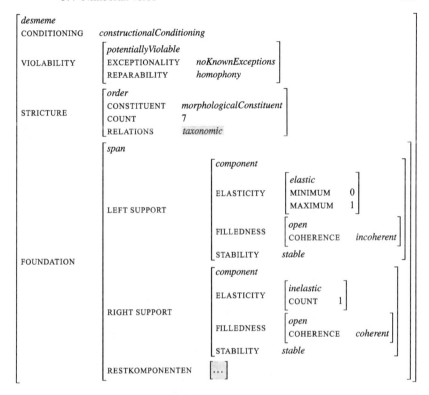

Figure 3.7 Nimboran verb template

no other position class is indicated as playing a special role in the template's organization.[14] This means the template only has two dedicated structural positions, the left support (Position 2) and right support (Position 7). The remaining feature of the foundation is the RESTKOMPONENTEN, which points to a set of RESTKOMPONENTE components – i.e., those which do not occupy a predefined foundational position, of which there are five in the Nimboran case, as given in Figure 3.8.

With respect to the properties of the components of the Nimboran template, many of these should be fairly straightforwardly derivable from Figure 3.6 and the discussion to this point. For instance, the left support (i.e., Position 2) is treated as incoherent since it is occupied by an apparently arbitrary class of two morphemes, while the right support, containing only person markers, is

---

[14] Inkelas (1993: 602–603) suggests that the Nimboran template could be analyzed as being built around a null "base," but this appears to be for theoretical reasons rather than empirical ones. I, therefore, do not adopt this analysis here.

128 Typologizing templates: case studies

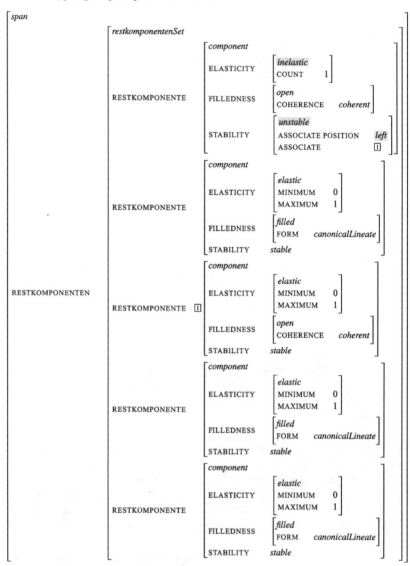

Figure 3.8 Nimboran verb template restkomponenten

treated as coherent. Similarly, the left support is not obligatory, and is, therefore, elastic with a maximum of one, and the right support is obligatory and, therefore, inelastic with a count of one. None of the components can be occupied by more than one element, making them canonical position classes. The

3.4 Nimboran verbs

current formalization does not encode any ordering relations among restkomponenten. So, their vertical positioning in Figure 3.7 is not meaningful, but one can see that three of them are analyzed as filled by canonical lineates. These correspond to Positions 3, 4, and 6, each of which can be occupied only by a single morpheme, as indicated in Figure 3.6. These are all elastic since these morphemes are not obligatorily present. The remaining two components are both open and coherent and correspond to Positions 5 and 7.

There is an additional indication that one of these components has a discontinuous dependency (i.e., it is of type *unstable*) with a component to its left. This is encoding the fact that, as described by Inkelas (1993: 573–574), though not exemplified here, the precise form of the Tense marker (Position 7) can be influenced by what morpheme, if any, fills the optional Directional–Locational Position 5. I follow the lead of her description in treating this dependency as asymmetric. This same component is also treated as inelastic due to the fact that Tense marking on the verb is treated as obligatory. These characteristics of the relevant component are shaded in Figure 3.8.

A simplified visual representation of the Nimboran template is presented in Figure 3.9 in order to make its structure clearer. The numbers under each component block correspond to those seen in Figure 3.6, zigzag lines are used to encode elastic components, shading is used to represent filled components, and the arrow pointing from the component representing Position 5 to the one representing Position 7 encodes the asymmetric discontinuous dependency holding between them.

More so than with the other templates to be examined here, the typological description of the Nimboran construction would quite clearly be "incomplete" as a synchronic description of the full range of Nimboran complexities. For instance, attested super-positions are not encoded since it is not clear how they should fit into a description language that is based on a two-way division between template-level features and component level features, with only limited possibilites for expressing relationships among components (e.g.,

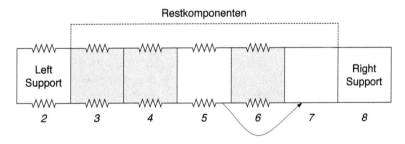

Figure 3.9 Schematization of the Nimboran verb template

130   Typologizing templates: case studies

discontinuous dependencies). Moreover, the Nimboran template schematized in Figure 3.6 may be the most general and pervasive template in the verbal system, but there also appear to be a number of lexico-constructional templates that overlap partly with this template involving co-occurrence restrictions with particles beyond those discussed here, exemplifying the phenomenon of templatic convergence (see Section 2.5.3) (see, e.g., the discussion of particle choice for different morphological forms of *kíb* 'beat' in Inkelas (1993: 588–589)). I would not be surprised, in fact, if a full templatic "description" of the Nimboran verb would involve, perhaps, a hundred or more templates. The extent to which information is left out of the formal description of the Nimboran verb is, ultimately, a function of the system's complexity, which is simply not found for the other cases examined here (but would most likely be comparable to any Athabaskan language had one been subject to this level of scrutiny).

A study of a larger number of templates would be required to determine whether Nimboran is especially unusual or not. If it turns out not to be, then this will probably mean changes are required to the description language to allow formal description of some of its features that, for now, appear to be "exotic."

3.5   Four templates found in Bantu verb stems

3.5.1   Templatic ordering in Bantu verbal extensions

The next four case studies consider a number of templatic restrictions in the ordering relations among the so-called extensions to the Bantu verb root. These are suffixes that are primarily used to encode various changes of valency to a verb's lexical argument structure (e.g., causativization, applicativization, reciprocalization, etc.). Three of the four case studies focus on quite similar templatic patterns involving relative ordering restrictions, and the value of including each of them here is not because they illustrate strikingly different phenomena but, rather, to demonstrate how the typological description language allows certain kinds of fine-grained variation to be effectively coded. The first two of these case studies cover Bantu languages in general, since the relevant templatic restrictions are widespread across the family and perhaps even reconstructible to Proto-Bantu. The third specifically involves Chichewa, which has developed an interesting strategy to deal with potential violations to a common Bantu ordering restriction. These case studies do not cover the whole of the ordering restrictions among Bantu suffixes; for instance, the restrictions on one common suffix, the Passive, will not be discussed. This is not due to the lack of templaticity in its ordering (see, e.g., Hyman (2003c)).

3.5 Four templates found in Bantu verb stems 131

Rather, in terms of illustrating the typology here, treating it would not have offered any templatic description particularly different from those that are already presented below.

The fourth case study in this section is quite different, involving a typologically unusual set of phonological constraints affecting, among other things, the linearization of consonants in verb stems in the Tiene language. It is included in this section because part of the diachronic source of the Tiene restrictions are the morphological ordering constraints seen in other Bantu languages, thus giving us a window into how templatic constraints can evolve over time.

Some of the data and analyses in this section have already been presented less systematically above in Sections 2.1, 2.3.5, 2.4.2, and 2.4.7, and the templates described in this section also present an instance of templatic convergence (see Section 2.5.3), where the analysis involves multiple, distinct templates converging on a single domain. This issue will be taken up in Section 3.5.6 after each case study is presented, with a particular focus being on the criteria that can be employed to determine when it is more appropriate to "split" a set of templatic restrictions than to "lump" them. While the analyses are broken up into different sections, each treating different sets of templatic restrictions, the overall discussion builds on the results of each preceding section. Because the templates described here build partly on my own work, and not all of the details to be discussed can already be found in published sources, the analytical discussion in this section will be more extensive than in most of the other case studies.

3.5.2 *Bantu causativizing suffixes*

Two key morphemes: the Causative and the Transitive
The first set of templatic constraints in the Bantu verb stem to be examined here involves two verbal suffixes that are generally associated with causativizing morphological processes. This case study and the immediately following one draw heavily on Good (2005) which, in turn, draws on Hyman (2003c). Each of these suffixes is illustrated in (23), giving data from the closely related languages Nkore and Nyoro.[15]

---

[15] Bantu language names in this section are followed by their Guthrie numbers in examples (Guthrie 1971). These are customarily used designations for Bantu languages. In some cases, the Guthrie numbers may be inexact due to the lack of a listing for a particular language/dialect in Guthrie (1971), in which case the Guthrie number of a closely related language/dialect is used. For detailed discussion of classification codes for Bantu languages, and their interpretation, see Maho (2001, 2003).

132 Typologizing templates: case studies

(23) a. Transitives and Causatives in Nkore (E.13)   (Bastin 1986: 116)
       -ham-a   'be.assured-FV'   "be assured"
       *-ham-**y**-a*   'be.assured-TRANS-FV' "confirm"
       *-ham-**is**-a*   'be.assured-CAUS-FV' "make confirm"
   b. Transitives and Causatives in Nyoro (E.11)   (Bastin 1986: 116)
       -og-a   'bathe-FV'   "bathe"
       *-og-**y**-a*   'bathe-TRANS-FV' "wash"
       *-og-**is**-a*   'bathe-CAUS-FV' "make wash"

In (23), two causativizing suffixes are found, which are here labeled the Transitive and the Causative following Good (2005). The choice of these labels is primarily intended to make sure each suffix can be clearly referred to rather than to assert a specific semantic analysis. The Transitive is generally segmentally reconstructed in Proto-Bantu as $*-i-$ (where i represents the highest front vowel in a seven vowel system) and the Causative is variously reconstructed $*-ic-$ or $*-ic-$ (see, e.g., Meeussen (1967: 92), Guthrie (1970: 215), Bastin (1986: 89–90), and Schadeberg (2003: 72)), but the distinction is not of particular significance here, and I adopt Guthrie's (1970) reconstructed vowel here merely for convenience.[16] In contemporary languages, the Transitive is more often attested as a *-y-*, a phonological process affecting a preceding consonant most generally known as spirantization (see Bostoen (2008)), an example of which will be seen below in (24), or a combination of the two. The Causative may be realized along the lines suggested by its reconstruction or its consonant may be subject to various lenition processes, with the suffix appearing as, for example, *-is-*, as seen in (23). This will be discussed further below. In addition, the vowel of the Causative is frequently subject to vowel harmony where it appears as a mid vowel *e* when preceded by another mid vowel (see Hyman (1999) for overview discussion).

The examples in (23) include a morpheme-by-morpheme gloss and a stem-level translation. In these examples, the Transitive suffix is used to mark direct causativization, as in, for example, a verb like *-og-y-a* 'wash,' while the Causative suffix is used to mark indirect causativization, as in *-og-is-a* 'make wash.' The verb stems all additionally appear with a so-called Final Vowel inflectional suffix that is found throughout Bantu, but has an opaque function (see Nurse (2008: 261–262) for comparative discussion). While its final ordering could perhaps be analyzed as templatic, its linearization patterns will not be analyzed here since the focus is on the relative ordering restrictions holding

---

[16] Some authors, such as Meeussen (1967) and Schadeberg (2003), treat the Causative suffix as having a form like $*-Vci$ rather than $*-Vc-$, but this seems best seen not as a monomorphemic form but, rather, as a concatenation of the Causative and the Transitive for reasons to be clarified below. See also Good (2005: fn. 10).

3.5 Four templates found in Bantu verb stems

among valency-changing morphemes.[17] A clearcut split in the semantic function of the Transitive and Causative morphemes, of the sort exemplified in (23), is not particularly common (Bastin 1986: 116). However, the presence of both morphemes in a given language is not especially rare, though many Bantu languages have lost one or the other of them (see, e.g., Good (2005: 19)). From the present perspective, the main point of interest is that, when the two morphemes co-occur, their order is strictly Causative before Transitive. This can be illustrated by examining the forms in (24), drawn from Ciyao.

(24) Ciyao (P.21)   (Ngunga 2000: 236)

-won-	<	**-bon-*	'see'
-won-el-	<	**-bon-id-*	'see-APPL'
-won-es-y-	<	**-bon-ic-i̧-*	'see-CAUS-TRANS'
-won-ec-es-y-	<	**-bon-ic-id-i̧-*	'see-CAUS-APPL-TRANS'

The verb stems in (24) (in this case not shown with the Final Vowel) illustrate verbs marked with the Causative, Applicative, and Transitive extensions. Proto-Bantu reconstructions (not included in the original source) are included for ease of exposition. The linear properties of the Applicative will be discussed in more detail in Section 3.5.3, and, here, it is only included as a means to make the ordering properties of the Causative and Transitive clearer. Ciyao shows morphologically bipartite marking of causativization requiring both the Causative and the Transitive in that order, as seen in the form *-won-es-y-* 'see.' An additional complication relates to the spirantization effects that the *-y-* can have on a preceding element, which were just alluded to above. In the data in (24), it triggers assibilation on both the Causative and the Applicative when their consonants are immediately followed by it. In both cases, this assibilation results in the extension's final consonant becoming *s*. The non-assibilated variant of the Applicative ends in an *l*, and, consistent with the reconstruction indicated above, the non-assibilated Causative ends in an *c*. Spirantization processes before the historical $*i$ vowel are quite common, and, in heteromorphemic contexts, the most frequent environment for them is in sequences where the second element is associated with the Transitive (see Bostoen (2008: 314)). This means that, even in languages where the Transitive is not a synchronically active suffix but the Causative has a shape like *-is-* (such as what is found in Ndebele (S.44) (Sibanda 2004: 46)), it may be the case that the synchronic Causative historically represents something along the lines of a fusion of the Causative and the Transitive.

---

[17] There is also a long-standing tradition which proposes a morphological domain, the verbal *base*, which includes the root and all suffixes except those appearing in final positions, such as the Final Vowel (see Meeussen (1967: 110)).

134 Typologizing templates: case studies

A final feature of the morphological realization of causativization in Bantu languages is that one finds an asymmetry where, in some languages, causativization can be marked with a combination of the Causative and Transitive (as seen in (24)) or just the Transitive, depending on various factors. This suggests that it is possible for there to be a long-distance dependency between the Causative and Transitive where the presence of the Causative is only allowed if a following Transitive is present as well. As seen in the survey of Good (2005: 19), the presence of this dependency is not found in all languages where both suffixes appear to be synchronically active (even if only partly productive). However, when one finds a dependency, it always appears to be the case that the Causative is dependent upon the presence of the Transitive, rather than the other way around. This observation is connected to the fact that some reconstructions of the Bantu causativization treat it as being marked with either a suffix like *-ici̧- or *-i̧- (see footnote 16 in this chapter). Such an analysis is comparable to the one presented here except that, rather than viewing the *-ici̧- as bimorphemic with an associated dependency of the Causative on the Transitive, they treat that sequence as a single morphological unit.

Nevertheless, the bimorphemic analysis seems justified for various reasons. The first is the formal identity between the second vowel of the "long" Causative suffix and the Transitive, whose reconstruction as a distinct causativizing morpheme is widely accepted, making a bimorphemic analysis initially plausible. The second is because of facts like those seen in (24), where there are synchronic morphological constructions causing the elements marking causativization to be separated from each other by another morpheme. Finally, though it is less concrete a factor, it is relevant here that Bastin (1986: 113–115) reconstructs the distribution of the longer sequence marking causativization as being at least partly driven by phonological factors, with the purely vocalic suffix appearing after consonant-final stems and the VCV form after vowel-final stems. This suggests that, historically, the *ic* sequence may have had a stabilizing function (see Gowlett (1984)), providing an appropriate morphophonological host environment for the Transitive given that the canonical Bantu verb stem ends in a consonant (see Meeussen (1967: 86) and Teil-Dautrey (2008: 60)). This gives us a further historical reason for treating the *ici̧* sequence as morphologically bipartite.

Two overlapping templates

Considering only those Bantu languages where the Transitive and Causative remain active synchronically as suffixes, such as Ciyao seen in (24), there, in fact, appear to be two different templatic constraints at work with respect to the linearization of the Causative and the Transitive. On the one hand, the Transitive always appears towards the end of the verb stem and, in particular, after any suffix with the shape -VC-, such as the Causative or the Applicative. On

3.5 Four templates found in Bantu verb stems 135

the other hand, there is also a converging, more specific template, that requires that the Causative be followed by the Transitive in many languages, as just discussed in Section 3.5.2. In other words, one template governs the general positioning of the Transitive, and the other imposes a narrower constraint on the positioning of the Causative.

Data exemplifying the Causative–Transitive ordering constraint has already been presented above in (24). Those examples also showed the Transitive's tendency to appear after other -VC- suffixes in that it was seen to follow both the Causative and the Applicative. Further evidence for this positioning constraint of the Transitive is seen in the forms in (25) drawn from Kinande.

(25) Kinande (D.42) (Hyman 1993: 13)

a. *-búl-*   'wonder'   "wonder"
    -búl-ị-   'wonder-TRANS   "ask"
    -búl-an-ị-   'wonder-RECP-TRANS'   "ask each other"

b. *-lim-*   'cultivate'   "cultivate"
    -lim-is-ị-   'cultivate-CAUS-TRANS'   "cause to cultivate"
    -lim-is-an-ị-   'cultivate-CAUS-RECP-TRANS'   "cause each other
                                           to cultivate"

c. **-song-*   'SONG'   *no meaning*
    -song-ị-   'SONG-TRANS'   "gather"
    -song-an-ị-   'SONG-RECP-TRANS'   "gather each other"

The examples in (25) give glosses and translations for a number of morphologically causativized verb forms in Kinande, including forms where a given verb is marked both for causativization and reciprocalization, the latter coded via the Reciprocal suffix, reconstructible with form *-an-* (see also Section 3.5.4). As with other languages already considered, Kinande marks causativization either using only the Transitive (as in (25a)) or a combination of the Causative and the Transitive (as in (25b)) (Mutaka & Kavutirwaki 2011: xxiv). As can be seen, in all of the verb forms, the Transitive follows the Reciprocal, again showing its tendency towards "final" positioning.[18] The forms in (25c) are somewhat striking in this regard since the verb meaning 'gather' shows a lexicalized Transitive, with the bare verb root *-song-* not able to appear on its own with any meaning. Despite this, the Transitive remains separable, appearing after the Reciprocal, running counter to an often expected association between lexicalization and morphological fusion (see Brinton &

---

[18] Reflexes of the Proto-Bantu Passive suffix also show positioning restrictions where they appear after -VC- suffixes, and they further generally appear after the Transitive as well (see Hyman (1993: 12)).

136   Typologizing templates: case studies

Traugott (2005: 47–57) for discussion). That is, the Transitive's positional restrictions appear to "outlive" its semantic independence.[19]

Having given a descriptive overview of the ordering restrictions of the Causative and Transitive, it is now possible to offer a formal description of their templatic properties in Figures 3.10 and 3.11. These templates are intended to describe what appears to have been the situation in Proto-Bantu as well as the situation of many contemporary Bantu languages, though, as should be clear from the immediately preceding discussion, various historical changes mean they will not apply uniformly across the family. Nevertheless, since the templates are not only probably reconstructible (see, e.g., Good (2005)) but also attested, they represent valid descriptions of templates, with the main question being the languages they apply to. In Figure 3.10, the restriction holding between the Causative and the Transitive is formalized, and in Figure 3.11, the final positioning of the Transitive is formalized.

A simplified visual presentation of the Bantu Causative–Transitive template described in Figure 3.10, using similar conventions to those already seen above, is given in Figure 3.12. The block representing the single restkomponente is slightly horizontally elongated to represent the fact that it can contain from zero to many elements (though it is somewhat less elongated than the blocks given for the Serbo-Croatian topicalization template presented earlier in Figure 2.15 since the latter had to contain at least one element). The block representing the verb root is vertically elongated to encode the fact that one component fills two templatic roles. The blocks representing the Causative and Transitive are shaded to represent the fact that these components are filled by specific morphemes, and an asymmetric dependency between them is indicated with an arrow. I do not give a visual representation for the Transitive final-positioning template described in Figure 3.11 since it would be more or less the same as the schematization in Figure 3.12, except for the removal of the component corresponding to the Causative and the associated dependency (and the necessary additional reclassification of the restkomponente as a right voussoir).

Many features of the templatic description have already been discussed, though some additional explanation is required for certain aspects of them. They are, therefore, discussed in more detail in the next section.

Further details on the two templates

A significant of aspect of the templatic descriptions in Figures 3.10 and 3.11 is that, unlike, for example, the Nimboran case discussed in Section 3.4, the verb root is formalized as part of the template, and the ordering relations among the

---

[19] This is not universally the case in Bantu languages, however. Sibanda (2004: 92–93) indicates that fusion and lexicalization of verbal suffixes appears to be the regular outcome in Ndebele.

3.5 Four templates found in Bantu verb stems

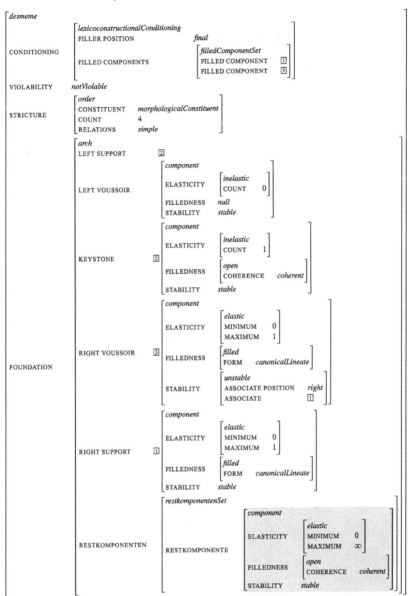

Figure 3.10 Bantu Causative–Transitive template

138 Typologizing templates: case studies

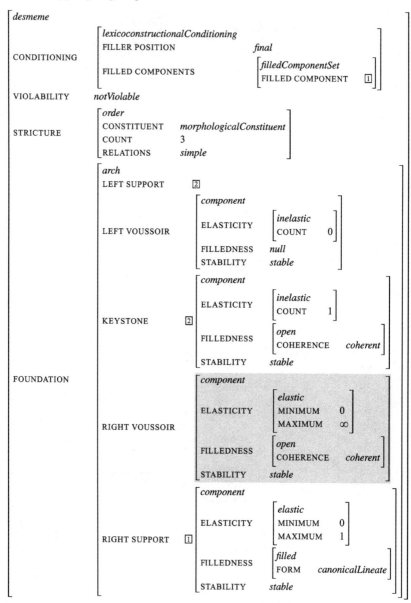

Figure 3.11 Bantu Transitive final-positioning template

3.5 Four templates found in Bantu verb stems

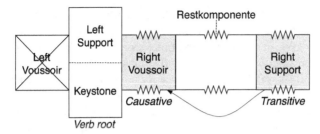

Figure 3.12 Schematization of the Bantu Causative–Transitive template

suffixes are treated as part of an arch template, rather than a span one, with the root serving as the keystone.[20] There are various interrelated reasons for this. Some will be more fully developed in this section, with other aspects presented in more detail in Section 3.5.3.[21]

The first reason why the verb root is treated as part of the template in these cases is that, in contrast to Nimboran, where there were reasons, independent of the template itself, to treat a set of verbal affixes as belonging to a grammatically distinct constituent (defined in phonological terms) from the root (Inkelas 1993: 563–566), in the case of the Bantu verb stem, the situation is quite the opposite: the verb stem – which consists, more or less, of the verb and following suffixes – has been explicitly considered to be a constituent on phonological and morphosyntactic grounds (see, e.g., Hyman (1993)).

The second reason relates to the fact that Bantu verbs have long been observed to be subject to various kinds of (potentially violable) constraints on their shape that, in effect, favor a -CVC- shape for roots and, thereby, when the final vowel is considered, a -CVCV shape for stems (see Meeussen (1967: 86)). This shape restriction is most usually emphasized in the context of minimality restrictions (see Section 2.4.3), where, for instance, roots that are shorter than -CVC- are seen to enter into specialized constructions that allow them to be "lengthened" in some way (see, e.g., Table 2.6). But, while such minimality effects can be particularly striking, it is important to bear in mind that a canonical -CVC- root shape (and accompanying -CVCV stem shape) restricts

---

[20] I will refer to the component not containing the suffixes of interest as the verb "root" in order to maintain a clear terminological distinction between the element that serves as the "base" for the suffixes and the constituent comprising that base and any following suffixes, which is referred to as the verb stem here. However, the root may in fact be morphologically complex and suffixed with extensions that precede the Causative. These are less productive, in general, than the extensions focused on here (see Schadeberg (2003: 72–79) for an overview of reconstructed extensions in Bantu). This terminological concern does not impact the typological characterization of the templates of interest here.

[21] Some of the discussion here adapts arguments made in Good (2003b: 234–273).

140   Typologizing templates: case studies

possible verb forms in other ways, with an important one being a kind of maximality restriction as well: that is, the verb root simultaneously tends to be both minimally -CVC- and, at the same time, *maximally* -CVC-. The maximality side of this restriction is more frequently violated than the minimality side, but there are still varying kinds of evidence for it. For instance, while Proto-Bantu reconstructions offer a fair number of roots of shape -CVCVC-, there are a much larger number of -CVC- roots (see, e.g., Teil-Dautrey (2008: 82–97)). Similarly, there are much greater restrictions on the segments that are allowed in the final VC portion of these longer roots than the initial CVC portion (see, e.g. Hyman (1993: 25) and Teil-Dautrey (2008: 62)). These restrictions, in effect, apply as well to the shape of the verbal extensions which make use of only a very limited range of the phonological contrasts available at the beginning of verb roots (Schadeberg 2003: 72). Accordingly, there is reason to consider a schema like -CVC- to represent not just a statement of a minimality restriction but also a weaker maximality one, manifested in various ways.

Moreover, as will be discussed in more detail Section 3.5.3, there is another piece of evidence that can be used to suggest there is a maximality restriction on the Bantu verb stem: while verbal extensions such as the Causative and the Applicative unambiguously result in violations of maximality, templatic constraints on their realization, in effect, limit the extent to which they can expand the root. They, thereby, also limit the extent to which maximality can be violated, and, while in some contemporary Bantu languages these templatic restrictions have been weakened, there is evidence that they applied in Proto-Bantu as well (see Good (2005)).

Finally, we should return to a feature of the -CVCV verb stem that has not yet been focused on: its imposition of a CV structure on the stem, as opposed to more complex syllable structures. Of course, syllable shape constraints such as this are general to Bantu phonology (Hyman 2003a: 43), and not limited to verbs. Nevertheless, this restriction seems relevant to understanding morphological patterns in Bantu languages. Suffixes with a shape like -VC-, such as the Causative and the Applicative, can "naturally" attach to -CVC- roots and allow the syllable structure to be maintained without any need for a special kind of repair. Single-vowel suffixes, such as the Transitive (as well as the Passive, which is not focused on here), however, do not result in such natural expansions of the root, especially given the morphologically obligatory presence of an inflectional Final Vowel. It has been suggested that this is connected with the asymmetry of the positioning of the -VC- suffixes, which are biased to appear closer root, and the -V- suffixes, which appear towards the end of the root (see Hyman (2003c: 262)). This implicates the root itself as one of the elements governing the overall properties of verbal extension placement, and, thereby, the templatic patterns of interest here.

3.5 Four templates found in Bantu verb stems   141

Thus, restrictions on the length and the shape of the verb root seem to be connected to the templates that govern the linear realization of the Bantu verbal suffixes, even if linear relationships among the suffixes themselves happen to be the most salient feature of these templates. The root is, therefore, treated as the keystone. In this particular case, the root is both the keystone and the left support in these templates, being at the left edge of the overall structure. This is indicated by the fact that the keystone and the left support share an inelastic component that must contain one element (since the root is obligatory but there can be only one).

In Figure 3.10, which describes the Causative–Transitive ordering restrictions, the Causative is further treated as the right voussoir in this template, since it appears immediately following the root, and it has a dependency with the Transitive, which is the right support since it appears at the end of the templatic structure. There is no left voussoir, since this is logically impossible given that the same component is both the keystone and the left support, and, therefore, a null component is included in that position (see Section 3.3 for further discussion of this convention). Finally, this templatic characterization formalizes the fact that the Causative and the Transitive need not be directly adjacent via the optional elastic restkomponente, which encodes the possibility that intervening verbal extensions may be present. This component is shaded in Figure 3.10 because it represents a kind of component which, in descriptive terms, has not yet been discussed. This component is treated as "infinite" in length, meaning, in effect, that more than one -VC- extension can appear between the Causative and Transitive, with the limitation not being determined by this specific template but, rather, other restrictions, whether templatic or not.

The templatic description language does not explicitly state that the restkomponente appears between the right voussoir and right support, since, at this point, it is not clear that this is a parameter of variation worth typologizing. However, if future research deemed this to be of interest, the description language could be extended as needed, presumably via the addition of a feature specifying a total ordering of a template's components. The lack of such a feature at present merely underscores that the goal of this study is typological comparison rather than "complete" synchronic description and the fact that the description language itself is understood to be an evolving object.

In Figure 3.11, which describes the final positioning of the Transitive, the overall description is similar to Figure 3.10, with the major difference being the that the (shaded) right voussoir is the optional, elastic component here which could be "infinite" in length, encoding the fact that more than one -VC- extension can appear before the Transitive, in a manner comparable to what was found for the restkomponente in Figure 3.10, as just discussed. In this case, the different nature of the templatic restrictions across these two templates means

142   Typologizing templates: case studies

that a component whose internal properties are the same ends up occupying two distinct structural positions.

These templates are also both conditioned by the presence of specific morphemes, and are, therefore, viewed as lexico-constructionally conditioned. In Figure 3.10, both the Causative and Transitive components (i.e., the right voussoir and right support) are listed as filled components in the construction, due to the fact that the dependency holding between the Causative and Transitive suggests both should be directly implicated in the templatic restriction. In Figure 3.11, only the Transitive (i.e., the right support) is listed as such. In both cases, the templates are treated as not violable, which appears to have been the case for Proto-Bantu and many daughter languages (Good 2005).[22] However, it should be pointed out that there are difficulties in applying the notion of violability in templates like this since doing so relies partly on one's model of compositional semantics. This issue will be explored in more detail towards the end of Section 3.5.3.

Finally, the logic of treating these templates as involving order stricture, rather than length stricture, should be fairly clear insofar as the linearization constraints are centered around the relative ordering of morphemes. At the same time, as indicated above (and as will be further developed in Section 3.5.3), it is worth bearing in mind that one effect of these ordering restrictions is to reduce the expansion possibilities of the verb stem and, thereby, limit its total length. The analyses in Figures 3.10 and 3.11 treat this as a secondary effect, but, from a comparative perspective, the Tiene data to be discussed in Section 3.5.5 suggests that, in cases like this, ordering restrictions can be reinterpreted as length restrictions, thus shifting a template from one stricture category into the other.

The next section treats a different templatic constraint in the Bantu verb stem involving ordering restrictions holding between the Causative and the Applicative. That section, as well as Sections 3.5.4 and 3.5.6, will also discuss additional conceptual issues in analyzing these templatic constraints.

3.5.3   Bantu causativization and applicativization

The Causative must precede the Applicative

The next templatic restriction in the Bantu verb stem to be considered here involves an ordering restriction among the Causative and Applicative suffixes where the Causative must precede the Applicative when the two co-occur. This

---

[22] This is not to say that there are no exceptions attested in any daughter languages. Various complications are found, especially regarding changes in the realization of the Transitive connected to its historical tendency to be associated with spirantization (see, e.g., Hyman (1994, 2003b), Good (2007a)), though these do not impact the validity of the templatic descriptions seen here as applying to a large number of languages and, therefore, being attested template types.

3.5 Four templates found in Bantu verb stems

restriction was introduced in Sections 1.4.3 and 2.4.7 and will be further developed here. As already discussed in Section 3.5.2, the Bantu Causative is one of the means through which a verb root may be causativized, adding causative semantics and a causer argument to the verb. The Applicative suffix, reconstructed as *-id-, is often attested as a form like -il- or -ir- and is also frequently subject to vowel harmony processes of the same type that affect the Causative discussed above in Section 3.5.2. The semantic contribution of the Applicative is not as straightforward as that of the Causative, and its effects are more visible in the syntactic domain. Abstracting away from a number of complications, its most salient characteristic is that, when it appears on a verb, it often allows for the realization of an additional unflagged object argument (see Peterson (2007) for general discussion of applicative constructions). The semantic role of that additional object can be varied, with benefactive semantics being quite typical, but other possibilities such as recipient or instrument being common as well.

Relevant data from Chichewa is presented in (26), adapted from Hyman & Mchombo (1992), and (27), drawn from Hyman (2003c: 248). The forms in (26) are associated with a gloss and a schematic presentation of their meaning intended primarily to illustrate scope relations.

(26) Chichewa (N.31b)

-mang-its-	'tie-CAUS'	[X cause Y to tie]
-mang-il-	'tie-APPL'	[Y tie for Z]
-mang-its-il-	'tie-CAUS-APPL'	[X cause [Y to tie with Z]] *or*
		[X [cause Y tie] with Z]
*-mang-il-its-	'tie-APPL-CAUS'	—

(27) Chichewa (N.31b)

a. *Alenjé   a-ku-líl-íts-il-a*   *mwaná ndodo.*
2.hunter 2-PROG-cry-CAUS-APPL-FV 1.child 10.sticks
"The hunters are [making [the child cry] with sticks]."

b. *Alenjé   a-ku-tákás-its-il-a*   *mkází   mthíko.*
2.hunter 2-PROG-stir-CAUS-APPL-FV 1.woman 9.spoon
"The hunters are [making [the woman stir with a spoon]]."

As seen in (26), Chichewa allows a Causative and Applicative suffix to appear on a verb in the order of Causative–Applicative but not Applicative–Causative. It might at first be suspected that the fact that Applicative–Causative order is disallowed is due to a syntactic or semantic restriction connecting morpheme order to semantic scope, along the lines of what has been called the Mirror Principle (see, e.g., Baker (1985:375, 1988) and Alsina (1999)).

144   Typologizing templates: case studies

However, as indicated in (26), and made clearer in (27), this ordering restriction is not obviously connected to semantic scope because the appearance of a Causative–Applicative combination on the verb is ambiguous for scope: it can be associated with a reading where the object associated with the Applicative falls outside the scope of the caused event associated with the Causative, as in (27a), where the instrumental object *ndodo* 'sticks' is used to induce the caused action but is not part of it. Or, it can be associated with one where the object falls within the scope of the caused event, as in (27b), where the instrumental object *mthíko* 'spoon' is used to perform the action being caused. These facts have been interpreted as deriving from a templatic restriction that says the Causative must precede the Applicative, when the two co-occur, regardless of their semantics (see, e.g., Hyman (2003c)). Moreover, Good (2005: 19) shows that this restriction has quite general provenance in Bantu, to the extent that available data on semantic interpretation allows us to see this clearly.

As was the case with the Transitive, as illustrated in (25), it is also possible to find cases where an Applicative has formed a lexicalized combination with a verb root but, nevertheless, retains its morphological independence, being separated from the root in the presence of a Causative. This demonstrates how the template can be instantiated even when one of the suffixes has, at least partially, been dissociated from its usual function. Relevant data, again from Chichewa, is provided in (28).

(28) Chichewa (N.31b)   (adapted from Hyman & Mchombo (1992: 359))

-uk-	'wake.up'	"wake up"
-uk-il-	'wake.up-APPL'	"rebel against"
*-uk-il-its-	'wake.up-APPL-CAUS'	—
-uk-its-il-	'wake.up-CAUS-APPL'	"cause to rebel against"

While there are various complications attested in some Bantu daughter languages, as discussed in Good (2005), we can describe the basic properties of this templatic restriction as in Figure 3.13. The overall description of this template is quite similar to that of the Causative–Transitive template given in Figure 3.10, with the most salient difference being the lack of any dependencies among the components. The right support corresponds to the Applicative and the right voussoir corresponds to the Causative, meaning this template simply describes a situation where one morpheme must follow another. An informal schematic representation of this template was provided in Chapter 2 in Figure 2.12.

Further details on the Causative–Applicative template

Given the discussion in Section 3.5.2, most features of the templatic description in Figure 3.13 have effectively been covered at this stage, but

3.5 Four templates found in Bantu verb stems

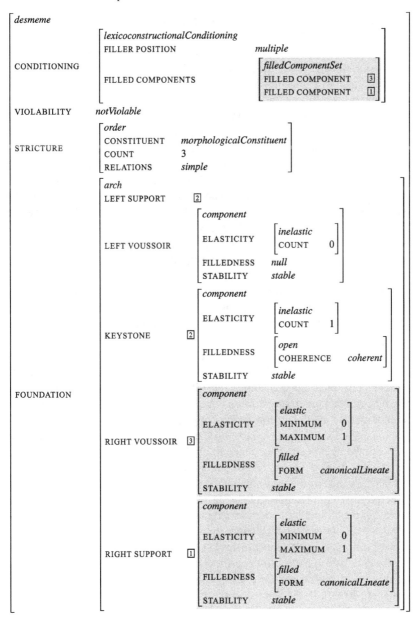

Figure 3.13 Bantu Causative–Applicative template

146   Typologizing templates: case studies

two bear remarking on. The first is the fact that, given that this is a lexico-constructional template, both the Causative and the Applicative are coded as driving the templatic restriction (via reference to both components in the FILLED COMPONENTS feature's value, which is shaded in Figure 3.13). The second is the fact that this template characterization treats the template as involving a restriction on adjacency of the two morphemes by specifying the right voussoir as consisting of an elastic component that can only be filled with a single element and which must immediately precede the right support by virtue of the fact that there are no restkomponenten that might intervene. (Each of these components is shaded in Figure 3.13.) In fact, based on the data provided so far, it might instead be better to treat this as involving a long-distance restriction on the Causative appearing before the Applicative in case other suffixes intervene, and one Bantu language where this appears to be the case, Ndebele, will be discussed shortly below. I will take up both of these issues in turn, i.e., the choice of morphemes taken to condition the appearance of the template and why the restriction is treated as involving strict adjacency rather than mere dependency.

The reason for the treating both morphemes as connected to the template's lexico-constructional conditioning is largely negative in nature: I am unaware of any evidence that would justify selecting one morpheme as the primary determinant of the templatic restriction over the other. The fact that the Causative is dependent on the Transitive in the template schematized in Figure 3.10 is positive evidence to implicate both morphemes in its lexico-constructional conditioning, and the fact that the Transitive has to appear after a class of morphemes, rather than a single morpheme, makes it reasonable for it alone to be included as a filler in the lexico-constructional conditioning of the template in Figure 3.11. However, for the Causative–Applicative restriction, there is no comparable positive evidence to claim either that both elements are the lexico-constructional fillers or just one of them.

Of course, it would presumably be possible to invoke some theoretical principle that might suggest choosing just one of these morphemes as being crucial in the template's lexico-constructional conditioning. For instance, Section 1.8.3 discussed proposals suggesting that a "no lookahead" constraint may apply to morphological constituents where the selection of an "inner" morpheme (i.e., a morpheme closer to a root) should not be dependent on the form of an "outer" morpheme (i.e., a morpheme further from the root) (see also Bobaljik (2000)). If one wanted to assume such a principle generally, it might argue for an analysis where the Applicative should be considered the crucial element for the template's conditioning since this would allow for an analysis where an "inner" Applicative would ban the appearance of an "outer" Causative, thus accounting for the templatic constraint against Applicative–Causative order in a way consistent with a "no lookahead" requirement.

3.5 Four templates found in Bantu verb stems

However, the moment we consider a principle based on any theory falling outside the descriptive theory embodied in the template description language developed in Chapter 2, we must be careful to ensure that the conditions of the theory can be applied generally to any templatic construction. In this case, it is simply unclear how a morphologically defined notion such as "no lookahead" could sensibly apply to morphophonological and syntactic constructions, making it inappropriate to invoke it here, at least without substantial adaptation. More problematic is the fact that, in effect, a constraint such as "no lookahead" is embedded within just the kind of theory of linearization whose adequacy the templatic description language developed here is designed to help test for in the first place (see Section 1.7). In particular, it allows for a sufficiently wide range of linearization patterns to be described that, if there are theoretically interesting gaps in them of the sort implied by a "no lookahead" constraint, it can help us detect them. This means, in general, that outside theories of linearization should not be invoked as factors in the typological coding decisions employed here in order to avoid "false" discoveries that are actually due to logical circularities in coding choices.

We can contrast, then, for instance how the potential choice of the Applicative as the morpheme involved in the template's lexico-constructional conditioning, as determined via the consideration of a specific theory of morphological linearization, differs from the choice of the Causative and the Transitive as filler morphemes in the template schematized in Figure 3.10 and the Transitive in Figure 3.11. In the first of these two cases, the decision was based on the presence of a dependency among the components, a principle that could be applied in any templatic construction without going beyond the description language used here. In the second, the choice was even more straightforward: the lexico-constructional conditioning type is defined with respect to the presence of a specific morpheme associated with the template, and, in this case, there is only one such morpheme, the Transitive. Unfortunately, these determinations leave us without a guiding principle for deciding what triggers the lexico-constructional conditioning in the case of the Causative–Applicative template, and the components corresponding to each of the relevant suffixes are, therefore, included in Figure 3.13 merely since there is no reason to exclude one or the other. This decision raises, in general, the problem of coding consistency in the face of such a complex system of typological characterization, an issue which will be returned to in Section 5.2.2, though not fully resolved here.

The final point to be addressed with respect to the templatic description in Figure 3.13 relates to the fact that the restriction appears generally to be characterized in terms of adjacency rather than simply "preceding" or "following." This is why, unlike the formal templatic characterizations given in Figures 3.10 and 3.11, the one in Figure 3.13 does not include an optional elastic component

148   Typologizing templates: case studies

corresponding to potentially intervening suffixes. Specific data that has bearing on the issue is provided in (29).

(29) Chichewa (N.31b)   (adapted from Hyman & Mchombo (1992: 354))
    -mang-il-an-   'tie-APPL-RECP'   "tie for each other"
    -mang-il-an-its-   'tie-APPL-RECP-CAUS'   "cause to tie for each other"
    *-mang-il-its-   'tie-APPL-CAUS'   —

As seen in (29), the ban on Applicative–Causative order, at least in some languages, is purely local. When another morpheme intervenes (in this case the Reciprocal, to be further discussed in Section 3.5.4), then a Causative can follow the Applicative as seen in the form *-mang-il-an-its-*. Data like that seen in (29) has rarely been looked for explicitly in analyses of Bantu suffix ordering. The same pattern is, however, also attested in Ikalanga (Mathangwane 2001: 404). In this case, the available evidence is too limited to say reliably what the Proto-Bantu situation might have been in this regard (see also Good (2005: 29–30)), though for purposes of exposition, I am treating the template characterized in Figure 3.13 as being "Bantu" in nature.

I am aware of one language where the ban on Applicative–Causative order has been reported as present even if another morpheme intervenes, though it is weaker in nature than the ban on an adjacent Applicative–Causative sequence. Specifically, in Ndebele, Sibanda (2004: 67) reports a verb form like **-sik-el-is-* 'cut-APPL-CAUS' as being fully ungrammatical, while also reporting that a form like *?-sik-el-an-is-* 'cut-APPL-RECP-CAUS' is degraded but not as bad (Sibanda 2004: 79). If we treat the form where the Reciprocal intervenes as actually disallowed, we can adapt the templatic restriction in Figure 3.13 to the one in Figure 3.14 to characterize the difference between the general Bantu pattern and the Ndebele one.

As can be seen, Figure 3.14 is quite similar to Figure 3.13, with the inclusion of one more component, which does not occupy a specific structural position but is, instead, included as a restkomponente. This optional elastic component, shaded in the figure, corresponds to a potentially intervening set of verbal extensions, in a manner parallel to the role of restkomponente in Figure 3.10, characterizing the Bantu Causative–Transitive template.[23] It, thus, is intended to encode the fact that, in Ndebele, this templatic constraint may involve a long-distance restriction rather than one conditioned only by adjacency. As with the Causative–Transitive template, nothing in this template specifically encodes that this other component must appear between the right voussoir and

---

[23] The actual facts of Ndebele morphology, in fact, appear to allow only one possible filler for this extra component, namely the Reciprocal suffix. However, this does not appear to be due to a templatic restriction but, rather, independent combinatorial constraints on Ndebele morphemes (see Sibanda (2004: 60–90) for a detailed overview of all the relevant ordering facts).

3.5 Four templates found in Bantu verb stems

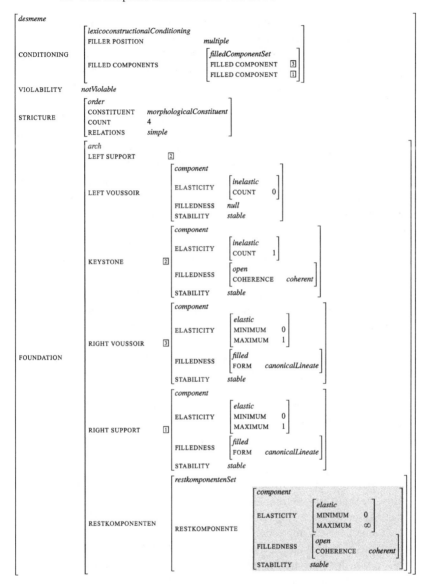

Figure 3.14 Ndebele variant of Causative–Applicative template

right support since not enough constructions like this have been encountered to justify adding this kind of specification to the description language. The simplified visual representation for the Causative–Transitive template given in Figure 3.12 could characterize this Ndebele template as well (excepting the details of the component labels).

150   Typologizing templates: case studies

The Causative–Applicative template as a maximality restriction
In justifying the details of the templatic descriptions given in Figures 3.10 and
3.11 above, there was discussion of the possibility that the Bantu verb stem
is governed not only by minimality restrictions, which have seen significant
attention, but also by weaker maximality restrictions, limiting deviation from
a -CVCV stem shape. In fact, the Causative–Applicative ordering restriction
can be understood as part of a "conspiracy" in this regard (see, e.g., Kisseberth (1970, 2011) for discussion of the notion of conspiracy in a phonological
context that is broadly applicable here). If the Causative and Applicative could
combine freely in ways that match their semantics, this would open up the
logical possibility of a "recursive" expansion where Causative and Applicative morphemes could repeat to express complex patterns of causativized and
applicativized semantics. While recursive morphology does not appear to be
especially common, it is not unattested (see, e.g., Inkelas & Orgun (1998)),
and there is no syntactic or semantic reason for the possibilities of Bantu verb
stem expansion to be limited for suffixes associated with an increase in valency
such as the Causative and the Applicative.

     Nevertheless, in the case of these particular suffixes, the template imposes
a clear limit on the extent to which the Causative and Applicative can expand
the verb: if there is an Applicative, a Causative cannot directly follow, making, for instance, patterns like Causative–Applicative–Causative impossible.
In Section 3.5.5, a case study will be given of the Bantu language Tiene that
suggests that, whatever the synchronic status of this generalization may be
in a language such as Chichewa, from a diachronic perspective, limitations on
expansion were, in at least one language, reanalyzed as being a primary driving
factor in the shape of the verb stem (in a quite complex way).

Violability and the Bantu templates
There are, unsurprisingly, some cases where difficulties in determining the
ideal application of the typological concepts employed here can arise. Violability, in the templatic domain, is one of these, since the general notion of
violability can apply to any manner of grammatical "violations" depending on
one's theoretical assumptions. For instance, if one were to adopt some version of the Mirror Principle (see, e.g., Baker (1985: 375, 1988) and Alsina
(1999)), which suggests, roughly speaking, that morpheme ordering should
be transparently relatable to syntactic interpretation, then verb forms where
the Causative–Applicative ordering is ambiguous for scope of causativization with respect to applicativization, as seen in, for instance (26) and (27),
could perhaps be considered some sort of "violation." Simply put, the different
scopes should be associated with different morpheme orders: when applicativization has semantic scope over causativization, as in (27a), one would
predict Causative–Applicative order, and, when causativization has semantic

3.5 Four templates found in Bantu verb stems 151

scope over applicativization, as in (27b), one would predict the disallowed Applicative–Causative order.

Thus, we can reasonably say that a verb form such as the one in (27b) violates the Mirror Principle, but this does not mean we would want to suggest it violates the template, since the template itself is not "aware" of the predictions of the Mirror Principle. Moreover, since the most straightforward analysis of Causative–Applicative order in a language like Chichewa is to suggest it is vague with respect to scope of causativization and applicativization, this implies that there is no semantic context which would demonstrate a violation of the template. Therefore, since there are neither surface violations of the templatic ordering nor clearcut contexts where it could be violated, it is categorized as *notViolable* here. Of course, alternative interpretations are possible: for instance, an analysis adhering to the Mirror Principle might suggest that Causative–Applicative order is not vague with respect to scope at some underlying level of representation and that the template forces some kind of morphological "metathesis" in surface forms, in which case we might treat the template as potentially violable.

As discussed just above in the context of justifying the treatment of the Causative–Applicative template as being conditioned by both the Causative and Applicative morphemes (see Figure 3.13), the general research strategy here is to limit the extent to which "external" theories are given consideration in terms of data coding for the simple reason that they complicate the extent to which the typological description language can be applied across a range of constructions. The Mirror Principle, for instance, is a theory of morphology, not syntax. So, if we adopt it in the analysis of morphological templates, it is not clear how to allow its assumptions to carry over consistently to syntactic ones. In the domain of violability, this means, in effect, that whether or not a template can be "violated" will be evaluated with respect to whether there are language-internal contexts where violation is possible, not whether there are violations with respect to a more general theoretical model. The case study in Section 3.5.4 immediately below will provide an example of the sort of data that is considered to be relevant in this regard here.

3.5.4   Chichewa Applicative and Reciprocal

The final templatic restriction associated with canonical Bantu verbal suffixing patterns to be examined here is not general to Bantu but is, rather, connected to a specific pattern in Chichewa. It also appears to be attested in similar ways elsewhere (see, e.g, Sibanda (2004: 80)), though its overall distribution is probably limited. It involves the realization of combinations of the Applicative and Reciprocal suffix, the latter of which adds reciprocal semantics to a given verb. The general Bantu pattern is that the Applicative must precede the Reciprocal

152   Typologizing templates: case studies

(see Hyman (2003c)). One result of this is that, as with the Causative and the Applicative, the Applicative–Reciprocal combination is ambiguous for scope of applicativization with respect to reciprocalization. However, there is also a strategy, which partly violates the templatic ordering constraint, that produces a verb with unambiguous semantics of applicativization with scope over reciprocalization. The illustrative forms in (30) are adapted from the discussion in Hyman (2003c: 253–254).

(30) Chichewa (N.31b)

-mang-il-	'tie-APPL'	[Y tie for Z]
-mang-an-	'tie-RECP'	[Y tie each other]
-mang-il-an-	'tie-APPL-RECP'	[Y tie [for each other]] *or* [[Y tie each other] for Z]
*-mang-an-il-	'tie-RECP-APPL'	—
-mang-an-il-an-	'tie-RECP-APPL-RECP'	[[Y tie each other] for Z]

Unlike causativization and applicativization in Chichewa, where the language provides no way to disambiguate their scopal readings, as can be seen in (30), the language's grammar does provide a way to partially disambiguate the scopal readings for applicativization and reciprocalization by providing an alternate form from the purely templatic one which specifies that reciprocalization has scope over causativization. But, this form partly violates the templatic Reciprocal–Causative restriction by appearing with two instances of the Reciprocal, one of which appears before the Applicative, in violation of the template, but the other of which appears after it, following the template. Importantly in the present context, the form that completely violates the template by placing the Reciprocal before the Applicative is not allowed.

The Chichewa Applicative–Reciprocal template is, thus, very much like the Causative–Applicative template with one key difference: it is potentially violable. When it is violated, a repair strategy is further employed that involves insertion of an extra element, in this case the Reciprocal "slot" after the Applicative must be filled with a copy of the Reciprocal. This is formally described in Figure 3.15. Other cases of insertion as a repair strategy are discussed in Sections 3.6 and 3.9.

For the reasons just discussed, the template characterization in Figure 3.15 is essentially the same as the one in Figure 3.13, except for its violability specification, which is shaded. The exceptionality of this template is indicated as being semantic in nature – that is, it is violated under specific semantic conditions (here, when there is unambiguous encoding of applicativization with scope over reciprocalization). The specific reason for the template's treatment as involving an adjacency restriction along the lines of what is also found in Figure 3.13 is somewhat different, however: for these suffixes, I am simply

3.5 Four templates found in Bantu verb stems

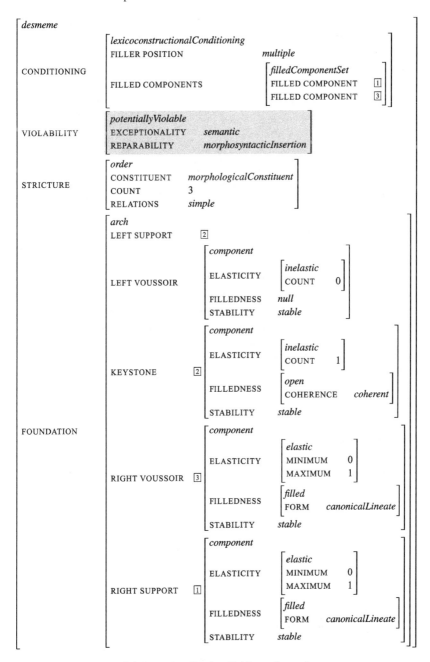

Figure 3.15 Chichewa Applicative–Reciprocal template

154   Typologizing templates: case studies

not aware of any instances where a morpheme could intervene between the Applicative and Reciprocal when both are present, due to other aspects of the language's verbal system.

Before moving on, it is worth noting that, comparable to the Causative–Applicative restriction, the Applicative–Reciprocal restriction that is general to Bantu (i.e., not just focusing on this specific Chichewa version of it), also in effect, acts to limit the length of stems (see Section 3.5.3).

3.5.5   Tiene verbs

Introducing Tiene

Tiene (B.81) is a Bantu language spoken in the Democratic Republic of Congo in the northwest of the Bantu-speaking area. Bantu languages of this region have long been recognized as diverging from the canonical Bantu type in surprising ways (Nurse & Philippson 2003: 5). The Tiene template to be discussed here, therefore, is quite distinct from the examples just discussed above in surface typological terms, meaning its place in this section may not be immediately obvious. It is included here, however, because, in diachronic terms, it represents a striking development from the relatively straightforward patterns in more canonical Bantu languages and, thereby, provides a window onto how templatic restrictions can develop in complex ways due to the reanalysis of the factors conditioning those restrictions.

The Tiene case was already introduced in Section 2.1, and is analyzed in detail in Hyman & Inkelas (1997) and Hyman (2010a).[24] These studies are based on Ellington (1977), which provides all the relevant data on the language and the first analysis of it, though it is the analysis of Hyman (2010a) which forms the primary basis of the templatic characterization to be given below. As with the preceding case studies, the template partly centers around restrictions in the realization of verbal suffixes, including a Causative and Applicative (the latter of which Ellington (1977: 109) labels the *directive*). These are etymologically connected to the suffixes with the same names already discussed. An additional suffix will also be considered, which I will refer to as the Stative here, following Hyman (2010a: 149). This suffix is associated with a Proto-Bantu extension reconstructible as *-ik- (see Meeussen (1967: 92) and Guthrie (1970: 216)) but goes under other labels as well, notably *neuter* (see Schadeberg (2003: 75)), which is also the original label used by Ellington (1977: 115).

---

[24] Hyman & Inkelas (1997: 97–98) specifically reject a "templatic" analysis of the Tiene facts that would invoke particular kinds of CV-skeleton templates (see Section 1.4.2). The present templatic analysis builds directly on their analysis of Tiene and does not seem to contradict their analysis insofar as the templatic description language developed here can describe a wider range of templatic restrictions than the CV templates they considered.

3.5 Four templates found in Bantu verb stems

Table 3.2 *Causative verb forms in Tiene*

STEM	CAUSATIVE	GLOSS
-lɛ	-lées-ɛ	'eat'
-bany-a	-baas-a	'be judged'
-mat-a	-maas-a	'go away'
-pal-a	-paas-a	'arrive'
-piin-a	-piis-ɛ	'be black'
-lab-a	-lasab-a	'walk'
-lók-a	-lósek-ɛ	'vomit'
-suɔm-ɔ	-sɔsɔb-ɔ	'borrow'
-tóm-a	-tóseb-ɛ	'send'

However, whatever label one gives this suffix, its Tiene etymology probably involves a conflation of two distinct morphemes, one of which corresponds to the general Bantu Stative and the other containing some kind of voiced coronal consonant (see Hyman (2010a: 149)).

Tiene verb forms providing illustration of the templatic patterns are given in Table 3.2 (for Causatives), Table 3.3 (for Applicatives), and Table 3.4 (for Statives). The tables give stems without an affix followed by stems with an affix. Like other Bantu languages, Tiene verb stems typically appear with a final vowel, which is parsed off in the examples where it occurs. The details of the formal realization of this vowel are complex, and will not be a focus of the present discussion.[25] The forms themselves are adapted from Ellington (1977).[26]

The constraints on Tiene stem shape

At first glance, the derivations of the Causative, Applicative, and Stative in Tiene may appear somewhat haphazard, certainly falling well outside the domain of canonical concatenative morphology that has, with some complications, characterized the Bantu data to this point. The derivational patterns seen in Tiene, are, in fact, best understood, not in terms of specific morphemes "extending" the verb stem but, rather, as something along the lines of "slotting" morphological material into the verb stem wherever strict phonotactic constraints allow. The relevant constraints for understanding the Tiene templatic

---

[25] Ellington (1977) provides a full overview of the rules involved in determining a verb's final vowel. Ellington (1977: 105) specifically discusses the rules for final-vowel assignment for derived stems, of special interest here.

[26] As discussed in Hyman (2010a: 150), Ellington (1977: 123–124) also discusses "vestigial" Reversive and Reciprocal extensions showing similar templatic patterns to the other data presented here. They are not a focus of the present discussion due to their unproductive status.

156 Typologizing templates: case studies

Table 3.3 *Applicative verb forms in Tiene*

STEM	APPLICATIVE	GLOSS
-ta	-téel-ɛ	'throw'
-síɛ	-síil-ɛ	'whittle'
-bót-a	-bóot-ɛ	'give birth'
-kas-a	-kaas-a	'fight for'
-sɔ́n-ɔ	-sɔ́ɔn-ɔ	'write'
-kony-a	-koony-ɛ	'plant'
-yal-a	-yaal-a	'spread'
-dum-a	-dunem-ɛ	'run fast'
-lɔŋ-ɔ	-lɔnɔŋ-ɔ	'load'
-súom-a	-sónem-ɛ	'buy'
-yɔb-ɔ	-yɔlɔb-ɔ	'bathe'
-yók-a	-yólek-ɛ	'hear'

Table 3.4 *Stative verb forms in Tiene*

STEM	STATIVE	GLOSS
-kaa	-kaal-a	'fasten'
-ból-a	-bólek-ɛ	'break'
-faas-a	-fasak-a	'drive'
-kóót-ɛ	-kótek-ɛ	'untie'
-yaat-a	-yatak-a	'split'
-vwuny-a	-vwunyeŋ-ɛ	'mix'
-sɔ́n-ɔ	-sɔ́nɔŋ-ɔ	'write'
-kab-a	-kalab-a	'divide'
-nyak-a	-nyalak-a	'tear'
-kam-a	-kanam-a	'twist'

restrictions are given in (31). They are adapted from Hyman (2010a: 152–153), but include features of the analysis of Hyman & Inkelas (1997), and are only relevant to the portion of verb stems not including the final vowel.[27] As indicated, some of the constraints refer to various segmental positions in the verb stem assuming a $-C_1VC_2VC_3-$ schema for longer verb stems. There are additional constraints on Tiene verb stems not discussed here, for instance involving patterns of vowel harmony, since there is no evidence that they are connected to the specific templatic restrictions to be typologically analyzed below.

[27] Hyman (2010a) sometimes discusses the Tiene restrictions in terms of verb stems with the final vowel. I only discuss stems without the final vowel since the templatic constraints appear to target this unit alone, at least with respect to the templates being analyzed here.

3.5 Four templates found in Bantu verb stems 157

(31) a. A derived verb stem is bimoraic (i.e., consisting of either one long vowel or two short vowels).
   b. C_2 must be coronal in a -$C_1VC_2VC_3$- structure.
   c. C_3 must be non-coronal in a -$C_1VC_2VC_3$- structure.
   d. C_2 and C_3 must show nasal harmony in a -$C_1VC_2VC_3$- structure.

The set of restrictions in (31) will be treated in the immediately following sections below as being associated with two distinct templates, one a length template (describing restriction (31a)) and the other an order template (describing (31b), (31c), and (31d)).[28]

A length template for the Tiene verb stem
The application of restriction (31a) is immediately visible in the data in Tables 3.2, 3.3, and 3.4 by inspecting the shapes of the derived verb stems which are always either -CVVC- or -CVCVC-, but, never, for instance, -CVVCV-, even when the shape of the non-derived verb stem would suggest this would be the case. Thus, a form like *-faas-* 'borrow' becomes *-fasak-* when derived with the Stative suffix, shortening its first vowel so as to adhere to this restriction.

This size restriction is comparable to ones already described for Turkish in Section 3.2. Its formal description is given in Table 3.16. One set of differences from the Turkish cases involves the reparability specification of the template, where, as just discussed, the repair strategy involves shortening of lexical forms. Another difference lies in the fact that this template involves a maximality restriction rather than a minimality one. This is coded by treating each of its components as inelastic, with a maximum size of one, as opposed to the elastic components found for the Turkish cases. These parts of the description are shaded in Figure 3.16.

An order template for segments in the Tiene verb stem

The basic consonantal restrictions and introducing the template The bimoraic size restriction of the Tiene verb stem is not particularly unusual, but the co-occurrence restrictions on consonants are of a cross-linguistically rare type, even if, as will be briefly discussed below, they seem diachronically

---

[28] While not a significant point of discussion in Hyman (2010a), Hyman & Inkelas (1997: 98) explicitly treat the Tiene stem as being subject to both a maximal and minimal bimoraic restriction, which is the basis for (31a). There is some ambiguity in the possible analysis of this restriction, for instance whether it should be treated as part of the templatic restrictions in and of themselves or whether it may be an epiphenomenon of independent (possibly templatic) restrictions on the lexical shapes of verbal elements. I treat it as resulting from a templatic restriction on the verb stem itself since, while there does not appear to be an explicit statement in this regard, it seems closest to the spirit of Hyman's (2010a) analysis.

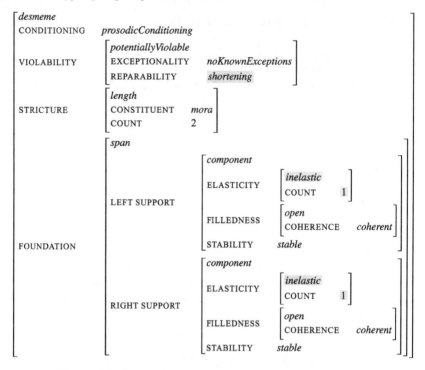

Figure 3.16 Tiene derived verb stem prosodic template

connected to the less unusual ordering restrictions discussed earlier in this section. Full description of the operation of these restrictions is given in Hyman (2010a), but, here, their basic manifestation will be summarized by considering the various sets of forms given in Tables 3.2, 3.3, and 3.4, with reference to the way the forms are divided into sets in each table. The first set of forms in each table gives the derived and non-derived forms of subminimal CV stems (see Section 2.4.3 for discussion of such stems in a Bantu context). Since the relevant verbal suffixes all contain only a single consonant, affixation processes create structures containing just two consonants. This, in effect, means that the constraints in (31b), (31c), and (31d) do not apply, and this gives us a reasonable window into the underlying consonants associated with the affixes. As can be seen, the Causative is associated with an *s* and the Applicative with an *l*. The realization of the Stative is more complex since in some cases it appears to be associated with the etymologically expected *k*, as in a verb stem like *-bólek-* 'break.STAT,' while in other cases, such as the form *-kaal-* 'fasten.STAT' based on a subminimal root, it is associated with an *l*. This issue will be returned to below.

3.5 Four templates found in Bantu verb stems

While it is possible to characterize these suffixes as being "associated with" certain segments, it is difficult to parse them out into clear affixal forms, and this is directly due to the segmental constraints listed in (31). For instance, the second block of Causative forms in Table 3.2 are all based on non-Causative forms whose stems end in coronal consonants. Since there cannot be two coronal consonants in the second and third consonant positions (due to the conjunction of (31b) and (31c)), it is not possible to realize both the *s* of the Causative and the final consonant of the stem, and, in this case, the resolution involves, in effect, deletion of the expected stem-final consonant. One also sees vowel lengthening in all forms which would not otherwise be bimoraic, which is not considered part of the segmental template being discussed here but is, rather, connected to the length template schematized in Figure 3.16. Various analyses are possible to capture the details of this pattern, but, for our purposes, one point to bear in mind is that it can be understood as the historical reflex of the fact that the Causative would have had a -VC- shape, and this long vowel, therefore, seems to reflect the etymological vowel of the suffix.[29]

The third block of forms in Table 3.2 gives cases where the Causative *s* and the final consonant of the verb stem both appear in Causative forms. However, rather than being part of a suffix, as would be expected on historical grounds, the *s* is infixed into the stem. This is due to the restriction that, in longer stems, coronals cannot appear in the third consonant position (see (31c)), making the second position the only licit slot for the Causative *s* to appear in.

The constraint on matching nasality for the second and third consonant positions given in (31d) results in denasalization of the final consonant for the last two forms in Table 3.2, producing, for instance, *-tóseb-* 'send.CAUS' rather than the expected **-tósem-*. Finally, the data for all the forms taken together illustrates a number of other processes affecting vowels as well, mostly connected to patterns of vowel harmony not directly connected to this template (see Ellington (1977: 122–123) for an overview).

The patterns for the Applicative (see Table 3.3), which is also associated with a coronal consonant, are largely the same as those for the Causative except for the fact that the Applicative *l* is, informally speaking, "weaker" than the Causative *s*. Thus, for coronal-final roots, for instance, we do not see the *l* replacing the root-final consonant, but, rather, it is the segment that fails to appear as expected and lengthening, thus, becomes the primary coding mechanism for applicativization. Similarly, the effect of the nasalization constraint is nasalization of the Applicative *l* to *n*, rather than denasalization of a stem-final nasal. It is because of these variable resolutions in the patterns of derivation,

---

[29] If the identity of this vowel is further recognized as some sort of vowel along the lines of *e* for both the Causative and Applicative suffixes, this would help account for the realization of the vowels in the Causative and Applicative forms of the -CV- stems in Tables 3.2 and 3.3.

160   Typologizing templates: case studies

i.e., with respect to the realization of *s* versus *l*, that the Tiene facts seem more effectively described in terms of constraints than rules.

The same constraints are active in the formation of the Stative, though, again the details of their resolution are different. The suffix shows apparent phonologically conditioned suppletive allomorphy (see Paster (2006)), where it appears with a *k* when Statives are derived from coronal-final stems and an *l* when they are derived from stems ending in non-coronals. (There are vowel differences as well, with the *l* forms apparently associated with non-front vowel features and the *k* forms with front vowel features, though the vowel harmony processes mentioned above obscure this picture.) This allomorphy appears suppletive due to the fact that, on the one hand, there is no obvious reason for there to be a phonologically predictable *k*~*l* alternation given other patterns of Tiene grammar, and, on the other hand, the fact that the affixes do not appear to be etymologically related (Hyman 2010a: 149)). (See Veselinova 2006: 1–31, 2013 for an overview discussion of issues surrounding suppletion, as well as Corbett (2007) for a discussion from the perspective of Canonical Typology.) At the same time, it must be immediately recognized that this suppletive pattern "solves" the problem of the exponence of the Stative when attached to different classes of stems: for stems ending in a coronal, the non-coronal *k* allomorph appears and occupies the third consonant position. For stems ending in a non-coronal, the coronal *l* allomorph appears and occupies the second consonant position. Nasal consonant harmony also affects the Stative in both cases, as with the other forms.

Having given a descriptive overview of the Tiene segmental template, its formal typological characterization is presented in Figure 3.17. The logic behind some aspects of the description should already be clear, for instance, the fact that it is treated as an order template, since it involves constraints on the realization of consonants in linearly defined positions. The details of the components themselves should also be fairly straightforward. One of the components in Figure 3.17 is a placeholder null component connected to the fact that the template is treated as having an arch foundation, which will be justified further below. This null component is structurally comparable to those found in the typological characterizations of the Bantu templates given in previous sections and connected to the fact that the element serving as the keystone, the first consonant of the stem, is also the left support. Each of the other components corresponds to one of the three consonants that can be present in a verb stem, with the keystone component, as just mentioned, corresponding to the first consonant in the stem, being inelastic of size one (since one consonant must always be present to create a verb root), and the other two corresponding to the second and third consonants of the verb (and assigned the structural positions of right voussoir and right support respectively). Both of these components are treated as optional (i.e., elastic with a minimum size of zero and

3.5 Four templates found in Bantu verb stems

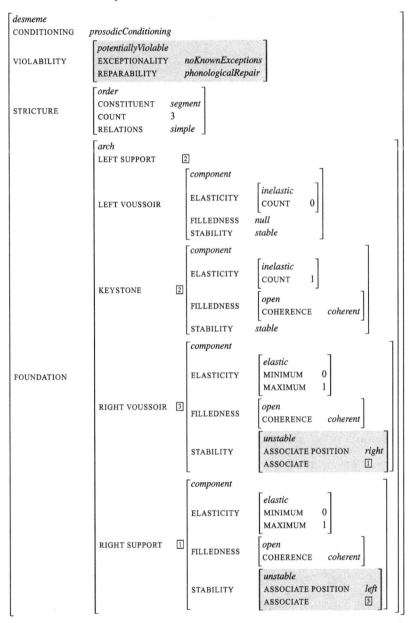

Figure 3.17 Tiene verb stem segmental template

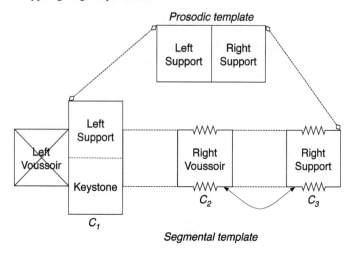

Figure 3.18 Schematization of the two Tiene templates

a maximum of one). All three of these components are further treated as open and coherent, reflecting the fact that their content can be described in terms of basic phonological classes. Additional aspects of the templatic description which require discussion are its violability and the symmetric dependency indicated for the second and third consonant positions, all of which are shaded in Figure 3.17 for readability. These, and other issues, are taken up shortly below.

The two Tiene templates are informally schematized, using the visually oriented format developed above, in Figure 3.18. In this case, the two templates are portrayed together and treated as "linked" to each other (via lines with diamond tips) to reflect the fact that they each can apply to the same morphologically definable domain. Most of the other conventions have already been seen above (e.g., the zigzag lines to indicate elastic components, arrows linking dependent components, etc.) except for the inclusion of empty boxes marked with dashed lines. These represent the vowels in the verb stem's segmental forms that are not treated as part of the template here (and which will be discussed further in the next section) but whose presence means the templatic components are not adjacent to each other.

Further details on the classification of the segmental restrictions Understanding further details of the description of the Tiene segmental template requires some additional discussion. First, the classification of the Tiene segmental template as an arch template rather than a span one is less straightforward than the other Bantu templates just discussed since, as a morphophonological template,

3.5 Four templates found in Bantu verb stems 163

rather than a morphosyntactic one, criteria for determining whether or not one component is privileged are not especially obvious. Indeed, this Tiene template perhaps lies in between the arch and span types and suggests that, as the database of templates is further developed, refinements to the categorization of foundations may be required (see also Section 3.10 and Section 3.12 for other cases suggesting the span/arch opposition may require further consideration). The critical question for determining the best way to characterize the Tiene segmental template in this regard is whether or not to accept Hyman's (2010a) characterization of the templatic restriction in terms of restrictions on *second* and *third* consonants in the stem or, rather, a logically possible alternative of *middle* and *final*. Relative characterizations like "second" and "third" can only be reckoned with respect to the first consonant, which would favor classifying it as a keystone, and the foundation as an arch type, while absolute characterization such as "middle" and "final" are consistent with a span type.

I opt for the former characterization here, largely following the descriptive lead of Hyman (2010a), for two reasons. First, the nature of the restrictions on the second and third consonants do not appear to be specific to the positions in the middle or the end of the stem but, rather, appear more arbitrary. For instance, I am not aware of any reason why the configuration where coronals should precede non-coronals is any more expected than the reverse in these positions. In other words, we are not dealing with a phenomenon like coda neutralization, where patterns of loss of phonemic contrast are so widespread as to present a reasonable candidate for a phonological universal (Kiparsky 2008: 45–49). Thus, a restriction on slots in the verb stem localized to the Tiene facts seems more in line with the descriptive facts than suggesting that "mediality" and "finality" are the crucial factor, and characterizing them in terms of their position with respect to the first consonant helps achieve this. Second, as discussed, there is a restriction on the second and third consonants where they exhibit nasal harmony, but neither the second nor third consonant is dominant with respect to the harmony. In the Causative (see Table 3.2), the second consonant triggers denasalization of the third consonant. In the Applicative and Stative (see Tables 3.3 and 3.4), the third consonant triggers nasalization of the second. What unifies these consonants in descriptive terms is the fact that they are non-initial, and, this, too, requires classifying them with respect to the first consonant, giving us another reason to treat it as a keystone.

There is a danger, of course, that, in making somewhat complex analytical arguments like these, it will become difficult to ensure consistent typological descriptions across constructions, since it is not as though the Tiene analysis just argued for can be straightforwardly seen as following from general coding principles. This issue will be taken up in general terms in Section 5.2.2.

Focusing on this specific case, however, it is important to bear in mind here that the stakes in choosing whether or not the Tiene segmental template is an arch or span template are not quite as great as they may seem due to the fine-grained nature of the data coding. One high-level classification would change, and specification of certain structural positions would change. For instance, there would be no keystone, and the current right voussoir (corresponding to the second consonant) would become a restkomponente. But, the descriptions of the components themselves will remain the same and the left and right supports will also remain unchanged. When the issue of rigorous comparison of templates is developed in Chapter 4, we will see, then, that, since it is possible to employ algorithms of comparison that consider essentially all of the features of a given template, rather than just privileging a few, changes in just one domain of typological classification for a given template will not necessarily have serious repercussions for how it compares with other templates.

The final two aspects of the typological description in Figure 3.17 that need to be considered are its violability and the dependency coded for the right voussoir and right support, which correspond to the second and third consonants in the stem respectively. Regarding violability, Hyman (2010a: 154–155) shows that the constraints on the realization of segments in Tiene verbs appear to show no known exceptions, even for cases of non-derived stems which happen to contain three consonants. There are noun stems which are exceptional, but the template being described here is treated as associated with verbs only, hence the indication that there are no known exceptions. Not enough data on Tiene is available to determine whether or how restrictions on nouns should be considered related to those on verbs. As we have seen, the verbal morphology of Tiene might be expected to produce exceptions to the segmental restrictions listed in (31) (hence the template's classification as potentially violable), but a variety of phonological repair strategies intervene to prevent any exceptions from appearing on the surface. Since these repair strategies are heterogenous, the specification for reparability in Figure 3.17 is simply given the general classification *phonologicalRepair*, though for future studies it is imaginable that it might be considered preferable to give a list of distinctive strategies (e.g., deletion, metathesis, nasalization, denasalization, etc.).

The nasal harmony relationship between the second and third consonants (see (31d)) is coded in Figure 3.17 by treating the corresponding right voussoir and right support components as each having a dependency on the other using the ASSOCIATE feature. The dependency is treated as symmetrical, with each component having the other as an associate, since, as discussed above, there is not a clear trigger–target asymmetry between the consonants where only one of them determines the nasal specification for both segments, as is

3.5 Four templates found in Bantu verb stems

usually the case in patterns of harmony (see Hansson (2010: 291–292) for further discussion of this interesting aspect of Tiene phonology).[30]

A final point to note about the typological description of the Tiene segmental template in Figure 3.17 is that it does not include any indication that its consonantal components are not adjacent but, rather, are separated by vowels, since these templatic patterns have been characterized as purely involving consonantal interactions. This is not because this is not a point of potential interest but, rather, is due to the fact that, of the case studies that have informed the present work, only the Tiene segmental template has this clearcut property where components can be separated by elements which do not factor into the template itself, making it of relatively little value as an aspect of typological variation to code at this point. Of course, if a larger range of CV-skeleton templates had been considered (see Section 1.4.2), adding information about templates with non-contiguous components would probably have been in order, though the details of how best to do this will have to await further study.[31]

Tiene and Proto-Bantu When we compare the Tiene template to what is seen in more "canonical" Bantu languages, it is striking how more or less the same historical morphological material has become part of two very different sets of templatic restrictions. Most Bantu languages show a templatic pattern involving restrictions on the relative ordering of individual morphemes. In Tiene, it appears that these restrictions, along with other aspects of verb stem morphology, have been reinterpreted as being primarily phonologically driven rather than morphosyntactically driven. There has not been significant work on the evolution of templatic restrictions (though see Good (2003b: 499–530) and Section 5.3), but, here, at least, we see that they can develop in ways that allow them to "live on" while taking quite different forms.

The general bridging context for this shift in the nature of the templatic restrictions is connected to the fact that the morphophonological restrictions

---

[30] Allowing each component to reference the other has a formal consequence of significance for automated processing of the templatic descriptions, as is done here (see Chapter 4). Namely, if the representation in Figure 3.17 were translated into a graph, it would no longer have the significant property of being "acyclic" since the cross-referencing of components in this way creates a single cycle. This could, in principle, affect the processing of the data, but the potential problems are ameliorated by the fact that, to this point, the need for cycles has been limited to coding of symmetrical dependencies among components. This means it is straightforward to handle these as a single exceptional case (see Section 3.12 for another example of such a dependency).

[31] Some of the other Bantu templates appear to have comparable properties involving a lack of component contiguity, as seen in, for instance, the opposition between Figures 3.13 and 3.14, where the former involves an immediate adjacency relation and the latter does not. However, in the case of these affixes, the presence or absence of an intervening morpheme has been seen to have an effect on the templatic restrictions themselves, suggesting they are part of the template. The Tiene vowels, on the other hand, seem to appear purely for independent phonological reasons without any impact on the consonantal templatic restrictions.

166 Typologizing templates: case studies

on the canonical Bantu verb stem (as discussed in Section 3.5.2), which can be detected independently from the templatic constraints, facilitate a reanalysis of morphologically driven constraints as phonologically driven.[32] Furthermore, as discussed in Section 3.5.3, restrictions like the one on Causative–Applicative order have, as a kind of "side effect," the limitation of the possibilities for the expansion of the verb stem. This means they play a role in limiting the maximal size of the Bantu verb stem, linking templatic patterns to morphophonological ones in ways that allow for Tiene-like reanalysis.

In a related vein, Good (2007a: 216–223) considers cases where the morphological patterns associated with certain Bantu verb suffixes, such as the Transitive, are reanalyzed as not being conditioned by the actual morphological presence of the Transitive but, rather, whether or not a verb stem has a phonological shape that makes it look like it has been marked with the Transitive. Abasheikh (1978: 66), for instance, discusses a special allomorph of the Applicative in Chimwiini which appears after all stems ending in *s*, *z*, *sh*, or *ñ*, which happen to be the only consonants causativized verbs end with due to the phonological effects of the Transitive on preceding stems (see Section 3.5.2). But, this allomorph is found whether or not the stem is synchronically causativized, meaning that the causativized verbs have merged with other verbs on morphophonological grounds with respect to this process. Further relevant cases are discussed in Good (2007a) and Hyman (2003b).

The path from such observations to a full account of the diachronic development of the templatic restrictions found in Tiene is not straightforward. However, they demonstrate how surface patterns in the Bantu verb stem open the door to morphophonological reanalysis of morphosyntactic patterns, thereby allowing the same set of surface constraints to shift from being driven by one class of templatic constraints to another.

3.5.6 The Bantu verb stem and templatic convergence

The final aspect of these Bantu templatic restrictions to be addressed relates to the fact that they instantiate a phenomenon that one could informally refer to as *templatic convergence* (see Section 2.5.3). That is, we see a number of different cases of templatic restrictions (e.g., Figures 3.10, 3.11, 3.13, and 3.15), all broadly similar but still with their own particularities, converging on a single domain, the Bantu verb stem. Unlike Hyman (2003c), I do not treat these as all deriving from a monolithic verb suffix template both because this would not

---

[32] The term *bridging context* in historical change is more usually associated with environments that permit syntactic change (see, e.g., Evans & Wilkins (2000: 550), Heine (2002: 84–85), and Enfield (2003: 28–30)). I extend its sense here to domains where the properties of morphosyntactic constituents and morphophonological constituents overlap in ways that allow restrictions in one domain to be reinterpreted as being conditioned by the other.

3.5 Four templates found in Bantu verb stems 167

allow us to capture fine-grained aspects of the variation among the templatic constraints found for the Bantu extensions and because, unlike, for instance, the Nimboran case (see Section 3.4), the templatic restrictions do not revolve around a set of positions which, when taken together, are analyzed as being integral to the formation of verbs in general. Rather, they involve derivational elements, whose templatic restrictions only become active in verbal formation when they are employed for independent syntactic/semantic reasons.

Nevertheless, it seems clear that, in describing these Bantu templates, we would not want to lose sight of the fact that it is almost certainly not coincidental that they converge on the same domain. Moreover, if the goal of the analyses here were to give a formal synchronic analysis of the range of templatic restrictions found in a given Bantu language, then we would want to ensure that our descriptions of these restrictions would unify into a larger templatic description whenever more than one of the relevant suffixes appears on the verb stem (see Francez & Winter (2012) for general discussion of unification). For typological investigation, the burden is not so high. However, some degree of formal specification of templatic convergence would clearly be valuable, and fortunately this is possible in the current database implementation (see Section 2.9 for relevant background).

Specifically, the graph-based nature of the database allows shared "nodes" to be reused across constructions when this is appropriate. In the present context, for instance, this allows us to define a single *BantuVerbStem* component, which serves as the keystone for all of the general Bantu templatic restrictions described in this section. Similarly, a single *BantuTransitive* component is reused across the templatic descriptions where possible. Thus, there is an explicit encoding of "shared" structure across the templates in many cases.

There are limitations to this, however. For instance, in a language like Chichewa, that has lost the Transitive, the structural description of the Causative component cannot justifiably include a dependency with the Transitive of the sort depicted in Figure 3.10. So, a different component description is required where the Causative lacks such a dependency. Therefore, it is not the case that we can simply "reuse" potentially overlapping material in all cases where there are clear relations. A comparable issue arises when considering the very similar templates depicted in Figures 3.13 and 3.14, characterizing the general Bantu Causative–Applicative template and its Ndebele variant, since it would clearly be sensible to code that these are templates that show something comparable to a cognate relationship (with the details dependent on one's specific Proto-Bantu reconstructions). At present, these types of relations, where there is significant, but not complete, overlap of the templatic properties of related languages, are not directly coded in the database, however. Capturing them would require levels of annotation beyond what is already found, for instance, involving the inclusion of specifications of etymological connections

168   Typologizing templates: case studies

and genealogical trees. Nothing in the technology of the database would prevent this; the limitations are simply connected to the need to keep the scope of the research manageable.

3.6   Chechen Preverbal *'a*

3.6.1   *A syntactic size template*

In shifting from the Bantu templates just described above in Section 3.5, to a template in Chechen, we are leaving the domain of morphology and moving into syntax. However, as we will see, the particular structure of the Chechen template is quite similar to some of the morphological templates already described, in particular, the Turkish templates discussed in Section 3.2 and the Tiene prosodic template discussed in Section 3.5.5. This is ultimately connected to the fact that it can be treated as a span template with a two-component length requirement, and a test for the description language used here is the extent to which it can treat the Chechen patterns as similar to those of length templates in morphological domains, while still allowing its distinguishing features to be coded.

Earlier discussions of some of the facts to be presented here can be found in Conathan & Good (2001), Good (2003a), and Good (2003b: 275–378). Much of the data in this case study is already reported in those publications. Similar patterns are also reported for the closely related Ingush language, and Peterson (2001) informs important aspects of the analysis to be presented here (see also Nichols (2011: 535–540)). Breaking from a pattern found in the other case studies, this section also includes data not appearing in previous sources. This is due to the fact that some of it is based on analyses of my own that have not been published. I have generally not included case studies of this sort so as to avoid the possibility that the work here would be biased too strongly towards my own templatic analyses, which may be skewed from those of other scholars by the nature of my interest in the topic.[33] However, the Chechen data would seem to merit exceptional consideration on "historical grounds": the descriptive overlap between the syntactic Chechen template and morphophonological templates in domains such as Turkish stems, which seem, at first, quite different from each other due to their appearance in very different grammatical environments, was a significant impetus for the generalizing approach to templates taken here. In this sense, the juxtaposition of, say, Chechen and Turkish has played a comparable role in this study to the comparison of Ingush and Abkhaz of Nichols (1986) that inspired the development of the head-marking/dependent-marking distinction or the comparison of English

---

[33] Of course, for some case studies, such as many of those discussed in Section 3.5, analyses developed in my earlier work are considered, but in these cases the initial templatic analyses had already been developed before my own work on the relevant phenomena.

3.6 Chechen Preverbal *'a*   169

and Atsugewi that inspired the model of motion events developed by Talmy (1985).

3.6.2   The positioning of Preverbal 'a

The Chechen template of interest here is lexico-constructionally conditioned, specifically appearing in contexts involving clausal cosubordination. In Chechen, cosubordination is partly coded via an enclitic which will here be termed Preverbal *'a*. It will be argued that this clitic is associated with a template imposing a restriction that its host must be an element which has a tight syntactic relationship with the verb that follows it. At the same time, despite a clear syntactic dimension to the template's conditioning, it will ultimately be analyzed as being closer to prosodic templates in typological terms than the more "purely" syntactic templates to be examined below, such as the topological fields analysis of the German clause (see Section 3.12).

Cosubordination refers to a kind of clausal linkage that shares some of the properties traditionally associated with coordination and some of the properties traditionally associated with subordination (see Foley & Van Valin (1984: 239–44) and Van Valin & LaPolla (1997: 453–454)). The data in (32) shows two distinct uses of Chechen Preverbal *'a* in cosubordinate contexts. It is used as a means to coordinate verb phrases in (32a) and as a marker of dependent clauses in chaining constructions in (32b) (see Longacre (2007: 374–376) for an introduction to the notion of clause chaining). Preverbal *'a* is glossed with "&" in the examples in this section and bolded in the introductory data.[34]

(32)   a.   *Maliika [loomax   hwal 'a jeelara,] [ohwa 'a*
            Malika   mountain.LAT up   & J.go.WP   down &
            joessara].
            J.descend.WP
            "Malika climbed up and down the mountain."
       b.   *Maliika, [tykana   'a jaghna,]   [zheina 'a iacna,]   c'a*
            Malika   store.DAT & J.go.CVANT book   & buy.CVANT home
            je'ara.
            J.come.WP
            "Malika went to the store, bought a book, and came back home."

Detailed justification for the analysis of Preverbal *'a* as a marker of cosubordination is given in Good (2003a). The core observation that guides

---

[34] The orthographic conventions for Chechen used here attempt to follow those of Nichols & Vagapov (2004), though there may be some minor differences based on different apprehensions of the words and/or variant forms produced by different consultants. Nichols & Vagapov (2004) also contains background information on Chechen grammar beyond what is covered here. The grammar of Nichols (2011) of the closely related language Ingush can also serve as a partial guide to the details of Chechen grammar.

170   Typologizing templates: case studies

the analysis can be seen in the juxtaposition of the sentences in (32), where the marker is found in two similar, though clearly distinct constructions which can be functionally unified using the notion of cosubordination. Since the actual syntactic function of Preverbal *'a* is not crucial for understanding its templatic properties, the reader is referred to Good (2003a) for further discussion.

The most salient formal indications that the two constructions exemplified in (32) are distinct relate to where Preverbal *'a* appears and what sort of verb form is found following it. In the verb phrase coordination construction exemplified in (32a), where each verb phrase is marked off by square brackets, Preverbal *'a* is found preceding two finite verbs, each of which appears with a Witnessed Past suffix (see Molochieva (2011) for discussion of the tense-aspect system of Chechen). In the chaining construction in (32b), Preverbal *'a* is only found preceding converbal forms that code for anteriority and not before the final finite verb. The example in (32b) illustrates the features that are generally common to chaining constructions in Chechen: a series of verb-final clauses headed by verbs in one of a few converbal forms all containing Preverbal *'a* are "chained" together into a larger sentence whose last verb is finite. (See Haspelmath (1995) for general discussion of the notion of converb.) Clauses in the chaining construction overwhelmingly tend to have a shared subject, which is generally only expressed once across the sentence (see Good (2003a: 123–129) for overview discussion). I will use the term *Chained Clause* below to refer to those clauses in the chaining construction headed by converbal forms and containing Preverbal *'a*, and these clauses are marked off by brackets in (32b).

Enclitics with the form *'a* are found in a range of Chechen constructions coding coordination, emphasis, or some combination of the two (with the latter function being roughly analogous to the use of English *too*).[35] (See Jeschull (2004) for a range of examples.) Whether these should all be treated as belonging to the same lexeme is not clear, but this does not affect the treatment of the template of interest here, which is limited to the preverbal use of *'a*. This use presumably bears at least some diachronic relationship to other instances of *'a*, but it alone is associated with specialized templatic properties that allow us to typologize it as being part of a lexico-constructional template.[36] The text example in (33) gives some sense of the range of uses

[35] The term *emphasis* is used here in order to be deliberately vague with respect to whether the "emphasis" should be equated with more theoretically elaborated notions such as focus or contrast. See Komen (2007b) for a descriptive and theoretical treatment of some aspects of focus in Chechen.

[36] As used here, the lexico-constructional categorization is agnostic as to whether the relevant templatic restrictions may be primarily associated with the lexical representation of a given element or the properties of the higher-level construction. This allows us to sidestep significant questions of synchronic analysis of the "source" of a template in a case study like this one.

3.6 Chechen Preverbal 'a

of enclitics with this form in Chechen. There are seven instances of 'a in this sentence. In this case, they are glossed as FOC to signal their different function from Preverbal 'a as markers of emphasis/coordination rather than cosubordination. With respect to the sequence hu~-'a, the element is transcribed as a suffix indicating its fixed role as a means to derive a word meaning something like *whatever* from the word *hu~* 'what.' The use of 'a after *valahw*, an Irrealis form, leads to a conventionalized concessive reading. The other instances of 'a are more transparently emphatic in their function.

(33) *Cyna~ chulaacaman maewna hu~ bu hwuona aelcha,*
3s.GEN content.GEN meaning what B.be.PRS 2s.DAT say.CVTEMP
daaxariahw 'a, duezaliahw 'a, micchanhwaa 'a, hu~-'a
life.ADV FOC family.ADV FOC everywhere FOC what-FOC
lielosh shaa valahw 'a, daggahw
engaged.in.CVSIM 3S.REFL V.be.CVIRR FOC heart.FOC.LOC
caw 'a dyycush, bagahw qi~ dyycush
one.NZ FOC D.tell.CVSIM mouth.ADV any.more D.tell.CVSIM
volu stag cq'aa 'a q'uonax xir vaac
V.be.PRS.PTCP person never FOC man be.FUT V.be.NEG.PRS
booxurg du iza.
speak.NZ D.be.PRS that
"Its meaning is that in life, in your family, everywhere, no matter what you are engaged in, anyone who thinks one thing and says another will never be a real person."

The examples in (34) illustrate that, while Preverbal 'a always appears immediately before the verb, its phonological hosts can be quite varied in nature, essentially constituting any element which would otherwise be expected to appear before the verb for syntactic reasons. Each of the examples is an instance of a simple chaining construction, comprising two clauses, with the one headed by a non-finite verb containing Preverbal 'a, as required by the chaining construction. An informal descriptive label is given for the verb phrases in the Chained Clauses in (34). The sequence of the host, Preverbal 'a, and verb is bolded in the examples.

(34) a. DEICTIC ELEMENT–VERB
*Maliikas Ahwmadna zheina **dwa 'a della**, dwa-jaghara.*
Malika.ERG Ahmed.DAT book DX & D.give.WP DX-J.go.WP
"Malika gave the book back to Ahmed and left."

172   Typologizing templates: case studies

b. PREVERB–VERB

*Ahwmada,   kiexat **jaaz**   'a dina,*   *zheina dueshu.*
Ahmed.ERG letter write & D.do.CVANT book   D.read.PRS
"Ahmed, having written a letter, reads a book."

c. OBJECT–VERB

*Ahwmad, **zhwala** 'a iacna,*   *vilxira.*
Ahmed   dog   & buy.CVANT V.cry.WP
"Ahmed bought a dog and cried."

d. SIMPLEX INTRANSITIVE

*Ahwmad, **wa**   'a   **wiina**,*   *dwa-vaghara.*
Ahmed   stay.INF &   stay.CVANT DX-V.go.WP
"Ahmed stayed (for a while) and left."

Chechen verbs frequently appear in morphologically complex structures wherein a verb stem is preceded by some sort of preverbal element which, in clauses not containing Preverbal *'a*, would normally be immediately adjacent to the verb in a compound-like fashion. In (34a), this element is a special kind of deictic marker, which will be referred to here as a Deictic Prefix (see Nichols (2011: 346–364) for description of a comparable set of deictic markers in Ingush). In (34b), one finds an element, termed a Preverb here, which combines with a light verb to encode the meaning 'write' (again, see Nichols (2011: 329–341) for description of comparable structures in Ingush). As an SOV language (if not a particularly rigid one), an object in Chechen will typically precede a transitive verb, in which case this, too, can be a host for Preverbal *'a*, as in (34c), assuming that there is no other element closer to the verb (see (34a) for a contrasting example). The status of Preverbal *'a* as an element whose syntactic position involves appearing *before* a verb even though it is enclitic to the preceding element is typologically unusual, as demonstrated by Peterson's (2001) analysis of the cognate clitic in Ingush, which has the same properties in this regard. (See also Cysouw (2005: 27).)[37]

For present purposes, however, the most interesting potential host for Preverbal *'a* is a Copy Infinitive, as exemplified (34d). The presence of this form in that example relates to the fact that there are two ordering restrictions on the appearance of the clitic, one of which has yet to be fully introduced. First, as already discussed, it must appear *before* the verb. Second, it must also appear *after* an element within a subpart of a verb phrase, which can roughly be characterized as the verb and additional non-adjunct elements. I will refer to this constituent as the Core Verb Phrase. In a sentence like (34d), where the

---

[37] It seems likely that there is a diachronic connection between the clitic's unusual positional properties and the presence of the template described here, though this will not be explored in the following discussion.

3.6 Chechen Preverbal *'a*

Chained Clause is headed by a simplex verb (i.e., a verb appearing without a Preverb, Deictic Prefix, or anything comparable) which is also intransitive, and, therefore, lacking an object, there is no element that "naturally" allows the second restriction to be fulfilled – i.e., no element which would otherwise be expected to appear in the verb phrase is available to serve as the host of Preverbal *'a*. In such cases, a Copy Infinitive, essentially a morphosyntactic copy of the verb heading the Chained Clause (see Conathan & Good (2001)), appears and serves as a host for Preverbal *'a*. This form is not otherwise associated with special semantics, nor can a non-templatic analysis for its appearance be found, as will be discussed in Section 3.6.3 shortly below.

It is sentences like (34d) that are key in showing the presence of a special templatic restriction associated with Preverbal *'a*, since they indicate that the positional patterning seen in examples like (34a), (34b), (34c), where the host of Preverbal *'a* is within the Core Verb Phrase, is not purely an accident of Chechen syntax but, rather, is being driven by a linearization constraint of some kind. The example in (35) provides a further example of the appearance of this Copy Infinitive, in this case in a sentence where Preverbal *'a* is used as part of the coding strategy for verb phrase coordination. Like (34d), it is appearing in a clause where the verbs are simplex and intransitive. The example in (36) provides another instance where the Copy Infinitive appears in a Chained Clause. The relevant clauses are enclosed in square brackets in the examples.

(35) *Maalik* [*viela   'a viilara,*]   [*vialxa   'a vilxara*].
     Malik   V.laugh.INF & V.laugh.WP V.cry.INF & V.cry.WP
     "Malik laughed and cried."

(36) *Kiexat,* [*daat'a 'a daett'a,*]   *telxara.*
     paper   tear.INF & tear.CVANT spoil.WP
     "The paper ripped and was spoiled."

While the Copy Infinitives in examples like (35) and (36) are not associated with any special semantics or pragmatics, a preverbal *'a* construction can be employed to encode emphatic coordinate semantics in the right circumstances. This is illustrated by the opposition between the sentences in (37). As mentioned above, the host for Preverbal *'a* must be an element of the Core Verb Phrase (e.g., excluding adjuncts). Thus, the basic strategy for constructing a Chained Clause with a simplex intransitive such as *wa* 'stay' is, as seen in (34d), to insert a Copy Infinitive, and this does not change with the addition of an adverbial element appearing before the verb, as seen in (37a), where the word *sialxana* 'yesterday' appears. It is possible for *'a* to appear following an

174   Typologizing templates: case studies

adjunct in a chained clause, however, as seen in (37b), but then the sentence is associated with additional emphatic meaning as indicated in the translation. In this case *'a* appears to simultaneously fill the role of coding the presence of a Chained Clause and of giving conjunctive and emphatic semantics to its host, as we only see one instance of the clitic rather than the two that might be expected. This pattern is reminiscent of what has been termed the *repeated morph constraint* in studies of morphology (Menn & MacWhinney 1984).

> (37) a. *Ahwmad, sialxana wa   'a wiina,   dwa-vaghara.*
>   Ahmed   yesterday stay.INF & stay.CVANT DX-V.go.WP
>   "Ahmed stayed yesterday and left."
>   b. *Ahwmad, sialxana 'a   wiina,   dwa-vaghara.*
>   Ahmed   yesterday FOC stay.CVANT DX-V.go.WP
>   "Ahmed stayed yesterday (too) and left."

The strongest argument for treating the Preverbal *'a* cosubordination construction as involving a template requiring Preverbal *'a* to be preceded by an element in the Core Verb Phrase is the appearance of the Copy Infinitive in sentences like (37a). It is, therefore, important to establish that there is no non-templatic explanation available to account for its presence. This is discussed in the next section.

3.6.3   Possible analyses that cannot account for the verbal copy

The appearance of the Copy Infinitive is taken as the most visible sign of a templatic constraint for Preverbal *'a*, since it is the most positive form of evidence that the clitic must be preceded by a word in the Core Verb Phrase. This analysis rests on the idea that we cannot account for the presence of this form in some non-templatic way. It is, of course, impossible to completely "prove" that there is no alternative account, but we can, at least, consider other possible accounts by examining analyses that have been given for superficially similar kinds of verb copying constructions seen in the world's languages and discussing why they cannot be straightforwardly applied to the Chechen case.[38] I will consider four such alternative analyses here. They are that the Copy Infinitive in cosubordinate constructions is: (i) some marker of topicalization; (ii) an instance of a clefted predicate; (iii) a cognate object; and

---

[38] Hargus & Tuttle (1997) provide a good example of the difficulties in "proving" that a given element is inserted purely to satisfy a templatic condition. They discuss a particular Athabaskan formative that had generally been considered to be present in some forms purely to satisfy a templatic restriction and propose a counter-analysis treating it as an affix which appears under predictable conditions.

3.6 Chechen Preverbal *'a*

(iv) a manifestation of patterns revolving around an unaccusative/unergative distinction among Chechen intransitives.

As will be seen, none of these possible analyses provides an effective account of the appearance of the Chechen Copy Infinitive. For the last possible analysis, due to limitations on the availability of data from Chechen, data from Ingush will be considered alongside Chechen data, though there is no reason to believe that Chechen will behave differently from Ingush in any crucial way. The choice of these specific four counteranalyses reflects the fact that, in other languages, these kinds of phenomena have been associated with verb copying and, in some cases, the fact that they have been specifically suggested to me as possible ways to analyze the appearance of the Copy Infinitive.

First, with respect to a topicalization analysis, the data in (38), drawn from Yiddish (Davis & Prince 1986: 90), provides a relevant cross-linguistic comparison.

(38) a. *redn   red   ikh mame-loshin*
       speak.INF speak.PRS.1s I   mama-language
       "As for speaking, I speak Yiddish."
     b. *veysn(/*visn) veyst   er gornit*
       know.INF?   know.PRS.3s he nothing
       "As for knowing, he knows nothing."

The Yiddish data in (38) shows superficial similarity with the Chechen Copy Infinitive construction, even down to a morphological idiosyncrasy, discussed for Chechen in Conathan & Good (2001), where the "infinitive" is not always necessarily the regular Infinitive but, rather, can be an apparently backformed element whose shape is based on the form of the inflected verb found later in the sentence. In the Yiddish data, this is seen in (38b), where the starred element gives the disallowed regular infinitive for the verb 'know' and the attested copy "infinitive" turns out to be phonologically more similar to the following inflected form by virtue of matching its vowel. Relevant data from Chechen is provided in Table 3.5. In the language, there is a small class of verbs where there is a suppletive (or partly suppletive) relation between the Infinitive and Present stems. As can be seen, in some cases, the Copy Infinitive can take on a form along the lines of what the Infinitive would be expected to be purely on the basis of the Present form. (As suggested by the data in Table 3.5, Infinitives in Chechen regularly end in *a*.) In the final case, for the verb 'go,' the creation of this "false" infinitive even involves undoing a pattern of vowel ablaut associated with verbs in the Present to produce an infinitive-like vowel in the form *duoda* which, otherwise, is not used in infinitival contexts.

To the extent that topicalization involves a kind of emphasis relation and, at least based on the translations in (38), a kind of contrastive emphasis, it would

176 Typologizing templates: case studies

Table 3.5 *Alternation in the realization of the Chechen Copy Infinitive (Conathan & Good 2001: 54)*

INFINITIVE	PRESENT	COPY INFINITIVE	GLOSS
dala	*lo*	*dala ~ la*	'give'
daˉ	*dahwa*	*daˉ ~ dahwa*	'bring'
dagha	*duedu*	*dagha ~ duoda*	'go'

not be unreasonable to suggest that there is more than coincidence involved in the formal overlap between these Yiddish and Chechen constructions, especially since the Chechen Copy Infinitive does have, among its functions, a kind of emphatic marking, as found for instance in negative imperatives (see Conathan & Good (2001: 49)). However, when appearing as a host for Preverbal *'a* in cosubordination constructions, consultants consistently report that there is no special emphasis on the verb (or any other element), and there is no evidence for this otherwise. Thus, while a diachronic connection cannot be ruled out, treating the Copy Infinitive's presence as resulting from something along the lines of topicalization is not a viable synchronic analysis. (Additionally, topicalization is usually understood as a process that involves the topicalized element appearing in a peripheral position, which we do not find in the Chechen case, though that difference is less relevant here.)

Another verb copying construction that shows surface similarity to the Chechen Copy Infinitive is the so-called predicate cleft construction.[39] The data in (39), drawn from Edo (Stewart 2001: 87) (earlier presented in Stewart (1998)), exemplifies the use of such constructions. The sentence in (39a) shows no predicate cleft structure, while (39b) shows its clefted equivalent. In the predicate cleft construction in Edo, a nominalized copy of the verb appears at the left edge of the clause, followed by a focus marker and an embedded clause with comparable structure to the non-clefted counterpart of the predicate cleft construction, though with a change in the tone pattern of the final verb (the exclamation mark in (39b) is used to transcribe tonal downstep).

(39) a. *Òzó kpòló.*
      Ozo be.big
      "Ozo is big."

---

[39] I am not aware of any typologically oriented overviews of predicate cleft constructions, and the most detailed work on them has been within the generative literature. Kandybowicz (2008: 79–81) provides introductory discussion as well as an extensive list of references on work on predicate cleft constructions done within the generative tradition. (See also Kandybowicz (2006: 144–146) for largely the same information.)

3.6 Chechen Preverbal 'a

b. *Ùkpɔ́lɔ́mwɛ̀n ɔ̀ré Òzó kpɔ́!lɔ́.*
NZ.be.big.NZ FOC Ozo be.big
"It is fat that Ozo is fat (not obese)."

Treating the appearance of the Chechen Copy Infinitive in cosubordination constructions as an instance of something like predicate cleft runs into one of the same problems as for the topicalization construction illustrated for Yiddish in (38). A predicate cleft construction is expected to be associated with some additional semantic or pragmatic force when set against its non-clefted counterpart. This is clearly the case in (39b), where the cleft construction encodes a contrastive reading for the verb's semantics. As already discussed, the Chechen Copy Infinitive is apparently not associated with any additional semantic/pragmatic force when appearing with Preverbal 'a. In addition, from a formal perspective, cleft constructions are generally understood to be biclausal in nature (see, e.g., Harris & Campbell (1995: 151–155) for overview discussion), but the Chechen Preverbal 'a construction does not show any evidence of being biclausal. If anything, the Copy Infinitive's role within the clause appears to be comparable to that of a verbal argument in terms of its positioning (though see below for a refinement of this characterization) rather than it showing evidence of being "fronted" or otherwise displaced.

Given the Copy Infinitive's linear overlap with a verbal object, another possibility would be to consider it to be analogous to a cognate object, an example of which, again from Edo, is given in (40) (Stewart 2001: 93).[40] In this example, an intransitive verb can be optionally followed by a nominal form which is based on the same root as the verb itself.

(40) *Òzó khián (òkhián).*
Ozo walk PFX.walk
"Ozo walked."

While it is not the case for cognate objects in general (see Bond & Anderson (2014)), for the cognate object seen in (40), there does not appear to be any special semantics associated with its presence (Stewart 2001: 93). This brings this construction more in line with the Chechen Copy Infinitive as employed in cosubordinate constructions. Moreover, there are languages where it is reported that cognate objects are obligatory in certain contexts, comparable to what is found for Chechen Copy Infinitives (see, e.g., Faraclas (1984: 5, 53) on the Cross River language Obolo). If the Chechen Copy Infinitive were a

---

[40] Bond & Anderson (2014) contains the most detailed overview of cognate object constructions that I am aware of.

178   Typologizing templates: case studies

kind of cognate object, its appearance could perhaps be interpreted as resulting from something like a "transitivity requirement" for verbs.

Storch (1999: 237–238, 2009: 128–130), for instance, accounts for the appearance of cognate objects in the Jukunoid language Hone by analyzing all verbs in the language as transitive. In those cases where a verb's semantics is not naturally associated with an object (e.g., a verb meaning 'be heavy' (Storch 2009: 129)), a cognate object can be employed to meet the transitivity requirement. We will see in Section 3.9 that there may be reasons to account for patterns involving such "expletive" objects templatically. But, even if we assume that there is a syntactic (i.e., non-templatic) account for them, there are problems applying this kind of analysis to Chechen. First, there is nothing object-like about the Chechen Copy Infinitive other than its preverbal positioning (which is also shared by clear non-objects such as preverbs and deictic elements, as seen in (34)). Chechen nouns show distinctive formal properties, such as being marked for case and being associated with verb agreement when serving as absolutive arguments (see Nichols (2011: 127–150) for discussion of case and agreement in Ingush and Nichols (2007a) for overview discussion of Chechen morphology). Chechen Infinitives, by contrast, are more verbal in nature, not being marked for case or triggering agreement. In addition, Chechen has productive nominalization strategies for verbs which are associated with forms other than the Infinitive (Good 2003a: 116–117).

There is, thus, no reason to consider the Chechen Copy Infinitive to be nominal. Moreover, even if it were nominal, there would be no obvious way to connect its appearance specifically to cosubordinate constructions. To do so would require some logic for arguing that cosubordination should be associated with higher verbal transitivity than other clausal functions, but, as a clause linkage construction, there is no reason to have such an expectation.

A final possibility for a non-templatic account of the appearance of the Copy Infinitive might be to suggest it is related to patterns of unaccusativity and unergativity in intransitives (see Perlmutter (1978) for the earliest formulation of this distinction, Levin & Rappaport Hovav (2005: 12–13) for recent overview discussion, and Wichmann (2008b: 5–6) and Donohue (2008: 50–51) for contextualization in a typological context). The unaccusative/unergative distinction, roughly connected to the agentivity of the subject of an intransitive, has been associated with the possibility of verbs appearing with cognate objects in English (see, e.g., Levin & Rappaport Hovav (1995: 40)), making it reasonable to see if it can help explain the presence of verbal copies in Chechen. In particular, generally intransitive verbs with relatively agentive subjects are expected to be more likely to appear with objects than generally intransitive verbs with relatively patientive subjects.

In fact, relevant data from Chechen indicating that the distinction between unaccusative and unergative verbs is not useful in understanding the

3.6 Chechen Preverbal 'a

appearance of the Copy Infinitive has already been presented in (35) and (36). The verbs in conjoined cosubordinate constructions in (35) (i.e., 'laugh' and 'cry') are seemingly semantically more agentive while the verb 'rip' in the cosubordinate construction in (36) is used to encode an action done on an inanimate patient and is, therefore, semantically more patientive. Regardless, in both cases, the Copy Infinitive appears. Moreover, in general, there is no evidence that Chechen grammar is sensitive to the unaccusative/unergative distinction, making this an unpromising area to look for a syntactic explanation for the appearance of the Copy Infinitive.

The pair of sentences in (41), drawn from Ingush, further illustrate the apparent insensitivity of the appearance of the Copy Infinitive to patterns of transitivity.[41] The verb *dyza* 'fill' is labile in Ingush, allowing for a transitive or intransitive reading. In the sentences in (41), exemplifying chaining constructions, the Absolutive argument of 'fill' is not found in the chained clause, but in the finite clause and is, therefore, not available to serve as a host for Preverbal 'a. In this case, the Copy Infinitive appears in the chained clauses in both sentences, even though in (41a) 'fill' is interpreted as intransitive and in (41b) it is interpreted as transitive.

(41) a. *Xygh   dyza   'a dyzaa,   piila wa-'ottadyr.*
       water.LOC fill.INF & fill.CVANT glass DX-put.CS.WP
       "(Someone) filled the glass and put it down."
    b. *Xygh   dyza   'a dyzaa,   piila t'ix-daxar.*
       water.LOC fill.INF & fill.CVANT glass pass-D.go.WP
       "The glass filled with water and fell over."

We have seen then that there is not good evidence to adopt any of the four possible non-templatic accounts for the appearance of the Chechen Copy Infinitive in cosubordinate constructions. Therefore, while it is impossible to definitively prove that there is no non-templatic explanation for its presence, at this stage, there is no viable competing explanation that I am aware of.[42]

3.6.4   The prosody of clitics with the shape 'a

In light of the fact that, as discussed in Section 1.8.2 and illustrated in Section 3.2, it has been noted that there is often a correlation between prosodic

---

[41] I am grateful to Johanna Nichols for assistance in gathering the data in (41).

[42] Haspelmath (2004: 9–10) points out that a very similar construction to the Chechen Copy Infinitive of interest here is found in the Tibeto-Burman language Hakha Lai (see Peterson & VanBik (2004: 348)), where an otherwise unexpected verb must be found before an emphatic conjunctive marker when intransitive verbs are conjoined. This perhaps suggests that such contexts are prone to developing templatic restrictions.

180   Typologizing templates: case studies

constituency and templates, it will be worthwhile here to briefly discuss the prosodic pattern of regular verb phrases in Chechen, as well as verb phrases containing Preverbal *'a*, especially since conjunctive clitics with the form *'a* are among a handful of tone-bearing morphemes in Chechen and, therefore, influence the prosodic structure of the verb phrases where they appear.[43]

The examples in (42) illustrate the basic prosodic high–low pitch pattern associated with verbs and a preceding element when the verb is clause-final (which is the usual verbal position), transcribed using an acute accent on an initial syllable to indicate an overall higher pitch on the first word and a grave accent on an initial syllable of the following verb to indicate an overall lower pitch (see Nichols (2011: 102) for description of parallel facts in Ingush). These transcriptions, of course, abstract away from various phonetic details, but they give a reasonable impression of the overall prosodic patterning. What is noteworthy in the present context is that the unit of verb and preceding element, which has already been shown to be syntactically relevant in the context of understanding the placement of Preverbal *'a*, is also associated with a specific prosodic generalization. However, it should be noted that this pattern is not limited merely to cases where the verb and preceding element are part of the Core Verb Phrase, as illustrated in (43), where the verb and the preceding subject also exhibit this same contour. There is, therefore, some overlap between this prosodic constituent and the morphosyntactic domain in which the templatic restriction operates, but it is not complete.

(42)   a. *Malika [dwá-jèdira]*.
          Malika   DX-J.run.WP
          "Malika ran away."
       b. *Ahwmad [óeghaz-vàghara]*.
          Ahmed   anger-V.go.WP
          "Ahmed got angry."

(43)   *Máliika jòelu*.
       Malika   J.laugh.PRS
       "Malika laughs."

The high–low prosodic contour found for a verb and preceding element seen in examples like (42) is also found in clauses containing Preverbal *'a*, with the additional complication that the clitic is associated with a high tone that falls on the immediately preceding syllable. This high tone is realized with a higher

---

[43] See Nichols (2011: 105–110) for description of the tone system of Ingush, which serves as a useful comparison case, and Komen (2007a: 15–17) for additional discussion of aspects of Chechen intonation, including limited discussion of tone in the language.

3.6 Chechen Preverbal *'a* 181

pitch than the regular phrasal high pitch and is transcribed with a double acute accent. As can be seen, if the word preceding Preverbal *'a* consists of only one syllable, the high tone associated with the clitic appears instead of the usual phrasal high tone. (The pitch on Preverbal *'a* itself is often lower than the high tone, but the clitic is often phonetically reduced in ways that make precise determination of its pitch impossible.)

(44) a. *Maliika loomax*   [*hwắl 'a jèelara*] [*óhwắ 'a jòessara*].
       Malika mountain.LAT up   & J.go.WP down & J.descend.WP
       "Malika climbed up and down the mountain."
    b. *Maliikina*   *Ahwmad* [*gắ*   *'a gìra*]   *Mariam* [*xázắ*   *'a*
       Malika.DAT Ahmed   see.INF & see.WP Mary   hear.INF &
       xèzara].
       hear.WP
       "Malika saw Ahmed and heard Mary."

As the examples in (44) indicate, the two-element combination where Preverbal *'a* appears is associated with a consistent pitch contour and, therefore, a prosodic constituent of some kind. There is no particular reason to believe that this alignment of the prosodic constituent with a template is, in some sense, driving the templatic restrictions as would be suggested if we were to attempt to extend the Prosodic Morphology Hypothesis (see Section 1.8.2) from morphology to syntax. However, it may not be unreasonable to speculate that the presence of this prosodic pattern played a role in a historical process in which Preverbal *'a* developed from a marker of emphatic coordination to clausal cosubordination with an associated templatic constraint where it was required to be preceded by an element in the Core Verb Phrase. In particular, the consistent prosodic pattern that would have been associated with Preverbal *'a* when following the preverbal element may have facilitated a reanalysis of the marker as a kind phrasal "infix," thereby allowing it to become morphosyntactically associated with both its prosodic host and the following verb. While such a historical account will remain speculative here, clear parallels can be drawn between it and the analysis of the historical development of endoclitics – i.e., infixing clitics – in Udi, a (distant) relative of Chechen, which appear in a roughly similar environment to Preverbal *'a* from a diachronic perspective and whose origin has been examined in detail by Harris (2000, 2002, 2008: 68–74).

3.6.5   *The Chechen cosubordination template*

Having covered the basic descriptive facts of the templatic restriction associated with Preverbal *'a*, it is now possible to characterize the template formally, which is done in Figure 3.19. This template will be treated as sharing salient

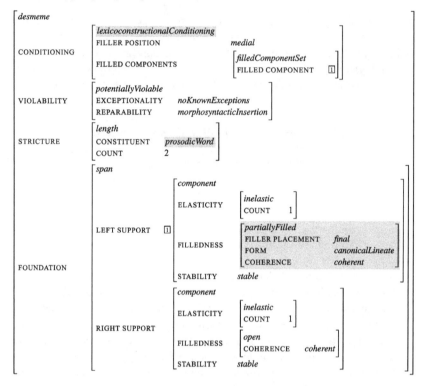

Figure 3.19 Chechen preverbal 'a template

features with various templates already discussed, such as the morphophonological templates described for Turkish in Section 3.2 and a number of the Bantu templates discussed in Section 3.5. Like the Turkish templates, it will be treated as a length restriction that can be stated over two units. This reflects the fact that the phonosyntactic "frame" in which Preverbal 'a is found can be seen as being two units in length: it is positioned syntactically in between two elements of a Core Verb Phrase, with the initial element of that phrase serving as its phonological host.

As discussed in Section 3.6.4, there is considerable overlap between the syntactic elements of this construction and prosodic constituency in Chechen, and characterizing the length restriction in terms of either syntactic or prosodic elements would be descriptively possible. I treat the template's stricture as being prosodic in nature, however, due to the phonological integration of Preverbal 'a with its host element, suggesting that this non-syntactic association forms a distinctive component of the construction from a templatic perspective. At the

3.6 Chechen Preverbal *'a*   183

same time, the template cannot be understood as being purely prosodically conditioned due to its sensitivity to the structure of the Core Verb Phrase. This aspect of its behavior is captured via its typological categorization as lexico-constructionally conditioned. The Chechen template, thus, illustrates a strength of the fine-grained scheme of typological characterization adopted here: we can straightforwardly characterize a template's environment as both phonological and syntactic in nature, as the data warrants. In this particular case, the template's STRICTURE feature is defined in prosodic terms, while its CONDITIONING feature is defined in lexico-syntactic terms. The relevant aspects of the templatic description illustrating this "split" classification are shaded in Figure 3.19.

Most of the other characteristics of the Chechen template specified in Figure 3.19 should be relatively familiar at this point. As a lexico-constructional template, at least one of its components must be filled, and, in this case, it is the left support, which is the component where Preverbal *'a* appears. The filler position at the level of the template is treated as medial since Preverbal *'a* appears neither at the left or right edge of the template. Lexico-constructional templates were already seen in Section 3.5, and, here, the main difference is that the lexical item which serves as part of the conditioning environment for the template (i.e., Preverbal *'a*) does not fully occupy its component, but only partially. This is indicated using the type *partiallyFilled* in the left support, with further specification that the filler is a canonical lineate found at the end of the component (i.e., having *final* placement), and this part of the templatic description is shaded in Figure 3.19.[44] This entire component is treated as *coherent* to reflect the fact that, even though the syntactic hosts for Preverbal *'a* are heterogenous (see (34)) they are prosodically homogenous and appear to consistently form a prosodic word with Preverbal *'a* when integrated with it. This is indicated by the prosodic patterns of phrases containing Preverbal *'a*, which retain the usual two-word high–low pattern even if augmented by an extra tone (see (44)). The right support of the template is a regular open and obligatory slot, which is also coherent by virtue of only being occupied by verbs,

---

[44] This Chechen analysis raises a logical descriptive possibility which the current typological description would not be able to straightforwardly formalize. If the "filler" of this template was not limited to a single lexical item but rather a class of items (e.g., a paradigm of cosubordinate markers differing across categories such as tense, polarity, person of subject, etc.), then there would be a component half of which is open and incoherent and the other half of which is open and coherent. This pattern may even be attested, since the data from Nganhcara discussed in Klavans (1985: 104) appears to fit this model, where the language has a class of case enclitics that must appear in penultimate position, in a kind of mirror-image pattern to second-position clitic phenomena, an example of which will be analyzed in Section 3.7. If such a pattern can be shown to be clearly attested, the description language for components will need to be extended to allow for "split" components in addition to partially filled ones.

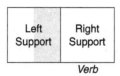

Figure 3.20 Schematization of the Chechen Preverbal 'a template

which also form prosodic words in the language.[45] Each of these components is treated as inelastic, reflecting the fact that this special lexico-constructional template is not "expandable," but, rather, centered on Preverbal 'a, making the template more similar, in this aspect, to the Tiene maximality restriction seen in Section 3.5.5 than the Turkish minimality restriction seen in Section 3.2.

The only additional features that bear remarking upon in the description in Figure 3.19 are those relating to its violability. The template is treated as potentially violable due to the presence of simplex intransitive verbs, such as the one seen in (34d). These would not produce a sufficiently large Core Verb Phrase for Preverbal 'a to have an appropriate host, leading to a possibly violated template, except for the fact that the repair strategy of Copy Infinitive insertion is available. This is indicated with the reparability type of *morphosyntacticInsertion*. Because this repair strategy is always invoked when the template would otherwise be violated, there are no known exceptions to the appearance of the template.[46]

The Chechen template can be informally schematized as in Figure 3.20. This schema is essentially the same as the one presented for the Tiene prosodic template above in Figure 3.18, except for the fact that the left support is indicated as partially filled via the gray coloring in its right half.

3.7 Serbo-Croatian *je*

From this point onward, the presentation of the typological analyses of the templates discussed in the case studies will be abbreviated compared to earlier case studies. This is partly due to the fact that, as more templates are described, it becomes easier to relate new templates to others whose formal characterizations have already been justified in detail. It is also due to the fact

---

[45] In using a term like *prosodic word* here, it is important to bear in mind that this is meant as a comparative concept rather than a universal category. In other words, the use of the label is a claim that the best conceptual "match" for this Chechen category, in typological terms, is some general notion of prosodic word, not that Chechen phonology neatly segregates its prosodic domains in a way that means there is an unambiguous synchronic prosodic word domain in the language. See Schiering et al. (2010) for relevant discussion.

[46] This analysis assumes that a sentence like (37) does not represent an exception to the template but, rather, the use of a different construction marking conjunctive emphasis which prevents "true" Preverbal 'a from being employed.

3.7 Serbo-Croatian *je* 185

that none of the remaining case studies are based on my own descriptive analyses, and it is, on the whole, more straightforward to re-cast already proposed templatic analyses (which are justified in the existing literature) into the typological description language than to justify the relevant templates in the first place.

The next case study, involving the placement of second-position verbal clitics in Serbo-Croatian, is based on the templatic treatment given in Zec & Inkelas (1990: 369), though it is adapted somewhat to take into account the wider picture of second-position clitics in the language. A general overview of the literature on second-position clitics was provided in Section 1.4.5. Not surprisingly, given the presence of second-position clitics in major European languages and the fact that they have long been of interest in studies of comparative Indo-European – with Wackernagel (1892) being an early work of particular significance (see Spencer & Luís (2012b: 39–41)) – there are many competing analyses of the linearization constraints on second-position clitics (see, e.g., Bošković (2001: 8–96)), some of which are not obviously templatic. Nevertheless, from a typological perspective, it is clear that the placement of such clitics is distinctive from more common syntactic word order patterns and that, somehow, this distinctiveness relates to a special linear position. This means, in effect, that any analysis that attempts to be non-templatic, for instance by resorting to abstract syntactic mechanisms, will usually involve some templatic "residue," such as the idea of a phonological filter operating on syntactic structures which violate a clitic's prosodic requirements (see, e.g., Bošković (2001: 83)).

The case study here will only cover cases where the placement of second-position clitics is defined with respect to the first word of the sentence. As discussed by Spencer & Luís (2012b: 48–50), Serbo-Croatian allows its second-position clitics to appear in a second position reckoned with respect to the first accented phrase of a clause as well. I assume that this variation is due to the presence of two distinct (though quite similar) templates that are in free variation with each other, in a manner comparable to the presence of pronunciation variants for canonical lineates. The template description language could straightforwardly describe the second template by simply altering the stricture characterization given in Figure 3.21 to apply to prosodic phrases rather than prosodic words.

While the data presented here primarily includes examples of the positioning of the auxiliary element *je*, second position in Serbo-Croatian is not occupied only by a single clitic, but, rather a clitic cluster, due to the fact that there is a relatively large class of second-position elements in the language which are allowed to co-occur (see, Franks & King (2000: 28–30) for an overview). In the examples below, this cluster happens to contain only one clitic, but this is merely for presentational simplicity and the fact that crucial data in Zec &

186   Typologizing templates: case studies

Inkelas (1990) involves the use of this clitic specifically. The template focused on in this section is, therefore, best understood as a characterization of the "external" templatic constraints of the entire clitic cluster, which also is subject to "internal" templatic constraints, forming a template within a template, a possibility discussed in Section 2.5.5. Initial data illustrating the positioning of the clitics of focus in this section, drawn from Halpern (1995: 15), is given in (45). In these examples, the relevant clitic has a function as a past auxiliary, but it can also be used as a copula (Franks & King 2000: 19).[47] As can be seen, the clitic must always remain in "second" position (which will be defined more precisely below) even as other words in the sentence are shifted to occupy different positions, and all the sentences in (45) have the same basic semantics (but, of course, their pragmatic force may differ). The formalization of this in the templatic description language used here will be discussed shortly below.

(45) a. *Čovek=je*   *voleo Mariju.*
          man.NOM=AUX.3S loved Mary.ACC
          "The man loved Mary."
      b. *Čovek=je Mariju voleo.*
      c. *Voleo=je Mariju čovek.*
      d. *Voleo=je čovek Mariju.*
      e. *Mariju=je čovek voleo.*
      f. *Mariju=je voleo čovek.*

The examples in (46), drawn from Zec & Inkelas (1990: 367), illustrate that possible hosts for second-position clitics like *je* cannot be just any word-like lexical item, as might be suggested by the data in (45). For instance, they cannot come immediately after the preposition in (46c) or the element glossed as 'so' in (46e).[48]

(46) a. *Petar=je*   *u kući.*
          Peter=AUX.3S in house
          "Peter is in the house."
      b. *U kući=je*   *Petar.*
          in house=AUX.3S Peter
          "Peter is in the house."

---

[47] This clitic is a member of a larger paradigm of past tense/copula markers associated with different subject person and number.

[48] Zec & Inkelas (1990) do not fully gloss the nouns in their examples for case, and I do not attempt here to analyze the nouns morphologically in this regard, even though Serbo-Croatian is a case-marking language (see, e.g., Wechsler & Zlatić (2000: 806) for a schematic overview). In (47), the forms glossed as past participles are also morphologically analyzable, though, again, I do not attempt to improve upon Zec & Inkelas's (1990) glosses.

3.7 Serbo-Croatian *je*   187

c.**U=je*   *kući   Petar.*
   in=AUX.3S house Peter
d. *A Petar=je   u kući.*
   so Peter=AUX.3S in house
   "So, Peter is in the house."
e.**A=je   Petar u kući.*
   so=AUX.3S Peter in house

Based on the data in (46), it might seem reasonable to analyze the ungrammaticality of sentences like (46c) and (46e) in morphosyntactic terms. Perhaps, for instance, the host of the clitic must be a word from an open lexical class. The examples in (47), however, argue in favor of the idea that the restriction is prosodic in nature, making this a template that might be labeled phonosyntactic, rather than strictly syntactic (Zec & Inkelas 1990: 368). Specifically, there are two conjunctions *ali* 'but' and *pa* (meaning something like 'and') which can be either accented or unaccented. When accented, they can host second-position clitics (see Browne (1974: 41) and Inkelas & Zec (1988: 238)). This suggests that second position in this case is prosodically defined rather than morphosyntactically defined, with the position reckoned with respect to the first prosodic word of a clause (identified, here, by the ability of an element to be accented). In (47a), a second position clitic (here, *nam*, a Dative first plural form) has as its host the word *niko* 'nobody,' which comes after the unaccented variant of the conjunction *ali*. When *ali* is accented (indicated with bolding), by contrast, as in (47b), the clitic appears after it and before *niko*.

(47) a. *Mi smo   zvonili, ali niko=nam   nije   otvorio.*
         1p AUX.1p rang   but nobody=1p.DAT NEG.AUX.3S opened
         "We rang but nobody opened the door for us."
      b. *Mi smo   zvonili,   **ali**=nam niko   nije   otvorio.*
         1p AUX.1p rang=1p.DAT but   nobody NEG.AUX.3S opened
         "We rang but nobody opened the door for us."

The final analytical assumption which should be made clear before moving on to the formal characterization of this template is that I assume, following Zec & Inkelas (1990: 369), that the prosodic unit formed when second-position clitics attach to a prosodic word is another prosodic word, rather than some dedicated category for word-clitic combinations, such as a "clitic group" (see Inkelas (1990: 242–244), Zec & Inkelas (1992)). (This assumption was also implicitly made above for the Chechen case study in Section 3.6.)

Based on this data, we can treat the second-position placement of Serbo-Croatian templatically in terms of an order template involving two components

188   Typologizing templates: case studies

as in Figure 3.21. One of these, the left support, consists of a partially filled component, in a manner comparable to the left support of the Chechen template formally characterized in Figure 3.19. The description of this component, in effect, characterizes the second-position placement of these clitics in an indirect way: they appear in that position by virtue of being finally positioned fillers in an initial component. A consequence of this characterization is that the template is also classified as having a span foundation, rather than an arch one, since neither of these two components appears to be privileged with respect to the other. It is the special internal properties of the first component that are taken to result in the "counting" properties of the template, rather than, say, reckoning the templatic positions directly from the clitic itself.[49]

As just discussed above, the filler element appearing in this second position is actually a templatic clitic cluster rather than a single clitic. Accordingly, the filler itself is characterized as a subtype of a desmeme, an *embedded-Desmeme*, and this aspect of the description is shaded in Figure 3.21. There is nothing internally distinct between a regular desmeme and an embedded one, but the distinction is made here to code a difference between (non-embedded) desmemes associated with a full typological description and desmemes that are not given a full description since they are not the object of formal modeling in a given instance. The nature of the description language employed here would allow for a full characterization of a desmeme within a desmeme – in this case an embedded clitic cluster template description within the larger second-position template. This is not done here simply to keep the study more manageable, in particular with respect to comparing templatic descriptions (see Chapter 4).

Since desmemes are considered to simply be a special kind of form comprising part of a sign, this template is considered to be lexico-constructionally conditioned, in a manner comparable to cases such as those seen in Section 3.5 and Section 3.6, where the fillers were canonical lineates rather than embedded desmemes.

Most of the remaining features of the templatic description in Figure 3.21 should be relatively straightforward at this point given that they are shared with other templates described above. So, I will only remark on two of their additional features. First, in the way the templatic restrictions are described in the source literature, there does not appear to be any means within Serbo-Croatian grammar for them to be violated, and, thus, the template is characterized as *notViolable*. One reason for this is that, at least in some cases where one

---

[49] It is possible to imagine a Serbo-Croatian-like language, where a second-position element shows no prosodic dependency on what precedes it, which could result in a templatic structure where that element resides in its own component and would serve as the keystone for the template. In fact, the German clause (see Section 3.12) is close to this, except that it contains more than one component after its "second" position (the *cf* position in Table 2.2).

3.7 Serbo-Croatian *je*

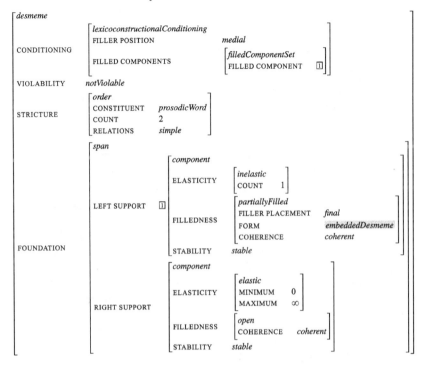

Figure 3.21 Serbo-Croatian second-position clitic template

can imagine a violation, for instance, when the meaning of the clitic is being emphasized, which might be associated with a special word order, a different, accented form of the relevant element is employed (see, e.g., Browne (1974) and Spencer & Luís (2012b: 49)).

Second, the right support here is treated as optional and elastic – effectively comprising the entire clause after second position. There may be syntactic contexts where the right support must contain some element, but there is not evidence that I am aware of which would argue for this being part of the templatic restrictions associated with these clitics, as opposed to being connected to other grammatical generalizations. An additional implication of the overall templatic description is that the elements that can fill the right-support component are characterized as having to be prosodic words but, unlike with the left support, I know of no specific evidence for this, as opposed to the fillers being, say, syntactic phrases. This aspect of the coding must be considered arbitrary from a typological perspective, though, from a practical perspective, it allows for the avoidance, at this stage, of consideration of how to code cases where

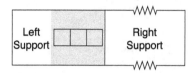

Figure 3.22 Schematization of the Serbo-Croatian second-position clitic template

components could be filled with a mixture of high-level types (e.g., one component of a template being filled by prosodic constituents and another syntactic ones).[50] I am not aware of a template where such an analysis seems necessary, which is why it has not yet been considered for the description language used here (see also Section 5.3.2).

This template is informally schematized in Figure 3.22. The schematization borrows from conventions seen earlier to indicate inelastic and elastic components (see, e.g., Figure 3.12) and partially filled components (see, e.g., Figure 3.20). It further encodes the fact that the filler is an embedded desmeme via the placement of a set of small blocks within the shaded area representing the filler.

3.8 Serbo-Croatian topicalization

The Serbo-Croatian topicalization template was already introduced in Section 2.4.7, and its characterization should be relatively straightforward at this point. Relevant data from Section 2.4.7 is repeated below in (48) (see Zec & Inkelas (1990: 373–374) and Inkelas & Zec (1995: 545–546)). The key feature of the templatic constraint involves a "heaviness" restriction where a constituent can appear in a peripheral topic position if it consists of at least two prosodic words (or, in the terms of Zec & Inkelas (1990), if it is prosodically "branching"). The fact that these constituents appear in a special peripheral position can be seen from the fact that the second-position clitics in (48) (see Section 3.7) are in surface "third" position rather than their usual surface second position.

(48) a. [[*Taj*]$_\omega$ [*čovek*]$_\omega$]$_\phi$ *voleo=je*   *Mariju.*
   that   man.NOM loved=AUX Mary.ACC
   'That man loved Mary.'

---

[50] Since components are not directly "aware" of the content of other components in the description language, the key coding issue surrounds how one would characterize the CONSTITUENT feature of a component's stricture in cases where the contents of a template's components might be mixed in this way.

3.9 Aghem clauses 191

b.*[[*Petar*]$_\omega$]$_\phi$ *voleo=je*   *Mariju.*
   Peter.NOM loved-AUX Mary.ACC
   'Peter loved Mary.'

c. [[*Petar*]$_\omega$ [*Petrović*]$_\omega$]$_\phi$ *voleo=je*   *Mariju.*
   Peter.NOM   Petrovic.NOM loved=AUX Mary.ACC
   'Peter Petrovic loved Mary.'

The sentences in (48a) and (48c) are both allowable instantiations of the topicalization construction since the relevant constituents each consist of two prosodic words. The sentence in (48b), by contrast, is disallowed since the constituent that is in the topicalized position only consists of a single prosodic word. The fact that (48b) is disallowed, while (48c) is allowed, is evidence for the analysis of this restriction as prosodic since, from a syntactic and semantic perspective, the two sentences hardly differ – all that has changed is the use of a one-word name versus a two-word name.

The Serbo-Croatian template can therefore be treated as a two-unit length template, as in Figure 3.23. It is comparable in its description to the Turkish templates seen in Section 3.2. As with the Turkish case, its two components are treated as being elastic with a minimum size of one unit. This encodes the fact that there is a two-unit minimum on the topicalized phrase, but also allows for arbitrarily longer units to be topicalized as independent syntactic restrictions might permit.[51]

The nature of this construction makes the templatic constraint potentially violable since Serbo-Croatian grammar permits syntactic constituents of less than two prosodic words (as in (48c)), but there are no reported actual exceptions, and there is also no general repair strategy for possible exceptions. This makes it more similar to the Turkish nominal template in Figure 3.1 than the Turkish verbal template in Figure 3.2.

An informal schematization of the Serbo-Croatian topicalization template, repeated from Figure 2.15, is given again in Figure 3.24.

3.9   Aghem clauses

The next case study represents the first of four instances of templatic restrictions on the overall shape of a clause and is based on data reported for the Bantoid language Aghem, as described by Watters (1979), though many of the basic facts apply to languages spoken in the same general region as Aghem as well (see, e.g., Good (2010)). Indeed, the pattern where all verbs

---

[51] Zec & Inkelas (1990) do not explicitly discuss upper bounds on the size of a topicalized constituent, and I simply assume it can be larger than two units or this would have been specified in their analysis. Limitations on the upper bound of its length would presumably be driven by non-templatic factors for a syntactic construction like this one.

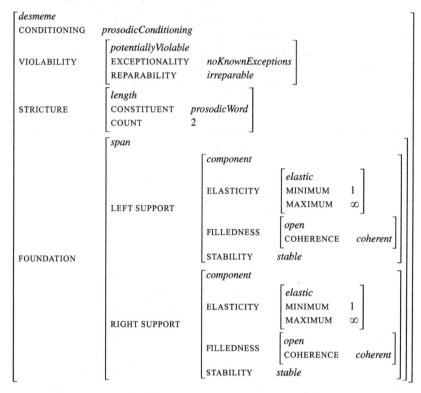

Figure 3.23 Serbo-Croatian topicalization template

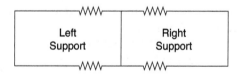

Figure 3.24 Schematization of the Serbo-Croatian topicalization template

in the Jukunoid language Hone have been analyzed as syntactically transitive (and, thereby, requiring an object) discussed in Section 3.6.3 may be connected diachronically to the pattern to be described in this section given that Jukunoid languages are also spoken in the same general region as Aghem and related to it.

The basic structure of the template is relatively straightforward. It can be characterized in terms of a schema along the lines of Subject-Aux-X-Verb-Y-Z, where X, Y, and Z are used to refer to variable classes of verbal arguments.

3.9 Aghem clauses

Which arguments appear in the X, Y, and Z positions is dependent their topicality/focality in complex ways, as described in detail by Watters (1979). Also, the "subject" position is not always occupied by the actor of a verb, as will be seen below, since the position of the actor is also connected to its topicality/focality. Watters (1979) does not explicitly lay out all the details of the templatic analysis assumed here, but he clearly signals a template-like analysis by referring to certain syntactic positions in linear terms, in particular emphasizing the importance of an Immediate Before Verb position ("X" in the schema just given above) and an Immediate After Verb positon ("Y" in the schema above). Some of the other positions not explicitly developed by Watters (1979) are inferred on the basis of the proposal of these two positions (see also Watters (1979: 173)).

There have been some attempts in the generative literature to give a non-templatic interpretation to Aghem clausal structure (see, e.g., Horvath (1995), Aboh (2007), and Hyman & Polinsky (2009)). (See also Hyman (2010b) for recent overview discussion of the relevant issues.) All are largely based on reinterpretations of the facts presented in Watters (1979), and none of these is as comprehensive as his treatment in covering the full range of word order facts, which why it is adopted here.[52] Initial data illustrating the properties of the Aghem template is provided in (49) (Watters 1979: 144).

(49)   a. *énáʔ mɔ̀   ñɨ́ŋ **nô***
          Inah DPST run FOC
          "Inah ran."
       b. *à   mɔ̀   ñɨ́ŋ énáʔ*
          DS DPST run Inah
          "*Inah* ran."

The example in (49a) gives an instance of the most frequent word order for intransitive clauses in Aghem, i.e., an SV pattern. In addition, after the verb one finds an element *nɔ̀*. This element can be associated with a focus reading along the lines of 'only,' in which case it modifies the preceding element (see Hyman (1979: 168)). (This element is affected by rules of tone sandhi. Thus, its tone marking may differ in the examples from its citation tone.) However,

---

[52] Moreover, the most thorough generative analysis, that of Hyman & Polinsky (2009: 224), is not able to analyze the Aghem facts without recourse to a device that, to the best of my knowledge, has not otherwise been proposed in the generative literature: this is an "operator" that assigns focus to the lowest constituent in the verb phrase in an abstract articulated phrase structure. Proposing the presence of this device, along with other details of their syntactic analysis, effectively redefines the notion of Immediate After Verb position in non-linear terms, while retaining a degree of analytical arbitrariness. It, therefore, seems reasonable, in the present context, to consider this analysis to still embody the invocation of a template, broadly construed, just under a different guise.

194 Typologizing templates: case studies

in (49a), this element does not make any clear semantic or pragmatic contribution but is, rather, there to fulfill a requirement that the Immediate After Verb position not be empty (Watters 1979: 166). The presence of this "dummy," or expletive, Focus marker in such contexts is a key piece of evidence for the templatic analysis of the Aghem clause, since it is part of the justification for positing a dedicated Immediate After Verb position. This position is reminiscent of the "slots" associated with slot-filler morphology of the sort discussed in Section 1.4.2.

The example in (49b) represents a different information structure configuration in a sentence with the same basic semantics as (49a), where the subject receives a focal interpretation in Immediate After Verb position. Since the subject now occupies this position, the expletive focus marker is no longer needed to fill it, and it is not found. However, the preverbal Subject position is no longer occupied by the actor of the verb and another dummy element, this one with the same shape as the marker of a third plural subject (Hyman 1979: 48), appears in this position, which also must be obligatorily filled. The treatment of this marker in this context as an expletive element is not novel here but is clearly indicated in the original description where it is glossed specifically as a "dummy subject" (abbreviated as DS in (49b)).

The examples in (50) give comparable data from clauses containing transitive verbs (Watters 1979: 146). In these cases, one does not find the expletive focus marker in Immediate After Verb position since the nature of the verb's semantics does not lead to the position being empty (at least in typical information structure contexts). The example in (50a) gives a clause showing the most common word order in the language for transitive clauses, SVO. In the examples in (50b) and (50c), the (bolded) subject is in Immediate After Verb position, which encodes its focal interpretation. The object also remains after the verb in Aghem (though not immediately after it), at least in the most common utterances of this type (but see Good (2010) for variant OVS patterns in comparable contexts in nearby languages). This leaves the Subject position without a "natural" argument, and the expletive subject marker again appears.

(50) a. *fɨ́l   á mɔ̀ zɨ́ kɨ́bɛ́*
       2.friend.B SM DPST eat 7.fufu.A
       "The friends ate fufu."

   b. *à mɔ̀ zɨ́ **ndúghɔ́** bɛ́'kɔ́*
      DS DPST eat who   fufu.B
      "Who ate the fufu?"

   c. *à mɔ̀ zɨ́ **á-fɨn**   bɛ́'kɔ́*
      DS DPST eat 2.friend.A 7.fufu.B
      "*The friends* ate fufu."

3.9 Aghem clauses

The example in (51) shows that multiple verbal arguments can appear after the Immediate After Verb position at the end of the clause. This is a ditransitive construction where the subject is focal (Watters 1979: 153) and is followed by a theme and benefactive argument respectively.

(51) à mɔ̀ zɔ́m á-fɨ́n   nzàŋ â bà?tòm°
DS DPST sing 2.friend.A Nzaŋ for 1.chief.B
"*The friends* sang Nzaŋ for the chief."

The data to this point has illustrated the Subject position, a verbal domain, the Immediate After Verb position, and a domain after the Immediate After Verb position. The verbal domain, however, can in fact be divided into an auxiliary position and a main verb position, as evidenced by the fact that, under appropriate information structure conditions, they can be separated from each other by verbal arguments appearing in Immediate Before Verb position. Relevant examples, containing a distant past auxiliary marker with form *mɔ̀*, are given in (52) (Watters 1979: 148–149, 154). As can be seen in (52c), more than one element can appear in this position. In that example, a theme and benefactive argument appear between the auxiliary *mɔ̀* and the verb *zɔ́m* 'sing.'

(52) a. fɨ́l   á   mɔ̀ bɛ́'kɨ   zɨ́ án 'sóm
2.friend.B SM DPST 7.fufu.B eat LOC 3.farm.B
"The friends ate fufu in the *farm*."

b. fɨ́l   á   mɔ̀ án 'sóm   zɨ́ kɨ́bɛ́
2.friend.B SM DPST LOC 3.farm.B eat 7.fufu.A
"The friends ate *fufu* in the farm."

c. à   mɔ̀ nzàŋ â bà?tóm zɔ́m á-fɨ́n
DS DPST Nzaŋ for 1.chief.B sing 2.friend.A
"It was the friends who sang Nzaŋ for the chief."

These examples, thus, establish six domains in the Aghem clause, a Subject position, an Auxiliary position, an Immediate Before Verb field, a Verb position, an Immediate After Verb position, and a Final field after the Immediate After Verb position. The Subject, Verb, and Immediate After Verb positions are obligatory. The others are optional, and two of the optional positions are elastic, the Immediate Before Verb field and the Final field.[53] The only

---

[53] I did not encounter an explicit statement in Hyman (1979), Anderson (1979) or Watters (1979), the three parts of the available Aghem sketch grammar, about whether multiple auxiliaries could appear adjacent to each other. If so, the Auxiliary slot may also be elastic. This change would not greatly affect the overall templatic analysis to be presented in Figure 3.25. The Verb slot may be morphosyntactically complex due to the presence of various postverbal aspectual markers (Anderson 1979: 94–97), but these are not treated as causing its slot to be elastic since they appear to be morphologically bound.

196   Typologizing templates: case studies

other aspect of the template that requires specific illustration relates to contexts where it is systematically violated. Relevant examples are given in (53) (Hyman 2010b: 98–100).

(53) a. *ò mɔ̀   bvɥ̀ nò*
         3s RPST fall FOC
         "He fell."
      b. *ò máà   bvɥ̀*
         3s RPST.FOC fall
         "He did fall."

As has already been seen, the Aghem clausal template is sensitive to information structure relations. This sensitivity is not just found with respect to the linear ordering of elements in the clause itself. The language also employs various strategies of word-level flagging of information structure relations (see Hyman (2010b) for overview discussion). In particular, as discussed in Anderson (1979: 97–99), Aghem has a set of "focused" auxiliaries which are used to encode something along the lines of polarity focus in the sense of Dik (1997: 31), where the truth of a statement is asserted. When one of these auxiliaries is employed, the Immediate After Verb position no longer needs to be filled, as seen in the opposition between (53a) and (53b). The clause in (53b) contains the auxiliary *máà*, which is associated with a polarity focus interpretation, and the *nò* element, which otherwise would be expected to be required, no longer appears.

Following Hyman & Watters (1984: 251–254), I treat auxiliaries such as the one in (53b) as being "inherently" focused: that is they are specified lexically for an abstract grammatical feature which plays a role in Aghem's system of encoding the relationship between grammatical relations and information structure in a way comparable to how case systems indirectly encode thematic roles (see, e.g., Horvath (1995) for a development of this idea for Aghem from a formal perspective and Evans (1997) and Bickel (2011) for discussion of how notions like grammatical relations should be expanded to cover a wider range of phenomena than those that are usually considered). In the present context, the data in (53) suggests (i) that there is a long-distance dependency between the Auxiliary position in the Aghem clausal template and the Immediate After Verb position, where the realization of the latter is potentially dependent on what occupies the former and (ii) that there are contexts (classified here as *lexical*) where an aspect of the template can be violated, namely the requirement that the Immediate After Verb position be filled.

Having covered these descriptive and analytical points, the formal characterization of the Aghem clausal template is given in Figure 3.25. It is a constructionally conditioned order template with six components, corresponding to the various slots and fields just described. It is, moreover, an arch template due to the fact that the functional and structural nature of the various components is determined via their linear relation with respect to the Verb position, which serves as the keystone.

Three of the components of the Aghem template, the left support, the keystone, and the right voussoir, corresponding to the Subject, Verb, and Immediate After Verb positions respectively, are treated as obligatory and having a size of one. The left voussoir and the right support, corresponding to the Immediate Before Verb position and the Final field, are characterized as elastic and optional. The remaining Auxiliary position does not occupy a dedicated structural role and is a restkomponente, treated as optional but only allowing one element to fill it if present. In addition, the right voussoir (e.g., the Immediate After Verb position) is treated as depending on the restkomponente corresponding to the Auxiliary for reasons just discussed in relation to the data in (53). This is coded as an asymmetric dependency under the assumption that it is the non-templatic choice of tense–aspect configuration which determines whether or not the Immediate After Verb position can exceptionally be empty, rather than the lack of an element in that position which governs the choice of auxiliary.

The only other aspects of the characterization in Figure 3.25 yet to be discussed relate to the details of its violability specification. It is treated as potentially violable since there are contexts where one might expect various required slots not to be filled, but, as seen in data like that in (49), there are dedicated repair strategies involving insertion of dummy elements to avoid such violations. Thus, repair can take place via morphosyntactic insertion. At the same time, violations of the template are found when certain lexical elements are present in the Auxiliary position (see (53)). The template is, therefore, specified as being subject to lexical exceptionality.

An informal schematization of the Aghem clausal template, making use of conventions introduced above (see, e.g., Figure 3.12), is given in Figure 3.26. The component characterizations included under the blocks (given merely for convenience) make use of the abbreviation Aux for *Auxiliary*, IBV for *Immediate Before Verb*, and IAV for *Immediate After Verb*.

3.10 Mande clauses

The next template to be considered, associated with clauses in Mande languages, is similar in some ways to the Aghem clausal template just discussed in Section 3.9. The discussion here is based primarily on Creissels (2006) and will specifically focus on data from Bambara. Creissels (2006) is part of a larger body of descriptive studies treating the Mande clause as subject to a

198 Typologizing templates: case studies

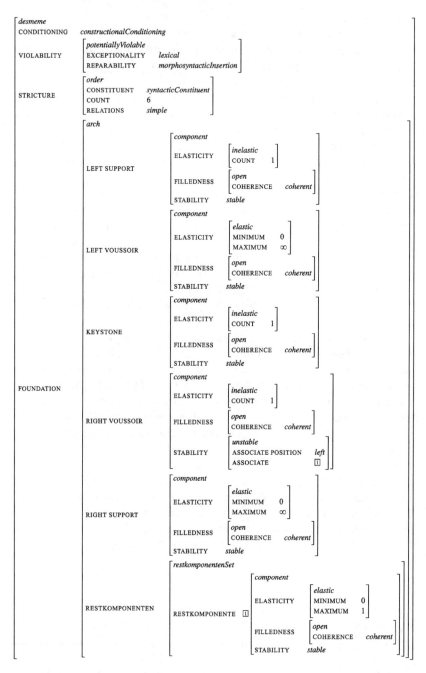

Figure 3.25 Aghem clausal template

3.10 Mande clauses

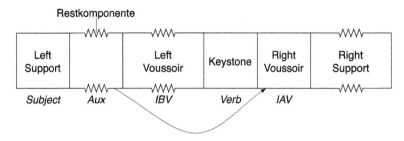

Figure 3.26 Schematization of the Aghem clausal template

rigid S-Aux-OVX word order constraint: the subject appears at the beginning of the clause, it is followed by a tense–mood–aspect "auxiliary" marker, one (and only one) object argument is then permitted before the verb, and all other verbal arguments follow the verb in the "X" position. As discussed by Creissels (2006), among others (see, e.g., Gensler (1994, 1997)), while this puts Mande languages into the general typological category of SOV, this is a rather unusual SOV pattern since, in general, SOV languages would allow multiple non-subject arguments before the verb rather than just one. Similar patterns are reported for languages spoken in the same general region as Mande languages (Güldemann 2007, Heath 2007, Carlson 2000), though often not with the same degree of rigidity, and, in fact, the Aghem pattern shows a roughly comparable structure. Indeed, while it is not in contact with Mande languages, it shows a range of grammatical features that suggest that it has been subject to a similar set of areal forces (see Güldemann (2008) for overview discussion). Thus, the surface similarity in the syntactic patterns of these languages is probably not coincidental.

Examples from Bambara illustrating the ordering restrictions, drawn from Creissels (2006: 37), are given in (54). While I characterize the second position as "Aux," for "auxiliary," following earlier work (see, e.g., Gensler (1994)), elements occupying this position do not actually have verbal properties (Creissels 2006: 41). Rather, they share with canonical auxiliaries the function of (partly) encoding "auxiliary" categories such as tense, mood, aspect, etc. Following Creissels (2006), they are glossed as Predicative Markers in the examples seen here.

(54) a. *sékù bɛ́ mǎdú kálán tùbàbùkán ꜜná*
Sekou PM Madou teach French POSTP
"Sekou is teaching French to Madou."
b. *sékù jé mǎdú délí wárí ꜜlá kúnùn*
Sekou PM Madou ask money POSTP yesterday
"Sekou asked Madou for money yesterday."

c. *sékù jé mădú nèní à mùsó ⁺ɲɛ́ná síɲɛ̀ fìlà*
Sekou PM Madou teach 3s wife POSTP time two
"Sekou insulted Madou twice in the presence of his wife."

d. *ù bɛ́nà fántà dí à mà mùsó ⁺yé*
3p PM Fanta give 3s POSTP wife POSTP
"They will give him Fanta as a wife."

Creissels (2006: 39) describes the Mande S-Aux-OVX pattern as, "absolutely rigid in the sense that it is neither restricted to particular types of clauses, nor conditioned by certain characteristics of the object [noun phrase]." This rigidity can be well illustrated in the opposition between the two sentences in (55), drawn from Creissels (2006: 39). They are roughly semantically equivalent. However, the preverbal object of the clause in (55a) appears unflagged, while, when in postverbal position in the clause in (55b), it is flagged with a postposition, suggesting it has been syntactically demoted. Creissels (2006: 39) characterizes this alternation in terms of an antipassive construction. It suggests that the preverbal position truly is a dedicated object position and a phrase cannot maintain its object status if it is not found there.

(55) a. *mădù bɛ́nà dúmúní ⁺bán*
Madou PM food finish
"Madou will finish the food."

b. *mădù bɛ́nà bán dúmúní ⁺nà*
Madou PM finish food POSTP
"Madou will finish the food."

The example in (55b) further illustrates the fact that the immediately preverbal position does not need to be filled with any element if syntactic constraints do not require it – that is, in templatic terms, it is an elastic component.

Given the clear statement from Creissels (2006) about the pervasiveness and rigidity of this constituency order pattern in Mande, the formal characterization of the template is relatively straightforward, and is given Figure 3.27. The main points requiring further explication are the characterization of the template's foundation and some features of specific components.

As can be seen, the characterization in Figure 3.27 analyzes the clausal template as consisting of five components, each corresponding to one of the five positions of the S-Aux-OVX schema. It is further classified as an arch template with the verb as the keystone, reflecting the fact that the verb is a "pivot" around which the various verbal arguments can be descriptively characterized in relation to it. However, based on the discussion to this point, the Auxiliary position would be another potential candidate for the keystone, since one could characterize both the Subject and Object position with respect to it. I do

3.10 Mande clauses

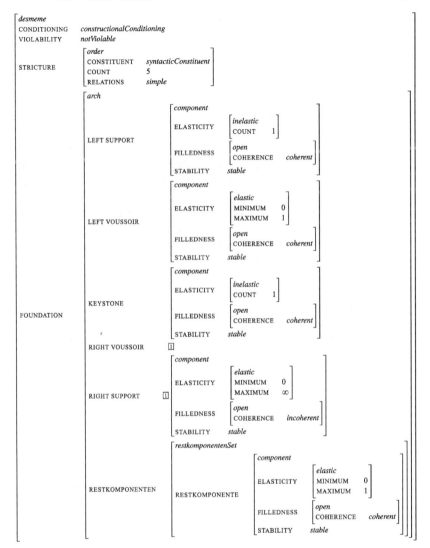

Figure 3.27 Mande clausal template

not consider this analysis for the Mande case because there are declarative contexts where this component is not filled (Creissels 2006: 41), at least in the reference language, Bambara, from which examples are drawn here. However, the fact that the positions of the verbal arguments can be characterized both in relation to the Auxiliary position (which is usually filled) and the Verb position suggests, perhaps, that the current two-way distinction between arch and span foundations is too limited and more complex configurations are possible, for instance involving multiple keystone-like positions (see also Section 3.5.5 for another case suggesting that the span/arch opposition may require further refinement and Section 3.12 for something possibly similar to the Mande case).[54]

As already discussed in relation to the example in (55b), the Object component is optional, hence the specification of the right voussoir position as elastic with a maximum size of one. Also, as just discussed above, the Auxiliary component (a restkomponente) can also be empty in some cases, which is why it, too, is treated as elastic with a maximum size of one. The "X" component, serving as the right voussoir and right support, is a typical field, meaning that it can be empty (as in (55a)) or contain multiple elements (as in (54b)), and is therefore characterized as being of any size. The Subject and Verb positions are characterized as inelastic of size one since Creissels (2006) does not suggest either is optional (with the exception that, in imperative constructions, no subject is present, which I assume results from the imposition of a separate syntactic construction from the one of focus here). All of the components are treated as open since they can be filled with a class of elements, and all are also treated as coherent, except for the final "X" position, given their straightforward functional characterization. As indicated in a sentence like (54b), the elements in the final position of the template only share the fact that they do not otherwise fit elsewhere in the template, which is why this component is treated as incoherent.

An informal schematization of the Mande template following conventions introduced above (see, e.g., Figures 3.5 and 3.26) is given in Figure 3.28.

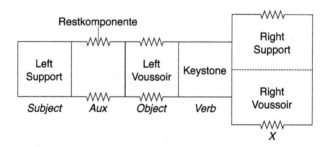

Figure 3.28 Schematization of the Mande clausal template

---

[54] A possible example of languages where this classificatory expansion might be valuable are those of the Songhay family, as described by Heath (2007: 91), which show a very Mande-like pattern, with the additional characteristic that the Auxiliary position must be filled, with a special kind of filler element appearing just in case it would otherwise be expected to be empty based on the morphosemantics characteristics of TMA encoding.

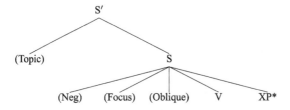

Figure 3.29 Meskwaki clausal structure following Dahlstrom (1993: 13)

3.11 Meskwaki clauses

The templatic analysis of Meskwaki (Fox) syntax considered here is based on the discussion given in Dahlstrom (1993, 1995). In Figure 3.29, her analysis of the structure of the Meskwaki clause is given. The templatic portion of the clause is that part of the structure that is under the node labeled S – i.e., the part of the syntactic structure which is "flat." A key feature of this structure which makes it templatic, beyond the fact that it is primarily described in terms of linear order, is the interleaving of constituents characterized with respect to discourse roles with those characterized with respect to syntactic roles (Dahlstrom 1995: 2). Only this part of the clause will be focused on here. See Dahlstrom (1993: 13–14, 1995: 6–9) for justification of the placement of the Topic position outside the rest of the clause.[55]

The sentences in (56) exemplify the various positions of the clausal template schematized in Figure 3.29.[56] In (56a), the typical position of subjects (as an "XP" argument) in postverbal position is illustrated. In (56b) two contrasted subjects appear before their verbs, signaling that they are focused. In (56c), the preverbal positioning of obliques is seen. In (56d), the position of a negative element as before the verb and also before a focused element is exemplified. Finally, (56e) gives an example of a Topic-Clause construction with a topical element falling outside the template of interest here.

(56) a. *e·h=mehkawa·či*   [*wa·koše·ha*]$_{XP}$
       PCL=find.3s>3sOBV.AOR   fox
       "the fox found him"   (Dahlstrom 1995: 4)

---

[55] Depending on whether or not the appearance of a Topic position before the rest of the elements of the clause is considered predictable or not, the whole Meskwaki clause structure may be analyzable as consisting of a template within a template (see Section 2.5.5).
[56] The morphological analysis in the examples in this section is adapted from Dahlstrom (1993, 1995) partly on the basis of additional information found in Dahlstrom (2003b: 6, 2003a: 152), Thomason (2003: 21), and Rhodes (2010). It should be considered approximate only. Since the relevant templatic patterns are syntactic in nature, this aspect of the presentation should have no impact on the typological analysis.

204   Typologizing templates: case studies

b. *a·kwi=na·hkači* [*ni·na nešihka*]$_{Focus}$ *ota·hi·nemi-ya·nini,* [*ki·na*
   not=also   1s   alone   possess.O2-1s.NEG   2s
   e·ye·ki]$_{Focus}$ *ke-tepe·neta*
   also   own.2s>3pINAM.INDP.IND
   "I do not possess them alone, you also own them."
                                                        (Dahlstrom 1995: 10)

c. [*kehčikami·ki*]$_{Oblique}$ *e·h=taši-komisahekoči*
   ocean.LOC   PCL=RR-swallow.3s>3sOBV.AOR
   meši·name·wani keki·wa·wa
   big.fish.OBV   2p.POSS.mother
   "The whale swallowed your mother in the ocean. "
                                                        (Dahlstrom 1995: 15)

d. [*a·kwi*]$_{Neg}$ [*mo·hči nekoti*]$_{Focus}$ *nesakečini*
   not   even   one   kill.1p>3s.NEG
   "We didn't even kill one."   (Dahlstrom 1995: 11)

e. *o·ni*   [*wi·nwa·wa*]$_{Topic}$ [*kapo·twe*
   and.then   3p   at.some.point
   e·h=neno·ta·ti·hiwa·či]$_S$
   PCL=understand.RECP.DIM.3p.AOR
   "And, as for them, at some point they understood each other."
                                                        (Dahlstrom 1995: 6)

Fuller illustration of the template can be found in Dahlstrom (1995). The basic analysis is quite clearly illustrated in Figure 3.29 and can be readily translated into the templatic description language employed here with only a few further remarks. First, Meskwaki shows second-position clitics (see Sections 1.4.5 and 3.7). Their positioning appears to be determined independently of the template of interest here (Dahlstrom 1995: 7–8), even though it operates over the same constituent, making this an apparent case of templatic convergence (see Section 2.5.3) rather than an additional complication with respect to the clausal template. Second, it may be the case that the elastic XP position of the template (see Figure 3.29) in fact is itself a template, since the principles underlying the ordering facts of multiple elements in that position are not yet fully worked out (Dahlstrom 1995: 13–16). Here, I simply assume the ordering of these elements is not templatic in the interests of expediency, but relatively little hinges on this given that the modeling of templates within templates is not a central concern at this stage of investigation (see Section 2.5.5).

Finally, there is evidence for the possibility of a discontinuous dependency between two components of the template, the Negative position and the Verb position. Relevant examples are provided in (57). In (57a), negation is not expressed with an element in the Negative positon, but via a Negative Preverb,

3.11 Meskwaki clauses

one of a class of elements normally expected to appear adjacent to the verb (Dahlstrom 1995: 16). However, Negative Preverbs can also be displaced to the Negative position, as seen in (57b). (In both examples, the template is found within an embedded clause.) Following Dahlstrom (1995: 16–18), I treat this as a discontinuous dependency with the Negative Preverb being dependent on the Verb.[57]

(57) a. *nekehke·nema·wa*   [[*ke·ko·hi*]Focus
          know.1s>3s.INDP.IND   anything
          e·h=pwa·wi·mi·čiči]
          PCL=NEG-eat.3s>3sINAM.AOR
          "I know he didn't eat anything."   (Dahlstrom 1995: 16)

      b. *nekehke·nema·wa*   [[*e·h=pwa·wi-*]Neg
          know.1s>3s.INDP.IND   PCL=NEG-
          [*ke·ko·hi*]Focus *-mi·čiči*]
          anything   -eat.3s>3sINAM.AOR
          "I know he didn't eat anything."   (Dahlstrom 1995: 16)

It is now possible to introduce the formal characterization of this Meskwaki clausal template, and it is provided in Figure 3.30. The description is largely a recharacterization of the more schematic representation in Figure 3.29 using the description language developed here.

The template consists of five components. Three of these are elastic with a maximum size of one, corresponding to the parenthesized positions in Figure 3.29. Another, the Verb position, is obligatory with a size of one. The last, corresponding to the XP position, is elastic without restrictions on its length (i.e., it functions as a field). In addition, this template is classified as an arch template with the Verb as the keystone, following the characterization of Dahlstrom (1995: 3) where the verb is treated as the "pivot or reference point for the other constituents." This makes the Oblique and XP components the left and right voussoirs respectively. The XP component is also the right support, with the Negative component serving as the left support. The Focus position is the sole restkomponente in the template. As just mentioned with respect to the data in (57), there is evidence that there can be a long-distance dependency between the Negative component and the Verb component, which is indicated by the left support having the keystone as an associate. Dahlstrom (1995) does not indicate any conditions under which the template can be violated, and it is accordingly classified as not violable here.

---

[57] Dahlstrom (1995: 18–21) discusses another apparent case of a discontinuous dependency involving a preverb where the Topic position is implicated. Since this position is not part of the template analyzed here, I do not model its behavior below in Figure 3.30.

206 Typologizing templates: case studies

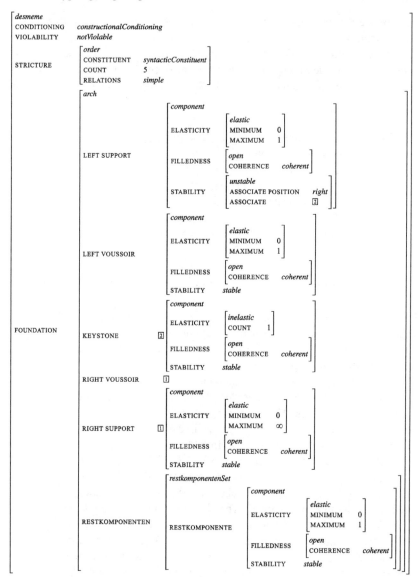

Figure 3.30 Meskwaki clausal template

An informal schematization of the Meskwaki clausal template, following conventions introduced above (see, e.g., Figures 3.5 and 3.28), is given in Figure 3.31. The labels for the blocks representing the templatic components are drawn from Figure 3.29.

3.12 German clauses

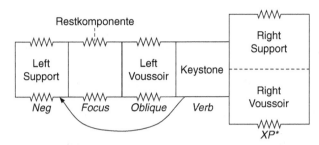

Figure 3.31 Schematization of the Meskwaki clausal template

3.12 German clauses

Key features of the template that are the subject of the final case study, the German clause, have already been presented in Sections 1.4.5 and 2.3.5, and the analysis on which the templatic characterization is based is carefully developed in Kathol (2000) (see also Kathol (1995)).[58] Accordingly, the treatment here will only be abbreviated. Overall, the properties of this template are largely comparable to those seen for Mande languages in Section 3.10 and Meskwaki in Section 3.11. The key feature of the templatic analysis of the German clause, which is adapted from the traditional topological field approach as discussed in Section 1.4.5, is the characterization of the linearization patterns of German clauses in terms of five positions, First Position (vf), Second Position (cf), Middlefield (mf), Verb Cluster (vc), and Postverbal Field (nf) (see Table 1.4). As discussed in Section 2.5.5, the Verb Cluster position may itself constitute a template, in which case this German template would represent an additional case of a template being embedded within a template (see Section 2.5.5), though I do not develop that possible analysis here, and it would only minimally affect the typological classification (see Section 3.7 for a case where such an analysis is partly developed).

Of these positions, only one is obligatory from a templatic perspective, the Second Position, which is occupied either by a verb or a complementizer-like element (e.g., a marker of clausal subordination). The rest are either filled or not based on syntactic principles independent of the template itself. Three of the positions are fields rather than slots – that is, they can be occupied by more than one element. These are the Middlefield, the Verb Cluster, and the Postverbal Field. As the only obligatory position, I treat the Second Position as a keystone, and classify the template as having an arch foundation. There

---

[58] As discussed in Section 1.4.5, I am aware that the templatic analysis of the German clauses is not uncontroversial. I included it here both because it is comparatively well known and because of the existence of work like Kathol (2000) which lays out the templatic analysis so explicitly. See also Section 1.7.

208 Typologizing templates: case studies

is, however, a descriptive tradition that treats both the Second Position and the Verb Cluster position as part of the *Satzklammer* 'clause bracket,' with Second Position serving as the *linke Satzklammer* 'left clause bracket' and the Verb Cluster as the *rechte Satzklammer* 'right clause bracket.' This characterization suggests that an alternative analysis of the German clause with two privileged keystone-like elements may merit consideration, a possibility also discussed above for Mande (see Section 3.10), though I leave this open as an area for future investigation.[59] None of the components of the template are coherent, which, in fact, has been the key motivating factor behind the German clause's templatic analysis in the first place.[60] Once the Second Position is established as the keystone, this means that the First Position is both the left support and the left voussoir, the Middlefield is the right voussoir, the Final Field is the right support, and the Verb Cluster is a restkomponente.

Like the Mande and Meskwaki cases (see Sections 3.10 and 3.11), this German template is associated with clauses in general and is not violable. Like Nimboran (see Section 3.4), the relationships among the template's components are taxonomic, as mentioned in Section 2.4.4, though the taxonomy is not especially elaborated. Specifically, two of the components, the Second Position and the Verb Cluster, have been grouped into the category *verbal* to indicate that they are where verbs can appear (Kathol 2000: 83). The formal characterization of the template is given in Figure 3.32. Most aspects of its categorization have been discussed, except for the issue of component dependencies. The German clausal template is the only one presented here which contains two dependencies (one symmetric and one asymmetric), and their encoding is shaded in Figure 3.32.

The two dependencies described for the components of the German clausal template both involve the keystone (i.e., Second Position), and relevant data is provided in (58) (see Kathol (2000: 58)). The fact that Second Position is implicated in the two dependencies could, perhaps, be taken as a further justification of its status as the keystone.

---

[59] If one were to treat the *Satzklammer* as a fundamental element in the German clausal template, this might prompt a refinement to the present analysis in a different way. The notion of "bracket" metaphorically suggests that these components, in some sense, "close off" the clause. If this is case, then they would appear to be more comparable to templatic supports than their current classifications as a keystone and restkomponente respectively, which might prompt a reconsideration of the German clause as containing a "*Satzklammer*" template inside a larger clausal structure. I do not pursue this possibility here since it is not raised by Kathol (2000), around which this case study is based.

[60] Some of the positions, however, can clearly be considered more coherent than others. The Middlefield, for instance, can be understood as the "default" position for verbal arguments (see, e.g., Kathol (2000: 83)), making it relatively incoherent, while the Verb Cluster, as its name indicates, generally contains verbal elements except for a limited class of exceptions (see, e.g., (58b)). Developing a more gradient notion of coherence may be a fruitful area of investigation in future studies.

3.12 German clauses

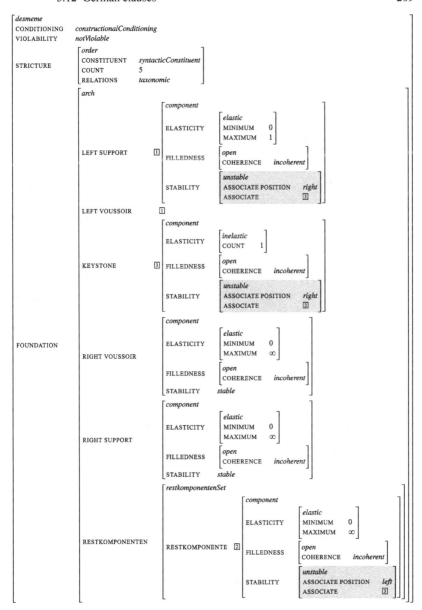

Figure 3.32 German clausal template

210 Typologizing templates: case studies

(58) a. *Peter wird   Paul anrufen.*
        Peter be.FUT.3s Paul PFX.call
        "Peter will call Paul up."
      b. *Peter ruft   Paul an.*
        Peter call.PRS.3s Paul PFX
        "Peter calls Paul up."
      c. *weil   Peter Paul anruft*
        because Peter Paul PFX.call.PRS.3s
        "because Peter will call Paul up"

In (58a) a future-coding construction is seen involving the use of an auxiliary verb in Second Position and an infinitival verb in the Verbal Cluster. The citation form for the verb is *anrufen* 'to call up,' but it is a member of a class of morphosyntactically complex verbs, with initial elements usually described as "separable" in the literature on German (see Müller (2002: 253–340) for an extensive overview). In the case of this verb, the relevant separable element has the form *an*, and it is simply glossed as a "prefix," though this categorization should not be treated as a definitive analysis. In a different construction, involving a verb marked in the Present tense, seen in (58b), the main verb appears in the Second Position (the usual position for finite verbs in non-subordinate clauses) but the element *an* remains in the Verb Cluster and, hence, has become "separated" from the verb. Since the combinations of verbs and these separable elements are lexically idiosyncratic and since they can, in some cases, appear in the same component, a sentence like (58b) can be viewed as exhibiting a dependency between these two elements across two different components. I am not aware of any specific evidence for treating this dependency as asymmetric since both elements must be present in the sentence in order for the relevant verbal meaning to be conveyed and the nature of the templatic analysis does not suggest that either element is found in a "displaced" position (along the lines of the Negative Preverbs seen in Meskwaki in (57)). This dependency is therefore treated as symmetric, with each component having the other as an associate. In Figure 3.32, it is the one encoded as holding between the keystone and the template's sole restkomponente.

A second, asymmetric, dependency is also seen in the examples in (58). This is connected to what material appears in Second Position. As seen in (58a), when this is a verbal element, another constituent can appear in the First Position. However, when Second Position is occupied by a complementizer-like element, as in (58c), which is an instance of a subordinate clause with the verb appearing in the Verbal Cluster component, the First Position cannot be filled (see, e.g., Höhle (1986: 329)). Thus, there is a dependency where the element in Second Position can block the appearance of an element in First Position,

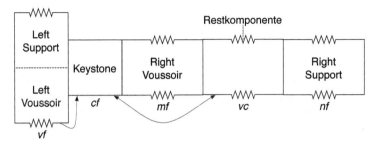

Figure 3.33 Schematization of the German clausal template

and an asymmetric dependency is indicated between these two components, i.e., the left support/left voussoir and the keystone in Figure 3.32.[61]

An informal schematization of the German clausal template following conventions introduced above (see, e.g., Figures 3.5 and 3.18) is given in Figure 3.33. The labels for the blocks representing the templatic components are drawn from Table 1.4 in Chapter 1.

The German clause is the final "templatic" case study to be considered here. In the next section, two desmemic constructions that would not generally be considered templatic are formally characterized using the template description language so that they can serve as comparative controls in Chapter 4.

3.13 Two non-templatic desmemes in English

3.13.1 Two templatic "controls"

The case studies discussed in previous sections of this chapter all had in common that there was something "unexpected" about their linearity which made them templatic, following the informal definition of the term provided in (6) in Chapter 1. One of the goals of the present study, of course, is not merely to understand how to compare templates to each other, but also to see how templatic linearization constraints are similar to and different from non-templatic linearization constraints. The foundational nature of the

---

[61] In analogy to the treatment of "blocking" elements in Nimboran, as discussed in Section 3.4, it would be possible to analyze this pattern in German as involving a similar kind of "straddling" via an additional layer of taxonomic classification. I do not pursue that possibility here since, while I can not find an explicit statement to that effect, the dependency analysis appears closer to the spirit of Kathol (2000). For similar reasons, I do not treat First Position as obligatorily filled (i.e., inelastic) and clauses containing complementizers as exceptional, in a manner that would be parallel to the analysis of sentences missing an element in the Immediate After Verb position in Aghem, as discussed in Section 3.9, though such a reanalysis does not, on the surface, seem implausible. These sorts of analytical indeterminacies get to the heart of the issue of consistency in coding, to be discussed in Section 5.2.2.

212   Typologizing templates: case studies

study is not designed to answer this question in any definitive way. Nevertheless, it would still be useful, for purposes of illustration, to describe some non-templatic patterns of linear stipulation which will then enter into the formal comparisons to be presented in Chapter 4 and serve as kind of analytical "controls." Accordingly, I characterize two English linearization patterns, involving the Plural suffix and the verb phrase, using the typological description language developed in Chapter 2 in this section, following the same basic approach seen in the case studies. They are developed in less detail due to the fact that the relevant English facts are well known and that they are not themselves templatic and, therefore, less illustrative of the complications involved when coding linearization constructions using the description language. They should, therefore, be treated more as possible examples of how to extend the description language to non-templatic constructions than definitive analyses.

3.13.2   The English plural

A characterization of the linearization restrictions governing the appearance of the English plural suffix -*s*, treated as a desmeme, is given in Figure 3.34. They are treated as part of an arch desmeme with the noun stem as the keystone and the suffix, a canonical lineate, as both the right voussoir and right support. The left voussoir and left supports are both treated as null. The template's conditioning is classified as lexico-constructional under the assumption that this linearization restriction is connected to the specific lexical identity of the suffix. (A constructional analysis would also be imaginable if we chose to generalize to the class of English inflectional affixes.) While there are irregular plurals in English, when this specific construction is employed, there are no exceptional cases (e.g., with the -*s* appearing as an infix for some nouns). So, the desmeme is classified as not being violable.

3.13.3   The English verb phrase

A partial characterization of the linearization restrictions found for the English verb phrase, treated as a desmeme, is given in Figure 3.35.

This desmeme consists of three components and is intended to represent the possibilities for a verb phrase where no arguments are flagged that can be schematized as V(IO)(DO) (i.e., a verb followed by an optional indirect object and an optional direct object, with the order of all elements, when appearing, being rigid). The construction is treated as an arch desmeme with the one obligatory component, corresponding to the verb, as the keystone, the indirect object

3.13 Two non-templatic desmemes in English

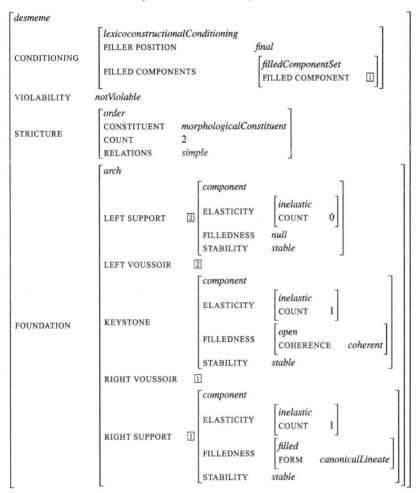

Figure 3.34 English plural suffix as a desmeme

component as the right voussoir, and the direct object component as the right support. The left support and left voussoir are assigned to a null component. The desmeme is treated as constructionally conditioned and not violable under the assumption that cases where it is not realized do not involve violations of the desmemic restrictions but, rather, invocation of different constructions (e.g., a V-DO-*to*-IO construction where the indirect object is marked with a preposition).

214   Typologizing templates: case studies

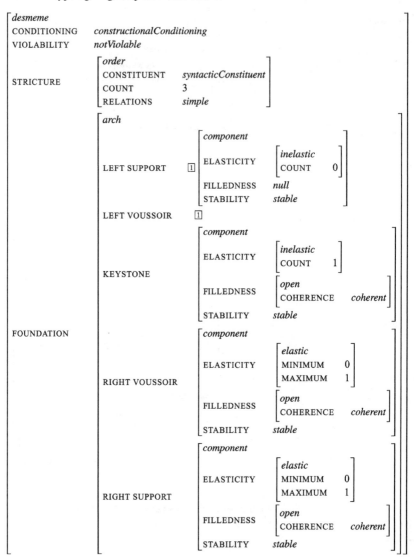

Figure 3.35 English verb phrase as a desmeme

3.14 Summary of the case studies

Case studies have now been presented for eighteen templatic constructions, some of which are quite similar to each other (e.g., the two Turkish templates presented in Section 3.2), and others of which are clearly quite distinct from each other (e.g., either of the Turkish templates when set against the Mande

3.14 Summary of the case studies

template in Section 3.10). The next step in this investigation is to systematically compare these templatic constructions, via their formal characterizations. The ultimate goal, of course, is to come to a better understanding of the typology of templatic constructions. The relatively limited sample size will prevent any strong conclusions from being reached but beginning investigations in this regard will be presented in the next chapter. However, the main goal of the next chapter is not so much to work out global patterns in templatic distributions but, rather, to consider how we can rigorously compare constructions using the relatively elaborate descriptions presented above. Now that we have moved beyond "atomic" classifications such as SOV, SVO, VSO, etc., to a richer feature-structure based specification, our methods for assessing the degrees of similarity and difference holding among two typologically characterized objects will have to become more sophisticated. The next chapter presents a proof of concept that, despite these complications, the task is nevertheless manageable.

Another concern that is lurking in the various case studies is the fact that, given the complexity of the description language, the extent of the choices that an analyst must make to translate existing analyses into formal characterizations is much greater than in a traditional study. This strongly increases the chances that "similar" constructions may be coded differently for purely accidental reasons. This issue is treated in Section 5.2.2 of the concluding chapter.

4 Typologizing templates: comparison

4.1 Comparing templatic descriptions

Chapter 2 developed a rich formal description language for templatic constructions, and Chapter 3 described a number of templates using that language. A major goal of this study is, however, not merely to describe templates but also to investigate their typology. The description language can, in fact, be understood as a claim regarding the descriptive typology of templatic constructions, but, as discussed in Section 1.6, templates are, in some sense, a wastebasket class. This makes knowing if a given descriptive typology is reasonably exhaustive, or, in some sense, "accurate," more difficult than for phenomena (e.g., word order) where our approaches to their analysis make laying out a logical space of possibilities more straightforward.

Accordingly, it is important to find some way to rigorously compare the templates described here, since it is by means of such comparison that we can begin to detect unexpected similarities and differences and determine which templatic descriptions deserve further scrutiny, perhaps because they are especially deviant from other descriptions. The process of such comparison is, therefore, further likely to allow for testing of the plausibility of existing templatic descriptions and to indicate where refinements are needed to the descriptive typology. Moreover, to the extent that it may permit the descriptive typology to "stabilize," it will lay the groundwork for the coding of a sufficiently large number of desmemes that the templatic patterns of the world's languages can be quantitatively explored in a systematic way, with an ultimate goal of determining the limits of templaticity and detecting universals in the patterning of templatic structures.

The present study is not able to achieve these latter goals, of course: the current database contains an insufficient number of templates. Moreover, work needs to be done on understanding what kinds of information can be reliably gleaned from logically possible approaches to comparison of the complex formal structures employed here. However, it is possible to work on a more limited problem which, nevertheless, represents a crucial step towards understanding the larger research questions posed by patterns of linear stipulation.

4.1 Comparing templatic descriptions

Recent advances in data processing technology allow us to develop the means through which the formal characterizations employed in this study can be rigorously compared for different purposes. The discussion below is, therefore, designed as a kind of "proof of concept" to demonstrate the general feasibility of the seemingly daunting task of extracting significant linguistic patterns from a database where the objects being described can be as different as the German clausal template (see Section 3.12), repeated in Figure 4.1, and the Turkish nominal stem template (see Section 3.2), repeated in Figure 4.2.

It is clear from superficial examination that the templates characterized in Figures 4.1 and 4.2 have relatively little in common, but they are still not different in every imaginable way, especially given the wide descriptive space that the template description language allows for. For instance, each contains one inelastic component of size one. But, how do we go from a lone observation such as this to objective comparison of all the desmemes that we might want to code?

The rest of this chapter takes up this question and addresses it in two ways. First, it establishes that, despite their formal complexity, the fact that the templatic descriptions employed here can be modeled as graphs, in the mathematical sense (see Section 2.9), opens them up to methods of algorithmic processing available for the comparison of graphs in general, thereby allowing us to tackle key problems in their typological comparison. In particular, this observation will facilitate an assessment of their holistic level of difference from each other and permit the identification of similar structural features even across dissimilar templatic structures. Second, this chapter shows that the structure of the database is rich enough to allow for subparts of templatic descriptions to be straightforwardly extracted to look for correlations among their features of the kind generally associated with statistical universals.

The basic structure and content of this chapter draws significantly on the analysis of clause linkage patterns in Bickel (2010), using it as an analytical model. The major difference is that Bickel (2010) employs a "multivariate" typology where each clause linkage construction is associated with a "flat" list of values across a range of features. However, of particular importance here is the fact that the typological descriptions involve articulated formal models where feature structures are typed and embedded. This allows for, among other things, a formal characterization of logical dependencies in the interrelationships of feature–value pairings (e.g., that only arch templates are associated with a keystone), which was a crucial desideratum for a description of complex structural objects such as templates. The drawback to this is that the methods of manipulating the data necessarily become more complex in various ways than when descriptions are "flat," but, as we will see, this is an obstacle that can be overcome in increasingly straightforward ways.

218   Typologizing templates: comparison

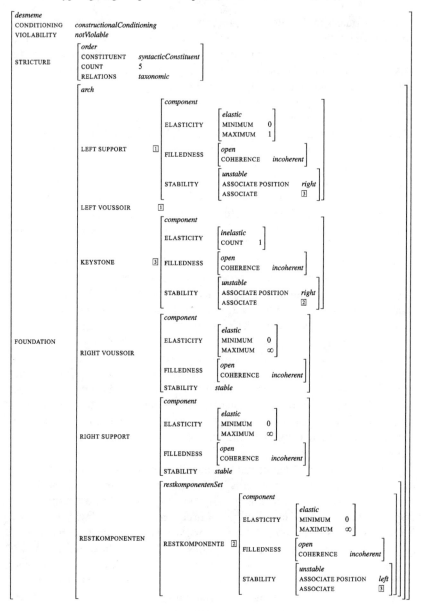

Figure 4.1 German clausal template

4.1 Comparing templatic descriptions

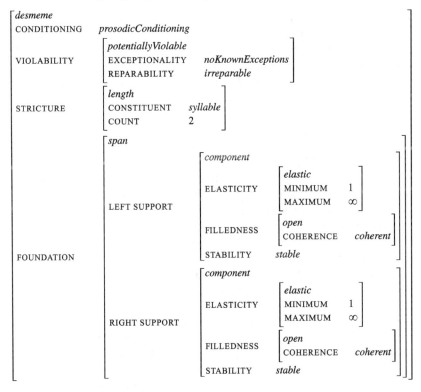

Figure 4.2 Turkish disyllabic minimal size restriction template for nouns

In Section 4.2 of this chapter, the typological problem of devising a metric of overall similarity for graph-based descriptions is considered, and this will provide us with a means for determining which of the templatic descriptions found in Chapter 3 are most similar to each other in a global way. In Section 4.3, a different technique will be used to detect "pockets" of similarity across templatic constructions, for instance, identifying which pair of components may be most similar to each other across two templates, even if the templates themselves are quite different. The goal will be to not only assess similarity on the basis of the "internal" properties of the templatic elements themselves but also to consider the wider environment that they are embedded within. Finally, in Section 4.4, the existing database will be explored in ways which would, in principle, allow us to attempt to extract universals from it, even though the size of the present database does not allow us to consider any of the "universals" that may be uncovered to be robust.

220   Typologizing templates: comparison

The discussion in this chapter will, therefore, serve to establish that future studies of templates attempting to find "true" universals and to explore their properties in a systematic way using the formalism developed here are clearly viable, even if it would take substantial effort to formally describe the large number of templatic restrictions that would be required to do so.[1]

4.2   From graphs to a similarity metric

4.2.1   The generality of graph structures

As already discussed in Section 2.9, templates characterized via the description language used here can be straightforwardly represented in the form of graphs, in the mathematical sense. For present purposes, this has a significant practical consequence since a range of disciplines (including linguistics) provide examples of the use graphs as a means to formally describe multifaceted phenomena, and various metrics have already been devised for exploring the properties of different graphs. Perhaps the most significant instance of their use has been within computer science, given the fact that the Web can be understood as a graph describing the interlinking of Web pages, making the exploitation of general techniques for exploring the properties of graphs of value in domains such as Web search (see, e.g., Kleinberg (1999), Melnik et al. (2002), and Jeh & Widom (2002)). Work within biology has also developed such techniques (see, e.g., Ogata et al. (2000), Heymans & Singh (2003)), as has chemistry (Rupp et al. 2007), and they have even been used in the development of processes for facilitating automatic grading (Naudé et al. 2010), among other things.[2] Zager (2005) and Zager & Verghese (2008) provide more general discussion of issues surrounding graph analysis, in particular in the areas of assessing graph similarity and matching comparable nodes across graphs from a computer science perspective, and Blondel et al. (2004) is a relevant work within applied mathematics which employs its proposed similarity metric to a linguistic domain in the detection of synonyms on the basis of dictionary entries. While I am not aware of previous work in theoretical or descriptive linguistics specifically using graph comparison algorithms, there is, of course, ample precedent for linguists to make use of data comparison tools from outside linguistics to arrive at results of relevance to the study of language (see, e.g., Nichols (1992), Gray & Atkinson (2003), Dunn et al. (2008), Nichols & Warnow (2008), Wichmann (2008a), and Bickel (2010), among many others).

---

[1] While not formally reviewed or fully documented, readers wishing to examine the various scripts and tools used to develop the analyses in this section can find them at https://github .com/jcgood/desmeme.

[2] A number of the works cited above were reported on in Melnik et al. (2013).

4.2 From graphs to a similarity metric

An examination of the works cited above reveals a wide range of proposed algorithms designed to compare graph structures in one way or another. To the extent that the use of graphs in typological investigation is novel here, there is no established precedent for choosing one of these over any other, nor is there any existing "baseline" across which the various methods can be compared. Given that the size of the database used here is inappropriate for statistical generalizations, I will not attempt to use it to establish any such comparative baseline but, rather, simply make use of algorithms to the extent that they can provide exemplary instances of the application of graph-based methods to typological investigation. I will begin in this section by employing a conceptually straightforward algorithm for holistic comparison of graph-based descriptions of templates that yields results which appear quite reasonable based on impressionistic investigation. Then, in Section 4.3, I will consider a more complex algorithm designed to uncover points of similarity across an arbitrary pair of template graphs.

4.2.2 A node-centric method for holistic graph comparison

As discussed above in Section 2.9, graphs are modeled as a series of nodes (also called vertices) joined by a series of arcs (also called edges), and the graphs used here are specifically directed because the arcs connecting the nodes are additionally associated with a "direction" that treats one node as the beginning of the arc and the other as the end. In addition, both nodes and arcs in the graphs used here are associated with labels. In the case of nodes, the labels specify the type of the node, and in the case of arcs, they specify the nature of the feature–value relationship holding between the relevant nodes. When developing a graph comparison algorithm for any set of graphs, the question then becomes how each of these kinds of information (e.g., the existence of nodes and arcs and their labels) should enter into calculations of similarity and difference.

A significant characteristic of the graph-based descriptions used here when it comes to considering such an algorithm is that there is a relatively high degree of redundancy holding between the information encoded in the labels on arcs and the nodes that they point to. Consider, for instance, the graph-based representation of the prosodic template associated with the Tiene derived verb stem given in Figure 4.3, whose feature value representation was given in Figure 3.16 in Section 3.5.5. In many cases, the label on an arc is fully predictable from the type associated with the node it points to. This is the case, for instance, for the VIOLABILITY, STRICTURE, and FOUNDATION features. The reason for this is that each of these nodes is associated with a type that, in the description language used here, is only ever the value of one of these features. In other cases, there is only partial predictability, such as with the components, since

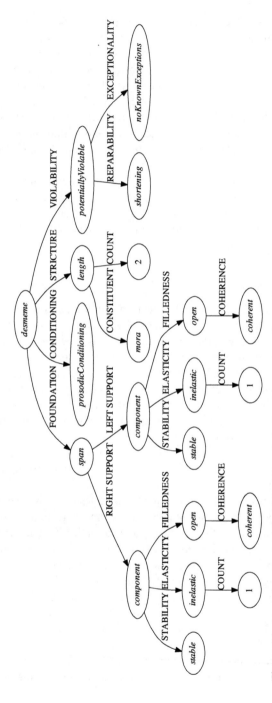

Figure 4.3 A graph representation of the Tiene derived verb stem prosodic template

4.2 From graphs to a similarity metric

each can have different roles in a foundation. However, there are many features that can never have components as their value, limiting the amount of extra information provided by the arc labels even in such cases.

Given the level of overlap between the information associated with arc labels and the information associated with node labels, one could create a simplified algorithm for comparing graph-based descriptions of templates by comparing only the nodes or the arcs across the templates in the database. Some information would be lost, but much would be retained, and, while such a strategy may not be appropriate for all applications, as we will see, it is still useful for performing initial global comparisons across a set of templates. In choosing between focusing on the information found in node or arc labels, the node information is of greater significance, since nodes are labeled for the subtypes associated with the given feature, while the feature labels on arcs, in many cases, only distinguish at the level of a higher type (e.g., there is a general arc label of FOUNDATION pointing to either *arch* or *span* node subtypes of *foundation*). The primary kind of information that is lost in focusing on nodes only is the specific features associated with components, for instance whether a given component is taking on the role of keystone, support, or voussoir, as well as cases where a given component is serving multiple roles (as found, for instance, in the German template seen in Figure 4.1 where the same component is both left voussoir and left support). A different comparison algorithm will be considered in Section 4.3 which incorporates information from both node and arc labels.[3]

The particular node-centric algorithm that will be adopted here is adapted from the simUI method of Gentleman (2013), devised for comparison of graph-based descriptions of genes as found in the Gene Ontology database (see Ashburner et al. (2000) and Falcon & Gentleman (2007)). To make the nature of this graph comparison method clear, one can consider the two schematic graphs depicted in Figure 4.4. The top graph and the bottom graph should be understood as each sharing the three gray nodes in the center of the graphs, and each having nodes that are not found in the other graph. Nodes that are not shared are black in the top graph and white in the bottom graph. In terms of the templatic descriptions used here, gray nodes can be understood as instances

---

[3] Even the relatively simple algorithm employed in this section could be minimally altered to include some of the information associated with arc labels if that were considered desirable. This could be done by subjecting a given graph to a stage of "pre-processing," where some information embedded in arcs is re-encoded within new nodes, for instance nodes specifically characterizing patterns of reentrancy. Such a procedure would represent something akin to a highly localized line graph transformation, where a graph's nodes and arcs are, in some sense, "inverted" with each other (see Bagga (2004) for a recent overview). Work in bioinformatics and complex systems analysis (among others) has considered the role of line graph transformations in the analysis of data encoded in graph-based descriptions (Nacher et al. 2004, Evans & Lambiotte 2010).

224   Typologizing templates: comparison

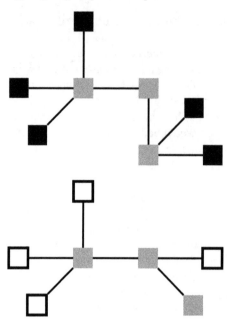

Figure 4.4 Schematic graphs for illustrating simUI graph comparison method

where two templates share a node of a specific type (e.g., the same foundation or stricture type), while black and white nodes can be understood as type specifications unique to each of the graphs. The arcs of these schematic graphs are not labeled because this particular algorithm ignores such information, as just discussed. (Indeed, it ignores arcs entirely, but they are retained in the schematizations for purposes of illustration.)

The simUI graph comparison method calculates a similarity score for any pair of graphs by dividing the number of nodes in the intersection of the two sets of nodes associated with each graph by the number of nodes in their union. This produces scores between zero and one, zero in the case where two graphs have no nodes in common and one in the case where all of their nodes are in common. For the schematic graphs in Figure 4.4, the intersection of the nodes is three – that is, the number of gray nodes – and the union is twelve – that is, the sum of the five black nodes, the four white nodes, and the three gray nodes. The similarity score of the graphs is, therefore, 3/12 or .25. Because the similarity scores must range between zero and one, they can be converted to distance scores by subtracting the similarity score from the number 1. In the example case, this would mean subtracting .25 from 1, yielding a distance of .75. Converting similarity to distance in this way will be useful below when this algorithm is used to create a set of pairwise distances across all of the templates

4.2 From graphs to a similarity metric 225

in the database which can then serve as input to visualization algorithms for examining overall patterns of similarity and difference (see Cysouw (2007a) for general discussion of visualization techniques for examining typological data).

In the description language used here, two templatic descriptions that are very similar to each other would get a similarity score of close to one and distance scores of close to zero. This is the case for the two Turkish templates discussed in Section 3.2, which differ only with respect to their reparability. At the same time, even the most divergent templates would never get a similarity score of exactly zero, since they would minimally share the base node of *desmeme* in their intersection and would probably at least share some nodes relating to the composition of their components. In principle, though, they could have a similarity score very close to zero if their graph representations contained very few nodes coded with the same types.

In Table 4.1, a set of pairwise templatic distances, determined via the algorithm just introduced, is given.[4] Distances are included for the eighteen templatic constructions, along with the two English templatic controls, discussed in Chapter 3.[5] As can be seen in the table, each template has a distance of zero from itself, and otherwise the distances range from a minimum of .09

---

[4] One could imagine adapting this algorithm in ways that are more sensitive to the specific objects being compared in this case, though I do not do so here given the exploratory nature of this work. Perhaps the most obvious alteration would be to not make use of a purely binary distinction when comparing nodes as being the "same" or "different" but to also allow for more gradient degrees of similarity. For instance, some templatic features have values which are integers (e.g., COUNT), and, rather than, in effect, assigning a pair of nodes with values of one and three a similarity score of zero, one could imagine giving them a similarity score along the lines of one-third. Similarly, a node in the graph specifying that a templatic component is *partiallyFilled* is treated as completely dissimilar from nodes specified as either *filled* or *empty*, even though partially filled components clearly bear more similarity to filled and empty components than components of the latter two types do to each other. Since the database used here defines its categories within an ontology, much of the information required to create more nuanced similarity metrics in such cases is coded even if it is not yet exploited.

[5] The abbreviated names in the first column of Table 4.1 refer to the templatic constructions discussed in Chapter 3 as follows: AghemClause, Aghem clausal template (Section 3.9, Figure 3.25); BantuCA, Bantu Causative–Applicative template (Section 3.5.3, Figure 3.13); BantuCT, Bantu Causative–Transitive template (Section 3.5.2, Figure 3.10); BantuVCy, Bantu Transitive final positioning template (Section 3.5.2, Figure 3.11); ChechenPreverbalA, Chechen Preverbal *'a* template (Section 3.6.5, Figure 3.19); ChichewaAR, Chichewa Applicative–Reciprocal template (Section 3.5.4, Figure 3.15); ChintangPrefixes, Chintang verbal prefix template (Section 3.3, Figure 3.3); EnglishPlural, English plural suffix as a desmeme (Section 3.13.2, Figure 3.34); EnglishVP, English ditransitive verb phrase as a desmeme (Section 3.13.3, Figure 3.35); GermanClause, German clausal template (Section 3.12, Figure 3.32); MandeClause, Mande clausal template (Section 3.10, Figure 3.27); MeskwakiClause, Meskwaki clausal template (Section 3.11, Figure 3.30); NdebeleCA, Ndebele Causative–Applicative template (Section 3.5.3, Figure 3.14); NimboranVerb, Nimboran verb template (Section 3.4, Figure 3.7); SerboCroatianJe, Serbo-Croatian second-position clitic template (Section 3.7, Figure 3.21); SerboCroatianTopicalization, Serbo-Croatian topicalization template (Section 3.8, Figure 3.23); TieneVerbProsodic, Tiene derived verb stem prosodic template

Table 4.1 *Pairwise distances among examined templates, including component nodes*

	1	2	3	4	5	6	7	8	9	10	11	12	13	14	15	16	17	18	19	20
AghemClause	0.00																			
BantuCA	0.66	0.00																		
BantuCT	0.54	0.28	0.00																	
BantuVCy	0.59	0.21	0.24	0.00																
ChechenPreverbalA	0.77	0.72	0.72	0.67	0.00															
ChichewaAR	0.63	0.11	0.35	0.29	0.68	0.00														
ChintangPrefixes	0.64	0.57	0.59	0.50	0.61	0.62	0.00													
EnglishPlural	0.72	0.41	0.49	0.37	0.56	0.48	0.32	0.00												
EnglishVP	0.50	0.34	0.43	0.30	0.77	0.41	0.43	0.57	0.00											
GermanClause	0.52	0.71	0.59	0.67	0.87	0.74	0.75	0.80	0.61	0.00										
MandeClause	0.31	0.55	0.44	0.49	0.78	0.59	0.57	0.67	0.33	0.45	0.00									
MeskwakiClause	0.36	0.59	0.43	0.54	0.83	0.63	0.65	0.73	0.40	0.38	0.21	0.00								
NdebeleCA	0.53	0.23	0.11	0.27	0.74	0.30	0.58	0.51	0.42	0.63	0.40	0.47	0.00							
NimboranVerb	0.51	0.62	0.53	0.64	0.76	0.61	0.75	0.75	0.61	0.59	0.49	0.51	0.52	0.00						
SerboCroatianJe	0.75	0.64	0.62	0.54	0.44	0.68	0.57	0.56	0.65	0.77	0.69	0.70	0.64	0.80	0.00					
SerboCroatianTopicalization	0.77	0.82	0.78	0.74	0.59	0.80	0.70	0.81	0.76	0.81	0.77	0.78	0.78	0.79	0.63	0.00				
TieneVerbProsodic	0.76	0.78	0.77	0.73	0.41	0.77	0.56	0.67	0.71	0.84	0.74	0.80	0.77	0.75	0.65	0.48	0.00			
TieneVerbSegments	0.56	0.50	0.50	0.47	0.73	0.49	0.59	0.67	0.33	0.61	0.54	0.53	0.55	0.61	0.71	0.70	0.65	0.00		
TurkishNominalMinimality	0.77	0.82	0.78	0.74	0.63	0.80	0.74	0.81	0.76	0.81	0.77	0.78	0.78	0.79	0.67	0.08	0.48	0.70	0.00	
TurkishVerbalMinimality	0.75	0.82	0.78	0.74	0.59	0.78	0.74	0.81	0.76	0.81	0.77	0.78	0.78	0.79	0.67	0.16	0.48	0.70	0.08	0.00

4.2 From graphs to a similarity metric

for the two very similar Turkish templates to a maximum of .85 for the distance of the German clause and the Meskwaki clause templates from the Chechen Preverbal *'a* template.[6]

It is not easy to extrapolate patterns directly from a set of distances like those given in Table 4.1. However, the information within them can be visualized using various methods, such as the NeighborNet algorithm (Bryant & Moulton 2004) as implemented in SplitsTree4 (Huson & Bryant 2006). This can create a splits graph (see Bandelt & Dress (1992a,b) and Dress & Huson (2004)) and produces a visualization of the distances among the templates as a network joining them together, as will be seen in Figure 4.5. NeighborNet has become relatively popular as a means of analyzing linguistic data for historical purposes, where its networks are open to interpretation as depictions of the evolution of linguistic features (see Bryant et al. (2005), Nichols & Warnow (2008: 776), Cysouw & Forker (2009: 590), and Heggarty et al. (2010: 3833–3834)). It has also been used for non-historical purposes, in a manner comparable to its application here, as in, for instance, Bickel (2010: 85), Cysouw & Comrie (2009), and Bakker et al. (2011). In such cases, the graph should be interpreted as depicting patterns of similarity and difference (according to whatever metric is being used) where the objects being compared cannot neatly be placed within a single taxonomic tree. Informally speaking, where the network appears less reticulated and more tree-like (see Wichmann et al. (2011)), objects appearing in the tree-like area are simultaneously relatively similar to each other and relatively dissimilar to the other objects being compared. Where the network is more reticulated (i.e., has an

(Section 3.5.5, Figure 3.16); TieneVerbSegments, Tiene verb stem segmental template (Section 3.5.5, Figure 3.17); TurkishNominalMinimality, Turkish disyllabic minimal size restriction template for nouns (Section 3.2; Figure 3.1); TurkishVerbalMinimality, Turkish disyllabic minimal size restriction template for verbs (Section 3.2; Figure 3.2).

[6] On the whole, the schematic representation of the comparison algorithm discussed above applies straightforwardly to the cases of the graphs used to describe the templates if one uses node labels to treat two nodes as the "same." However, an issue arises for node labels that can be repeated, such as those for components. In effect, the way distance is calculated in such cases here is that, wherever possible, repeatable nodes are "matched" with each other in pairs until there are no more possible matches. Thus, for instance, if a template with two component nodes is compared to one with five, they will be treated as having two matching nodes and three non-matching nodes for the *component* type. Those interested in the full details of the implementation of this procedure will find the copies of the scripts used to calculate the distances at https://github.com/jcgood/desmeme. The scripts also implement a pre-processing stage for the templatic descriptions that is required, but of no theoretical import, wherein some information found in the template graphs in the actual database is removed for the purposes of comparison since it is not typologically relevant, e.g., metadata indicating the source of the templatic description. This same pre-processing was applied in the creation of the feature structure representations given for the various templates in Chapter 3. Accordingly, the descriptions presented there are the same as those that entered into the calculation of the distance measures seen in this chapter.

228   Typologizing templates: comparison

appearance closer to that of a net), this means that the patterns of similarity and dissimilarity are not as clearcut.

Given this background, it is now possible present a general picture of the extent to which the different templates in the database are similar to each other. This will be done in the following section, where splits graphs will be presented based on data like that in Table 4.1, with an additional way of measuring the distance among templates, removing most information about components, presented as well.

Before moving on, it will be helpful at this point return to an issue discussed in Section 2.5.5: The status of templates embedded within templates. As discussed, there are clear cases of descriptions of templates whose components contain other templates (see, e.g., the Serbo-Croatian second-position clitic template in Section 3.7). However, the full formal characterization of these in the database has been avoided to this point. The reasons for this are practical, not conceptual, in nature, and the greatest practical barrier involves developing appropriate measures of comparison for cases of templates containing templates. For instance, the similarity metric just introduced is not able to distinguish nodes which belong to a higher-level template from those belonging to an embedded template, which would most likely result in templates containing templates to diverge from other templates in ways which reflect the properties of the embedded templates more than the overall template itself. Of course, it would be possible to alter this metric (or devise different ones), which would mitigate such problems, but pursuing this has not been deemed a priority at this stage of investigation.

4.2.3   An overall view of templatic similarity in the database

In Figure 4.5, a split graph is presented based on the distances given in Table 4.1. From it one can get an overview of which templates are most alike in terms of the overlap among their nodes. There are various clusters among the templates that are visible. One of these contains the Bantu templates involving verb extension ordering discussed in Section 3.5. Given that all of these templates operate over a similar unit within a language family and impose restrictions on relative ordering, its presence is not particularly surprising. More interesting is the somewhat weaker link between the Tiene segment template and the English verb phrase, though, as will be discussed shortly below, this appears to be largely connected to the fact that there are similarities among the components in both sets of templates, rather than due to their higher-level properties. Another noteworthy cluster involves the various clausal templates, suggesting that templatic constructions at the clausal level, in general, may show high levels of similarity in their form. The Nimboran verb also appears to be relatively close to the clausal templates, which is more surprising, though it

4.2 From graphs to a similarity metric

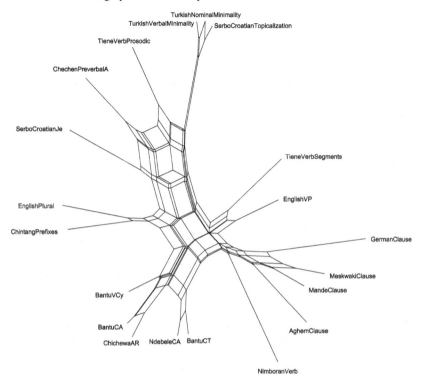

Figure 4.5 Split graph for similarity among templates, including components

is clear from its description that is probably an unusual case in cross-linguistic terms. Towards the top of the figure, one sees a clustering of templates that are found in diverse morphosyntactic contexts but which share an important property of being length templates consisting of two components, which gives them many overlapping nodes. A final cluster worth noting is the small one linking the English plural construction to the Chintang verbal prefix template. Here, the two straightforward affixal constructions are patterning together, revealing that the Chintang template may, in some sense, be the least "templatic" of the templates surveyed here, with its only unexpected linearization property being its choice of host and with its other properties being more canonically affixal. This result is not especially surprising, though clearly there is some value in verifying it in this way. (However, as will be seen in Figure 4.6 below, this similarity between the two templates is largely driven by shared nodes among components rather than higher-level templatic features.)

In addition to visualizing clustering patterns, a further way in which Figure 4.5 represents similarity and difference is in the lengths of the paths that

230 Typologizing templates: comparison

would connect any two templates in the graph. For instance, the path between the two Turkish templates is quite short, reflecting their closeness. By contrast, even though the Nimboran verb template clusters with the clausal templates, the path connecting it to them is relatively long, indicating it is not nearly as similar to those clausal templates as the Turkish templates are to each other.

The nature of the node-based graph comparison algorithm used to generate the distances in Table 4.1 means that there will be an inherent bias towards treating templates with similar numbers of components as more alike than templates with different numbers of components, since all of the nodes associated with the template's components will contribute to the distance scores. Thus, for instance, two templates that were very similar except for the fact that one had a large number of components and the other very few will come out as relatively different because it is impossible for the nodes associated with the "extra" components of the template with more components to be the same as any nodes in the template with fewer components. In order to see what effect this has on the overall picture of template similarity seen in Figure 4.5, we can modify the distance metrics in ways the minimize the impact of the number of components. For instance, in Table 4.2, a new set of distance measures is given where all nodes relating to components (i.e., from a node labeled *component* downwards in the graph) are excluded from the template comparison. For these distance measures, the only information about the components in the template is found in the value of the COUNT feature associated with the template's stricture. The new distances range from zero (i.e., sharing all non-component nodes), for the pairing of the Mande clause and Meskwaki clause templates, to .95, for a number of the clausal templates with the Chechen Preverbal *'a* template and a number of the two-unit prosodic templates with the Bantu Causative–Transitive template and the Ndebele Causative–Applicative template.

The overall picture of similarity that emerges from this revised distance measure can be seen in Figure 4.6. A number of the more coherent clusters from Figure 4.5 remain, for instance constituting the various Bantu templates (excluding those associated with the Tiene verb), many of the two-unit prosodic templates, and the clausal templates. At the same time, a number of other templates have shifted. For instance, the Chintang verbal prefix template is no longer closely linked to the English plural construction, the English verb phrase now patterns more closely with the clausal templates, and the Serbo-Croatian second-position clitic construction no longer clusters closely with the other two-unit templates.

Of course, these remarks do not exhaust the observations that can be made based on an examination of Figures 4.5 and 4.6. At the same time, given the relatively limited size of the database, as well as the fact that it is based on a convenience sample, it would seem premature to arrive at strong conclusions on the basis of these results. What is clear, however, is that the comparatively

Table 4.2 *Pairwise distances among examined templates, excluding component nodes*

AghemClause	0.00																			
BantuCA	0.76	0.00																		
BantuCT	0.71	0.38	0.00																	
BantuVCy	0.76	0.18	0.25	0.00																
ChechenPreverbalA	0.84	0.83	0.84	0.83	0.00															
ChichewaAR	0.65	0.31	0.56	0.43	0.72	0.00														
ChintangPrefixes	0.64	0.62	0.64	0.62	0.81	0.75	0.00													
EnglishPlural	0.76	0.33	0.25	0.18	0.76	0.53	0.50	0.00												
EnglishVP	0.54	0.50	0.64	0.50	0.94	0.67	0.40	0.62	0.00											
GermanClause	0.57	0.73	0.67	0.73	0.95	0.83	0.58	0.73	0.45	0.00										
MandeClause	0.46	0.64	0.57	0.64	0.95	0.76	0.45	0.64	0.30	0.20	0.00									
MeskwakiClause	0.46	0.64	0.57	0.64	0.95	0.76	0.45	0.64	0.30	0.20	0.00	0.00								
NdebeleCA	0.71	0.25	0.17	0.38	0.84	0.47	0.64	0.38	0.64	0.67	0.57	0.57	0.00							
NimboranVerb	0.71	0.83	0.78	0.83	0.78	0.79	0.81	0.83	0.81	0.67	0.75	0.75	0.78	0.00						
SerboCroatianJe	0.83	0.57	0.60	0.57	0.50	0.71	0.50	0.46	0.71	0.81	0.73	0.73	0.60	0.83	0.00					
SerboCroatianTopicalization	0.89	0.94	0.95	0.94	0.46	0.89	0.79	0.88	0.94	0.94	0.94	0.94	0.95	0.75	0.73	0.00				
TieneVerbProsodic	0.89	0.94	0.95	0.94	0.57	0.89	0.87	0.88	0.94	0.94	0.94	0.94	0.95	0.75	0.81	0.36	0.00			
TieneVerbSegments	0.69	0.67	0.76	0.67	0.83	0.63	0.71	0.75	0.62	0.81	0.73	0.73	0.76	0.76	0.82	0.73	0.73	0.00		
TurkishNominalMinimality	0.89	0.94	0.95	0.94	0.57	0.89	0.87	0.88	0.94	0.94	0.94	0.94	0.95	0.75	0.81	0.20	0.36	0.73	0.00	
TurkishVerbalMinimality	0.82	0.94	0.95	0.94	0.46	0.83	0.87	0.88	0.94	0.94	0.94	0.94	0.95	0.75	0.81	0.36	0.36	0.73	0.20	0.00

232   Typologizing templates: comparison

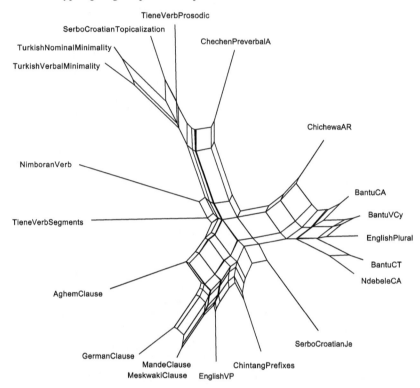

Figure 4.6 Split graph for similarity among templates, excluding components

complex formalism used here does not present an insurmountable barrier to rigorous typological comparison. One simply needs to devise or adapt appropriate metrics and apply them consistently. What the "ideal" metrics may be for typological studies of this kind must, at this point, however, be left as an open question.

Before moving on, it is worth addressing a final point regarding the presentation of split graphs as in Figures 4.5 and 4.6. Overall, it is not clear how much more we have learned from examining them than we might have learned by simply looking at the various formal descriptions of templates by hand – for instance, it does not take a sophisticated algorithm to reveal that prosodic templates consisting of two components all have quite a bit in common. The logic of examining such methods, in fact, is not to explore the composition of the database as it stands now – after all, twenty different templatic constructions (including the two English controls) is not all that many. Rather, the goal is to ensure that, if the database were to be scaled to hundreds, or even thousands,

4.3 Detecting similar subparts of templates

of constructions – which would presumably be required to properly investigate patterns of linear stipulation – methods are available which would allow for systematic examination of similarities and differences among all the constructions in the database, even when comparison by hand becomes infeasible. This goal seems attainable, largely due to the fact that other fields (especially biology) have already been concerned with working with large graph-based datasets.

In the next section, a different method of graph comparison will be explored that makes use of information in both nodes and edges in order to find nodes across a pair of graphs that are most similar to each other in terms of their overall environment within the graph. Again, the goal will be to establish that methods already exist to examine different facets of similarity and dissimilarity in graph-based descriptions of data, rather than to arrive at definitive conclusions.

4.3 Detecting similar subparts of templates

4.3.1 Examining nodes and arcs in graph comparison

The graph similarity algorithm described above in Section 4.2 provided a relatively simple way of arriving at an overall set of similarity scores across pairings of templatic constructions. In this section, a more complex algorithm will be introduced that adapts the *similarity flooding* approach of Melnik et al. (2002).[7] It is considered here for two reasons. First, unlike the simUI method discussed above, it takes into account the information contained in both node labels and arc labels, and thus provides an example of how the latter kind of information can be used to assess graph similarity. Second, it is designed to assess similarity not across graphs as a whole but, rather, for pairs of nodes across two graphs, thus showing how rich, graph-based representations can be exploited for varying purposes.

To situate this discussion in a more usual typological context, the previous section described an approach that was akin to assessing the similarity of basic clausal word orders by assigning categories like SOV, SVO, VSO, etc., similarity scores based on more than just a holistic pattern of linearization. For instance, it would be as if one considered whether or not the verb and object were adjacent or the subject preceded the object for each type when comparing basic word orders. In this section, we will consider how to assess the extent to which, say, the subject of an SVO language is more or less like the object in an OVS language, based on some multivariate classification of these types –

---

[7] The longer, unpublished technical report of Melnik et al. (2001), upon which Melnik et al. (2002) is based, was also consulted in adapting the similarity flooding algorithm to the data of interest here.

234   Typologizing templates: comparison

in other words, one is trying to assess the similarity of substructures within a larger structure.

It should be made clear that the choice of employing the similarity flooding algorithm in comparing templates here is somewhat opportunistic as well: it has already been developed, is well described, and associated with available implementations.[8] The algorithm itself is based on two quite distinct procedures. The first takes two graphs as input to a process that creates a kind of "merged" graph, specifically termed a *pairwise connectivity graph*. This represents those parts of the graphs which share structure on the basis of comparison of arc labels and will be described in more detail in Section 4.3.2. The second procedure is iterative in nature and uses the structure of the pairwise connectivity graph to assign scores to pairs of nodes, ranking them for their overall similarity to each other when compared against the other possible pairings of nodes across the graphs. This will be described in detail in Section 4.3.3.

The two procedures are logically distinct. The first represents a powerful way of determining, of all possible pairs of nodes across two graphs, which are likely to be similar to each other based on their overall context in terms of the nodes and arcs which they are connected to both directly and indirectly. The second has a comparable goal to the simUI algorithm, discussed in Section 4.2 – to find a way to quantify patterns of graph similarity so as to facilitate rigorous comparison – though, as will be seen, the quantification is achieved in a very different way. In any future efforts adapting this algorithm for typological work, the first part of the procedure is likely to be maintained more or less as it is described here since it applies quite generally to any pair of graphs. The second part, however, needs to take the actual domain being modeled into account in assigning various numeric scores to different pairings of nodes across graphs, for reasons that will be made clearer in Section 4.3.3.

After the version of the algorithm employed here is introduced, illustrative examples of its application to specific pairs of templates will be discussed in Section 4.3.4.

4.3.2   *Pairwise connectivity graphs*

The similarity flooding algorithm is based on an intuition that two elements are more similar to each other to the extent that are found in similar contexts. From a formal perspective, this is understood to be the case when a given pair of nodes across two graphs shares more arcs with the same label in a subgraph of their original graph than another pair of nodes shares. To assess the extent that two nodes are found in a comparable contexts across two graphs,

---

[8]   The implementation used here can be found at https://github.com/jcgood/desmeme and is based on the version written in Perl by Shohei Kameda found on the Comprehensive Perl Archive Network (CPAN; www.cpan.org).

4.3 Detecting similar subparts of templates

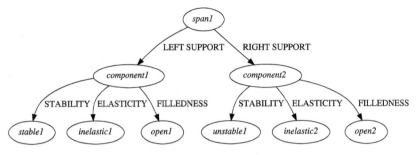

Figure 4.7 First schematic graph to illustrate pairwise connectivity

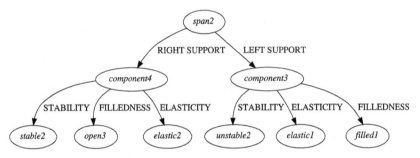

Figure 4.8 Second schematic graph to illustrate pairwise connectivity

a pairwise connectivity graph is constructed on the basis of those parts of the graphs where arc labels are shared.

The nature of this process is probably best illustrated through example. In Figures 4.7 and 4.8, two sample representations are given of fragment descriptions of possible template foundations. (The nature of the process through which pairwise connectivity graphs are created would make presentation of the entire pairwise connectivity graph for a full templatic description impractical for illustration and is also why the foundation descriptions are abbreviated, for instance by not including all the component features seen elsewhere.) Unlike the other graph-based presentations of templatic descriptions presented to this point (see, e.g., Figure 4.3), the node labels are suffixed with integers. These are purely used to help differentiate the nodes being referred to when discussing the formation of the pairwise connectivity graph based on these two graphs and have no theoretical or descriptive significance.

As can be seen, Figures 4.7 and 4.8 describe two span foundations associated with two components, each with its own features and values. Focusing on the components, if we were to examine these graphs impressionistically, there is a sense in which *component1* in Figure 4.7 and *component3* in Figure 4.8 are

236   Typologizing templates: comparison

similar insofar as they are both serving as left supports. At the same time, *component1* and *component4* also have salient similarities in that both are stable and open, therefore sharing two out of three of their feature values. By contrast, *component1* and *component3* do not share any feature values, though they are not completely dissimilar in that regard insofar as they are actually specified for those features (as are all components). In Figure 4.9, an initial formalization of these intuitions regarding similarity is presented in the form of a pairwise connectivity graph, in the sense developed in Melnik et al. (2002). This is not the final version of the pairwise connectivity graph that will be used to assess node similarity, but this intermediate representation is useful for purposes of illustration.

The pairwise connectivity graph in Figure 4.9 is constructed as follows: for any given arc label shared across the two graphs (e.g., LEFT SUPPORT), the nodes at the origin of the arc (e.g., *span1* and *span2*) are paired together to create a new composite node (e.g., *span1/span2*) and the nodes at the destination of the arc (e.g., *component1* and *component3*) are similarly paired together (e.g., *component1/component3*) and joined by an arc of that same original type. This results in, for instance, the LEFT SUPPORT arc in Figure 4.9 connecting the span nodes of the two graphs in Figures 4.7 and 4.8 with two component nodes. Since these two component nodes themselves share three features (FILLEDNESS, STABILITY, and ELASTICITY) further node pairs are joined across these features, as also seen in Figure 4.9. The same pairing process applies to the right supports of the two original foundation graphs as well, and in any other instances where two nodes share an arc label, even if the arc labels are repeated in the graph. Thus, for instance, *component2* appears in two places in the pairwise connectivity graph. It pairs with the other right support, *component4*, as well as with the other component in the graph in Figure 4.8, *component3*, since each of these components also share the FILLEDNESS, STABILITY, and ELASTICITY features.

As can be seen in Figure 4.9, the process through which a pairwise connectivity graph is created will not necessarily result in a graph where all the nodes are connected, reflecting the fact that nodes may only share arcs across limited parts of the original graphs. Thus, there are three subgraphs which are disconnected from each other in the pairwise connectivity graph created from the graphs in Figures 4.7 and 4.8. This corresponds to the fact that two of the component node pairs across the graphs are cases where the nodes share the same role in the foundation (and are, therefore, connected to the paired span foundation node), while the other two play different roles in the foundation and are, therefore, "detached" from that portion of the graph when the pairwise connectivity graph is formed.

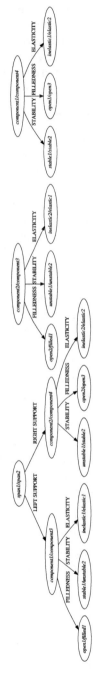

Figure 4.9 Pairwise connectivity graph for the graphs in Figures 4.7 and 4.8

238   Typologizing templates: comparison

The pairwise connectivity graph can be understood as a representation of the extent to which any given pair of nodes across two graphs are found in a comparable context. The next step of the similarity flooding algorithm is to make use of this representation to come up with a quantitative measure of similarity across pairs of nodes, which is discussed in Section 4.3.3 immediately below.

4.3.3   *Pairwise connectivity graphs and nodal similarity*

The construction of a pairwise connectivity graph, such as the one presented in Figure 4.9, represents, in some sense, the "similarity" step of the similarity flooding algorithm. The next step is to apply an iterative procedure through which each node pairing receives a numeric score that potentially reflects both the nature of the pairing itself (e.g., whether two nodes of the same type paired or not) as well as the similarity scores of nearby nodes. This follows from an intuition that the similarities between two nodes should reflect both the properties of the nodes themselves and the extent to which the nodes they are connected to are also similar.

The specific iterative process employed here adapts that of Melnik et al. (2002) to reflect the fact that the input data is somewhat different. The first step involves converting the pairwise connectivity graphs of the sort seen in Figure 4.9 to graphs of the form given in Figure 4.10.[9] This transformation involves: (i) removing the original arc labels, (ii) adding arcs in the opposite direction from their original one for all pairs of composite nodes, and (iii) assigning each arc a numeric weighting calculated by dividing the number of outgoing arcs from each node by one (so that the total weighting across all of the outgoing arcs of a given composite node will always add up to one). The effect of this is to transform the original graph into a kind of network, where, on the one hand, the similarity scores of nearby nodes can be "transmitted" to each other, but, on the other hand, the amount of information transmitted from a node to its neighbors is inversely proportional to the number of neighbors it has.[10] This network then becomes the basis of an iterative process

---

[9] Graphs such as those in Figures 4.9 and 4.10 (as well as comparable graphs seen elsewhere in this book) have been automatically generated from an abstract specification using the DOT graph description language and the Graphviz toolkit (Gansner & North 2000). One result of this automatic rendering of the graphs is that their layout may be altered as the details of their content change. This explains why the same sets of nodes and basic arc relations are presented quite differently between Figures 4.9 and 4.10.

[10] The procedure through which the arc weighting is determined here differs from that presented in Melnik et al. (2002). (Following Melnik et al. (2001: 9), it is reasonable to compute this in different ways.) Melnik et al. (2002) assign weightings in a way that is inversely proportional to the number of neighbors formed from arcs that originally shared labels. This is reasonable for their example cases, but, in the graphs developed here, there is generally only one arc with a given label leading from any node, which would not result in such weightings having any meaningful effect. The procedure adopted here is based on the following logic: (i) it produces

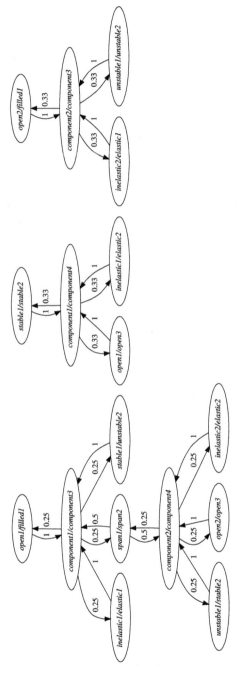

Figure 4.10 Transformation of the pairwise connectivity graph in Figure 4.9 for flooding

240   Typologizing templates: comparison

for calculating a similarity score for each composite node. This can be taken as a metric for the similarity of the pair of nodes across the original graphs that formed the composite node. The application of this iterative process is reminiscent of the use of simple recurrent networks associated with connectionist models of cognitive processes employing neural networks, which may be familiar to some readers (see, e.g., Jordan (1986, 1997) and Elman (1990, 1991)).

The similarity flooding algorithm in general does not specify all of the details required for its application. So, the description of its iterative application here should be taken as specific to the present investigation. The first step is to assign an initial score between zero and one to each composite node which will serve as the input to the initial iteration. Here, the score is assigned as follows: if two nodes are of the same type, they are given a score of one. Otherwise, they are given a score of .5 (to reflect the fact that, while their types may be different, they must still be near subtypes of a higher supertype due to the way the description language is constructed). In Table 4.3 the similarity scores for the composite nodes in Figure 4.10 are given, with the "zero" iteration reflecting this initial weighting and the following columns labeled with integers corresponding to the scores of subsequent iterations.

Once the initial weightings are set, the iteration begins. Each node adds to the similarity score of its neighbors in proportion to its own similarity score multiplied by the weighting label on its outgoing arcs. In a case like the *unstable1/stable2* pairing (found at the bottom of the leftmost subgraph in Figure 4.10), this means that all of its weight (.5) is added to the weight of *component2/component4* since it has only one outgoing arc. This process of similarity distribution is not "destructive." So, *unstable1/stable2* retains the original .5 similarity score even after its similarity is transmitted to *component2/component4*. At the same time, *unstable1/stable2* also sees its similarity score increased on this iteration by .25 (to .75) due to the similarity contribution from *component2/component4*, which starts with a score of one and transmits one-quarter of that score to each of its neighboring nodes. This process is applied across all node pairings along with a normalization procedure to keep the similarity scores between one and zero across the nodes in the pairwise connectivity graph. (This is done by dividing all final scores by whatever the highest score ends up being among all the nodes of the graph.) In the case of the first iteration, *component1/component4* and *component2/component4* would both be tied for the highest similarity score of 3.5, and this becomes

clear differences across the arcs in terms of weightings and (ii) the nature of the iterative process assigning similarity scores to be described below causes scores to "flow" back and forth between neighbors, meaning that, if the outgoing flow from a node with many neighbors is not attenuated somehow, its similarity scores will quickly increase in ways which seem to make meaningful cross-node comparison more difficult.

4.3 Detecting similar subparts of templates 241

Table 4.3 *Application of four iterations of similarity flooding procedure*

NODE↓ ITER→	0	1	2	3	4
component1/component3	1	0.86	0.86	0.86	0.87
component1/component4	1	1	1	1	1
component2/component3	1	0.86	0.86	0.86	0.86
component2/component4	1	1	1	1	0.99
inelastic1/elastic1	0.5	0.21	0.21	0.21	0.21
inelastic1/elastic2	0.5	0.24	0.29	0.31	0.32
inelastic2/elastic1	0.5	0.24	0.26	0.27	0.28
inelastic2/elastic2	0.5	0.21	0.23	0.24	0.24
open1/filled1	0.5	0.21	0.21	0.21	0.21
open1/open3	1	0.38	0.36	0.35	0.34
open2/filled1	0.5	0.24	0.26	0.27	0.28
open2/open3	1	0.36	0.3	0.28	0.26
span1/span2	1	0.43	0.45	0.46	0.46
stable1/stable2	1	0.38	0.36	0.35	0.34
stable1/unstable2	0.5	0.21	0.21	0.21	0.21
unstable1/stable2	0.5	0.21	0.23	0.24	0.24
unstable1/unstable2	1	0.38	0.33	0.31	0.3

the factor by which all the similarity scores are divided. Thus, for example, the new score of the *unstable1/stable2* node, just discussed, would become .75/3.5, which is around .21, as given in the table.

After the scores are all calculated and normalized, the entire process repeats, producing a new set of normalized scores that feed into the next iteration. Iteration continues until some predefined condition is reached. For the example developed here (as well as for the results discussed below in Section 4.3.4), following Melnik et al. (2001: 121), this condition is determined by calculating when the differences between the similarity scores across the current iteration and the immediately previous iteration fall below a predetermined threshold.[11]

The final results of the application of this process to the example graphs are seen in Table 4.3, which gives the composite node similarity scores across the four iterations that were required before the predefined termination threshold was reached. The scores clearly delineate the four logically possible

[11] The threshold used here is based on the measure of the Euclidean distance of the residual vector found by the subtraction of the similarities across the composite nodes in one iteration from those of the immediately preceding iteration. That is, the difference in the similarity scores across each pair of nodes is squared, and, then, the distance is calculated as the square root of the sum of these squared distances. An arbitrary cutoff of .05 is used here such that when the Euclidean distance between scores across an iteration and its immediately preceding iteration is less than or equal to .05, the algorithm terminates. Determination of an "ideal" cutoff threshold will have to await further research, but .05 seems to work here for expository purposes.

242   Typologizing templates: comparison

component pairs as more similar to each other than any of the other node pairs. The least similar component pair (*component2/component3*) has a similarity of score .86, with the next most similar pair of nodes (*span1/span2*) having a score of only .46. Based on the graphs in Figures 4.7 and 4.8, this seems like a reasonable result: the components share a number of features and also are found in similar overall positions in their respective graphs. (Of course, things will be somewhat different when full templatic graphs are considered in Section 4.3.4 since there will be many more nodes to consider in a wider range of environments.)

Moreover, the relative ranking of component pairs also seems reasonable: the *component1/component4* and *component2/component4* pairings are almost equally similar with a clear break between them and the other pairs, reflecting that fact that the *component1/component4* pairing shares more values of its features than the other component pairs, and the fact that the *component2/component4* pairing shares one value (represented by *open1/open2*) as well as having overlapping positioning in the rest of the graph by virtue of both of its source nodes serving in the role of RIGHT SUPPORT. By contrast, the *component2/component4* pairing shares only one feature, namely *unstable1/unstable2*, and does not share wider structural context, and the *component1/component3* pairing shares no component features but does share structural context. Thus, both these pairings seem impressionistically less similar to the other pairings while being similar to each other (in that each is lacking similarity in one domain while having it another). This is in line with the scores they received via this algorithm.

It is important to bear in mind that, given the nature of the graph-based templatic descriptions being used here, nodes that are "centrally" located in the template graph, in the sense of having many connections to other nodes (e.g., foundation nodes which are both pointed to by the *desmeme* node and point to component nodes), will be biased towards having higher scores than peripheral nodes, which will be comparatively lacking in connections. Thus, some aspects of the scoring seen in cases like the exemplary data in Table 4.3 should be viewed as artifacts of the description language rather than as substantive linguistic results, for example the fact that the component features have lower similarity scores than other features. At the same time, when we look within sets of nodes of a single type, the comparisons can be considered to represent non-artifactual results. For instance, the *inelastic1/elastic1* composite node has a considerably lower similarity score than the *inelastic1/elastic2* node, even though both represent an elastic–inelastic "mismatch" and would otherwise seem quite similar. This reflects the fact that *inelastic1/elastic2* is found in an overall environment of higher graph similarity than *inelastic1/elastic1*, most saliently represented by the higher similarity score

4.3 Detecting similar subparts of templates 243

for its one neighbor, *component1/component4*, than for the one neighbor of *inelastic1/elastic1*, *component1/component3*.[12]

The next section presents some sample results from the application of the version of the similarity flooding algorithm developed above to representative pairs of templates from the database. Before moving on, it seems worthwhile to emphasize an important positive feature of this algorithm: it is general in nature and not specific to templatic descriptions. Therefore, there is nothing, in principle, preventing its use with any kind of typological description that is well characterized using graphs.

4.3.4 Some sample results from the database

In this section, using three examples of templatic descriptions, the results of the application of the variant of the similarity flooding algorithm used here will be presented for two pairs of templates (one templatic description will be used twice). The three templates to be considered are the Chechen Preverbal *'a* template discussed in Section 3.6, the Mande clause template discussed in Section 3.10, and the Aghem clause template discussed in Section 3.9. First, the Chechen and Mande templates will be compared, and then the Mande and Aghem templates. The logic of these choices is that they represent a pairing of two templates that are relatively structurally dissimilar, Chechen and Mande, and two that are relatively structurally similar, Mande and Aghem (see, e.g., the distance measures in Table 4.1). This will allow for examination of the application of the algorithm in two distinct contexts to see what kinds of results arise in each.

The formal characterization for the Chechen template in the form of a feature structure was presented in Figure 3.19 and for the Mande template in Figure 3.27. In this section, it will be helpful to present them instead in graph-based form, as in Figure 4.11 for Chechen and Figure 4.12 for Mande. The node labels are adapted for ease of reference in cases where there are distinct nodes of the same type within and across the templates, in a manner comparable to what was presented in Figures 4.7 and 4.8. In particular, nodes in

---

[12] By contrast, the relative scores of the *inelastic1/elastic2* an *inelastic2/elastic2* nodes (.32 vs. .24 for the final iteration) in Table 4.3 are not as intuitive given that they seem to be in quite similar overall environments. Here, the crucial factor seems to be the .25 outgoing weighting on the *component2/component4* node, which limits the extent to which its comparatively high similarity score can be transmitted to the *inelastic2/elastic2* node. Insofar as this result seems counterintuitive, it suggests that the means of assigning weights to arc edges should perhaps be modified in some way. Since the goal here is to explore the use of graph similarity algorithms to establish the feasibility of typology using complex structural representations of the sort developed here, rather than to defend specific metrics or come to conclusions based on the results of those metrics, I leave this issue open since the present application of similarity flooding seems sufficient for establishing feasibility.

244 Typologizing templates: comparison

Table 4.4 *Similarity scores for the Chechen (Figure 4.11) and Mande (Figure 4.12) templates*

CHECHEN/MANDE	SIMILARITY
component-c2/component-m1	1.00
component-c1/component-m1	0.99
component-c1/component-m5	0.99
component-c1/component-m3	0.92
component-c2/component-m5	0.92
component-c1/component-m2	0.92
component-c1/component-m4	0.91
component-c2/component-m3	0.83
component-c2/component-m2	0.83
desmeme/desmeme	0.77
component-c2/component-m4	0.75
span/arch	0.65
length/order	0.63
prosodicWord/syntacticConstituent	0.21
lexicoconstructionalConditioning/constructionalConditioning	0.19
potentiallyViolable/notViolable	0.19

the Chechen template of repeated types (such as component nodes) are suffix with a string such of form *-cn* (where *n* is an integer), and comparable nodes in the Mande template are appended with *-mn*. Nodes whose values are integers (e.g., the values of a feature like COUNT) are indicated with the name of the relevant feature in lowercase and italics, followed by the integer of their value, followed by a suffix of the form just described. Thus, *count1-c1* refers to a count value of one for a Chechen COUNT feature and *minimum0-m3* refers to a minimum value of zero for a MINIMUM in Mande (e.g., for an elastic component). The MAXIMUM100-M1 label refers to a maximum that was coded as infinity in the feature structure representation of the Mande clause template. This reflects the fact that, in the database, 100, rather than the infinity symbol, is used as a placeholder for "no maximum." With respect to the similarity flooding calculations, these alterations to the labels are irrelevant since they were not factored into the comparison itself in any crucial way.

In Table 4.4, similarity scores are given across select node pairs for the Chechen and Mande template graphs seen in Figures 4.11 and 4.12.[13] The chosen nodes are those which were part of the pairwise connectivity graph but not

[13] The full set of similarity scores across all desmemes discussed in Chapter 3 for node pairs that had a similarity greater than or equal to .05 can be found in the file FloodingSimilarities.txt at https://github.com/jcgood/desmeme/blob/master/FloodingSimilarities.txt.

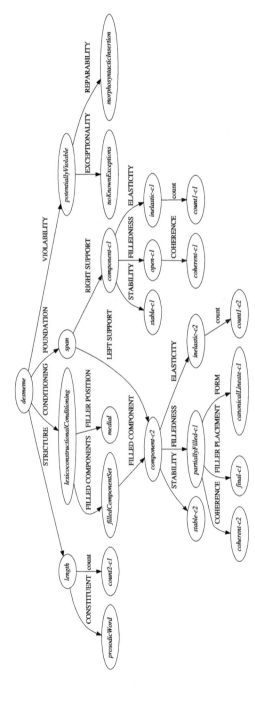

Figure 4.11 The Chechen template in Figure 3.19 as a graph

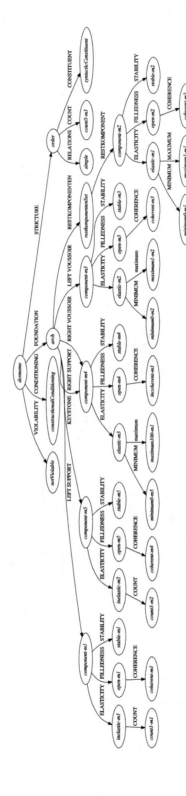

Figure 4.12 The Mande template in Figure 3.27 as a graph

4.3 Detecting similar subparts of templates 247

those with integer values or serving as component features, since this allows us to focus on similarities across higher-level features of the templates. As can be seen, the two greatest points of similarity, following the algorithm employed here, hold between the pairings of *component-c2/component-m1*, *component-c1/component-m1*, and *component-c1/component-m5*, reflecting the fact that the Chechen template's components share many features with the Mande template's left support and keystone. In addition, the *component-c2/component-m1* pairing involves two left supports, which further raises its score by placing the two components in a comparatively large pairwise connectivity graph. Similarly, the *component-c1/component-m4* pairing also scores comparatively high, reflecting the fact that these two components each serve in the role of right support in their respective templates, even though their internal features do not otherwise overlap considerably. The other component pairing similarities simply reflect greater or lesser similarities among component-level features. Further aspects of the remaining pairings will be discussed below when the Chechen and Mande template similarity scores are contrasted with the Mande and Aghem ones.

A graph-based representation of the Aghem clausal template, containing the same information as the feature structure representation in Figure 3.25 and following the labeling conventions discussed above for the Chechen and Mande templates, is given in Figure 4.13. In Table 4.5, similarity scores are given across select node pairs for the Aghem and Mande template graphs, parallel to what was given in Table 4.4.

As can be seen in Table 4.5, the overall patterns of similarity for the Aghem and Mande templates are somewhat distinctive from those for the Chechen and Mande templates. For instance, for Aghem and Mande, the foundation node pairing of *arch/arch* gets the highest similarity score, reflecting the overall similarity in the foundations of the two templates, each consisting of a relatively large number of components arranged in an arch foundation. Moreover, the position of the foundation node in the "middle" of the graph biases its similarity score towards being high, all other things being equal (see Section 4.3.3). The fact that the similarity scores for the components in Table 4.5 are lower than those for Table 4.4 should not, therefore, be taken as an indication that they are somehow less similar to each other than in the Chechen and Mande case. This is because the similarity flooding algorithm only produces a relative ranking of similarity. What this means then is that, for the Chechen and Mande case, high-level structural patterns of greater similarity were not detected, but only low-level ones at the level of the component were, while this was not the case for Aghem and Mande precisely because there was a high-level similarity at the level of the foundation.

Beyond this, the component pairing rankings in Table 4.5 follow patterns already seen above. Component similarity is a function of shared

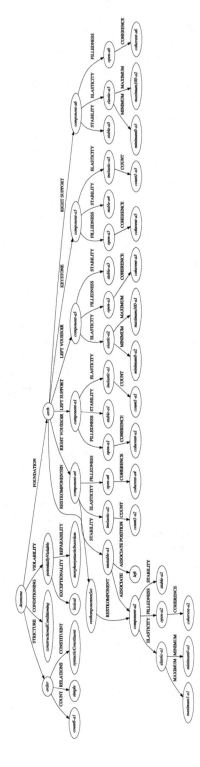

Figure 4.13 The Aghem template in Figure 3.25 as a graph

4.3 Detecting similar subparts of templates

Table 4.5 *Similarity scores for the Aghem (Figure 4.13) and Mande (Figure 4.12) templates*

AGHEM/MANDE	SIMILARITY
arch/arch	1.00
component-a2/component-m2	0.63
order/order	0.62
component-a5/component-m5	0.61
component-a1/component-m1	0.61
component-a3/component-m3	0.61
component-a6/component-m4	0.58
desmeme/desmeme	0.57
component-a5/component-m1	0.56
component-a1/component-m5	0.56
component-a6/component-m3	0.54
component-a6/component-m2	0.54
component-a3/component-m2	0.54
component-a2/component-m3	0.54
component-a6/component-m5	0.52
component-a6/component-m1	0.52
component-a5/component-m3	0.52
component-a5/component-m2	0.52
component-a3/component-m5	0.52
component-a3/component-m1	0.52
component-a2/component-m5	0.52
component-a2/component-m1	0.52
component-a1/component-m3	0.52
component-a1/component-m2	0.52
component-a4/component-m5	0.51
component-a4/component-m1	0.51
component-a3/component-m4	0.50
component-a2/component-m4	0.50
component-a4/component-m4	0.49
component-a5/component-m4	0.47
component-a1/component-m4	0.47
component-a4/component-m3	0.46
component-a4/component-m2	0.46
syntacticConstituent/syntacticConstituent	0.16
simple/simple	0.16
constructionalConditioning/constructionalConditioning	0.14
potentiallyViolable/notViolable	0.14

component-level features and shared positions within the graph structure (e.g., having the same role in the template's foundation). As can be seen, there are many more component pairings than for Table 4.4, simply reflecting the greater number of components found across the two graphs. In terms of relative ranking, however, there are some points worth noting with respect to Table 4.4

250 Typologizing templates: comparison

in comparison with Table 4.5. For instance, the similarity of the stricture nodes is comparatively greater for Table 4.5, reflecting their shared *order* type and, as a consequence, greater number of shared features as well (due to the presence of the RELATIONS feature in both). The *desmeme/desmeme* pairing also appears ahead of a number of the component pairings (unlike what is seen in Table 4.4), again reflecting the overall greater similarity of the Aghem and Mande templates to each other, when set against the Chechen and Mande templates.[14]

Other pairings, involving the constituent, conditioning, and violability types, are ranked towards the bottom of the similarity scale in both of the comparisons, which reflects their "peripheral" position in the graph. This will generally result in lower scores due to the nature of the "flooding" aspect of the algorithm which causes higher scores to often be found in more central nodes (see Section 4.3.3), as just discussed. Still, it must be emphasized that the fact that such nodes are identified as similar at all represents some degree of success for the algorithm insofar as all pairings were detected automatically rather than being "hand picked."

The examination of these two pairs of templates would thus seem to establish that it is possible to use available algorithms to help determine which parts of two templates are most similar (or dissimilar). Here, it has been seen that the greatest similarities between the Chechen and Mande templates can be found only at the level of components, while, for the Aghem and Mande templates, it is at the level of the foundation where this is found (which, in turn, implies a fair amount of similarity in the components themselves). Unlike the simpler procedure in Section 4.2, similarity flooding considers information as encoded on both the nodes and the arcs, allowing it to more effectively exploit the fine-grained nature of the typological descriptions used here.

It may be worth bringing up here a point that was also raised at the end of Section 4.2.3: what has the application of this algorithm told us that we would not have already known? For instance, one could manually inspect the Chechen, Aghem, and Mande templates and discover fairly quickly that the Aghem and Mande templates have much more similar foundations than either does to the Chechen template. The goal at this stage, however, is not to use this method as a tool to make specific discoveries but, instead, to explore the power of complex representations of typological descriptions that can be represented in the form of graphs and ensure their feasibility for use in studies employing larger samples. Here, we have seen that there are ways to automate the comparison of subparts of the templatic descriptions. This means that, as the database

---

[14] Though not done here, since all templates contain a desmeme node, one could, in principle, use the scores of the paired desmeme nodes as generated by the similarity flooding algorithm as another means of producing a set of similarity or distance scores across all the templates, in parallel to the one presented in Section 4.2.3.

4.4 Exploiting the database to detect typological universals

scales upward, it will be possible to systematically compare templates not just holistically but also taking their structural pieces into consideration. Indeed, since the similarity flooding algorithm is general in nature, this point applies not only to characterizations of templates but to any grammatical object (e.g., a clause) which could be effectively typologized using a formalism that can be represented as a graph.

4.4 Exploiting the database to detect typological universals

As a final examination of how a graph-based database can be used to conduct different kinds of typological investigation, the possibility of looking for correlations among the coded categories in order to detect statistical universals will be considered in this section. Even more so than with the discussion in Sections 4.2 and 4.3, the limits of a small database are fully apparent here, since it is essentially impossible to consider any quantitative generalizations coming out of it to be robust at this point. At the same time, it will be made clear that the graph-based formalism is hardly an obstacle to the discovery of statistical patterns in the database using existing methods for a straightforward reason: many of these methods are generally designed to operate on data presentable in a tabular format, where a given set of objects are characterized across a fixed set of categories. Since a graph structure is richer than a table, one need only transform graph-based data into tabular data by extracting a subset of the information it encodes, at which point it is amenable to more traditional kinds of processing.

The data presented in Table 4.6 will be used in this section as an illustrative example. For each template, a set of values has been extracted for the template's violability, conditioning, exceptionality, reparability, foundation, stricture, relations, constituent type, and number of components (i.e., what is labeled *count* in the table) (see Section 2.2 for discussion of these features). This extraction "flattens" the description of the templates considerably, for example by excluding information relating to components, and the specific features chosen are intended to represent salient high-level properties of templates. The extraction of the features in this way is quite trivial since it merely represents selecting specific features across the various template graphs – a kind of manipulation which is much more straightforward than, for instance, applying the similarity flooding algorithm to a pair of graphs, as just discussed in Section 4.3 above. In Table 4.6 feature labels are abbreviated in the interests of presentation and a value of "—" means that the given template was not specified for the relevant feature. In all cases, this is not due to missing information but, rather, logical dependencies among features and values (e.g., *span* templates are not associated with the RELATIONS feature in the description language).

Table 4.6 *Extraction of select features across the templates in the database*

TEMPLATE	VIOL	CONDITIONING	EXCEPTION	REPAIR	FOUND	STRICT	RELATIONS	CONSTITUENT	COUNT
AghemClause	potentially	constructional	lexical	insertion	arch	order	simple	syntactic	6
BantuCA	notViolable	lexicoconstructional	—	—	arch	order	simple	morphological	3
BantuCT	notViolable	lexicoconstructional	—	—	arch	order	simple	morphological	4
BantuVCy	notViolable	lexicoconstructional	—	—	arch	order	simple	morphological	3
ChechenPreverbalA	potentially	lexicoconstructional	noneKnown	insertion	span	length	—	prosodicWord	2
ChichewaAR	potentially	lexicoconstructional	semantic	insertion	arch	order	simple	morphological	2
ChintangPrefixes	notViolable	constructional	—	—	arch	order	simple	prosodicWord	2
EnglishPlural	notViolable	lexicoconstructional	—	—	arch	order	simple	morphological	2
EnglishVP	notViolable	constructional	—	—	arch	order	simple	syntactic	3
GermanClause	notViolable	constructional	—	—	arch	order	taxonomic	syntactic	5
MandeClause	notViolable	constructional	—	—	arch	order	simple	syntactic	5
MeskwakiClause	notViolable	constructional	—	—	arch	order	simple	syntactic	5
NdebeleCA	notViolable	lexicoconstructional	—	—	arch	order	simple	morphological	4
NimboranVerb	potentially	constructional	noneKnown	homophony	span	order	taxonomic	morphological	7
SerboCroatianJe	notViolable	lexicoconstructional	—	—	span	order	simple	prosodicWord	2
SerboCroatianTopicalization	potentially	prosodic	noneKnown	irreparable	span	length	—	prosodicWord	2
TieneVerbProsodic	potentially	prosodic	noneKnown	shortening	span	length	—	mora	2
TieneVerbSegments	potentially	prosodic	noneKnown	phonological	arch	order	simple	segment	3
TurkishNominalMinimality	potentially	prosodic	lexical	irreparable	span	length	—	syllable	2
TurkishVerbalMinimality	potentially	prosodic	lexical	insertion	span	length	—	syllable	2

4.4 Exploiting the database to detect typological universals 253

Once the data represented in graph form is reformulated along the lines of what is seen in Table 4.6, any number of statistical tests can be performed on the distributions of the feature values (i.e., the values of the typological variables), and, here, I will make use of the methods presented in Bickel (2010: 86–92), where they are discussed in more detail. At heart, the methods he employs are intended to find statistically significant correlations among variables, as is the case with many kinds of statistical tests. The main difference between them and methods that may be more familiar is that they are designed to look for correlations across large sets of variables rather than simply testing for a correlation between a pair of variables. Tests of the latter kind would be sensible if we were considering some specific narrow hypothesis, for instance that the components of arch templates tend to be syntactic constituents more often than for span templates. However, when one has a database coding at a fine-grained level, it would clearly be desirable to search for significant correlations across all available variables since this would help uncover universals that might otherwise go undetected.

However, simply "fishing" for universals by, for instance, testing all possible pairwise combinations of variables raises a number of problems.[15] For instance, if one uses a standard statistical threshold where α is set to .05 and looks at more than twenty pairings of variables, one would expect at least one false positive. In the case of the variables presented in Table 4.6, since there are nine of them, this yields thirty-six possible pairs of variables, which makes it clearly inappropriate to simply test for significance across all pairs using, for instance, a chi-square test. Another issue that arises is that, if there is a significant correlation between a pair of variables, say A and B, as well as a correlation between a pair like B and C, if one also finds a correlation between A and C, one cannot immediately know if this results from distinct patterns or if one of the correlations is an artifact of the others. For instance, perhaps the variable C is somehow constraining both A and B, in a way that makes the correlation between A and B fully predictable if one knows the value for C.

The approach taken by Bickel (2010: 86–92) attempts to address these concerns and provides a relatively straightforward way to look for typological implications using a method that also has a reasonable theoretical interpretation. First, rather than looking specifically for pairwise correlations between all variables, one instead estimates their *mutual information*. This can informally be understood as a measurement of the extent to which knowledge of the distribution of the values of one feature allows one to predict the distribution of the values of another. On its own, this method does not allow one

---

[15] Indeed, this sort of approach could be viewed (pejoratively) as involving a "fishing expedition." This would perhaps be a problem if the goal was to do hypothesis testing in an experimental context. However, the exemplary use of the methods discussed below is intended, instead, to be an exercise in hypothesis raising.

254 Typologizing templates: comparison

Table 4.7 *Predictability scores across different templatic features*

Violability	—								
Conditioning	0.03	—							
Exceptionality	0.01	0.00	—						
Reparability	0.01	0.00	0.00	—					
Foundation	0.09	0.02	0.01	0.00	—				
Stricture	0.13	0.11	0.00	0.00	0.25	—			
Relations	0.02	0.04	0.00	0.04	0.06	0.01	—		
Constituent	0.02	0.29	0.00	0.00	0.13	0.17	0.02	—	
Count	0.02	0.05	0.05	0.03	0.13	0.06	0.05	0.19	—

to predict how particular values of the features being compared correlate, but it can give an indication of the extent to which information about one feature helps predict the values of another, which, following Bickel (2010), seems reasonable as a step towards devising typological implications of the traditional kind. Further technical details on this procedure can be found in Bickel (2010), which, in particular, builds on the work of Hausser & Strimmer (2009) on estimating mutual information for gene association networks in biology. This is due to the fact that their methods are specifically designed to work with comparatively small sample sizes of the sort that are typical in many domains of typological investigation.

Based on the data in Table 4.6, the data in Table 4.7 presents the mutual information scores across each of the pairs of features. In the present context, the actual numeric values for these mutual information scores is less significant than whether or not they are non-zero (meaning that there is some degree of significant predictability found between them) and how they compare among one another (higher mutual information means greater predictability).[16]

The mutual information scores presented in Table 4.7 have not been corrected for artifacts of the type described above where correlations across overlapping pairs of variables may not actually be reflective of a direct connection in the distributions of the values for two of the features, but, rather,

---

[16] The calculation of the mutual information estimates seen in this section was done in R (R Core Team 2013) using the *entropy* package of Hausser & Strimmer (2013), following the procedure described in Bickel (2010). Potential statistical artifacts were removed (see Table 4.8) using the *aracne.a* method of the *parmigene* package with an epsilon of .05, as described in Sales & Romualdi (2012) (see also Margolin et al. (2006)). Bickel (2010) did not explicitly mention the implementation of the procedure for removing artifacts, but this may be the exact same, or a very close version, of his procedure following the discussion in Bickel (2010: 87–88). As discussed in Margolin et al. (2006), the procedure used to remove potential artifacts can result in false negatives – that is, it may treat some non-zero mutual information estimates as artifacts that actually represent meaningful mutual information. The extent to which this might inhibit discovery of significant linguistic generalizations is in need of further research. The scripts and other resources used to make the calculations discussed in this section can be found at https://github.com/jcgood/desmeme.

4.4 Exploiting the database to detect typological universals   255

Table 4.8 *Predictability scores across different templatic features without potential artifacts*

Violability	—							
Conditioning	0.00	—						
Exceptionality	0.01	0.00	—					
Reparability	0.01	0.00	0.00	—				
Foundation	0.09	0.00	0.01	0.00	—			
Stricture	0.13	0.00	0.00	0.00	0.25	—		
Relations	0.02	0.04	0.00	0.04	0.06	0.00	—	
Constituent	0.00	0.29	0.00	0.00	0.13	0.17	0.02	—
Count	0.00	0.00	0.05	0.03	0.13	0.00	0.05	0.19	—

only indicative of an indirect one. In Table 4.8, mutual information scores that have removed potential artifacts are presented (see footnote 16 for further details). Thus, for instance, the .03 mutual information estimate for the pairing of violability and conditioning seen in Table 4.7 is not found in Table 4.8 because it was deemed a possible result of some other confluence of mutual information patterns (e.g., the fact that stricture is a better predictor of both violability and conditioning than either are of each other).

Since, as stated at various points above, the current database is not appropriate for reaching definitive statistical conclusions, it is not sensible to explore in detail all the positive mutual information values seen in Table 4.8. However, for the purposes of illustration, some of the higher-valued ones are worth considering. The highest mutual information score, for example, at .29, is between the templates' constituent features and conditioning features. This seems reasonable: if a template is, for instance, constructionally conditioned, we might expect its components to be more likely to be defined in morphosyntactic terms. This need not strictly be the case, as seen, for instance in the case of Chintang (see Table 4.6), but it would seem to fall out from a more general linguistic principle that there is a kind of harmony between the conditioning environment of a linguistic unit and its makeup in terms of constituency.

We can further explore the specific contours of this pattern with respect to the database by calculating the extent to which the probability that the values of each of the features actually predicts the values of the other (since mutual information, on its own, does not reveal any sort of directionality). Following Bickel (2010: 87), this can be accomplished by dividing the mutual information estimate by the entropy of the distribution of the values associated with each of the features (in the sense of *entropy* as developed within information theory (Shannon 1948)).[17] Using this method, the probability of the distribution (in terms of frequency) of constituency given conditioning is .19 and the

[17] I do not repeat the details of how these calculations are made here and, instead, refer the interested reader to Bickel (2010: 87).

256   Typologizing templates: comparison

probability of conditioning given constituency is .27, suggesting that it is the constituency which more strongly predicts conditioning, rather than the other way around, at least in the current dataset.

A final way to examine the relationships like that between conditioning and constituency is to determine if there any specific patterns in the ways the values of the features correspond to each other which can be seen as specifically contributing to the relatively high mutual information estimate for the features. Following Bickel (2010: 88–89), this can be done by considering the distribution of attested pairings of the values across the two features with respect to the logically possible pairings in order to calculate cases where what is attested differs in statistically significant ways from what would be predicted if the distribution of the pairings were random. Using methods described in Meyer et al. (2006) and Zeileis et al. (2007), and implemented in Meyer et al. (2013), in the present database, there are two pairings which are identified as significantly contributing to the comparatively high level of mutual information between the conditioning and constituent features: these are the pairing of the constructional conditioning environment with components comprising syntactic units and the prosodic conditioning environment with components comprising syllables. Such results are readily interpretable as being in line with descriptive intuitions regarding construction types and subconstituents.

To pick one other example, we can consider the relatively high mutual information estimate for the stricture and foundation features. It would not seem unreasonable for these features to have some kind of relationship to each other. There are long-standing lines of research that have linked length templates to prosodic units (see Section 1.8.2) in ways which would suggest they should be unlikely to have comparatively articulated arch foundations, and, instead, have span foundations, which are good at characterizing two-unit restrictions of the sort commonly found in prosodic templates.[18] Moreover, to the extent that order templates seem to often involve three or more units, it would not be surprising to find that they are more likely to be arch templates, where the ordering can be reckoned with respect to a head-like keystone element, given how well this would parallel other types of linguistic structure (e.g., syntactic constituency) where ordering is relevant and is typically analyzed with respect to the positioning of heads.

---

[18] It would be possible to use the database to explore specific connections between length templates and templates whose constituents involve prosodic units by exploiting the fact that the typological categories used within it are defined within an ontology. In this particular case, various phonological categories generally deemed to be prosodic constituents are all grouped together as types under the supertype *prosodicConstituent*, meaning this connection among them is discoverable in machine-readable form. The current ontology used in the database is presented in the Appendix.

4.5 The feasibility of graph-based typology

Following the procedure just adopted above in the examination of the conditioning and constituency features, we can first calculate the extent to which the distributions of the foundation and stricture features can be understood to predict each other. The probability of the foundation feature's distribution given that of the stricture feature is .39, and the probability of the stricture feature's distribution given the foundation feature is .44. These relatively close probabilities suggest a two-way implication where the patterning of each feature helps predict the other in more or less equal fashion.[19]

What we have seen in this section, then, is that employing a graph-based database does not offer any significant impediment to using quantitative methods to detect "classical" kinds of typological generalizations associated with implicational patterns. Transforming the graphs into the less informative tabular format, as in Table 4.6, is straightforward, and, to the extent that there is a barrier to such work, it is simply that the process of describing typological objects in the manner done here is more time consuming than for more typical approaches, resulting in reduced sample sizes and, thereby, less robust statistical patterns.

4.5 The feasibility of graph-based typology

We have seen in this chapter that typological comparison over complex objects of the sort used here – what one might call *graph-based typology* – is feasible, even if significant work remains for us to understand what kinds of methods are most effective for robustly extracting different kinds of generalizations from such data. In particular, it is possible to do holistic cross-constructional comparison (Section 4.2), detect similar nodes within a graph (Section 4.3), and transform graph-based data in ways that allow for the detection of correlations which can be interpreted as classical statistical universals (Section 4.4).

This establishes that the approach to typologizing templates developed here as one which could form an effective foundation for a larger-scale study with a sample size sufficient to extract statistically significant results. It also suggests that whole new kinds of typological studies could be undertaken for patterns which can be well described via feature structures due to the fact that they can be represented straightforwardly as graphs. To the extent that feature structures are already well established as a means for fine-grained descriptive analysis

---

[19] As discussed by Bickel (2010: 88), there are also methods for determining which specific feature values may be most significant in producing the observed patterns of predictability. These would clearly be of use with a database that was large enough to be considered to give truly representative results. If we apply the methods he proposes to the case of the foundation and stricture features, the pairing of a template with a length stricture and a span foundation is the only one that represents a statistically significant association. This indicates that, perhaps, span templates are more restricted than arch templates (with the general caveat of the small sample size still applying here).

of synchronic grammars, one can imagine a range of possibilities for comparing linguistic structures which have scarcely been possible to this point. For instance, rather than simply treating languages as SVO, SOV, VSO, etc., one could compare full-fledged clausal descriptions, yielding a level of accuracy in comparison across large samples going well beyond what traditionally typology has allowed.

5 Moving forward

5.1 Next steps in the study of templatic constructions

The previous chapters of this book have examined how we can define templatic constructions, describe them, and compare them. A number of issues remain open which cannot be fully explored here, but they clearly merit consideration and will be briefly discussed in this chapter. These can be divided into two broad classes: (i) how can work within the general framework developed here be effectively extended (Section 5.2)? (ii) what has the present study taught us about the kinds of theoretical questions regarding templates that have animated the field until now (Section 5.3)?

5.2 Extending the present study

5.2.1 What is a valid sample?

A key limitation of the present study, which was felt especially acutely in Chapter 4, is that its limited sample size did not allow for the collection of robust statistical generalizations. The reasons for not having a larger sample were largely practical in nature: the difficulties in studying a "wastebasket" class of object such as templates (see Section 1.5), which further exhibit significant internal structural complexity, meant that devising an appropriate description language, and testing it for adequacy, is, in many respects, a more difficult endeavor than has been the case for earlier typological investigations. Of course, the approach taken here would have been completely impractical before the development of methods of data encoding, storage, and processing which only came into being quite recently. This largely explains why typological studies, to this point, have made use of highly reduced systems of categorization.

Nevertheless, the present work has established the feasibility of typologizing templatic constructions using a rich description language (and, by extension, many other similar "wastebasket" phenomena). Moreover, consistent with the experiences of work in the AUTOTYP project (Bickel & Nichols 2002) (see Section 2.7), after coding around the first ten or so templatic constructions, the

260   Moving forward

description language began to stabilize to the point that, even when a new construction prompted modifications to its structure or content, these were comparatively limited in nature. It can still take an extensive amount of time to go from a published description of a templatic construction to one that is encoded in the database. However, at this point, the time required at the encoding stage is relatively trivial, and the bulk of effort is, instead, spent in fully modeling the template's properties given that available descriptions may often be somewhat telegraphic regarding templatic features deemed to be of interest here.

Given the relative stability of the structure of the database at present, it then becomes reasonable to seriously consider just what kind of sample would be needed for us to have some general faith that the database is representative enough of templatic diversity to yield worthwhile results. Work on the issue of creating balanced samples in typology has generally focused on finding a balance among sampled *languages* along some important parameter (e.g., genealogical relations (Dryer 1989, Bickel 2008)). Here, however, we are dealing with constructions, not languages, which expands the sample space considerably, since one language could have many templatic constructions. How, then, do we determine when a sample has "sufficient" coverage across all possible points of variation? This issue was discussed to some extent in Section 2.8, but it seems reasonable to briefly take it up again here in the context of understanding how the present study can be built upon in the future.

Of course, there cannot be a one-size-fits-all answer to the question of sampling since the shape of a sample will depend in large part on the nature of the questions being asked. The question that has (often implicitly) structured the discussion here is a relatively unstructured one: what is the general range of attested templatic variation? Within the context of this broad question, various other, more specific questions present themselves: are there correlations between the grammatical domain where a template operates and the shape of the relevant templatic restrictions? Do certain kinds of templatic properties co-occur especially frequently?

These questions are all oriented towards the universe of constructions in and of themselves, but there are other topics one may want to examine relating to the distribution of templatic constructions within a language. Some of the issues were discussed in Section 2.5, for instance involving cases where templates are found embedded within other templates or where multiple templates seem to target the same domain. Earlier, these issues were raised mostly in the context of how best to analyze a given set of templatic restrictions, but one could also consider them when probing questions of overall patterns of "templaticity" in a grammar, with perhaps one of the most obvious ones being whether a language's being highly templatic in one grammatical domain (e.g., the verb) results in it being less templatic in another domain (e.g., the clause). This question seems particularly significant given the interest there has been

5.2 Extending the present study

in how complex verbal morphology relates to so-called non-configurational syntax in recent decades (see Section 2.8).

On top of this, of course, one could also consider patterns of templaticity across linguistic areas and families. The survey of Bickel & Nichols (2013), for instance, suggests that verbs in languages of the Americas are, on the whole, characterized by a relatively high degree of morphological synthesis. This is in accord with the fact that some of the most famously "templatic" languages are found in the Americas (see Section 1.4.3) and suggests that templaticity is likely to be subject to areal effects. We have, moreover, seen from the Bantu case studies in Section 3.5 that there are genealogical factors at play as well in the development and inheritance of templates (which should hardly be considered surprising given that templates are essentially a kind of linguistic form, parallel to canonical lexical items, albeit of an abstract type, as discussed in Section 2.1).

Accepting that different kinds of samples are needed to address different sorts of questions and given how little we actually do know about templatic constructions across languages and grammatical domains, the most fruitful way to sample constructions for the next stages of investigation would probably involve an eclectic strategy combining multiple sampling "subprojects." Each would be structured to help test and refine the design of the database to allow it to be used to address a range of questions while, at the same time, involving sample sizes within each subproject that are large enough for there to be some assurance that one could use them to derive relatively robust results. Examples of subprojects I envision being of value in this regard are, for instance: (i) A small set of exceptionally well-described languages (on the order of three to five) could be sampled and all of the known patterns of linear stipulation in their grammars could be collected in order to produce a set of "linear grammars" that can be used to pilot the study of patterns of templaticity within languages. (ii) A specific functional grammatical domain could be chosen that would be expected to be well-described across a large number of languages so that data on patterns of templaticity within that domain could be collected and described across a genealogically and areally balanced sample, with the most obvious candidate being the expression of verbs in syntactic contexts associated in general with higher degrees of morphological complexity (e.g., the main verb of a finite transitive clause). (iii) A subset of the languages from the second subproject, to the extent that available descriptions allow, could be additionally examined for their patterns of templaticity in another well-described general domain (e.g., ordering of elements in a transitive clause) so that intragrammatical patterns of templaticity could be examined rigorously.

These subprojects, taken together, would also hopefully result in the more opportunistic detection and encoding of a large sample of templatic constructions in general, but lacking in the above list is a subproject along the lines

262   Moving forward

of: (iv) Grammars of the languages of the world could simply be "scoured" for any and all templatic constructions found within them to allow us to better assess the range of attested templatic possibilities. Such a subproject has, in fact, primarily informed the present work. However, it is clearly hard to look for a grammatical oddity, such as a template, in any systematic fashion because available descriptive grammars have not, to this point, been structured in a way which would allow all of the templatic constraints in a language to be readily detected. Moreover, templates themselves are only likely to be invoked as descriptive devices under specific conditions, as will be discussed in Section 5.2.3, which means that many "templates" (or, more generally, desmemes) will be obscured given the way linguistic description usually operates. This further hinders our ability to simply construct a database of templates by directly looking for their description in grammars.

At this stage, therefore, it seems more sensible to embark on more tractable subprojects with the hope that, over time, they will help reveal more and more of the world's templatic diversity. Moreover, ultimately, to the extent that the efforts of such subprojects yield results of interest, language descriptions more explicitly attuned to templatic patterns may be produced which will greatly facilitate making further discoveries of interesting template types in the future.

5.2.2   Achieving consistency in coding

A more practical issue that has been alluded to, but not yet adequately addressed, relates to the concerns surrounding replicability in data coding. This is, in general, a significant issue for typology since, unless one can ensure that similar criteria will be applied to the coding of similar kinds of data across languages, it becomes difficult, if even possible, to ensure replicability of typological results (see, e.g., Nichols et al. (2006) and Haspelmath & Siegmund (2006: 74)). As discussed in Dryer (1995), even a seemingly straightforward typological notion such as "unmarked" or "neutral" word order will not necessarily be interpreted the same way across sources. What happens, therefore, when the typological coding system involves the combination of many novel categories (e.g., stricture and foundation), each potentially associated with its own set of novel subcategories (e.g., arch and span foundations), as well as the expression of structural relationships (e.g., support, voussoir, and keystone)?

In simple terms, such a coding system reaches a level of complexity where full replicability of coding across typologists (or even the same typologist over time) cannot be considered achievable. The challenge then becomes to minimize inconsistency in coding and also to have some understanding of (i) how much of a mismatch across coders can be expected and (ii) how much this level of mismatch is likely to affect the overall results of a given study. In the present

5.2 Extending the present study

context, the issue of coding reliability has been mitigated in various ways. First and foremost, only one individual (the author) was directly involved in coding the data in this particular instance. Thus, inconsistency across coders is not an issue. Second, the relatively small number of constructions coded has meant that the coding of each could be set against the coding of the others more or less directly, again helping consistency to be maintained. Finally, since the structure of this book devoted considerable space to case studies, the logic of the coding decisions in the present database is laid out in more detail than is generally typical of typological studies – and, thus, more readily open to inspection.

However, if this research were expanded so that, say, hundreds, or even thousands, of desmemes were coded, none of these three conditions would be likely to hold. What would be required is the development of explicit strategies to maximize coding consistency as well as targeted research into the limits of consistency and the impacts of inconsistent coding on the research results. For instance, formal protocols could be developed enumerating operationalized definitions for the various concepts used in the description language, especially those that, here, required a degree of subtlety in their application, such as the notion of keystone (see Section 2.4.5) or the determination of when a template should be considered potentially violable (see Section 2.4.3). Perhaps the most important operationalized definition in this regard would be deciding precisely which sets of templatic restrictions should be treated as belonging to a single template in the first place (see also Section 2.5.3).

Similarly, once one acknowledges that it is impossible to become completely consistent in coding when using an elaborated system such as the one developed here, it becomes clear that a topic of research must become discovering what the average inter-coder level of consistency can be expected to be (see Bybee et al. (1994: xvii) for relevant discussion). This would allow for the quantification of part of the uncertainty in the results of a study like this one, thereby providing extra context for their interpretation. The most straightforward way to gather data relevant to inter-coder reliability would simply be to ask two individuals to code the same set of templates on the basis of published descriptions to see the extent to which they arrive at the same result. If they are found to be fairly inconsistent, this would suggest a need for more detailed protocols of the sort just mentioned above, or perhaps a refinement to the typological description language so that only more "reliable" categories are included.

A related question is that, for a given method of comparison or data extraction, how much would it matter for the ultimate conclusions if some of the data were miscoded? For instance, the graph similarity algorithm described in Section 4.2 treats all component nodes equally. Given that even the simplest template descriptions in the present study have around twenty nodes

264   Moving forward

(see, e.g., the Turkish templates in Section 3.2), the misclassification of one of these would not have a major impact on results derived from using that similarity metric. Indeed, at many points during the work described here, the data had to be recoded for various reasons – correction of mistakes, reanalyses, ensuring consistent coding of existing database entries with new ones, etc. – and, impressionistically, these recodings appeared to have relatively minimal impact on the graph similarity scores on the whole. Of course, it would be better to back up such impressions with systematically collected data on the impact of coding "mistakes," where one could investigate the degree of robustness of the results of the application of any metric given a set of changes to the data coding. This, too, would allow for a more accurate sense of how to interpret the results of any quantitative investigation of templatic properties.

Finally, there may be technical solutions to some problems surrounding coding consistency. The current database tool enforces key restrictions embodied in the template description language on the encoding of templatic constructions, for instance only allowing a template to have a keystone component if it has an arch foundation. However, further levels of data validation could, in principle, be implemented that would help maintain data consistency. To pick one example, as seen in Figure 2.1, a template's stricture is associated with a COUNT feature, indicating its number of components. In all of the case studies developed in Chapter 3, this information is redundant – since one could arrive at the value of the COUNT feature simply by counting components. This redundancy is included due to the fact that it is imaginable that there could be a typological study of templates where a deliberate choice would be made not to include descriptions of all the components of a template if this information was not especially important for the questions being investigated. However, it clearly would be desirable to have automatic mechanisms in place that detected cases where the number of encoded components would not match the value for the COUNT feature of a template's stricture, since this could, in some cases, represent a coding error. Similarly, the current database system would allow for the encoding of clearly mistaken templatic restrictions, such as cases where a given component is simultaneously serving as a keystone and a voussoir, a definitional impossibility. To the extent that additional degrees of data validation could be put in place to detect issues like these, coding reliability could be improved at relatively low cost.

5.2.3   *"Invisible" templates*

At the end of Section 2.4.3, an issue was alluded to regarding an (unsurprising) bias in the morphophonological literature towards describing templatic

5.2 Extending the present study

patterns which become especially "visible" by virtue of being violable in some way. Thus, for instance, the Turkish templates discussed in Section 3.2 have been the subject of significant theoretical work precisely because they can result in some expected forms simply being ineffable. However, it is easy to imagine a language more or less identical to Turkish, but lacking the crucial class of subminimal roots which make the presence of a template especially clear. It seems counterintuitive that such a language would then be treated as simply lacking those templatic constraints, but they might easily go unnoticed or simply be considered an accidental surface fact of word realization, rather than representing a true grammatical generalization.

Within the syntactic literature, there is a different kind of bias wherein very common patterns of linearization, such as SVO word order in English, are not considered templatic, but less common patterns, such as so-called verb-second order, may be given templatic analyses, as is the case with many Germanic languages (see Sections 1.4.5 and 3.12). However, an English-like language, in principle, presents analytical ambiguity: its SVO word order could be due to predictable patterns of phrase structure or due to a templatic restriction on constituent ordering. Metatheoretical principles such as Occam's Razor may favor one analysis over another, as could specific language-internal facts, but, as a general rule, it is not possible to tell when a "common" linearization pattern may or may not be templatic (or, at least, desmemic).

We are left then with the significant problem that the present state of language description, if anything, underreports template-like phenomena. Of course, as discussed in Section 1.5, the term *template* is not theoretically precise, since it is partly defined by linguist's expectations regarding linearization. This is where the somewhat broader notion of desmeme (see Section 2.1) becomes valuable, but, to the extent that grammars generally only discuss desmemes in detail when they rise to the level of "unexpectedness" found in templates, our picture of linear stipulation must be seen as quite limited, and, in some respects, we may even know more about exotic patterns of stipulation than commonplace ones, since the latter have not been deemed of sufficient interest to be investigated at the same level of detail (unless they happen to be associated with some kind of special repair strategy). Perhaps the best way to address this issue in future work would be to undertake a kind of project alluded to in Section 2.8: this would involve collecting and coding all examples of constructions (whether phonological, morphological, or syntactic) involving linear stipulation from an exceptionally well-described language, in order to produce something along the lines of a "desmemic grammar." A study like this could provide an example for similar investigations of other languages and help distance us from an inherent bias in only focusing on linear stipulation when it appears "special."

266   Moving forward

5.3   Explaining templates

5.3.1   To what extent are templates "real"?

As discussed in Section 1.2, this work has quite deliberately avoided making "theoretical" claims of the sort often associated with linguistic analysis, regarding, for example, issues such as the grammatical reality of templates or their possible cognitive representation. The reasoning behind this is relatively straightforward: it is my view that we simply do not know enough about patterns of linear stipulation to begin to address abstract theoretical questions such as these in a sufficiently rigorous way. The focus has, therefore, been on developing a more adequate descriptive framework for them.

This position may be surprising in light of the relatively extensive theoretical literature on morphophonological and morphosyntactic templates (see Sections 1.4.2 and 1.4.3). However, it is important to bear in mind that previous work has generally focused on only limited aspects of linear stipulation. The Prosodic Morphology Hypothesis, discussed in Section 1.8.2, for instance, limits its scope to a subset of morphophonological templatic phenomena. It considers the possible shapes of reduplicated elements or size restrictions on morphological units, such as those associated with the length template for the Tiene verb stem discussed in Section 3.5.5. However, in and of itself, it has nothing to say about other features of morphophonological templates, such as those relating to segmental ordering of the sort also seen in the Tiene verb stem and discussed in the same section.

Similarly, the Prosodic Morphology Hypothesis has little to say directly about a well-known class of phenomena in reduplicative constructions, describable as "fixed segmentism" (see Alderete et al. (1999)), wherein a reduplicant appears with segments not found in the base, but which are a part of the specific reduplication construction. Some instances of fixed segmentism, for example the replacement involved in the English construction exemplified by *table-shmable* (see Nevins & Vaux (2007)), are clearly amenable to a templatic analysis involving the replacement of one element with another in a specific linearly definable position. But, since these patterns involve segmental replacement rather than prosodic size restrictions, they represent phenomena which appear to be clearly morphophonological but outside the scope of the Prosodic Morphology Hypothesis.

As discussed in Section 1.4.3, in the morphosyntactic domain, there is a body of work seriously assessing the actual need for templates in morphosyntactic analysis in the first place. However, this work, too, is somewhat limited in nature, and tends not to be focused on the existence of linear stipulation in morphosyntactic constructions, per se, but rather on the highly elaborated templates sometimes proposed in the descriptive literature, with the templates proposed for the Athabaskan verb being a particular source of controversy (see,

5.3 Explaining templates

e.g., Rice (2000)). In fact, it seems likely to be the case that the Athabaskan verb should not be characterized simply in terms of a series of "unstructured" slots (see Section 3.1). In the approach taken here, this does not call for a non-templatic analysis but, rather, a more nuanced one than seen in work oriented towards more traditional description. In other words, even if we can simplify the Athabaskan "template," this does not obviate the need to investigate the desmemic properties of the Athabaskan verb (see also Rice (2000: 394–395)).

This leads us to the question posed in the title of this section, one which is probably of more interest to many linguists than the core focus of this work: are templates "real," in some sense, or simply epiphenomena of description? If by "real," we mean something like "cognitively real," then I cannot say much, since issues of cognitive representations fall too far outside the scope of my expertise.[1]

If by "real," however, we mean that templates represent kinds of descriptive objects that are rendered necessary given common approaches to the representation of grammatical constructions, then, in a broad sense, the unavoidable answer is that templates must be considered to be "real." Even if the especially ornate templates proposed in cases like that of Athabaskan languages are not strictly necessary for the characterization of linear stipulation in the verb, it is impossible to suggest that grammars do not involve a significant amount of logically unnecessary stipulation. This is revealed by the overwhelming predominance of prefixes and suffixes over mobile affixes (see Section 1.5); the paucity of languages allowing for morphological "scrambling" (see Section 3.3 for one example of this rarity), even though "free" word order is well attested; or the fact that freely ordered ambipositions are much less common than their fixed prepositional and postpositional cousins (see Libert (2006) and Hagège (2010: 114–124)). Of course, nothing prevents an analyst from recharacterizing linear stipulation in non-linear terms, as found in, for instance, Kayne (1994), where mandatory movement operations in some languages replace the need for stipulating ordering patterns at the phrasal level. Here, however, such recharacterizations would be considered to just be desmemes in another guise. They may, of course, additionally make predictions regarding the kinds of desmemes that are likely to be attested, but this does not change their nature as stipulations of some kind.

The interesting question, therefore, is not whether templates are "real." Absent terminological contortions, it seems hard to imagine that they are not.

---

[1] There has been work on this topic, especially in the context of the nature of lexical representation for speakers of Semitic languages, given that these languages are famous for the presence of morphophonological templatic patterns based on consonantal roots (see Section 1.4.2) and are spoken by relatively accessible populations. Twist (2006: 47–51) provides a relatively recent overview of such work.

268   Moving forward

Rather, we should focus on what kinds of variation we see among desmemes and how they pattern in grammars. To this point, research into them has been divided across phonology, morphology, and syntax, often in the context of looking at the specific properties of chimeric categories which blend linear properties with morphophonological and morphosyntactic ones into a single unit, such as affixes or words (see Section 2.1). This is understandable given the way the field of linguistics has divided itself, but this study has shown that we can also look at desmemes in a more general way, independent of how they are "bundled" together with other grammatical objects.

I would like to conclude this section by returning to an issue first raised in Section 1.2 and remarking on an unfortunate tendency in some analytical traditions that, I believe, has hindered our ability to see linearization patterns as involving richly articulated structures of interacting elements, as is assumed to be the case here. This is the frequent conflation of the object typically used to represent a linguistic form, the string, with the form itself (see McCawley (1998: 2–3) for relevant discussion). This can make it appear, for instance, that the linearization properties of a syntactic structure primarily involve the concatenation of "strings" of words and that words, in turn, are merely the concatenation of "strings" of morphemes.[2] However, as the case studies in Chapter 3 should make abundantly clear, there is much more to linearization than concatenation. I think most linguists are aware of this, in principle, though accidents of linguistic practice often make linearization seem more simple than it really is.

5.3.2   Are there impossible templates?

Even though the core sample used for this study was comparatively small, significantly more literature on templates was examined overall (see Chapter 1), and this allows us to consider questions regarding whether "anything goes" when it comes to templates or if there may be limits on possible templatic structures – or even just very strong statistical tendencies. The description language developed in Chapter 2.1 is deliberately intended to allow for the description of "impossible" templates so as to not prematurely delimit the typological space of templates that we might consider and, thereby, prevent us from detecting interesting patterns. Therefore, we must not turn to it for our understanding of the limits of templates but, at this stage, base our conclusions

---

[2] This conflation of "linguistic form" with "string" seems to be a particularly prominent feature of generative approaches to syntax, going back to Chomsky (1957: 26–30). However, it is hardly limited to Chomskyan approaches. For example, standard treatments of Head-driven Phrase Structure Grammar, as seen in textbooks such as Sag et al. (2003), reveal a similar bias when one sets the limited nature of the phonological representations they provide (typically just orthographic strings) against the framework's elaborated syntactic and semantic representations (though see Bird (1992, 1995), Bird & Klein (1994)).

5.3 Explaining templates 269

on those templates that have been proposed in the literature, even if they are controversial.

What is interesting in the present context is that, even if we were to accept the "reality" (see Section 5.3.1) of the most elaborated and controversial templates, such as that of the Athabaskan verb as developed by Kari (1989), it is still possible to imagine kinds of templates that would not be merely controversial but, rather, appear to be wholly unattested (or at least undescribed). For instance, one dominant feature of templates appears to be that there is a high degree of homogeneity among their components. One may find a length template where a given constituent must consist of two units characterizable as syllables, but not one where one component must be a syllable and the other a tense–mood–aspect morpheme. This particular pattern has been robust enough that, in fact, it is embedded in the current description language by the fact that a template's stricture is associated with a single CONSTITUENT specification since, to this point, there has been no need to have to code a list of "mixed" constituents for a template (but see Section 3.7).

Another kind of template that has yet to be encountered, but is somewhat easier to imagine (and allowed by the description language), would be one whose stricture involves a length restriction but has an arch, rather than a span, foundation. It seems to often be the case that length templates involve constructions where the restriction is over two components (one of which may be elastic), but, this does not mean that one of those components could not be privileged in a keystone-like way. Hyman & Udoh (2007), for instance, describe a pattern in Leggbó verbs which, on the surface, seems describable as length harmony. In verb forms consisting of two syllables, the vowel of the first syllable must be long if the vowel of the second is also long, in a harmony-like fashion, potentially resulting in surface alternations. Ultimately, they offer a metrical analysis of the pattern which does not characterize the alternation in this particular way (Hyman & Udoh 2007: 84). However, if the length harmony analysis had been maintained, a templatic analysis involving a length stricture, with the second syllable acting as a keystone determining the length of the first, would seem possible, thus resulting in a two-unit length template with a keystone. I am not aware of a clear case of such a template, however, and even if they do exist, it seems likely that they are relatively rare, if not necessarily unattested.

We can also consider the properties of components when looking at whether there may be some "impossible" kinds of templates. For instance, the current descriptive scheme for component elasticity would allow for the specification of components with any number of minimum or maximum sizes, which clearly goes beyond what could be imaginably attested – e.g., an elastic component that could have only between seven and thirty-one elements filling it would certainly be linguistically impossible. However, there are less absurd possibilities

270   Moving forward

that I have not yet explicitly encountered, such as an elastic component that could be occupied by zero to two components. A Mande-like language (see Section 3.10) which allowed up to two non-subject arguments before the verb would contain such a component. So, such a template would seem imaginable, if not yet attested. Nevertheless, there may very well be severe limitations on the precise sizes of components.

The discussion here just scratches the surface of potential templatic "impossibilities." Nevertheless, the existence of the templatic description language and its application to a number of case studies now makes a range of questions about possible and impossible templates much more straightforward to consider than was previously the case.

5.3.3   Where do templates come from?

Perhaps the most significant question not yet addressed here is understanding where templates "come from."[3] Their status as grammatical "outliers" would seem to preclude a synchronic universalist account, but it may be the case that specific templates could be accounted for partly in functional terms. Hyman (2003c: 264), for example, suggests that the Bantu suffix ordering templates discussed above (see Section 3.5) may fulfill the useful function of allowing speakers and hearers to "just fix the order and not worry about" trying to get morpheme order to align with semantic scope given that this information will usually be retrievable from the discourse context anyway. However, a general functional explanation for all templatic patterns seems difficult.

The most fruitful avenue of investigation for understanding how templates arise is likely to be primarily historical in nature – with the question being what kinds of pathways of change are liable to result in patterns of templaticity in grammars?[4] Of particular interest in this regard are patterns of historical change wherein elements which were formerly either freely ordered in linear terms, or had their order determined by functional considerations (broadly construed), become fixed in their ordering. The fixing of the order of just a pair of elements would not result in a "template" in the usual sense, but it would result in a desmeme and, thereby, a greater degree of templaticity in a given construction.[5]

However, the picture is almost certainly not as straightforward as simply treating templates as "frozen" linearity (e.g., along the lines of Givón's (1971)

---

[3] See Good (2008) for discussion of different possible modes of explanation for the properties of grammatical objects.

[4] Good (2003b: 508–530) discusses issues related to those briefly introduced here.

[5] Work such as that of Schiering (2006), focusing on the phonological side of grammaticalization (rather than its better-studied semantic aspect) is likely to also yield results of interest for the study of the development of templates.

5.3 Explaining templates

understanding of certain morphological patterns as deriving relatively directly from older, more free syntactic structures). Mithun (2000: 245–252), for instance, suggests that, once a templatic pattern is established, an existing templatic "slot" can analogically attract elements with similar functions to those which already occupy it. She, thus, suggests that an existing template, in some sense, can reinforce itself.[6] Harris (2008: 68–74) (based on Harris (2002)) discusses something comparable, where the ordering of a class of elements within the Udi verb shifted from being morphologically predictable to a more templatic ordering. In particular, these elements show unexpected behavior as endoclitics due to a historical combination of univerbation, where formerly independent elements fused into a single word, and analogical change, where even words that were not historically univerbated began to behave as though they, too, were part of the univerbated class (see also Harris (2000) and Good (2003b: 511–516)).

Of course, such anecdotal examples can hardly stand in for a full-fledged examination of the historical forces that result in the development of templatic constructions, and work is especially needed to understand the rise of syntactic templates given the relative lack of research that has been undertaken on historical syntax as compared to historical morphology and phonology. Nevertheless, if we want to truly understand why templates are the way they are, it seems essential to consider not simply the templates of the world's languages in terms of their grammatical states but also in terms of the processes which resulted in those states, echoing suggestions of Greenberg (1978, 1995) for the study of typology in general.

---

[6] See also footnote 6 in Chapter 1 for reference to the Principle of Templatic Attraction of Leer (1991: 92), which is supposed to target formally similar elements.

Appendix
Specification of template description language

This appendix gives a specification of the ontological structure of the linguistic aspects of the database used in this study (and, therefore, leaves out things such as information relating to referencing sources of the data, administrative notes, etc.). It represents two primary kinds of information, a taxonomic structure of categories (referred to as *types* below) and the typological features associated with each category (see Chapter 2 for further discussion). The symbols used in the specification are described in Table A.1. An additional convention is that a subtype should be understood as inheriting any features associated with its supertype. The specification also indicates whether a feature's value is an instance of a given type, a string representation, or a specification of a type or set of types (in which case no qualifier is given unless a set of types is involved). As discussed in Section 2.3.2, the ontological structure is designed for this particular study and is not intended to be "complete" in all respects. For purposes of database maintenance, each of the terms in the specification is associated with a specific namespace (see Bray et al. (2009)). These are not included here. The machine-readable form of this specification, along with the database itself and accompanying processing scripts, can be found at https://github.com/jcgood/desmeme.

The types employed in this study, and their associated features, are given below, along with brief descriptions. The prefix *gold* attached to certain types is used for terms drawn from the General Ontology for Linguistic Description

Table A.1 *Conventions used to describe the database ontology*

SYMBOL	DESCRIPTION
⊢	A top-level *type*
↳	A *subtype* of the preceding type
•	A FEATURE–*value* pairing associated with the preceding *type*
→	A pairing of a FEATURE and a *value*

Specification of template description language   273

(GOLD) (Farrar & Langendoen 2003, 2009, Farrar & Lewis 2007), whose current version can be found at http://linguistics-ontology.org. Full descriptions of the features are given after the types are specified.

⊢ *coherence*   A supertype for characterizing whether the elements that can fill a given component are of a coherent functional class or not.

- NAME → string representation of *name*

↳ *coherent*   A type that specifies that a given component is filled with a functionally coherent class of elements. It is associated with a feature specifying that class.

- CLASS → *grammaticalCategory*

↳ *incoherent*   A type that specifies that a given component is not filled with a functionally coherent class of elements. It is associated with a feature allowing a set of the functional classes that it is associated with to be specified.

- CLASSES → set of *grammaticalCategory*

⊢ *component*   A type for templatic components. This is one of the fundamental types in the typology.

- NAME → string representation of *name*
- ELASTICITY → instance of *elasticity*
- FILLEDNESS → instance of *filledness*
- STABILITY → instance of *stability*

⊢ *conditioning*   A supertype for characterizing the grammatical locus of some observable set of templatic restrictions, for instance, whether a template targets phonological elements or morphosyntactic ones. All templates are associated with some conditioning.

- NAME → string representation of *name*

↳ *morphosyntacticConditioning*   A type for characterizing cases where a template's conditioning environment is morphosyntactic in nature.

↳ *constructionalConditioning*   A type for characterizing cases where a template's conditioning environment is constructional (i.e., morphological or syntactic) in nature.

↳ *lexicoconstructionalConditioning*   A type for characterizing cases where a template's conditioning environment is lexico-constructional in nature, that is where it involves a constructional environment where a specific lexical item or set of lexical items must also appear.

- FILLED COMPONENTS → instance of *filledComponentSet*
- FILLER POSITION → *position*

274   Specification of template description language

↳ *phonologicalConditioning* A type for characterizing cases where a template's conditioning environment is phonological in nature.

↳ *prosodicConditioning* A type for characterizing cases where a template's conditioning environment is prosodic in nature.

⊢ *constituent* A supertype for characterizing the kind of constituents that a given set of templatic restrictions applies over.

↳ *morphosyntacticConstituent* A supertype for specifying that the linguistic constituents that a set of templatic restrictions applies over are morphosyntactic in nature.

↳ *morphologicalConstituent* A type for specifying that the linguistic constituents that a set of templatic restrictions applies over are morphological in nature (e.g., morphemes within a word).

↳ *syntacticConstituent* A type for specifying that the linguistic constituents that a set of templatic restrictions applies over are syntactic in nature (e.g., phrases in a clause).

↳ *phonologicalConstituent* A supertype for specifying that the linguistic constituents that a set of templatic restrictions applies over are phonological in nature.

↳ *prosodicConstituent* A type for specifying that the linguistic constituents that a set of templatic restrictions applies over are prosodic in nature (e.g., a phonological phrase). The labels of the subtypes should be readily interpretable for their category.

↳ *gold:Mora*

↳ *gold:Syllable*

↳ *prosodicWord*

↳ *segment* A type for specifying that the linguistic constituents that a set of templatic restrictions applies over consist of segments

⊢ *elasticity* A supertype for characterizing the overall size of a component, including whether or not its size is fixed or variable.

- NAME → string representation of *name*

↳ *elastic* A type that specifies that a given component can potentially be filled with a varying number of elements. It is associated with features specifying the maximum and minimum number of elements it can contain.

- MAXIMUM → integer
- MINIMUM → integer

Specification of template description language

↳ *inelastic* A type that specifies that a given component must be filled with a fixed number of elements (usually just one). It is associated with a feature specifying the number of elements it must contain.

- COUNT → integer

⊢ *exceptionality* A supertype for characterizing the nature of observed exceptions to a given templatic pattern.

↳ *attestable* A supertype for those cases where exceptionality appears to be possible based on a language's overall grammatical patterns.

    ↳ *lexical* A type for cases where the exceptions to a templatic pattern are lexically conditioned.

    ↳ *semantic* A type for cases where the exceptions to a templatic pattern are semantically conditioned.

↳ *noKnownExceptions* A type for cases where a language's grammar suggests there could be potential surface violations of a template, but where no actual surface violations are attested.

⊢ *filledComponentSet* A type that serves as a container for the set of components (most typically just one) that are filled in a given template. The FILLED COMPONENT feature can be repeated as needed.

- NAME → string representation of *name*
- FILLED COMPONENT → instance of *component*

⊢ *filledness* A supertype for characterizing the nature of the class of elements that is found within a given component, for instance whether it can be occupied by only one morpheme or an entire class of morphemes.

- NAME → string representation of *name*

↳ *filled* A type that specifies that a given component is always fully or partly occupied by a specific element (e.g., a specific morpheme). If the type is not specified as *partiallyFilled*, then the use of this type should be interpreted as "completely filled."

- FILLER CLASS → *grammaticalCategory*
- FORM → instance of *form*

    ↳ *partiallyFilled* A subtype that inherits its properties from both the *filled* and *open* types and that specifies that a given component is internally complex with part of its material always consisting of a specific element and part of its material drawn from a set of elements.

    - FILLER PLACEMENT → *position*

↳ *null* A value for the FILLEDNESS feature of null components (i.e., components serving as placeholders for positions not found in a given template).

↳ *open* A type that specifies that a given component's fillers are always fully or partly drawn from a class of elements (e.g., morphemes of a particular semantic type). If the type is not specified as *partiallyFilled*, then the use of this type should be interpreted as "completely open."

- COHERENCE → instance of *coherence*

Specification of template description language

↳ *partiallyFilled* A subtype that inherits its properties from both the *filled* and *open* types and that specifies that a given component is internally complex with part of its material always consisting of a specific element and part of its material drawn from a set of elements.

- FILLER PLACEMENT → *position*

⊢ *form* A supertype that could encompass various kinds of linguistic forms. In the present taxonomy, it serves as the supertype only for lineates.

- NAME → string representation of *name*
- GOLD:INLANGUAGE → instance of *language identifier*

↳ *lineate* A supertype for types of linguistic form that involve stipulation of linear ordering. A template is a subtype of lineate.

↳ *canonicalLineate* A type for sets of linearization restrictions that are considered to be "normal" and, therefore, not templatic. The linear specifications associated with most lexical items would fall into this type.

- LIAISON → *liaison*
- TRANSCRIPTION → instance of *transcription*

↳ *desmeme* A type for sets of of linearization restrictions that are not predictable and are not associated with the ordering of segments or suprasegments of a lexical item. Templates can be understood as a subclass of desmemes, though they are not given formal status in this ontology due to problems with devising a precise definition for them.

- CONDITIONING → instance of *conditioning*
- FOUNDATION → instance of *foundation*
- FUNCTION → *grammaticalCategory*
- STRICTURE → instance of *stricture*
- VIOLABILITY → instance of *violability*

↳ *embeddedDesmeme* A subtype of desmeme used for cases where a component of a template is itself a desmeme. This category does not logically require its own type, but this is useful in the present database since the templatic properties of embedded desmemes are not fully encoded within it.

⊢ *foundation* A supertype for subtypes that classify the nature of the relationships holding among a template's components, including partial indication of their relative order.

- NAME → string representation of *name*
- LEFT SUPPORT → instance of *component*
- RESTKOMPONENTEN → instance of *restkomponentenSet*

Specification of template description language 277

- RIGHT SUPPORT → instance of *component*

↳ *arch* A type of foundation whose components are analyzed as organized around a single privileged component. It has five predefined structural positions, the keystone (for the privileged component), the left and right voussoirs, and the left and right supports.

- KEYSTONE → instance of *component*
- LEFT VOUSSOIR → instance of *component*
- RIGHT VOUSSOIR → instance of *component*

↳ *span* A type of foundation without a privileged component around which the other components are organized. Its only predefined structural positions are the left and right supports.

⊢ *grammaticalCategory* A supertype for general grammatical categories that can be used to specify the function and conditioning of a given template or the possible fillers of components. These types do not enter into the typological comparison at present but are included due to their potential interest for purposes of reference and for future studies. A number of these types are drawn from the GOLD ontology. Those that are not should be interpretable on the basis of their labels or the descriptions of the relevant templates in Chapter 3 of this book.

↳ *TenseMoodAspect*
  ↳ *tense*
↳ *adjunct*
↳ *adpositionalPhrase*
↳ *argument*
↳ *clauseChaining*
↳ *consonant*
↳ *coronalConsonant*
↳ *focal*
↳ *focus*
↳ *gold:Complementizer*
↳ *gold:MainClause*
↳ *gold:Mora*
↳ *gold:Noun*
↳ *gold:Object*
  ↳ *gold:DirectObject*
  ↳ *gold:IndirectObject*
↳ *gold:Stem*
↳ *gold:Subject*
↳ *gold:Syllable*
↳ *gold:Verbal*
  ↳ *finite*

278 Specification of template description language

↳ *gold:Auxiliary*
↳ *gold:VerbalParticle*
↳ *locative*
↳ *negative*
↳ *nonCoronalConsonant*
↳ *oblique*
↳ *personReference*
  ↳ *objectReference*
  ↳ *subjectReference*
↳ *plural*
↳ *prosodicWord*
↳ *topical*
↳ *topicalization*
↳ *valency*

⊢ *liaison*   A supertype for characterizing prosodic dependencies for a given form, for instance, whether it can be understood as prosodically independent or is dependent on a host in some general way.

↳ *dependent*   A type for characterizing forms that are dependent (e.g., affixes or clitics). Only one subtype is defined in the present typology, for characterizing suffixing elements, since this is all that has been required to code the data to this point.

  ↳ *sinistrous*   A type of dependence for elements which lean "left" on their hosts, e.g., suffixes and enclitics.

↳ *independent*   A type of liaison for forms which are not prosodically dependent.

⊢ *position*   A supertype for referring to linear positions as needed in the descriptions of the templates.

  • NAME → string representation of *name*

↳ *associatePosition*   A supertype for the positional specifications of components with dependencies on other components.

  ↳ *left*   A type specifying that a component is dependent on a component appearing before it in the template.

  ↳ *right*   A type specifying that a component is dependent on a component appearing after it in the template.

↳ *fillerPosition*   A supertype for the position of a filler element in a lexico-constructional template. This position is evaluated with respect to the whole template, not just the component that the filler is found in.

  ↳ *final*   A type specifying that the filler of a lexico-constructional template is in the final position of the template.

  ↳ *medial*   A type specifying that the filler of a lexico-constructional template is in a medial position in the template.

  ↳ *multiple*   A type specifying that there are multiple fillers in a lexico-constructional template.

Specification of template description language 279

⊢ *relations*   A supertype for subtypes classifying the nature of the relations holding among a template's components.

↳ *simple*   A type for classifying the components in a template where their categorial relationship to each other is simply that they are part of the same template.

↳ *taxonomic*   A type for classifying the components in a template in cases where they can be divided up into distinct categories, creating taxonomic relationships among them.

⊢ *reparability*   A supertype for characterizing kinds of possible repair strategies for potential violations of templatic restrictions.

↳ *irreparable*   A type indicating that potential violations to a template, when they occur, cannot be repaired.

↳ *reparable*   A supertype indicating that potential violations to a template, when they occur, can be repaired.

↳ *morphosyntacticRepair*   A supertype indicating that potential violations to a template, when they occur, can be repaired using a morphosyntactic strategy.

↳ *homophony*   A type indicating that potential violations to a template, when they occur, can be repaired by allowing a surface construction to exhibit otherwise unexpected homophony.

↳ *morphosyntacticInsertion*   A type indicating that potential violations to a template, when they occur, can be repaired via the insertion of a morphosyntactic element whose appearance would not otherwise be expected.

↳ *phonologicalRepair*   A type indicating that potential violations to a template, when they occur, can be repaired using a phonological strategy.

↳ *shortening*   A type indicating that potential violations to a template, when they occur, can be repaired by shortening a constituent that would otherwise be expected to have a longer form than the one that appears on the surface.

⊢ *restkomponentenSet*   A type for a container where those components not occupying predefined structural slots in a template can be listed as part of a template's foundation. The RESTKOMPONENTE feature can be repeated as needed.

- NAME → string representation of *name*
- RESTKOMPONENTE → instance of *component*

⊢ *stability*   A supertype for characterizing dependencies among components, in particular for cases where the nature of the content of one component can be somehow dependent on what is found in another component.

- NAME → string representation of *name*

↳ *stable*   A type that specifies that a given component does not exhibit any dependencies with any other component.

280 Specification of template description language

↳ *unstable* A type that specifies that a given component exhibits a dependency with another component. Only one dependency can be specified per component since the need for more than one has not yet arisen in the database.

- ASSOCIATE → instance of *component*
- ASSOCIATE POSITION → instance of *associatePosition*

⊢ *stricture* A supertype for subtypes that give a high-level classification of the nature of the linear stipulations associated with a given template, in particular whether they involve restrictions on the length of a constituent or the order of its components.

- NAME → string representation of *name*
- CONSTITUENT → *constituent*
- COUNT → integer

↳ *length* A type for classifying a template whose linear stipulations involve a restriction on the size of a constituent.
↳ *order* A type for classifying a template whose linear stipulations involve a restriction on the order of a set of elements.

- RELATIONS → *relations*

⊢ *transcription* A type that specifies a given string is a transcriptional representation of some linguistic form.

- NAME → string representation of *name*
- TRANSCRIPTION STRING → string representation of *transcription*

⊢ *violability* A supertype for subtypes that characterize whether or not the linearization restrictions of a given template can be violated and what repair strategies may be activated in cases of potential violations.

- NAME → string representation of *name*

↳ *notViolable* A type for indicating that, given other aspects of a language's grammar, there is not the potential for a specific template to be violated.
↳ *potentiallyViolable* A type for indicating that, given other aspects of a language's grammar, there is the potential for a specific template to be violated, in which case further specification is given regarding the nature of exceptions to the template and what repair strategies (if any) may be applied to those exceptions.

- EXCEPTIONALITY → *exceptionality*
- REPARABILITY → *reparability*

Specification of template description language 281

The various features employed in this study are given below, with brief descriptions for each feature. Each of these features is used for at least one of the types above.

- NAME   A string representation of the name for an instance of a type used for purposes of reference.

- ASSOCIATE   A feature for specifying the component that another component is dependent upon.

- ASSOCIATE POSITION   A feature for specifying the position of a component that another component is dependent upon with respect to the component itself.

- CLASS   A feature for specifying the class of elements which appear in a coherent component.

- CLASSES   A feature for specifying a set of classes for the elements which can appear in an incoherent component.

- COHERENCE   A feature for specifying the coherence of a component.

- CONDITIONING   A feature for specifying the environment that conditions the appearance of a template.

- CONSTITUENT   A feature for specifying the kind of constituent a set of templatic restrictions operates over.

- COUNT   A feature for cases where a given type can be associated with a fixed countable number of subunits. Its precise interpretation is dependent on the type it is associated with (e.g., a component versus a stricture type).

- ELASTICITY   A feature for specifying the elasticity of a component.

- EXCEPTIONALITY   A feature for specifying the nature of attested exceptions to a given set of templatic restrictions.

- FILLED COMPONENT   A feature for specifying that a given component in a template is filled.

- FILLED COMPONENTS   A feature which points to a container for those components which are filled within a template.

- FILLEDNESS   A feature for specifying the filledness of a component.

- FILLER CLASS   A feature for specifying the class of an element which serves as a filler for a component.

- FILLER PLACEMENT   A feature for specifying where, in a partially filled component, the filler element appears.

- FILLER POSITION   A feature for specifying where, in a lexico-constructional template, filler elements appear.

- FORM   A feature for characterizing a given object as an instance of a linguistic form. It is primarily used to classify filler elements in a template.

282   Specification of template description language

- FOUNDATION   A feature which points to the foundation of a template.

- FUNCTION   A feature for specifying the general function of a given template in the context of a language's grammar.

- KEYSTONE   A feature which characterizes a component in an arch template as a keystone (i.e., as privileged with respect to the foundation's organization).

- LEFT SUPPORT   A feature which characterizes a component in a template as a left support (i.e., as the leftmost component in the template).

- LEFT VOUSSOIR   A feature which characterizes a component in an arch template as a left voussoir (i.e., as the component immediately to the left of the keystone).

- LIAISON   A feature for specifying the prosodic dependency (or lack thereof) of a specific linguistic form.

- MAXIMUM   A feature for specifying the maximum size of an elastic template. In the database itself, this is set to 100 for cases where there is no templatically prescribed limit on the size of a component.

- MINIMUM   A feature for specifying the minimum size of an elastic template.

- RELATIONS   A feature for specifying the nature of the relations holding among the components of an order template (e.g., whether there are taxonomic relations holding among them).

- REPARABILITY   A feature for specifying the nature of any strategies available for repairing potential violations of a template's restrictions.

- RESTKOMPONENTE   A feature which classifies a component as not belonging to any of the specially classified structural slots of a given template.

- RESTKOMPONENTEN   A feature which points to a container for those components which do not belong to any of the specially classified structural slots of a given template.

- RIGHT SUPPORT   A feature which characterizes a component in a template as a right support (i.e., as the rightmost component in the template).

- RIGHT VOUSSOIR   A feature which characterizes a component in an arch template as a right voussoir (i.e., as the component immediately to the right of the keystone).

- STABILITY   A feature for specifying a component's stability (i.e., whether or not it shows a dependency with another component).

- STRICTURE   A feature which points to a characterization of the stricture of a template.

- TRANSCRIPTION   A feature for specifying a linguistic transcription that some form is associated with.

- TRANSCRIPTION STRING   A feature which specifies that a string is being used to represent a transcription.

- VIOLABILITY   A feature for specifying whether or not a set of templatic restrictions is potentially violable or not.

- gold:inLanguage   A feature for specifying the language a given form is found in.

References

Abasheikh, Mohammed. 1978. The grammar of Chimwi:ni causatives. Ph.D. dissertation, University of Illinois.

Aboh, Enoch O. 2007. Leftward focus versus rightward focus: The Kwa-Bantu conspiracy. In Nancy C. Kula & Lutz Marten (eds.), *Bantu in Bloomsbury: Special issue on Bantu linguistics* (SOAS Working Papers in Linguistics, volume 15), 81–104. London: SOAS.

Aikhenvald, Alexandra Y. 2007. Typological distinctions in word-formation. In Timothy Shopen (ed.), *Language typology and syntactic description*, volume III: *Grammatical categories and the lexicon* (second edition), 1–65. Cambridge University Press.

Akmajian, Adrian, Susan M. Steele & Thomas Wasow. 1979. The category AUX in universal grammar. *Linguistic Inquiry* 10. 1–64.

Alderete, John, Jill Beckman, Laura Benua, Amalia Gnanadesikan, John McCarthy & Suzanne Urbanczyk. 1999. Reduplication with fixed segmentism. *Linguistic Inquiry* 30. 327–364.

Allemang, Dean & James Hendler. 2011. *Semantic Web for the working ontologist: Effective modeling in RDFS and OWL* (second edition). Amsterdam: Elsevier.

Alsina, Alex. 1999. Where's the mirror principle? *The Linguistic Review* 16. 1–42.

Anceaux, J. C. 1965. *The Nimboran language: Phonology and morphology*. The Hague: M. Nijhoff.

Anderson, Stephen C. 1979. Verb structure. In Larry M. Hyman (ed.), *Aghem grammatical structure: With special reference to noun classes, tense-aspect and focus marking*, 73–136. Los Angeles: University of Southern California Department of Linguistics.

Anderson, Stephen R. 1992. *A-morphous morphology*. Cambridge University Press.

1993. Wackernagel's revenge: Clitics, morphology, and the syntax of second position. *Language* 69. 68–98.

1996. How to put your clitics in their place or why the best account of second-position phenomena may be something like the optimal one. *The Linguistic Review* 13. 165–191.

2000. Toward an optimal account of second position phenomena. In Joost Dekkers, Frank van der Leeuw & Jeroen van de Weijer (eds.), *Optimality theory: Phonology, syntax, and acquisition*, 302–333. Oxford University Press.

2005. *Aspects of the theory of clitics*. Oxford University Press.

Arnold, Doug & Evita Linardaki. 2007. A data-oriented parsing model for HPSG. In Anders Søgaard & Petter Haugereid (eds.), *Proceedings of the 2nd International*

284 References

Workshop on Typed Feature Structure Grammars (TFSG '07), 1–8. Copenhagen: Center for Sprogteknologi.

Aronoff, Mark. 1994. *Morphology by itself: Stems and inflectional classes*. Cambridge, MA: MIT Press.

1998. Isomorphism and monotonicity: Or the disease model of morphology. In Steven G. Lapointe, Diane K. Brentari & Patrick M. Farrell (eds.), *Morphology and its relation to phonology and syntax*, 419–425. Stanford: CSLI.

Ashburner, Michael, Catherine A. Ball, Judith A. Blake, David Botstein, Heather Butler, J. Michael Cherry, Allan P. Davis, Kara Dolinski, Selina S. Dwight, Janan T. Eppig, Midori A. Harris, David P. Hill, Laurie Issel-Tarver, Andrew Kasarskis, Suzanna Lewis, John C. Matese, Joel E. Richardson, Martin Ringwald, Gerald M. Rubin & Gavin Sherlock. 2000. Gene ontology: Tool for the unification of biology. *Nature Genetics* 25. 25–29.

Asudeh, Ash & Ida Toivonen. 2010. Lexical-Functional Grammar. In Bernd Heine & Heiko Narrog (eds.), *The Oxford handbook of linguistic analysis*, 425–458. Oxford University Press.

Awóyalé, Yíwọlá. 1988. *Complex predicates and verb serialization*. Cambridge, MA: Lexicon Project, Center for Cognitive Science, MIT.

Axelrod, Melissa. 1993. *The semantics of time: Aspectual categorization in Koyukon Athabaskan*. Lincoln: University of Nebraska Press.

Baerman, Matthew. 2006. Nimboran (Trans-New Guinea). In *Typological database on deponency*. Guildford, UK: Surrey Morphology Group, CMC, University of Surrey. www.smg.surrey.ac.uk/deponency/Examples/Nimboran.htm.

Bagemihl, Bruce. 1991. Syllable structure in Bella Coola. *Linguistic Inquiry* 22. 589–646.

Bagga, Jay. 2004. Old and new generalizations of line graphs. *International Journal of Mathematics and Mathematical Sciences* 2004. 1509–1521.

Baker, Mark C. 1985. The mirror principle and morphosyntactic explanation. *Linguistic Inquiry* 16. 373–415.

1988. *Incorporation: A theory of grammatical function changing*. University of Chicago Press.

1996. *The Polysynthesis Parameter*. Oxford University Press.

2010. Formal Generative Typology. In Bernd Heine & Heiko Narrog (eds.), *The Oxford handbook of linguistic analysis*, 285–312. Oxford University Press.

Baker, Mark C. & Jim McCloskey. 2007. On the relationship of typology to theoretical syntax. *Linguistic Typology* 11. 285–296.

Bakker, Peter, Aymeric Daval-Markussen, Mikael Parkvall & Ingo Plag. 2011. Creoles are typologically distinct from non-creoles. *Journal of Pidgin and Creole Languages* 26. 5–42.

Bandelt, Hans-Jürgen & Andreas W. M. Dress. 1992a. A canonical decomposition theory for metrics on a finite set. *Advances in Mathematics* 92. 47–105.

1992b. Split decomposition: A new and useful approach to phylogenetic analysis of distance data. *Molecular Phylogenetics and Evolution* 1. 242–252.

Barrett-Keach, Camillia N. 1986. Word-internal evidence from Swahili for Aux/Infl. *Linguistic Inquiry* 17. 559–664.

Bastin, Yvonne. 1986. Les suffixes causatifs dans les langues bantoues. *Africana Linguistica* 10. 55–145.

References 285

Bauer, Laurie & Salvador Valera. 2005. Conversion or zero-derivation: An introduction. In Laurie Bauer & Salvador Valera (eds.), *Approaches to conversion/zero-derivation*, 7–17. Münster: Waxmann.

Bender, Emily M. 2000. Syntactic variation and linguistic competence: The case of AAVE copula absence. Ph.D. dissertation, Stanford University.

Bender, Emily M., Dan Flickinger & Stephan Oepen. 2002. The Grammar Matrix: An open-source starter-kit for the rapid development of cross-linguistically consistent broad-coverage precision grammars. In John Carroll, Nelleke Oostdijk & Richard Sutcliffe (eds.), *Proceedings of the Workshop on Grammar Engineering and Evaluation at the 19th International Conference on Computational Linguistics*, 8–14. Taipei, Taiwan.

den Besten, Hans. 1983. On the interaction of root transformations and lexical deletive rules. In Werner Abraham (ed.), *On the formal syntax of the Westgermania: Papers from the 3rd Groningen Grammar Talks, Groningen, January 1981*, 47–131. Amsterdam: Benjamins.

Bickel, Balthasar. 2007. Typology in the 21st century: Major current developments. *Linguistic Typology* 11. 239–251.

2008. A refined sampling procedure for genealogical control. *Sprachtypologie und Universalienforschung* 61. 221–233.

2010. Capturing particulars and universals in clause linkage: A multivariate analysis. In Isabelle Bril (ed.), *Clause-hierarchy and clause-linking: The syntax and pragmatics interface*, 51–102. Amsterdam: Benjamins.

2011. Grammatical relations typology. In Jae Jung Song (ed.), *The Oxford handbook of linguistic typology*, 399–444. Oxford University Press.

Bickel, Balthasar, Goma Banjade, Martin Gaenszle, Elena Lieven, Netra Prasad Paudyal, Ichchha Purna Rai, Manoj Rai, Novel Kishore Rai & Sabine Stoll. 2007. Free prefix ordering in Chintang. *Language* 83. 43–73.

Bickel, Balthasar, Bernard Comrie & Martin Haspelmath. 2008. The Leipzig Glossing Rules: Conventions for interlinear morpheme by morpheme glosses. www.eva .mpg.de/lingua/pdf/LGR08.02.05.pdf.

Bickel, Balthasar, Kristine A. Hildebrandt & René Schiering. 2009. The distribution of phonological word domains: A probabilistic typology. In Janet Grijzenhout & Barış Kabak (eds.), *Phonological domains: Universals and deviations*, 47–75. Berlin: De Gruyter Mouton.

Bickel, Balthasar & Johanna Nichols. 2002. Autotypologizing databases and their use in fieldwork. In *Proceedings of the International Workshop on Resources and Tools in Field Linguistics, Las Palmas, 26–27 May 2002*. Nijmegen: ISLE and DOBES. www.mpi.nl/lrec/2002/papers/lrec-pap-20-BickelNichols.pdf.

2007. Inflectional morphology. In Timothy Shopen (ed.), *Language typology and syntactic description*, volume III: *Grammatical categories and the lexicon* (second edition), 169–240. Cambridge University Press.

2013. Inflectional synthesis of the verb. In Matthew S. Dryer & Martin Haspelmath (eds.), *The World Atlas of Language Structures online*. Leipzig: Max Planck Institute for Evolutionary Anthropology. http://wals.info/chapter/22.

Bird, Steven. 1992. Finite-state phonology in HPSG. In Christian Boitet (ed.), *Proceedings of the fifteenth International Conference on Computational Linguistics (COLING-92)*, 74–80. Grenoble: IVR Imprimerie.

286   References

1995. *Computational phonology: A constraint-based approach.* Cambridge University Press.

Bird, Steven & Ewan Klein. 1994. Phonological analysis in typed feature systems. *Computational Linguistics* 20. 455–491.

Bisetto, Antonietta & Sergio Scalise. 2005. The classification of compounds. *Lingue e Linguaggio* 2. 319–332.

Bizer, Christian, Tom Heath & Tim Berners-Lee. 2009a. Linked data – The story so far. *International Journal on Semantic Web and Information Systems* 5. 1–22.

Bizer, Christian, Jens Lehmann, Georgi Kobilarov, Sören Auer, Christian Becker, Richard Cyganiak & Sebastian Hellmann. 2009b. DBpedia – A crystallization point for the Web of Data. *Web Semantics: Science, Services and Agents on the World Wide Web* 7. 154–165.

Bjerre, Tavs, Eva Engels, Henrik Jørgensen & Sten Vikner. 2008. Points of convergence between functional and formal approaches to syntactic analysis. *Working Papers in Scandinavian Syntax* 82. 131–166.

Blackings, Mairi & Nigel Fabb. 2003. *A grammar of Ma'di.* Berlin: Mouton.

Blevins, James P. 2011. Feature-based grammar. In Robert D. Borsley & Kersti Börjars (eds.), *Non-transformational syntax: Formal and explicit models of grammar.* Chichester: Wiley-Blackwell.

Blevins, Juliette. 1995. The syllable in phonological theory. In John A. Goldsmith (ed.), *The handbook of phonological theory*, 206–244. Oxford: Blackwell.

Blondel, Vincent D., Anahí Gajardo, Maureen Heymans, Pierre Senellart & Paul Van Dooren. 2004. A measure of similarity between graph vertices: Applications to synonym extraction and web searching. *SIAM Review* 46. 647–666.

Bloomfield, Leonard. 1962. *The Menomini language.* New Haven: Yale University Press.

Bobaljik, Jonathan David. 2000. The ins and outs of contextual allomorphy. In Kleanthes K. Grohmann & Caro Struijke (eds.), *University of Maryland Working Papers in Linguistics*, volume 10, 35–71. College Park, MD: University of Maryland Department of Linguistics.

2002. A-chains at the PF-interface: Copies and covert movement. *Natural Language and Linguistic Theory* 20. 197–267.

Bonami, Olivier & Gilles Boyé. 2007. French pronominal clitics and the design of Paradigm Function Morphology. In Geert Booij, Luca Ducceschi, Bernard Fradin, Emiliano Guevara, Angela Ralli & Sergio Scalise (eds.), *On-line proceedings of the Fifth Mediterranean Morphology Meeting*, 291–322. Università degli Studi di Bologna.

Bond, Oliver & Gregory D. S. Anderson. 2014. The functions of Cognate Head-Dependent Constructions: Evidence from Africa. *Linguistic Typology* 18. 215–250.

Bonet, Eulàlia. 1991. Morphology after syntax: Pronominal clitics in Romance. Ph.D. dissertation, MIT.

1995. Feature structure of Romance clitics. *Natural Language and Linguistic Theory* 13. 607–647.

Booij, Geert E. 2010a. Construction morphology. *Language and Linguistics Compass* 4. 543–555.

2010b. *Construction morphology.* Oxford University Press.

References

Bostoen, Koen. 2008. Bantu Spirantization: Morphologization, lexicalization and historical classification. *Diachronica* 25. 299–356.

Bottazzini, Umberto. 1986. *The higher calculus: A history of real and complex analysis from Euler to Weierstrass.* New York: Springer.

Bouma, Gosse & Gertjan van Noord. 1998. Word order constraints on verb clusters in German and Dutch. In Erhard W. Hinrichs, Andreas Kathol & Tsuneko Nakazawa (eds.), *Syntax and semantics*, volume 30: *Complex predicates in nonderivational syntax*, 43–72. San Diego: Academic Press.

Bošković, Željko. 2001. *On the nature of the syntax-phonology interface.* Amsterdam: Elsevier.

Bray, Tim, Dave Hollander, Andrew Layman, Richard Tobin & Henry S. Thompson (eds.). 2009. *Namespaces in XML 1.0* (third edition). World Wide Web Consortium. www.w3.org/TR/2009/REC-xml-names-20091208/.

Brentari, Diane. 1993. Establishing a sonority hierarchy in American Sign Language: The use of simultaneous structure in phonology. *Phonology* 10. 281–306.

2005. Representing handshapes in sign languages using morphological templates. In Helen Leuninger & Daniela Happ (eds.), *Gebärdensprachen: Struktur, Erwerb, Verwendung Linguistische Berichte*, Sonderheft 13, 145–177. Hamburg: Helmut Buske.

Bresnan, Joan. 2001. *Lexical-functional syntax.* Oxford: Blackwell.

Bresnan, Joan & Sam A. Mchombo. 1987. Topic, pronoun, and agreement in Chicheŵa. *Language* 63. 741–782.

Brickley, Dan & R. V. Guha (eds.). 2004. *RDF vocabulary description language 1.0: RDF Schema.* W3C Recommendation. www.w3.org/TR/rdf-schema/.

Brinton, Laurel J. & Elizabeth Closs Traugott. 2005. *Lexicalization and language change.* Cambridge University Press.

Broadbent, Sylvia M. 1964. *The Southern Sierra Miwok language.* Berkeley: University of California Press.

Broselow, Ellen. 1995. Skeletal positions and moras. In John A. Goldsmith (ed.), *The handbook of phonological theory*, 175–205. Oxford: Blackwell.

Brown, Dunstan & Marina Chumakina. 2012. What there might be and what there is: An introduction to Canonical Typology. In Dunstan Brown, Marina Chumakina & Greville G. Corbett (eds.), *Canonical morphology and syntax*, 1–19. Oxford University Press.

Browne, Wayles E. 1974. On the problem of enclitic placement in Serbo-Croatian. In Richard D. Brecht & Catherine V. Chvany (eds.), *Slavic transformational syntax*, 36–52. Ann Arbor: Department of Slavic Languages and Literatures, University of Michigan.

Bryant, David, Flavia Filimon & Russell D. Gray. 2005. Untangling our past: Languages, trees, splits and networks. In Ruth Mace, Clare J. Holden & Stephen Shennan (eds.), *The evolution of cultural diversity: A phylogenetic approach*, 67–83. University College London Press.

Bryant, David & Vincent Moulton. 2004. Neighbor-Net: An agglomerative method for the construction of phylogenetic networks. *Molecular Biology and Evolution* 21. 255–265.

Bybee, Joan L. 1985. *Morphology: A study of the relation between meaning and form.* Amsterdam: Benjamins.

288 References

Bybee, Joan L., William Pagliuca & Revere Perkins. 1994. *The evolution of grammar: Tense, aspect, and modality in the languages of the world.* University of Chicago Press.

Caballero, Gabriela & Alice C. Harris. 2012. A working typology of multiple exponence. In Ferenc Kiefer, Mária Ladányi & Péter Siptár (eds.), *Current issues in morphological theory: (Ir)regularity, analogy, and frequency*, 163–188. Amsterdam: Benjamins.

Cain, William. 1893. *Theory of voussoir arches* (second edition). New York: D. Van Nostrand.

Cairns, Charles E. & Mark H. Feinstein. 1982. Markedness and the theory of syllable structure. *Linguistic Inquiry* 13. 193–225.

Campbell, Amy M. 2012. The morphosyntax of discontinuous exponence. Ph.D. dissertation, University of California, Berkeley.

Carlson, Robert. 2000. Event-views and transitivity in the Supyire verbal system. *Cahiers Voltaïques/Gur Papers* 5. 39–58.

Carpenter, Bob. 1992. *The logic of typed feature structures.* Cambridge University Press.

Carstairs-McCarthy, Andrew. 1999. *The origins of complex language: An inquiry into the evolutionary beginnings of sentences, syllables, and truth.* Oxford University Press.

Chappell, Hilary. 2006. Reproducibility: A summing up. *Linguistic Typology* 10. 124–128.

Chiarcos, Christian, Sebastian Hellmann & Sebastian Nordhoff. 2012. Introduction and overview. In Christian Chiarcos, Sebastian Nordhoff & Sebastian Hellmann (eds.), *Linked data in linguistics: Representing and connecting language data and language metadata*, 1–12. Berlin: Springer.

Chomsky, Noam. 1957. *Syntactic structures.* The Hague: Mouton.

1965. *Aspects of the theory of syntax.* Cambridge, MA: MIT Press.

Cogill-Koez, Dorothea. 2000. A model of signed language classifier predicates as templated visual representation. *Sign language & linguistics* 3. 209–236.

Comrie, Bernard. 1976. *Aspect.* Cambridge University Press.

Conathan, Lisa & Jeff Good. 2001. Morphosyntactic reduplication in Chechen and Ingush. In Arika Okrent & John Boyle (eds.), *Proceedings of the Chicago Linguistic Society 36-2: The panels*, 49–61. Chicago Linguistic Society.

Connolly, John H. 1983. Placement rules and syntactic templates. In Simon C. Dik (ed.), *Advances in functional grammar*, 247–266. Dordrecht: Foris.

1991. *Constituent order in Functional Grammar: Synchronic and diachronic perspectives.* Berlin: Walter de Gruyter.

Copestake, Ann. 2002. *Implementing typed feature structure grammars.* Stanford: CSLI.

Corbett, Greville G. 2005. The canonical approach in typology. In Zygmunt Frajzyngier, Adam Hodges & David S. Rood (eds.), *Linguistic diversity and language theories*, 25–49. Amsterdam: Benjamins.

2007. Canonical typology, suppletion, and possible words. *Language* 83. 8–42.

2012. *Features.* Cambridge University Press.

Corina, David & Wendy Sandler. 1993. On the nature of phonological structure in sign language. *Phonology* 10. 165–207.

References 289

Creissels, Denis. 2006. S-O-V-X constituent order and constituent order alternations in West African languages. In Rebecca T. Cover & Yuni Kim (eds.), *Proceedings of the thirty-first annual meeting of the Berkeley Linguistics Society: Special session on languages of West Africa*, 37–51. Berkeley Linguistics Society.

Cristofaro, Sonia. 2009. Grammatical categories and relations: Universality vs. language-specificity and construction-specificity. *Language and Linguistics Compass* 3. 441–479.

Croft, William. 1995. Modern syntactic typology. In Masayoshi Shibatani & Theodora Bynon (eds.), *Approaches to language typology*, 85–144. Oxford University Press.

2000. *Explaining language change: An evolutionary approach*. Harlow: Longman.

2001. *Radical Construction Grammar: Syntactic theory in typological perspective*. Oxford University Press.

Crowhurst, Megan J. 1991. Minimality and foot structure in metrical phonology and prosodic morphology. Ph.D. dissertation, University of Arizona.

Crysmann, Berthold. 1999. Morphosyntactic paradoxa in Fox. In Gosse Bouma, Erhard W. Hinrichs, Geert-Jan M. Kruijff & Richard T. Oehrle (eds.), *Constraints and resources in natural language syntax and semantics*. Stanford: CSLI.

2000. Clitics and coordination in linear structure. In Birgit Gerlach & Janet Grijzenhout (eds.), *Clitics in phonology, morphology and syntax*, 121–159. Amsterdam: Benjamins.

2002. Constraint-based coanalysis: Portuguese cliticisation and morphology-syntax interaction in HPSG. Ph.D. dissertation, Deutsches Forschungszentrum für Künstliche Intelligenz and Universität des Saarlandes.

Culicover, Peter W. 1999. *Syntactic nuts: Hard cases, syntactic theory, and language acquisition*. Oxford University Press.

Curry, Haskell B. 1961. Some logical aspects of grammatical structure. In Roman Jakobson (ed.), *Structure of language and its mathematical aspects*, 56–68. Providence, RI: American Mathematical Society.

Cysouw, Michael. 2005. Morphology in the wrong place: A survey of preposed enclitics. In Wolfgang U. Dressler (ed.), *Morphology and its demarcations*, 17–37. Amsterdam: Benjamins.

2007a. New approaches to cluster analysis of typological indices. In Peter Grzybek & Reinhard Köhler (eds.), *Exact methods in the study of language and text*, 61–76. Berlin: Mouton.

2007b. A social layer for typological databases. In Andrea Sansò (ed.), *Language resources and linguistic theory*, 59–66. Milan: FrancoAngeli.

Cysouw, Michael & Bernard Comrie. 2009. How varied typologically are the languages of Africa. In Rudolf Botha & Chris Knight (eds.), *The cradle of language*, 189–203. Oxford University Press.

Cysouw, Michael & Diana Forker. 2009. Reconstruction of morphosyntactic function: Nonspatial usage of spatial case marking in Tsezic. *Language* 85. 588–617.

Dahl, Östen. 2008. An exercise in *a posteriori* language sampling. *Sprachtypologie und Universalienforschung* 61. 208–220.

Dahlstrom, Amy. 1993. The syntax of discourse functions in Fox. In David A. Peterson (ed.), *Proceedings of the nineteenth annual meeting of the Berkeley Linguistics Society: Special session on syntactic issues in Native American languages*, 11–21. Berkeley Linguistics Society.

290 References

1995. *Topic, focus, and word order problems in Algonquian: The Belcourt lecture.* Winnipeg: Voices of Rupert's Land.

2003a. Focus constructions in Meskwaki (Fox). In Miriam Butt & Tracy Holloway King (eds.), *The proceedings of the LFG '03 conference*, 145–163. Stanford: CSLI.

2003b. Warrior powers from an underwater spirit: Cultural and linguistic aspects of an illustrated Meskwaki text. *Anthropological Linguistics* 45. 1–56.

Davis, Lori & Ellen Prince. 1986. Yiddish verb-topicalization and the notion of 'lexical integrity'. In Ann M. Farley, Peter T. Farley & Karl-Erik McCullough (eds.), *Proceedings of the Chicago Linguistic Society 22-1: Main session*, 90–97. Chicago Linguistic Society.

Davis, Stuart & Donna Jo Napoli. 1994. *A prosodic template in historical change: The passage of the Latin second conjugation into Romance.* Turin: Rosenberg and Sellier.

Di Meola, Claudio. 2003. Grammaticalization of postpositions in German. In Hubert Cuyckens, Thomas Berg, René Dirven & Klaus-Uwe Panther (eds.), *Motivation in language*, 203–222. Amsterdam: Benjamins.

Diestel, Reinhard. 1997. *Graph theory.* New York: Springer.

Dik, Simon C. 1997. *The theory of functional grammar*, part 1: *The structure of the clause* (second, revised edition). Berlin: Mouton.

Dixon, R. M. W. & Alexandra Y. Aikhenvald. 2002. Word: A typological framework. In R. M. W. Dixon & Alexandra Y. Aikhenvald (eds.), *Word: A cross-linguistic typology*, 1–41. Cambridge University Press.

Donohue, Mark. 2008. Semantic alignment systems: What's what, and what's not. In Søren Wichmann & Mark Donohue (eds.), *The typology of semantic alignment*, 24–75. Oxford University Press.

Downing, Laura J. 2006. *Canonical forms in prosodic morphology.* Oxford University Press.

Dress, Andreas W. M. & Daniel H. Huson. 2004. Constructing splits graphs. *IEEE/ACM Transactions on Computational Biology and Bioinformatics* 1. 109–115.

Dryer, Matthew S. 1989. Large linguistic areas and language sampling. *Studies in Language* 13. 257–292.

1995. Frequency and pragmatically unmarked word order. In Pamela Downing & Michael Noonan (eds.), *Word order in discourse*, 405–435. Amsterdam: Benjamins.

1997a. Are grammatical relations universal? In Joan L. Bybee, John Haiman & Sandra A. Thompson (eds.), *Essays on language function and language type: Dedicated to T. Givón*, 115–143. Amsterdam: Benjamins.

1997b. On the six-way word order typology. *Studies in Language* 21. 69–103.

2006. Descriptive theories, explanatory theories, and basic linguistic theory. In Felix Ameka, Alan Dench & Nicholas Evans (eds.), *Catching language: The standing challenge of grammar writing*, 207–234. Berlin: Mouton de Gruyter.

2007. Word order. In Timothy Shopen (ed.), *Language typology and syntactic description*, volume I: *Clause structure* (second edition), 61–131. Cambridge University Press.

2013a. On the six-way word order typology, again. *Studies in Language* 37. 267–301.

2013b. Order of subject, object and verb. In Matthew S. Dryer & Martin Haspelmath (eds.), *The World Atlas of Language Structures online*. Leipzig: Max Planck Institute for Evolutionary Anthropology. http://wals.info/chapter/81.

References 291

Dryer, Matthew S. & Martin Haspelmath (eds.). 2013. *The World Atlas of Language Structures online*. Leipzig: Max Planck Institute for Evolutionary Anthropology. http://wals.info/.

Dunn, Michael, Stephen C. Levinson, Eva Lindström, Ger Reesink & Angela Terrill. 2008. Structural phylogeny in historical linguistics: Methodological explorations applied in Island Melanesia. *Language* 84. 710–759.

Ekundayo, S. Ayotunde & F. Niyi Akinnaso. 1983. Yoruba serial verb string commutability constraints. *Lingua* 60. 115–133.

Ellington, John. 1977. Aspects of the Tiene language. Ph.D. dissertation, University of Wisconsin.

Elman, Jeffrey L. 1990. Finding structure in time. *Cognitive Science* 14. 179–211.

1991. Distributed representations, simple recurrent networks, and grammatical structure. *Machine Learning* 7. 195–225.

Enfield, N. J. 2003. *Linguistic epidemiology: Semantics and grammar of language contact in mainland Southeast Asia*. London: RoutledgeCurzon.

2006. Heterosemy and the grammar-lexicon trade-off. In Felix Ameka, Alan Dench & Nicholas Evans (eds.), *Catching language: The standing challenge of grammar writing*, 297–320. Berlin: Mouton de Gruyter.

Engberg-Pedersen, Elisabeth. 2010. Factors that form classifier signs. In Diane K. Brentari (ed.), *Sign languages*, 252–283. Cambridge University Press.

Epps, Patience. 2008. *A grammar of Hup*. Berlin: Mouton de Gruyter.

Evans, Nicholas. 1997. Role or cast? Noun incorporation and complex predicates in Mayali. In Alex Alsina, Joan Bresnan & Peter Sells (eds.), *Complex predicates*, 397–430. Stanford: CSLI.

2008. Reciprocal constructions: Towards a structural typology. In Ekkehard König & Volker Gast (eds.), *Reciprocals and reflexives: Theoretical and typological explorations*, 33–103. Berlin: Mouton de Gruyter.

Evans, Nicholas & David Wilkins. 2000. In the mind's ear: The semantic extensions of perception verbs in Australian languages. *Language* 76. 546–592.

Evans, Tim S. & Renaud Lambiotte. 2010. Line graphs of weighted networks for overlapping communities. *The European Physical Journal B* 77. 265–272.

Falcon, S. & R. Gentleman. 2007. Using GOstats to test gene lists for GO term association. *Bioinformatics* 23. 257–258.

Fanselow, Gisbert & Caroline Féry. 2002. Ineffability in grammar. In Gisbert Fanselow & Caroline Féry (eds.), *Resolving conflicts in grammar: Optimality Theory in syntax, morphology, and phonology*, 265–307. Hamburg: Helmut Buske.

Faraclas, Nicholas G. 1984. *A grammar of Obolo*. Bloomington: Indiana University Linguistics Club.

Farrar, Scott. 2012. An ontological approach to Canonical Typology: Laying the foundations for e-linguistics. In Dunstan Brown, Marina Chumakina & Greville G. Corbett (eds.), *Canonical morphology and syntax*, 239–261. Oxford University Press.

Farrar, Scott & D. Terence Langendoen. 2003. A linguistic ontology for the semantic web. *Glot International* 7. 97–100.

2009. An OWL-DL implementation of GOLD: An ontology for the Semantic Web. In Andreas Witt & Dieter Metzing (eds.), *Linguistic modeling of information and markup languages: Contributions to language technology*, 45–66. Berlin: Springer.

292   References

Farrar, Scott & William D. Lewis. 2007. The GOLD Community of Practice: An infrastructure for linguistic data on the Web. *Language Resources and Evaluation* 41. 45–60.

Fillmore, Charles J., Paul Kay & Mary Catherine O'Connor. 1988. Regularity and idiomaticity in grammatical constructions: The case of *let alone*. *Language* 64. 501–538.

Foley, William A. & Robert D. Van Valin, Jr. 1984. *Functional syntax and universal grammar*. Cambridge University Press.

Forkel, Robert. 2014. The Cross-Linguistic Linked Data project. In Christian Chiarcos, John Philip McCrae, Petya Osenova & Cristina Vertan (eds.), *Proceedings of the third Workshop on Linked Data in Linguistics: Multilingual knowledge resources and natural language processing (LDL-2014)*, 61–66. Paris: European Language Resources Association.

Francez, Nissim & Shuly Winter. 2012. *Unification grammars*. Cambridge University Press.

Franks, Steven & Tracy Holloway King. 2000. *A handbook of Slavic clitics*. Oxford University Press.

Freeland, L. S. 1951. *Language of the Sierra Miwok*. Baltimore: Waverly.

Gansner, Emden R. & Stephen C. North. 2000. An open graph visualization system and its applications to software engineering. *Software: Practice and Experience* 30. 1203–1233.

Gennari, John H., Mark A. Musen, Ray W. Fergerson, William E. Grosso, Monica Crubézy, Henrik Eriksson, Natalya F. Noy & Samson W. Tu. 2003. The evolution of Protégé: An environment for knowledge-based systems development. *International Journal of Human-Computer Studies* 58. 89–123.

Gensler, Orin D. 1994. On reconstructing the syntagm S-Aux-O-V-Other to Proto-Niger-Congo. In Kevin E. Moore, David A. Peterson & Comfort Wentum (eds.), *Proceedings of the twentieth annual meeting of the Berkeley Linguistics Society: Special session on historical issues in African linguistics*, 1–20. Berkeley Linguistics Society.

1997. Grammaticalization, typology, and Niger-Congo word order: Progress on a still-unsolved problem. *Journal of African Languages and Linguistics* 18. 57–93.

Gentleman, R. 2013. *Visualizing and distances using GO*. www.bioconductor.org/ packages/2.13/bioc/vignettes/GOstats/inst/doc/GOvis.pdf.

Geuder, Wilhelm & Miriam Butt. 1998. Introduction. In Miriam Butt & Wilhelm Geuder (eds.), *The projection of arguments: Lexical and compositional factors*, 1–20. Stanford: CSLI.

Givón, Talmy. 1971. Historical syntax and synchronic morphology: An archaeologist's fieldtrip. In Douglas Adams, Mary Ann Campbell, Victor Cohen, Julie Lovins, Edward Maxwell, Carolyn Nygren & John Reighard (eds.), *Proceedings of the Chicago Linguistic Society 7*, 394–415. Chicago Linguistic Society.

Goldberg, Adele E. & Laura Suttle. 2010. Construction grammar. *Wiley Interdisciplinary Reviews: Cognitive Science* 1. 468–477.

Goldsmith, John A. 1990. *Autosegmental and metrical phonology*. Oxford: Blackwell.

2011. The syllable. In John A. Goldsmith, Jason Riggle & Alan C. L. Yu (eds.), *The handbook of phonological theory* (second edition), 164–196. Chichester: Wiley-Blackwell.

Good, Jeff. 2003a. Clause combining in Chechen. *Studies in Language* 27. 113–170.

References

2003b. Strong linearity: Three case studies towards a theory of morphosyntactic templatic constructions. Ph.D. dissertation, University of California, Berkeley.

2005. Reconstructing morpheme order in Bantu: The case of causativization and applicativization. *Diachronica* 22. 3–57.

2007a. Slouching towards deponency: A family of mismatches in the Bantu verb stem. In Matthew Baerman, Greville G. Corbett, Dunstan Brown & Andrew Hippisley (eds.), *Deponency and morphological mismatches*, 203–230. Oxford University Press.

2007b. Strong linearity, weak linearity, and the typology of templates. In Matti Miestamo & Bernhard Wälchli (eds.), *New challenges in typology: Broadening the horizons and redefining the foundations*, 11–33. Berlin: Mouton.

2008. Introduction. In Jeff Good (ed.), *Linguistic universals and language change*, 1–19. Oxford University Press.

2010. Topic and focus fields in Naki. In Ines Fiedler & Anne Schwarz (eds.), *The expression of information structure: A documentation of its diversity across Africa*, 35–67. Amsterdam: Benjamins.

2011. The typology of templates. *Language and Linguistics Compass* 5. 731–747.

2012. Deconstructing descriptive grammars. *Language Documentation & Conservation* Special Publication no. 4. 2–32.

Good, Jeff & Calvin Hendryx-Parker. 2006. Modeling contested categorization in linguistic databases. In *Proceedings of E-MELD Workshop 2006: Tools and standards: The state of the art*. Lansing, Michigan. June 20–22. http://e-meld.org/workshop/2006/papers/GoodHendryxParker-Modelling.pdf.

Good, Jeff & Alan C. L. Yu. 1999. Affix-placement variation in Turkish. In Jeff Good & Alan C. L. Yu (eds.), *Proceedings of the twenty-fifth annual meeting of the Berkeley Linguistics Society: Special session on Caucasian, Dravidian, and Turkic linguistics*, 63–74. Berkeley Linguistics Society.

2005. Morphosyntax of two Turkish subject pronominal paradigms. In Lorie Heggie & Francisco Ordóñez (eds.), *Clitics and affix combinations*, 315–341. Amsterdam: Benjamins.

Gordon, Matthew K. 1999. Syllable weight: Phonetics, phonology, and typology. Ph.D. dissertation, University of California, Los Angeles.

2006. *Syllable weight: Phonetics, phonology, and typology*. New York: Routledge.

Gowlett, Derek F. 1984. Stabilization in Bantu. *African Studies* 43. 187–203.

Gray, Russell D. & Quentin D. Atkinson. 2003. Language-tree divergence times support the Anatolian theory of Indo-European origin. *Nature* 426. 435–439.

Greenberg, Joseph H. 1963. Some universals of grammar with particular reference to the order of meaningful elements. In Joseph H. Greenberg (ed.), *Universals of human language*, 73–113. Cambridge, MA: MIT Press.

1978. Diachrony, synchrony, and language universals. In Joseph H. Greenberg (ed.), *Universals of human language*, 61–91. Stanford: Stanford University Press.

1995. The diachronic typological approach to language. In Masayoshi Shibatani & Theodora Bynon (eds.), *Approaches to language typology*, 145–166. Oxford University Press.

Güldemann, Tom. 2007. Preverbal objects and information structure in Benue-Congo. In Enoch O. Aboh, Katharina Harmann & Malte Zimmerman (eds.), *Focus strategies in African languages: The interaction of focus and grammar in Niger-Congo and Afro-Asiatic*, 83–112. Berlin: Mouton de Gruyter.

294 References

2008. The Macro-Sudan belt: Towards identifying a linguistic area in northern Sub-Saharan Africa. In Bernd Heine & Derek Nurse (eds.), *A linguistic geography of Africa*, 151–185. Cambridge University Press.

Gupta, Anil. 2012. Definitions. In Edward N. Zalta (ed.), *The Stanford encyclopedia of philosophy* (Fall 2012 edition). http://plato.stanford.edu/archives/fall2012/entries/definitions/.

Guthrie, Malcolm. 1970. *Comparative Bantu: An introduction to the comparative linguistics and prehistory of the Bantu languages*, volume 4. Farnborough: Gregg.

1971. *Comparative Bantu: An introduction to the comparative linguistics and prehistory of the Bantu languages*, volume 2. Farnborough: Gregg.

ten Hacken, Pius. 2007. *Chomskyan linguistics and its competitors*. London: Equinox.

Hagège, Claude. 2010. *Adpositions*. Oxford University Press.

Hale, Ken. 1983. Warlpiri and the grammar of non-configurational languages. *Natural Language and Linguistic Theory* 1. 5–47.

2001. Navajo verb stem position and the bipartite structure of the Navajo conjunct sector. *Linguistic Inquiry* 32. 678–693.

Hale, Ken & Jay Keyser. 1993. On argument structure and the lexical expression of syntactic relations. In Ken Hale & Jay Keyser (eds.), *The view from building 20: A festschrift for Sylvain Bromberger*, 53–108. Cambridge, MA: MIT Press.

Halle, Morris & Jean-Roger Vergnaud. 1980. Three dimensional phonology. *Journal of linguistic research* 1. 83–105.

Halpern, Aaron. 1995. *On the placement and morphology of clitics*. Stanford: CSLI.

Hansen, Cynthia. 2011. Expressing reality status through word order: Iquito irrealis constructions in typological perspective. Ph.D. dissertation, University of Texas at Austin.

Hansson, Gunnar Ólafur. 2010. *Consonant harmony: Long-distance interaction in phonology*. Berkeley: University of California Press.

Hargus, Sharon. 1988. *The lexical phonology of Sekani*. New York: Garland.

2007. *Witsuwit'en grammar: Phonetics, phonology, morphology*. Vancouver: University of British Columbia Press.

2010. Athabaskan phonetics and phonology. *Language and Linguistics Compass* 4. 1019–1040.

Hargus, Sharon & Siri G. Tuttle. 1997. Augmentation as affixation in Athabaskan languages. *Phonology* 14. 177–220.

2003. Review of *Morpheme order and semantic scope: Word formation in the Athapaskan verb*. *Anthropological Linguistics* 45. 94–116.

Harley, Heidi & Rolf Noyer. 1999. Distributed morphology. *GLOT International* 4.4. 3–9.

Harris, Alice C. 2000. Where in the word is the Udi clitic? *Language* 76. 593–616.

2002. *Endoclitics and the origins of Udi morphosyntax*. Oxford University Press.

2008. On the explanation of typologically unusual structures. In Jeff Good (ed.), *Linguistic universals and language change*, 54–76. Oxford University Press.

Harris, Alice C. & Lyle Campbell. 1995. *Historical syntax in cross-linguistic perspective*. Cambridge University Press.

Haspelmath, Martin. 1995. The converb as a cross-linguistically valid category. In Martin Haspelmath & Ekkehard König (eds.), *Converbs in cross-linguistic perspective: Structure and meaning of adverbial verb forms – adverbial participles, gerunds*, 1–56. Dordrecht: Kluwer.

References 295

2004. Coordinating constructions: An overview. In Martin Haspelmath (ed.), *Coordinating constructions*, 1–39. Amsterdam: Benjamins.

2005. Argument marking in ditransitive alignment types. *Linguistic Discovery* 3. 1–21.

2007. Pre-established categories don't exist: Consequences for language description and typology. *Linguistic Typology* 11. 119–132.

2010. Comparative concepts and descriptive categories in cross-linguistic studies. *Language* 86. 663–687.

Haspelmath, Martin, Matthew S. Dryer, David Gil & Bernard Comrie (eds.). 2005. *The world atlas of language structures*. Oxford University Press.

Haspelmath, Martin & Sven Siegmund. 2006. Simulating the replication of some of Greenberg's word order generalizations. *Linguistic Typology* 10. 74–82.

Haspelmath, Martin & Uri Tadmor (eds.). 2009. *World loanword database*. Munich: Max Planck Digital Library. http://wold.livingsources.org/.

Hausser, Jean & Korbinian Strimmer. 2009. Entropy inference and the James-Stein estimator, with application to nonlinear gene association networks. *Journal of Machine Learning Research* 10. 1469–1484.

2013. *Entropy: Estimation of entropy, mutual information and related quantities*. http://CRAN.R-project.org/package=entropy. R package version 1.2.0.

Hayes, Bruce. 1995. *Metrical stress theory: Principles and case studies*. University of Chicago Press.

Hayes, Bruce & May Abad. 1989. Reduplication and syllabification in Ilokano. *Lingua* 77. 331–374.

Heath, Jeffrey. 1984. *A functional grammar of Nunggubuyu*. Canberra: AIATSIS.

2007. Bidirectional case-marking and linear adjacency. *Natural Language and Linguistic Theory* 25. 83–101.

Heggarty, Paul, Warren Maguire & April McMahon. 2010. Splits or waves? Trees or webs? How divergence measures and network analysis can unravel language histories. *Philosophical Transactions of the Royal Society B: Biological Sciences* 365. 3829–3843.

Heggie, Lorie & Francisco Ordóñez. 2005. Clitic ordering phenomena: The path to generalizations. In Lorie Heggie & Francisco Ordóñez (eds.), *Clitics and affix combinations*, 1–29. Amsterdam: Benjamins.

Heine, Bernd. 1968. *Die Verbreitung und Gliederung der Togorestsprachen*. Berlin: Dietrich Reimer.

2002. On the role of context in grammaticalization. In Ilse Wischer & Gabriele Diewald (eds.), *New reflections on grammaticalization*, 83–101. Amsterdam: Benjamins.

Hendricks, Sean. 1999. Reduplication without template constraints: A study in bare-consonant reduplication. Ph.D. dissertation, University of Arizona.

Heymans, Maureen & Ambuj K. Singh. 2003. Deriving phylogenetic trees from the similarity analysis of metabolic pathways. *Bioinformatics* 19 (Supplement 1). i138–i146.

Hockett, Charles F. 1950. Peiping morphophonemics. *Language* 26. 63–85.

1954. Two models of grammatical description. *Word* 10. 210–234.

1958. Two models of grammatical description. In Martin Joos (ed.), *Readings in linguistics: The development of descriptive linguistics in America since 1925*,

296   References

386–399. New York: American Council of Learned Societies (originally published as Hockett (1954)).

Höhle, Tilman. 1986. Der Begriff "Mittelfeld", Anmerkungen über die Theorie der topologischen Felder. In Albrecht Schöne (ed.), *Kontroversen alte und neue: Akten des 7. Internationalen Germanisten-Kongresses, Göttingen 1985*, volume 3, 329–340. Tübingen: Niemeyer.

Hoijer, Harry. 1971. Athapaskan morphology. In Jesse Sawyer (ed.), *Studies in American Indian languages*, 113–147. Berkeley: University of California Press.

Hopper, Paul J. & Sandra A. Thompson. 1980. Transitivity in grammar and discourse. *Language* 56. 251–299.

Hornstein, Norbert, Jairo Nunes & Kleanthes K Grohmann. 2005. *Understanding minimalism*. Cambridge University Press.

Horvath, Julia. 1995. Structural focus, structural case, and the notion of feature-assignment. In Katalin É. Kiss (ed.), *Discourse configurational languages*, 28–64. Oxford University Press.

Huang, C.-T. James. 1982. Logical relations in Chinese and the theory of grammar. Ph.D. dissertation, MIT.

2003. The distribution of negative NPs and some typological correlates. In Yen-hui Audrey Li & Andrew Simpson (eds.), *Functional structure(s), form and interpretation: Perspectives from East Asian languages*, 262–280. London: RoutledgeCurzon.

Huson, Daniel H. & David Bryant. 2006. Application of phylogenetic networks in evolutionary studies. *Molecular biology and evolution* 23. 254–267.

Hyman, Larry M. 1979. Phonology and noun structure. In Larry M. Hyman (ed.), *Aghem grammatical structure: With special reference to noun classes, tense-aspect and focus marking*, 1–72. Los Angeles: University of Southern California Department of Linguistics.

1993. Conceptual issues in the comparative study of the Bantu verb stem. In Salikoko S. Mufwene & Lioba Moshi (eds.), *Topics in African linguistics*, 3–34. Amsterdam: Benjamins.

1994. Cyclic phonology and morphology in Cibemba. In Jennifer Cole & Kisseberth Charles (eds.), *Perspectives in phonology*, 81–112. Stanford: CSLI.

1999. The historical interpretation of vowel harmony in Bantu. In Jean-Marie Hombert & Larry Hyman (eds.), *Bantu historical linguistics: Theoretical and empirical perspectives*, 235–295. Stanford: CSLI.

2003a. Segmental phonology. In Derek Nurse & Gérard Philippson (eds.), *The Bantu languages*, 42–58. London: Routledge.

2003b. Sound change, misanalysis, and analogy in the Bantu causative. *Journal of African Languages and Linguistics* 24. 55–90.

2003c. Suffix ordering in Bantu: A morphocentric approach. In Geert Booij & Jaap van Marle (eds.), *Yearbook of morphology 2002*, 245–281. Dordrecht: Kluwer.

2009. The natural history of verb-stem reduplication in Bantu. *Morphology* 19. 177–206.

2010a. Affixation by place of articulation: The case of Tiene. In Jan Wohlgemuth & Michael Cysouw (eds.), *Rara and rarissima: Collecting and interpreting unusual characteristics of human languages*, 145–184. Berlin: De Gruyter Mouton.

References 297

2010b. Focus marking in Aghem: Syntax or semantics. In Ines Fiedler & Anne Schwarz (eds.), *The expression of information structure: A documentation of its diversity across Africa*, 95–115. Amsterdam: Benjamins.

Hyman, Larry M. & Sharon Inkelas. 1997. Emergent templates: The unusual case of Tiene. In Viola Miglio & Bruce Morén (eds.), *University of Maryland Working Papers in Linguistics*, volume 5, 92–116. College Park, MD: University of Maryland Department of Linguistics.

Hyman, Larry M., Sharon Inkelas & Galen Sibanda. 2009. Morphosyntactic correspondence in Bantu reduplication. In Kristin Hanson & Sharon Inkelas (eds.), *The nature of the word: Essays in honor of Paul Kiparsky*, 273–309. Cambridge, MA: MIT Press.

Hyman, Larry M. & Sam A. Mchombo. 1992. Morphotactic constraints in the Chichewa verb stem. In Laura Buszard-Welcher, Lionel Wee & William Weigel (eds.), *Proceedings of the eighteenth meeting of the Berkeley Linguistics Society, general session and parassession*, 350–363. Berkeley Linguistics Society.

Hyman, Larry M. & Maria Polinsky. 2009. Focus in Aghem. In Malte Zimmerman & Caroline Féry (eds.), *Information structure: Theoretical, typological, and experimental perspectives*, 206–233. Oxford University Press.

Hyman, Larry M. & Imelda Udoh. 2007. Length harmony in Leggbó: A counteruniversal? In Peter K. Austin & Andrew Simpson (eds.), *Endangered languages* (*Linguistische Berichte*, sonderheft 14), 73–92. Hamburg: Helmut Buske.

Hyman, Larry M. & John R. Watters. 1984. Auxiliary focus. *Studies in African Linguistics* 15. 233–273.

Hymes, Dell H. 1955. Positional analysis of categories: A frame for reconstruction. *Word* 11. 10–23.

1956. Na-Déné and positional analysis of categories. *American Anthropologist* 58. 624–638.

Ide, Nancy, Alessandro Lenci & Nicoletta Calzolari. 2003. RDF instantiation of ISLE/MILE lexical entries. In *Proceedings of the ACL 2003 Workshop on Linguistic Annotation: Getting the model right (LingAnnot '03)*, 30–37. Stroudsburg, PA: Association for Computational Linguistics.

Inkelas, Sharon. 1990. *Prosodic constituency in the lexicon*. New York: Garland.

1993. Nimboran position class morphology. *Natural Language and Linguistic Theory* 11. 559–624.

Inkelas, Sharon & Cemil Orhan Orgun. 1995. Level ordering and economy in the lexical phonology of Turkish. *Language* 71. 763–793.

1998. Level (non)ordering in recursive morphology. In Steven G. Lapointe, Diane K. Brentari & Patrick M. Farrell (eds.), *Morphology and its relation to phonology and syntax*, 360–392. Stanford: CSLI.

Inkelas, Sharon & Draga Zec. 1988. Serbo-Croatian pitch accent: The interaction of tone, stress, and intonation. *Language* 64. 227–248.

1995. Syntax-phonology interface. In John A. Goldsmith (ed.), *The handbook of phonological theory*, 535–549. Oxford: Blackwell.

Inkelas, Sharon & Cheryl Zoll. 2007. Is grammar dependence real? A comparison between cophonological and indexed constraint approaches to morphologically conditioned phonology. *Linguistics* 45. 133–171.

Itô, Junko. 1986. Syllable theory in prosodic phonology. Ph.D. dissertation, University of Massachusetts.

298   References

1988. *Syllable theory in prosodic phonology*. New York: Garland.

1989. A prosodic theory of epenthesis. *Natural Language and Linguistic Theory* 7. 217–260.

Itô, Junko & Jorge Hankamer. 1989. Notes on monosyllabism in Turkish. In Junko Itô & Jeff Runner (eds.), *Phonology at Santa Cruz*, volume 1, 61–69. Syntax Research Center, University of California, Santa Cruz.

Jakobson, Roman & Linda Waugh. 1979. *The sound shape of language*. Bloomington: Indiana University Press.

Jeh, Glen & Jennifer Widom. 2002. SimRank: A measure of structural-context similarity. In *Proceedings of the Eighth ACM SIGKDD International Conference on Knowledge Discovery and Data Mining (KDD '02)*, 538–543. New York: Association for Computing Machinery.

Jelinek, Eloise. 1984. Empty categories, case, and configurationality. *Natural Language and Linguistic Theory* 2. 39–76.

Jeschull, Liane. 2004. Coordination in Chechen. In Martin Haspelmath (ed.), *Coordinating constructions*, 241–265. Amsterdam: Benjamins.

Joos, Martin. 1958. Preface. In Martin Joos (ed.), *Preface*, v–vii. New York: American Council of Learned Societies.

Jordan, Michael I. 1986. *Serial order: A parallel distributed processing approach (ICS report 8604)*. Institute for Cognitive Science, University of California, San Diego.

1997. Serial order: A parallel distributed processing approach. In John W. Donahoe & Vivian Packard Dorsel (eds.), *Neural-network models of cognition: Biobehavioral foundations*, 471–495. Amsterdam: Elsevier.

Kandybowicz, Jason. 2006. Conditions on multiple copy spell-out and the syntax-phonology interface. Ph.D. dissertation, University of California, Los Angles.

2008. *The grammar of repetition: Nupe grammar at the syntax-phonology interface*. Amsterdam: Benjamins.

Kari, James. 1989. Affix positions and zones in the Athapaskan verb. *International Journal of American Linguistics* 55. 424–455.

1990. *Ahtna Athabaskan dictionary*. Alaska Native Language Center, University of Alaska Fairbanks.

1992. Some concepts in Ahtna Athabaskan word formation. In Mark Aronoff (ed.), *Morphology now*, 107–131. Albany: SUNY Press.

Kathol, Andreas. 1995. Linearization-based German syntax. Ph.D. dissertation, The Ohio State University.

1998. Constituency and linearization of verbal complexes. In Erhard W. Hinrichs, Andreas Kathol & Tsuneko Nakazawa (eds.), *Syntax and semantics*, volume 30: *Complex predicates in nonderivational syntax*, 221–270. San Diego: Academic Press.

2000. *Linear syntax*. Oxford University Press.

Kay, Paul & Charles J. Fillmore. 1999. Grammatical constructions and linguistic generalizations: The what's X doing Y? construction. *Language* 75. 1–33.

Kayne, Richard S. 1994. *The antisymmetry of syntax*. Cambridge, MA: MIT Press.

Keenan, Edward L. 1976. Towards a universal definition of subject. In Charles N. Li (ed.), *Subject and topic*, 303–333. New York: Academic Press.

Kenstowicz, Michael. 1994. *Phonology in Generative Grammar*. Oxford: Blackwell.

References

Kepser, Stephan & Uwe Mönnich. 2008. Graph properties of HPSG feature structures. In *Proceedings of FGVienna: The 8th Conference on Formal Grammar*, 111–122. Stanford: CSLI.

Kim, Yuni. 2010. Phonological and morphological conditions on affix order in Huave. *Morphology* 20. 133–163.

Kimball, Geoffrey D. 1991. *Koasati grammar*. Lincoln: University of Nebraska Press.

Kiparsky, Paul. 1982a. From Cyclic Phonology to lexical phonology. In Harry van der Hulst & Norval Smith (eds.), *The structure of phonological representations (part I)*, 131–175. Dordrecht: Foris.

1982b. Lexical morphology and phonology. In *Linguistics in the morning calm: Selected papers from SICOL-1981*, 3–91. Seoul: Hanshin.

2008. Universals constrain change; change results in typological generalizations. In Jeff Good (ed.), *Linguistic universals and language change*, 23–53. Oxford University Press.

Kisseberth, Charles W. 1970. On the functional unity of phonological rules. *Linguistic Inquiry* 1. 291–306.

2011. Conspiracies. In Marc van Oostendorp, Colin J. Ewan, Elizabeth Hume & Keren Rice (eds.), *The Blackwell companion to phonology*, volume III: *Phonological processes*, 1644–1665. Malden, MA: Wiley-Blackwell.

Klavans, Judith. 1985. The independence of syntax and phonology in cliticization. *Language* 61. 95–120.

Kleinberg, Jon M. 1999. Authoritative sources in a hyperlinked environment. *Journal of the ACM* 46. 604–632.

Kleinberg, Jon M., Ravi Kumar, Prabhakar Raghavan, Sridhar Rajagopalan & Andrew S. Tomkins. 1999. The Web as a graph: Measurements, models, and methods. In Takano Asano, Hideki Imai, D.T. Lee, Shin-ichi Nakano & Takeshi Tokuyama (eds.), *Computing and Combinatorics: Fifth annual international conference (COCOON'99)*, 1–17. Berlin: Springer.

Koenig, Jean-Pierre & Karin Michelson. 2012. The (non)universality of syntactic selection and functional application. In Christopher Piñon (ed.), *Empirical issues in syntax and semantics 9*, 185–205. Paris: Colloque de syntaxe et sémantique à Paris. www.cssp.cnrs.fr/eiss9/.

Komen, Erwin R. 2007a. *Chechen stress and vowel deletion: An optimality theory approach*. ROA 923, Rutgers Optimality Archive.

2007b. Focus in Chechen. M.A. thesis, Leiden University.

Laudan, Larry. 1977. *Progress and its problems: Towards a theory of scientific growth*. Berkeley University of California Press.

Leer, Jeff. 1991. The schetic categories of the Tlingit verb. Ph.D. dissertation, University of Chicago.

Levin, Beth & Malka Rappaport Hovav. 1995. *Unaccusativity: At the syntax–lexical semantics interface*. Cambridge, MA: MIT Press.

2005. *Argument realization*. Cambridge University Press.

Lewis, Geoffrey L. 1967. *Turkish grammar*. Oxford University Press.

Libert, Alan. 2006. *Ambipositions*. Munich: LINCOM.

Lillo-Martin, Diane. 2002. Where are all the modality effects? In Richard P. Meier, Kearsy Cormier & David Quinto-Pozos (eds.), *Modality and structure in signed and spoken language*, 241–262. Cambridge University Press.

300 References

Longacre, Robert E. 2007. Sentences as combinations of clauses. In Timothy Shopen (ed.), *Language typology and syntactic description*, volume II: *Complex constructions* (second edition), 372–420. Cambridge.

Lounsbury, Floyd G. 1953. *Oneida verb morphology*. New Haven: Yale University Press.

Maganga, Clement & Thilo C. Schadeberg. 1992. *Kinyamwezi: Grammar, texts, vocabulary*. Cologne: Rüdiger Köppe.

Maho, Jouni. 2001. The Bantu area: (towards clearing up) A mess. *Africa and Asia: Göteborg Working Papers on Asian and African Languages and Literatures* 1. 40–49.

2003. A classification of the Bantu languages: An update of Guthrie's referential system. In Derek Nurse & Gérard Philippson (eds.), *The Bantu languages*, 639–651. London: Routledge.

Malchukov, Andrej, Martin Haspelmath & Bernard Comrie. 2010. Ditransitive constructions: A typological overview. In Andrej Malchukov, Martin Haspelmath & Bernard Comrie (eds.), *Studies in ditransitive constructions: A comparative handbook*, 1–64. Berlin: Walter de Gruyter.

Manova, Stela & Mark Aronoff. 2010. Modeling affix order. *Morphology* 20. 109–131.

Margolin, Adam, Ilya Nemenman, Katia Basso, Chris Wiggins, Gustavo Stolovitzky, Riccardo Favera & Andrea Califano. 2006. ARACNE: An algorithm for the reconstruction of gene regulatory networks in a mammalian cellular context. *BMC Bioinformatics* 7 (Supplement 1). S7.

Mathangwane, Joyce T. 2001. Suffix ordering in the Ikalanga verb stem: A case against the Repeated Morph Constraint. *South African Journal of African Languages* 21. 396–409.

Matthews, Peter H. 1991. *Morphology* (second edition). Cambridge University Press.

McCarthy, John. 1979. Formal problems in Semitic morphology and phonology. Ph.D. dissertation, MIT.

1981. A prosodic theory of nonconcatenative morphology. *Linguistic Inquiry* 12. 373–418.

1989. Linear order in phonological representation. *Linguistic Inquiry* 20. 71–99.

McCarthy, John & Alan S. Prince. 1990. Foot and word in Prosodic Morphology: The Arabic broken plural. *Natural Language and Linguistic Theory* 8. 209–282.

1993. *Prosodic morphology: Constraint interaction and satisfaction*. New Brunswick, NJ: Rutgers University Center for Cognitive Science. RuCCS Technical Report TR-3.

1995. Prosodic morphology. In John A. Goldsmith (ed.), *The handbook of phonological theory*, 318–366. Oxford: Blackwell.

1996. *Prosodic morphology 1986*. New Brunswick, NJ: Rutgers University Center for Cognitive Science. RuCCS Technical Report TR-32.

McCawley, James D. 1998. *The syntactic phenomena of English* (second edition). University of Chicago Press.

McCrae, John Philip, Dennis Spohr & Philipp Cimiano. 2011. Linking lexical resources and ontologies on the Semantic Web with lemon. In Grigoris Antoniou, Marko Grobelnik, Elena Simperl, Bijan Parsia, Dimitris Plexousakis, Pieter De Leenheer & Jeff Pan (eds.), *The Semantic Web: Research and applications: Eighth Extended Semantic Web Conference (ESWC 2011): Proceedings*, part I, 245–259. Berlin: Springer.

References 301

McDonough, Joyce. 1990. Topics in the phonology and morphology of Navajo verbs. Ph.D. dissertation, University of Massachusetts.

2000a. Athabaskan redux: Against the position class as a morphological category. In Wolfgang U. Dressler, Oskar Pfeiffer, Markus Pöchtrager & John R. Rennison (eds.), *Morphological analysis in comparison*, 155–178. Amsterdam: Benjamins.

2000b. On a bipartite model of the Athabaskan verb. In Theodore B. Fernald & Paul R. Platero (eds.), *The Athabaskan languages: Perspectives on a Native American language family*, 139–166. Oxford University Press.

2003. *The Navajo sound system*. Dordrecht: Kluwer.

McFarland, Teresa Ann. 2009. The phonology and morphology of Filomeno Mata Totonac. Ph.D. dissertation, University of California, Berkeley.

McLendon, Sally. 1975. *A grammar of Eastern Pomo*. Berkeley: University of California Press.

Meeussen, A. E. 1967. Bantu grammatical reconstructions. *Africana Linguistica* 3. 79–121.

Melnar, Lynette R. 2004. *Caddo verb morphology*. Lincoln: University of Nebraska Press.

Melnik, Sergey, Hector Garcia-Molina & Erhard Rahm. 2001. *Similarity flooding: A versatile graph matching algorithm and its application to schema matching (extended technical report)*. Stanford InfoLab. http://ilpubs.stanford.edu:8090/497/.

2002. Similarity flooding: A versatile graph matching algorithm and its application to schema matching. In Rakesh Agrawal, Klaus Dittrich, & Anne H. H. Ngu (eds.), *Proceedings of the eighteenth International Conference on Data Engineering*, 117–128. New York: IEEE.

2013. *A decade after flooding*. http://sergey.melnix.com/pub/melnik-icde13.pptx.

Mel'čuk, Igor. 1993. *Cours de morphologie générale (théorique et descriptive)*, volume I: *Introduction et Première partie: Le mot*. Les Presses de l'Université de Montréal.

1994. *Cours de morphologie générale (théorique et descriptive)*, volume II: *Deuxième partie: Significations morphologiques*. Les Presses de l'Université de Montréal.

1996. *Cours de morphologie générale (théorique et descriptive)*, volume III: *Troisième partie: Moyens morphologiques; Quatrième partie: Syntactiques morphologiques*. Les Presses de l'Université de Montréal.

1997. *Cours de morphologie générale (théorique et descriptive)*, volume IV: *Cinquième partie: Signes morphologiques*. Les Presses de l'Université de Montréal.

2000. *Cours de morphologie générale (théorique et descriptive)*, volume V: *Sixième partie: Modèles morphologiques; septième partie: Principes de la description morphologique*. Les Presses de l'Université de Montréal.

2006. *Aspects of the theory of morphology*. Berlin: Mouton.

Menn, Lise & Brian MacWhinney. 1984. The repeated morph constraint: Toward an explanation. *Language* 60. 519–541.

Mester, R. Armin. 1990. Patterns of truncation. *Linguistic Inquiry* 21. 478–485.

Meyer, David, Achim Zeileis & Kurt Hornik. 2006. The strucplot framework: Visualizing multi-way contingency tables with vcd. *Journal of Statistical Software* 17. 1–48.

302   References

Meyer, David, Achim Zeileis & Kurt Hornik. 2013. *vcd: Visualizing categorical data*. http://CRAN.R-project.org/package=vcd. R package version 1.3-1.

Michaelis, Laura A. 2010. Sign-based construction grammar. In Bernd Heine & Heiko Narrog (eds.), *The Oxford handbook of linguistic analysis*, 155–176. Oxford Univesity Press.

Michaelis, Susanne Maria, Philippe Maurer, Martin Haspelmath & Magnus Huber (eds.). 2013. *The Atlas of Pidgin and Creole Language Structures online*. Leipzig: Max Planck Institute for Evolutionary Anthropology. http://apics-online.info/.

Mihalicek, Verdrana. 2012. Serbo-Croatian word order: A logical approach. Ph.D. dissertation, The Ohio State University.

Miller, Philip H. & Ivan A. Sag. 1997. French clitic movement without clitics or movement. *Natural Language and Linguistic Theory* 15. 573–639.

Mithun, Marianne. 2000. The reordering or morphemes. In Spike Gildea (ed.), *Reconstructing grammar: Comparative linguistics and grammaticalization*, 231–255. Amsterdam: Benjamins.

Molochieva, Zarina. 2011. Aspect in Chechen. *Linguistic Discovery* 9. 104–121.

Moran, Steven. 2012. Using linked data to create a typological knowledge base. In Christian Chiarcos, Sebastian Nordhoff & Sebastian Hellmann (eds.), *Linked data in linguistics: Representing and connecting language data and language metadata*, 129–138. Berlin: Springer.

Moravcsik, Edith A. 2010. Conflict resolution in syntactic theory. *Studies in Language* 34. 636–669.

Müller, Stefan. 2002. *Complex predicates: Verbal complexes, resultative constructions, and particle verbs in German*. Stanford: CSLI.

Mutaka, Ngessimo M. & Kambale Kavutirwaki. 2011. *Kinande/Konze–English dictionary with an English–Kinande index*. Trenton, NJ: Africa World Press.

Myers, Scott P. 1987. Tone and the structure of words in Shona. Ph.D. dissertation, University of Massachusetts.

Nacher, Jose C., Nobuhisa Ueda, Takuji Yamada, Minoru Kanehisa & Tatsuya Akutsu. 2004. Clustering under the line graph transformation: Application to reaction network. *BMC Bioinformatics* 5. 207.

Naudé, Kevin A., Jean H. Greyling & Dieter Vogts. 2010. Marking student programs using graph similarity. *Computers and Education* 54. 545–561.

Nespor, Marina & Irene Vogel. 1986. *Prosodic phonology*. Dordrecht: Foris.

Nevins, Andrew & Bert Vaux. 2007. Metalinguistic, shmetalinguistic: The phonology of shm-reduplication. In David W. Kaiser Jonathan E. Cihlar, Amy L. Franklin & Irene Kimbara (eds.), *Proceedings of the Chicago Linguistic Society 39-1: Main session*, 703–722. Chicago Linguistic Society.

Newmeyer, Frederick J. 1998. *Language form and language function*. Cambridge, MA: MIT Press.

Ngunga, Armindo. 2000. *Lexical phonology and morphology of Ciyao*. Stanford: CSLI.

Nichols, Johanna. 1986. Head-marking and dependent-marking grammar. *Language* 62. 56–119.

    1992. *Linguistic diversity in space and time*. University of Chicago Press.

    2007a. Chechen morphology (with notes on Ingush). In Alan S. Kaye (ed.), *Morphologies of Asia and Africa (including the Caucasus)*, 1161–1180. Winona Lake, IN: Eisenbrauns.

References 303

2007b. What, if anything, is typology? *Linguistic Typology* 11. 231–238.

2011. *Ingush grammar*. Berkeley: University of California Press.

Nichols, Johanna, Jonathan Barnes & David A. Peterson. 2006. The robust bell curve of morphological complexity. *Linguistic Typology* 10. 96–106.

Nichols, Johanna & Balthasar Bickel. 2013. Locus of marking: Whole-language typology. In Matthew S. Dryer & Martin Haspelmath (eds.), *The world atlas of language structures online*. Leipzig: Max Planck Institute for Evolutionary Anthropology. http://wals.info/chapter/25.

Nichols, Johanna & Arbi Vagapov. 2004. *Chechen–English and English–Chechen dictionary*. London: RoutledgeCurzon.

Nichols, Johanna & Tandy Warnow. 2008. Tutorial on computational linguistic phylogeny. *Language and Linguistics Compass* 2. 760–820.

Nordhoff, Sebastian. 2012. Linked data for linguistic diversity research: Glottolog/Langdoc and ASJP Online. In Christian Chiarcos, Sebastian Nordhoff & Sebastian Hellmann (eds.), *Linked data in linguistics: Representing and connecting language data and language metadata*, 191–200. Berlin: Springer.

Nordlinger, Rachel. 2010. Verbal morphology in Murrinh-Patha: Evidence for templates. *Morphology* 20. 321–341.

Noyer, Rolf. 1991. The Mirror Principle revisited: Verbal morphology in Maung and Nunggubuyu. In Jonathan David Bobaljik & Tony Bures (eds.), *Papers from the third Student Conference in Linguistics, 1991* (MIT Working Papers in Linguistics, volume 14), 195–209. Cambridge, MA: MIT Department of Linguistics and Philosophy.

1994. Mobile affixes in Huave: Optimality and morphological well-formedness. In Eric Duncan, Donka Farkas & Philip Spaelti (eds.), *The proceedings of the twelfth West Coast Conference on Formal Linguistics*, 67–82. Stanford: CSLI.

1998. Impoverishment theory and morphosyntactic markedness. In Steven G. Lapointe, Diane K. Brentari & Patrick M. Farrell (eds.), *Morphology and its relation to phonology and syntax*, 264–285. Stanford: CSLI.

2001. Clitic sequences in Nunggubuyu and PF convergence. *Natural Language and Linguistic Theory* 19. 751–826.

Nurse, Derek. 2008. *Tense and aspect in Bantu*. Oxford University Press.

Nurse, Derek & Gérard Philippson. 2003. Introduction. In Derek Nurse & Gérard Philippson (eds.), *The Bantu languages*, 1–12. London: Routledge.

Ogata, Hiroyuki, Wataru Fujibuchi, Susumu Goto & Minoru Kanehisa. 2000. A heuristic graph comparison algorithm and its application to detect functionally related enzyme clusters. *Nucleic acids research* 28. 4021–4028.

Paster, Mary. 2006. A survey of phonological affix order with special attention to Pulaar. In Leah Bateman & Cherlon Ussery (eds.), *Proceedings of the thirty-fifth annual meeting of the North East Linguistic Society*, volume 2, 491–506. Amherst, MA: Graduate Linguistics Student Association.

2009. Explaining phonological conditions on affixation: Evidence from suppletive allomorphy and affix ordering. *Word Structure* 2. 18–37.

Perlmutter, David M. 1968. Deep and surface constraints in syntax. Ph.D. dissertation, MIT.

1970. Surface structure constraints in syntax. *Linguistic Inquiry* 1. 187–255.

1971. *Deep and surface structure constraints in syntax*. New York: Holt Rinehart and Winston.

304   References

1978. Impersonal passives and the Unaccusative Hypothesis. In Jeri J. Jaeger, Anthony C. Woodbury, Farrell Ackerman, Christine Chiarello, Orin D. Gensler, John Kingston, Eve E. Sweetser & Kenneth W. Whistler (eds.), *Proceedings of the fourth annual meeting of the Berkeley Linguistics Society*, 157–189. Berkeley Linguistics Society.

1992. Sonority and syllable structure in American Sign Language. *Linguistic Inquiry* 23. 407–442.

Pesetsky, David. 2009. Against taking linguistic diversity at "face value." *Behavioral and Brain Sciences* 32. 464–465.

Peterson, David A. 2001. Ingush *ʔa*: The elusive type 5 clitic? *Language* 77. 144–155.

2007. *Applicative constructions*. Oxford University Press.

Peterson, David A. & Kenneth VanBik. 2004. Coordination in Hakha Lai (Tibeto-Burman). In Martin Haspelmath (ed.), *Coordinating constructions*, 333–356. Amsterdam: Benjamins.

Pike, Kenneth L. 1967. *Language in relation to a unified theory of the structure of human behavior*. The Hague: Mouton.

Plank, Frans (ed.). 2006. *Das grammatische Raritätenkabinett: A leisurely collection to entertain and instruct*. http://typo.uni-konstanz.de/rara.

Poser, William J. 1990. Evidence for foot structure in Japanese. *Language* 66. 78–105.

Prince, Alan S. 1983. Relating to the grid. *Linguistic Inquiry* 14. 19–100.

1987. Planes and copying. *Linguistic Inquiry* 18. 491–509.

R Core Team. 2013. *R: A language and environment for statistical computing*. Vienna: R Foundation for Statistical Computing. www.R-project.org/.

Radford, Andrew. 1997. *Syntactic theory and the structure of English: A minimalist approach*. Cambridge.

Ramchand, Gillian & Charles Reiss. 2007. Introduction. In Gillian Ramchand & Charles Reiss (eds.), *The Oxford handbook of linguistic interfaces*, 1–13. Oxford University Press.

Rappaport Hovav, Malka & Beth Levin. 1998. Building verb meanings. In Miriam Butt & Wilhelm Geuder (eds.), *The projection of arguments: Lexical and compositional factors*, 97–134. Stanford: CSLI.

Revithiadou, Anthi. 2006. Prosodic filters on syntax: An interface account of second position clitics. *Lingua* 116. 79–111.

Rhodes, Richard A. 2010. Relative root complement: A unique grammatical relation in Algonquian syntax. In Jan Wohlgemuth & Michael Cysouw (eds.), *Rara and rarissima: Collecting and interpreting unusual characteristics of human languages*, 305–324. Berlin: De Gruyter Mouton.

Rice, Keren. 1993. The structure of the Slave (northern Athabaskan) verb. In Sharon Hargus & Ellen M. Kaisse (eds.), *Phonetics and phonology 4: Studies in lexical phonology*. San Diego: Academic Press.

2000. *Morpheme order and semantic scope: Word formation in the Athapaskan verb*. Cambridge University Press.

2011. Principles of affix ordering: An overview. *Word Structure* 4. 169–200.

van Riemsdijk, Henk. 2002. The unbearable lightness of GOing. *Journal of Comparative Germanic Linguistics* 5. 143–196.

Rose, Sharon. 1996. Inflectional affix order in Ethio-Semitic. In Jacqueline Lecarme, Jean Lowenstamm & Ur Shlonsky (eds.), *Studies in Afroasiatic grammar: Papers*

References

from the second conference on Afroasiatic languages, Sophia Antipolis, 1994, 337–359. The Hague: Holland Academic Graphics.

2003. The formation of Ethiopian Semitic internal reduplication. In Joseph Shimron (ed.), *Language processing and acquisition in languages of Semitic, root-based, morphology*, 79–97. Amsterdam: Benjamins.

Rupp, Matthias, Ewgenij Proschak & Gisbert Schneider. 2007. Kernel approach to molecular similarity based on iterative graph similarity. *Journal of Chemical Information and Modeling* 47. 2280–2286.

Sadock, Jerrold M. 2012. *The modular architecture of grammar*. Cambridge University Press.

Sag, Ivan A., Thomas Wasow & Emily M. Bender. 2003. *Syntactic theory: A formal introduction* (second edition). Stanford: CSLI.

Sales, Gabriele & Chiara Romualdi. 2012. *parmigene: Parallel mutual information estimation for gene network reconstruction.* http://CRAN.R-project.org/package=parmigene.

Sandler, Wendy & Diane Lillo-Martin. 2006. *Sign language and linguistic universals*. Cambridge Unversity Press.

Sapir, Edward. 1921. *Language: An introduction to the study of speech*. New York: Harcourt, Brace and Company.

Sapp, Christopher D. 2006. Verb order in subordinate clauses: From Early High New German to modern German. Ph.D. dissertation, Indiana University.

2011. *The verbal complex in subordinate clauses from medieval to modern German*. Amsterdam: Benjamins.

Saussure, Ferdinand de. 1916/1959. *Course in general linguistics* (translated by Wade Baskin). New York: McGraw Hill.

Scalise, Sergio & Antonietta Bisetto. 2009. The classification of compounds. In Rochelle Lieber & Pavol Štekauer (eds.), *The Oxford handbook of compounding*, 34–53. Oxford University Press.

Schadeberg, Thilo C. 2003. Derivation. In Derek Nurse & Gérard Philippson (eds.), *The Bantu languages*, 71–89. London: Routledge.

Schiering, René. 2006. Cliticization and the evolution of morphology: A cross-linguistic study on phonology in grammaticalization. Ph.D. dissertation, University of Constance. http://nbn-resolving.de/urn:nbn:de:bsz:352-opus-18728.

Schiering, René, Balthasar Bickel & Kristine A. Hildebrandt. 2010. The prosodic word is not universal, but emergent. *Journal of Linguistics* 46. 657–709.

Sezer, Engin. 2001. Finite inflection in Turkish. In Eser Erguvanlı Taylan (ed.), *The verb in Turkish*, 1–45. Amsterdam: Benjamins.

Shannon, Claude E. 1948. A mathematical theory of communication. *The Bell System Technical Journal* 27. 379–423, 623–656.

Shannon, Thomas F. 2000. On the order of (pro)nominal arguments in Dutch and German. In Thomas F. Shannon & Johan P. Snapper (eds.), *The Berkeley Conference on Dutch Linguistics 1997: The Dutch language at the millennium*, 145–196. Lanham, MD: University Press of America.

Sibanda, Galen. 2004. Verbal phonology and morphology of Ndebele. Ph.D. dissertation, University of California, Berkeley.

Simons, Gary F. 2005. Beyond the brink: Realizing interoperation through an RDF database. In *Proceedings of E-MELD 2005: Linguistic ontologies and data*

306   References

categories for language resources. Cambridge, MA, July 1–3. http://e-meld.org/workshop/2005/papers/simons-paper.pdf.

Simpson, Jane & Meg Withgott. 1986. Pronominal clitic clusters and templates. In Hagit Borer (ed.), *Syntax and semantics 19: The syntax of pronominal clitics*, 149–174. New York: Academic Press.

Sims, Andrea D. 2006. Minding the gaps: Inflectional defectiveness in a paradigmatic theory. Ph.D. dissertation, The Ohio State University.

Smith, Norval. 1985. Spreading, reduplication and the default option in Miwok nonconcatenative morphology. In Harry van der Hulst & Norval Smith (eds.), *Advances in non-linear phonology*, 363–380. Dordrecht: Foris.

Sobkowiak, Mikołaj. 2011. When 16th-century Polish poetry meets modern Danish syntax: A study of an odd case. *Folia Scandinavica* 12. 305–314.

Speas, Margaret. 1984. Navajo prefixes and word structure typology. In Margaret Speas & Richard Sproat (eds.), *Papers from the January 1984 MIT Workshop in Morphology* (MIT Working Papers in Linguistics, volume 7), 86–109. Cambridge, MA: MIT Department of Linguistics and Philosophy.

1987. Position classes and morphological universals. In Paul D. Kroeber & Robert E. Moore (eds.), *Native American languages and grammatical typology: Papers from a conference at the University of Chicago, April 22, 1987*, 199–214. Bloomington: Indiana University Linguistics Club.

1990. *Phrase structure in natural language.* Dordrecht: Kluwer.

Spencer, Andrew. 1991. *Morphological theory: An introduction to word structure in generative grammar.* Oxford: Blackwell.

2003. Putting some order into morphology: Reflections on Rice (2000) and Stump (2001). *Journal of Linguistics* 39. 621–646.

Spencer, Andrew & Ana R. Luís. 2012a. The canonical clitic. In Dunstan Brown, Marina Chumakina & Greville G. Corbett (eds.), *Canonical morphology and syntax*, 123–150. Oxford University Press.

2012b. *Clitics: An introduction.* Cambridge University Press.

Stanley, Richard John. 1969. The phonology of the Navaho verb. Cambridge, MA: MIT Ph.D. dissertation.

Stassen, Leon. 2000. AND-languages and WITH-languages. *Linguistic Typology* 4. 1–54.

Steele, Susan M. 1976. On the count of one. In Alphonse G. Juilland (ed.), *Linguistic studies offered to Joseph Greenberg on the occasion of his sixtieth birthday*, 591–613. Saratoga, CA: Anma Libri.

Steele, Susan M., Adrian Akmajian, Richard Demers, Eloise Jelinek, Chisato Kitagawa, Richard T. Oehrle & Thomas Wasow. 1981. *An encyclopedia of AUX: A study in cross-linguistic equivalence.* Cambridge, MA: MIT Press.

Steinhauer, Hein. 1997. The 4306 forms of the Nimboran verbal paradigm. In Udom Warotamasikkhadit & Thanyarat Panakul (eds.), *Papers from the fourth annual meeting of the Southeast Asian Linguistics Society*, 111–127. Tempe, AZ: Arizona State University, Program for Southeast Asian Studies.

Štekauer, Pavol, Salvador Valera & Lívia Kortvélyessy. 2012. *Word-formation in the world's languages: A typological survey.* Cambridge University Press.

Stewart, Osamuyimen T. 1998. The Serial Verb Construction parameter. Ph.D. thesis, McGill University.

References 307

2001. *The Serial Verb Construction parameter.* New York: Garland.

Storch, Anne. 1999. *Das Hone und seine Stellung im Zentral-Jukunoid.* Köln: Köppe.

2009. Hone. In Gerrit J. Dimmendaal (ed.), *Coding participant marking construction types in twelve African languages*, 123–140. Amsterdam: Benjamins.

Stump, Gregory T. 1993. Position classes and morphological theory. In Geert Booij & Jaap van Marle (eds.), *Yearbook of morphology 1992*, 129–180. Dordrecht: Kluwer.

1997. Template morphology and inflectional morphology. In Geert Booij & Jaap van Marle (eds.), *Yearbook of morphology 1996*, 217–241. Dordrecht: Kluwer.

2001. *Inflectional morphology: A theory of paradigm structure.* Cambridge University Press.

2006. Template morphology. In Keith Brown (ed.), *Encyclopedia of language and linguistics*, volume 12, 559–562. Oxford: Elsevier.

Stump, Gregory T. & Raphael A. Finkel. 2013. *Morphological typology: From word to paradigm.* Cambridge University Press.

Talmy, Leonard. 1985. Lexicalization patterns: Semantic structure in lexical forms. In Timothy Shopen (ed.), *Language typology and syntactic description: Grammatical categories and the lexicon*, 57–149. Cambridge: University Press.

Teil-Dautrey, Gisèle. 2008. Et si le proto-bantu était aussi une langue... avec ses contraintes et ses déséquilibres. *Diachronica* 25. 54–110.

Thomason, Lucy. 2003. The proximate and obviative contrast in Meskwaki. Ph.D. dissertation, University of Texas.

Tuttle, Siri G. & Sharon Hargus. 2004. Explaining variability in affix order: The Athabaskan areal and third person prefixes. In Gary Holton & Siri G. Tuttle (eds.), *Working Papers in Athabaskan Languages*, number 4, 70–98. Fairbanks, AK: Alaska Native Language Center.

Twist, Alina. 2006. A psycholinguistic investigation of the verbal morphology of Maltese. Ph.D. dissertation, University of Arizona.

Urbanczyk, Suzanne. 1996. Reduplication and prosodic morphology in Lushootseed. Ph.D. dissertation, University of Massachusetts.

2006. Reduplicative form and the root-affix asymmetry. *Natural Language and Linguistic Theory* 24. 179–240.

Ussishkin, Adam. 2000. The emergence of fixed prosody. Ph.D. dissertation, Univesity of California, Santa Cruz.

2005. A fixed prosodic theory of nonconcatenative templatic morphology. *Natural Language and Linguistic Theory* 23. 169–218.

Uszkoreit, Hans. 1987. *Word order and constituent structure in German.* Stanford: CSLI.

Vajda, Edward. 2004. *Ket.* Munich: LINCOM.

Van Valin, Robert D. Jr. & Randy J. LaPolla. 1997. *Syntax: Structure, meaning, and function.* Cambridge University Press.

Veselinova, Ljuba N. 2006. *Suppletion in verb paradigms: Bits and pieces of the puzzle.* Amsterdam: Benjamins.

2013. Suppletion. In *Oxford Bibliographies Online: Linguistics.* Oxford University Press. www.oxfordbibliographies.com/view/document/obo-9780199772810/obo-9780199772810-0125.xml.

Vihman, Marilyn M. & William Croft. 2007. Phonological development: Toward a "radical" templatic phonology. *Linguistics* 45. 683–725.

308 References

Wackernagel, Jacob. 1892. Über ein Gesetz der indogermanischen Wortstellung. *Indogermanische Forschungen* 1. 333–436.

Watters, John R. 1979. Focus in Aghem: A study of its formal correlates and typology. In Larry M. Hyman (ed.), *Aghem grammatical structure: With special reference to noun classes, tense-aspect and focus marking*, 137–197. Los Angeles: University of Southern California Department of Linguistics.

Wechsler, Stephen & Larisa Zlatić. 2000. A theory of agreement and its application to Serbo-Croatian. *Language* 76. 799–832.

Wetta, Andrew C. 2011. A construction-based cross-linguistic analysis of V2 word order. In Stefan Müller (ed.), *Proceedings of the 18th International Conference on Head-driven Phrase Structure Grammar, University of Washington*, 248–268. Stanford: CSLI.

Whitman, John. 2008. The classification of constituent order generalizations and diachronic explanation. In Jeff Good (ed.), *Linguistic universals and language change*, 233–252. Oxford University Press.

Whorf, Benjamin Lee. 1945. Grammatical categories. *Language* 21. 1–11.

  1956. *Language, thought, and reality: Selected writing of Benjamin Lee Whorf.* Cambridge, MA: MIT Press.

Wichmann, Søren. 2008a. The emerging field of language dynamics. *Language and Linguistics Compass* 2. 442–455.

  2008b. The study of semantic alignment: Retrospect and state of the art. In Søren Wichmann & Mark Donohue (eds.), *The typology of semantic alignment*, 3–23. Oxford Unversity Press.

Wichmann, Søren, Eric W. Holman, Taraka Rama & Robert S. Walker. 2011. Correlates of reticulation in linguistic phylogenies. *Language Dynamics and Change* 1. 205–240.

Wojdak, Rachel. 2008. *The linearization of affixes: Evidence from Nuu-chah-nulth.* Dordrecht: Springer.

Wunderlich, Dieter. 2006. Introduction: What the theory of the lexicon is about. In Dieter Wunderlich (ed.), *Advances in the theory of the lexicon*, 1–25. Berlin: Mouton de Gruyter.

Yip, Moira. 1989. Cantonese morpheme structure and linear ordering. In E. Jane Fee & Katherine Hunt (eds.), *The proceedings of the eighth West Coast Conference on Formal Linguistics*, 445–456. Stanford: CSLI.

Young, Robert W. 2000. *The Navajo verb system: An overview.* Albuquerque: University of New Mexico Press.

Yu, Alan C. L. 2007. *A natural history of infixation.* Oxford University Press.

Yu, Alan C. L. & Jeff Good. 2000. Morphosyntax of two Turkish subject pronominal paradigms. In Masako Hirotani, Andries W. Coetzee, Nancy Hall & Ji-Yung Kim (eds.), *Proceedings of thirtieth annual meeting of the North East Linguistic Society*, 759–773. Amherst: GLSA.

Zager, Laura A. 2005. Graph similarity and matching. Ph.D. dissertation, MIT.

Zager, Laura A. & George C. Verghese. 2008. Graph similarity scoring and matching. *Applied Mathematics Letters* 21. 86–94.

Zec, Draga & Sharon Inkelas. 1990. Prosodically constrained syntax. In Sharon Inkelas & Draga Zec (eds.), *The phonology-syntax connection*, 365–378. Stanford: CSLI.

References

309

1992. The place of clitics in the prosodic hierarchy. In Dawn Bates (ed.), *The proceedings of the tenth West Coast Conference on Formal Linguistics*, 505–519. Stanford: CSLI.

Zeileis, Achim, David Meyer & Kurt Hornik. 2007. Residual-based shadings for visualizing (conditional) independence. *Journal of Computational and Graphical Statistics* 16. 507–525.

Zwicky, Arnold M. 1977. *On clitics*. Bloomington: Indiana University Linguistics Club.

Author index

Abad, May, 11
Abasheikh, Mohammed, 166
Aboh, Enoch O., 193
Aikhenvald, Alexandra Y., 24, 77, 110
Akinnaso, F. Niyi, 19
Akmajian, Adrian, 91
Akutsu, Tatsuya, 223
Alderete, John, 266
Allemang, Dean, 101
Alsina, Alex, 143, 150
Anceaux, J. C., 118, 120–122, 124, 125
Anderson, Gregory D. S., 177
Anderson, Stephen C., 195, 196
Anderson, Stephen R., 12, 20, 25, 43, 45
Arnold, Doug, 95
Aronoff, Mark, 13, 25, 28, 41, 106
Ashburner, Michael, 223
Asudeh, Ash, 96
Atkinson, Quentin D., 220
Auer, Sören, 102
Awóyalé, Yíwolá, 19
Axelrod, Melissa, 15

Baerman, Matthew, 118
Bagemihl, Bruce, 16
Bagga, Jay, 223
Baker, Mark C., 5, 25, 29, 43, 63, 79, 97, 100, 143, 150
Bakker, Peter, 227
Ball, Catherine A., 223
Bandelt, Hans-Jürgen, 227
Banjade, Goma, 109–115
Barnes, Jonathan, 262
Barrett-Keach, Camillia N., 15
Basso, Katia, 254
Bastin, Yvonne, 132–134
Bauer, Laurie, 36
Becker, Christian, 102
Beckman, Jill, 266

Bender, Emily M., 19, 37, 44, 48, 52, 57, 62, 78, 90, 91, 93–95, 268
Benua, Laura, 266
Berners-Lee, Tim, 101
Bickel, Balthasar, xii, 4, 5, 35, 39, 46, 48, 52, 53, 76, 96–100, 104, 109–115, 184, 196, 217, 220, 227, 253–257, 259–261
Bird, Steven, 268
Bisetto, Antonietta, 77
Bizer, Christian, 101, 102
Bjerre, Tavs, 18
Blackings, Mairi, 20
Blake, Judith A., 223
Blevins, James P., 91, 93, 94
Blevins, Juliette, 16
Blondel, Vincent D., 220
Bloomfield, Leonard, 14
Bošković, Željko, 30, 32, 185
Bobaljik, Jonathan David, 79, 146
Bonami, Olivier, 15
Bond, Oliver, 177
Bonet, Eulália, 15
Booij, Geert E., 21
Bostoen, Koen, 132, 133
Botstein, David, 223
Bottazzini, Umberto, 28
Bouma, Gosse, 92
Boyé, Gilles, 15
Bray, Tim, 272
Brentari, Diane, 12, 17
Bresnan, Joan, 93, 96
Brickley, Dan, 45, 103
Brinton, Laurel J., 136
Broadbent, Sylvia M., 9
Broselow, Ellen, 9
Brown, Dunstan, 46, 48, 52
Browne, Wayles E., 187, 189
Bryant, David, 227
Butler, Heather, 223
Butt, Miriam, 20

Author index

311

Bybee, Joan L., 43, 263

Caballero, Gabriela, 57
Cain, William, 76
Cairns, Charles E., 16
Califano, Andrea, 254
Calzolari, Nicoletta, 103
Campbell, Amy M., 57
Campbell, Lyle, 177
Carlson, Robert, 199
Carpenter, Bob, 93
Carstairs-McCarthy, Andrew, 43
Chappell, Hilary, 4
Cherry, J. Michael, 223
Chiarcos, Christian, 101
Chomsky, Noam, 5, 268
Chumakina, Marina, 46, 48, 52
Cimiano, Philipp, 103
Cogill-Koez, Dorothea, 22
Comrie, Bernard, xii, 34, 42, 46, 105, 227
Conathan, Lisa, 168, 173, 175, 176
Connolly, John H., 19
Copestake, Ann, 93, 94
Corbett, Greville G., 28, 46, 47, 91, 93, 96, 160
Corina, David, 12
Creissels, Denis, 41, 197, 199–202
Cristofaro, Sonia, 35
Croft, William, 8, 35, 46, 55
Crowhurst, Megan J., 17
Crubézy, Monica, 103
Crysmann, Berthold, 15, 16
Culicover, Peter W., 34
Curry, Haskell B., 40
Cyganiak, Richard, 102
Cysouw, Michael, xii, 103, 172, 225, 227

Dahl, Östen, 104
Dahlstrom, Amy, 19, 203–205
Daval-Markussen, Aymeric, 227
Davis, Allan P., 223
Davis, Lori, 175
Davis, Stuart, 11
Demers, Richard, 91
den Besten, Hans, 19
Di Meola, Claudio, 73
Diestel, Reinhard, 100, 101
Dik, Simon C., 19, 196
Dixon, R. M. W., 24, 110
Dolinski, Kara, 223
Donohue, Mark, 178
Downing, Laura J., 7, 11, 35, 72, 99
Dress, Andreas W. M., 227
Dryer, Matthew S., 4, 5, 24, 25, 30, 31, 33–35, 52, 53, 102, 104, 260, 262

Dunn, Michael, 220
Dwight, Selina S., 223

Ekundayo, S. Ayotunde, 19
Ellington, John, 154, 155, 159
Elman, Jeffrey L., 240
Enfield, N. J., 20, 166
Engberg-Pedersen, Elisabeth, 22
Engels, Eva, 18
Eppig, Janan T., 223
Epps, Patience, 20
Eriksson, Henrik, 103
Evans, Nicholas, 46, 166, 196
Evans, Tim S., 223

Fabb, Nigel, 20
Falcon, S., 223
Fanselow, Gisbert, 69
Faraclas, Nicholas G., 177
Farrar, Scott, 56, 79, 102, 273
Favera, Riccardo, 254
Feinstein, Mark H., 16
Fergerson, Ray W., 103
Féry, Caroline, 69
Filimon, Flavia, 227
Fillmore, Charles J., 20, 55
Finkel, Raphael A., 15
Flickinger, Dan, 95
Foley, William A., 169
Forkel, Robert, 102
Forker, Diana, 227
Francez, Nissim, 82, 93, 167
Franks, Steven, 91, 185, 186
Freeland, L. S., 9, 10, 66, 67
Fujibuchi, Wataru, 220

Gaenszle, Martin, 109–115
Gajardo, Anahí, 220
Gansner, Emden R., 238
Garcia-Molina, Hector, 220, 233, 236, 238, 241
Garrett, Andrew, xii
Gennari, John H., 103
Gensler, Orin D., 199
Gentleman, R., 223
Geuder, Wilhelm, 20
Gil, David, 34
Givón, Talmy, 43, 270
Gnanadesikan, Amalia, 266
Goldberg, Adele E., 20
Goldsmith, John A., 9, 77
Good, Jeff, 1, 3, 13, 20, 25, 30, 35, 63, 79, 101, 103, 110–112, 131–134, 136, 139, 140, 142, 144, 148, 165, 166, 168–170, 173, 175, 176, 178, 191, 194, 270, 271

312 Author index

Gordon, Matthew K., 16
Goto, Susumu, 220
Gowlett, Derek F., 72, 134
Gray, Russell D., 220, 227
Greenberg, Joseph H., 34, 271
Greyling, Jean H., 220
Grohmann, Kleanthes K, 79
Grosso, William E., 103
Guha, R. V., 45, 103
Güldemann, Tom, 199
Gupta, Anil, 26
Guthrie, Malcolm, 131, 132, 154

ten Hacken, Pius, 4
Hagège, Claude, 267
Hale, Ken, 15, 20, 100
Halle, Morris, 9
Halpern, Aaron, 15, 20, 186
Hankamer, Jorge, 70
Hansen, Cynthia, 73
Hansson, Gunnar Ólafur, 165
Hargus, Sharon, 9, 15, 16, 38, 58, 105, 120, 174
Harley, Heidi, 118
Harris, Alice C., 57, 177, 181, 271
Harris, Midori A., 223
Haspelmath, Martin, xii, 34, 35, 42, 45–47, 62, 96, 102, 105, 170, 179, 262
Hausser, Jean, 254
Hayes, Bruce, 11, 17
Heath, Jeffrey, 16, 199, 202
Heath, Tom, 101
Heggarty, Paul, 227
Heggie, Lorie, 15
Heine, Bernd, 76, 166
Hellmann, Sebastian, 101, 102
Hendler, James, 101
Hendricks, Sean, 11, 35
Hendryx-Parker, Calvin, 101, 103
Heymans, Maureen, 220
Hildebrandt, Kristine A., 35, 46, 99, 100, 184
Hill, David P., 223
Hockett, Charles F., 25, 45
Höhle, Tilman, 17, 210
Hoijer, Harry, 1, 2
Hollander, Dave, 272
Holman, Eric W., 227
Hopper, Paul J., 46
Hornik, Kurt, 256
Hornstein, Norbert, 79
Horvath, Julia, 193, 196
Huang, C.-T. James, 32
Huber, Magnus, 102
Huson, Daniel H., 227

Hyman, Larry M., xii, 13, 14, 29, 38, 42, 63, 66, 67, 71, 72, 80, 89, 130–132, 135, 139, 140, 142–144, 148, 152, 154–158, 160, 163, 164, 166, 193–196, 269, 270
Hymes, Dell H., 15, 75

Ide, Nancy, 103
Inkelas, Sharon, 7, 13, 20, 34, 57, 70–72, 82, 89, 99, 106, 117–121, 123–127, 129, 130, 139, 150, 154, 156, 157, 185–187, 190, 191
Issel-Tarver, Laurie, 223
Itô, Junko, 7, 16, 17, 70

Jakobson, Roman, 12
Jeh, Glen, 220
Jelinek, Eloise, 91, 100
Jeschull, Liane, 170
Joos, Martin, 5
Jordan, Michael I., 240
Jørgensen, Henrik, 18

Kameda, Shohei, 234
Kandybowicz, Jason, 176
Kanehisa, Minoru, 220, 223
Kari, James, 7, 9, 13–15, 58, 75, 269
Kasarskis, Andrew, 223
Kathol, Andreas, 18, 19, 59, 60, 75, 91, 92, 207, 208, 211
Kavutirwaki, Kambale, 135
Kay, Paul, 20, 55
Kayne, Richard S., 25, 30, 267
Keenan, Edward L., 46
Kenstowicz, Michael, 77
Kepser, Stephan, 95
Keyser, Jay, 20
Kim, Yuni, 24
Kimball, Geoffrey D., 14
King, Tracy Holloway, 91, 185, 186
Kiparsky, Paul, 36, 119, 163
Kisseberth, Charles W., 150
Kitagawa, Chisato, 91
Klavans, Judith, 183
Klein, Ewan, 268
Kleinberg, Jon M., 102, 220
Kobilarov, Georgi, 102
Koenig, Jean-Pierre, 100
Komen, Erwin R., 170, 180
Kortvélyessy, Lívia, 36, 77
Kumar, Ravi, 102

Lambiotte, Renaud, 223
Langendoen, D. Terence, 56, 79, 273
LaPolla, Randy J., 7, 21, 32, 169
Laudan, Larry, 31

Author index

Layman, Andrew, 272
Leer, Jeff, 15, 58, 271
Lehmann, Jens, 102
Lenci, Alessandro, 103
Levin, Beth, 21, 178
Levinson, Stephen C., 220
Lewis, Geoffrey L., 70, 71
Lewis, Suzanna, 223
Lewis, William D., 56, 79, 273
Libert, Alan, 267
Lieven, Elena, 109–115
Lillo-Martin, Diane, 12, 29
Linardaki, Evita, 95
Lindström, Eva, 220
Longacre, Robert E., 169
Lounsbury, Floyd G., 14
Luís, Ana R., 15, 28, 91, 185, 189

MacWhinney, Brian, 174
Maganga, Clement, 15
Maguire, Warren, 227
Maho, Jouni, 131
Malchukov, Andrej, 46, 105
Manova, Stela, 13
Margolin, Adam, 254
Matese, John C., 223
Mathangwane, Joyce T., 148
Matthews, Peter H., 45
Maurer, Philippe, 102
McCarthy, John, 9–11, 23, 24, 35, 70, 88, 266
McCawley, James D., 31, 94, 268
McCloskey, Jim, 5, 97
McCrae, John Philip, 103
McDonough, Joyce, 12, 15, 31, 120
McFarland, Teresa Ann, 15
Mchombo, Sam A., 63, 96, 143, 144, 148
McLendon, Sally, 14
McMahon, April, 227
Meeussen, A.E, 132–134, 139, 154
Mel'čuk, Igor, 12, 40, 46
Melnar, Lynette R., 15
Melnik, Sergey, 220, 233, 236, 238, 241
Menn, Lise, 174
Mester, R. Armin, 1, 6
Meyer, David, 256
Michaelis, Laura A., 20, 90
Michaelis, Susanne Maria, 102
Michelson, Karin, 100
Mihalicek, Verdrana, 17, 40
Miller, Philip H., 15, 16
Mithun, Marianne, 57, 58, 271
Molochieva, Zarina, 170
Mönnich, Uwe, 95
Moran, Steven, 101
Moravcsik, Edith A., 94

Moulton, Vincent, 227
Müller, Stefan, 210
Musen, Mark A., 103
Mutaka, Ngessimo M., 135
Myers, Scott P., 15

Nacher, Jose C., 223
Napoli, Donna Jo, 11
Naudé, Kevin A., 220
Nemenman, Ilya, 254
Nespor, Marina, 25, 35
Nevins, Andrew, 266
Newmeyer, Frederick J., 4, 5
Ngunga, Armindo, 133
Nichols, Johanna, xii, 4, 5, 30, 35, 46, 48, 53, 79, 96–98, 104, 110, 168, 169, 172, 178–180, 220, 227, 259, 261, 262
van Noord, Gertjan, 92
Nordhoff, Sebastian, xiii, 101
Nordlinger, Rachel, 16
North, Stephen C., 238
Noy, Natalya F., 103
Noyer, Rolf, 16, 24, 30, 118
Nunes, Jairo, 79
Nurse, Derek, 132, 154

O'Connor, Mary Catherine, 55
Oehrle, Richard T., 91
Oepen, Stephan, 95
Ogata, Hiroyuki, 220
Ordóñez, Francisco, 15
Orgun, Cemil Orhan, 70, 106, 150

Pagliuca, William, 263
Parkvall, Mikael, 227
Paster, Mary, 24, 29, 113, 160
Paudyal, Netra Prasad, 109–115
Perkins, Revere, 263
Perlmutter, David M., 12, 15, 178
Pesetsky, David, 27
Peterson, David A., 143, 168, 172, 179, 262
Philippson, Gérard, 154
Pike, Kenneth L., 12, 18
Plag, Ingo, 227
Plank, Frans, 27
Polinsky, Maria, 193
Poser, William J., 1, 2
Prince, Alan S., 11, 23, 35, 70, 77, 88
Prince, Ellen, 175
Proschak, Ewgenij, 220

R Core Team, 254
Radford, Andrew, 32
Raghavan, Prabhakar, 102
Rahm, Erhard, 220, 233, 236, 238, 241

314   Author index

Rai, Ichchha Purna, 109–115
Rai, Manoj, 109–115
Rai, Novel Kishore, 109–115
Rajagopalan, Sridhar, 102
Rama, Taraka, 227
Ramchand, Gillian, 8
Rappaport Hovav, Malka, 21, 178
Reesink, Ger, 220
Reiss, Charles, 8
Revithiadou, Anthi, 20
Rhodes, Richard A., 203
Rice, Keren, 1, 7, 9, 13, 15, 16, 30, 36, 37, 57, 120, 267
Richardson, Joel E., 223
van Riemsdijk, Henk, 17
Ringwald, Martin, 223
Romualdi, Chiara, 254
Rose, Sharon, 11, 15
Rubin, Gerald M., 223
Rupp, Matthias, 220

Sadock, Jerrold M., 8, 19, 25
Sag, Ivan A., 15, 16, 19, 44, 48, 52, 57, 62, 78, 90, 91, 93, 94, 268
Sales, Gabriele, 254
Sandler, Wendy, 12
Sapir, Edward, 31
Sapp, Christopher D., 19
Saussure, Ferdinand de, 9
Scalise, Sergio, 77
Schadeberg, Thilo C., 15, 132, 139, 140, 154
Schiering, René, 35, 46, 99, 100, 184, 270
Schneider, Gisbert, 220
Schuh, Russell G., 12
Senellart, Pierre, 220
Sezer, Engin, 112
Shannon, Claude E., 255
Shannon, Thomas F., 18
Sherlock, Gavin, 223
Sibanda, Galen, 71, 72, 133, 136, 148, 151
Siegmund, Sven, 262
Simons, Gary F., 103
Simpson, Jane, 7, 12, 15, 23, 34, 36–38
Sims, Andrea D., 70
Singh, Ambuj K., 220
Smith, Norval, 9
Sobkowiak, Mikołaj, 18
Speas, Margaret, 15
Spencer, Andrew, 15, 16, 28, 36, 38, 91, 185, 189
Spohr, Dennis, 103
Stanley, Richard John, 15
Stassen, Leon, 46
Steele, Susan M., 91
Steinhauer, Hein, 118, 120

Štekauer, Pavol, 36, 77
Stewart, Osamuyimen T., 176, 177
Stoll, Sabine, 109–115
Stolovitzky, Gustavo, 254
Storch, Anne, 178
Strimmer, Korbinian, 254
Stump, Gregory T., 7, 12, 13, 15, 16, 36–38, 45
Suttle, Laura, 20

Tadmor, Uri, 102
Talmy, Leonard, 169
Teil-Dautrey, Gisèle, 134, 140
Terrill, Angela, 220
Thomason, Lucy, 203
Thompson, Henry S., 272
Thompson, Sandra A., 46
Tobin, Richard, 272
Toivonen, Ida, 96
Tomkins, Andrew S., 102
Traugott, Elizabeth Closs, 136
Tu, Samson W., 103
Tuttle, Siri G., 9, 15, 16, 38, 174
Twist, Alina, 267

Udoh, Imelda, 269
Ueda, Nobuhisa, 223
Urbanczyk, Suzanne, 11, 266
Ussishkin, Adam, 9, 11
Uszkoreit, Hans, 92

Vagapov, Arbi, 169
Vajda, Edward, 15
Valera, Salvador, 36, 77
Van Dooren, Paul, 220
Van Valin, Robert D. Jr., 7, 21, 32, 169
VanBik, Kenneth, 179
Vaux, Bert, 266
Verghese, George C., 220
Vergnaud, Jean-Roger, 9
Veselinova, Ljuba N., 160
Vihman, Marilyn M., 8
Vikner, Sten, 18
Vogel, Irene, 25, 35
Vogts, Dieter, 220

Wackernagel, Jacob, 185
Walker, Robert S., 227
Warnow, Tandy, 220, 227
Wasow, Thomas, 19, 44, 48, 52, 57, 62, 78, 90, 91, 93, 94, 268
Watters, John R., 191, 193–196
Waugh, Linda, 12
Wechsler, Stephen, 186
Wetta, Andrew C., 19

Author index

Whitman, John, 34
Whorf, Benjamin Lee, 15, 47, 75
Wichmann, Søren, 178, 220, 227
Widom, Jennifer, 220
Wiggins, Chris, 254
Wilkins, David, 166
Winter, Shuly, 82, 93, 167
Withgott, Meg, 7, 12, 15, 23, 34, 36–38
Wojdak, Rachel, 28
Wunderlich, Dieter, 21

Yamada, Takuji, 223

Yip, Moira, 23
Young, Robert W., 15
Yu, Alan C. L., 43, 110–113

Zager, Laura A., 220
Zec, Draga, 7, 20, 57, 82, 99, 185–187, 190, 191
Zeileis, Achim, 256
Zlatić, Larisa, 186
Zoll, Cheryl, 34
Zwicky, Arnold M., 20

Language index

Abkhaz, 168
Aghem, 191–199, 211, 225, 243, 247–250
Ahtna, 13
Athabaskan, 1, 2, 9, 15, 30, 32, 58, 75, 105, 106, 120, 126, 130, 174, 266, 267, 269
Atsugewi, 169

Bambara, 41, 197, 199, 201
Bantoid, 79
Bantu, 14, 59, 63, 64, 68, 71, 72, 79–85, 89, 90, 106, 130–146, 148, 150, 151, 154, 155, 158, 160, 162, 165–168, 182, 225, 228, 230, 261, 270

Caddo, 15
Cantonese, 23
Chechen, 168–184, 187, 188, 225, 227, 230, 243–245, 247, 250
Chichewa, 13, 14, 63, 72, 130, 143, 144, 148, 150–154, 167, 225
Chintang, 110–117, 225, 229, 230, 255
Ciyao, 133, 134

Dutch, 18

Eastern Pomo, 14
Edo, 176, 177
English, 10, 20, 21, 23, 32, 36, 40, 51, 55, 57, 71, 94, 105, 168, 170, 178, 212–214, 225, 228–230, 232, 265, 266

Filomeno Mata Totonac, 15

German, 17–19, 57, 59–64, 73, 75, 76, 79, 91, 92, 126, 169, 188, 207–211, 217, 218, 225, 227
Ghana-Togo Mountain languages, 76
Greek, 44

Hakha Lai, 179

Hone, 178, 192

Indo-European, 185
Ingush, 168, 172, 175, 178–180

Japanese, 1, 2

Ket, 15
Kinande, 135
Kinyamwezi, 15
Koasati, 15

Leggbó, 269

Mande, 41–43, 197, 199–202, 207, 208, 214, 225, 230, 243, 244, 246, 247, 249, 250, 270
Menomini, 14
Meskwaki, 19, 203–208, 210, 225, 227, 230
Mohawk, 57, 59

Na-Dene, 15
Navajo, 15
Ndebele, 71–73, 133, 136, 146, 148, 149, 167, 225, 230
Nganhcara, 183
Nimboran, 75, 106, 117–130, 136, 139, 167, 208, 211, 225, 228, 230
Nkore, 132
Nyoro, 132

Obolo, 177
Oneida, 14

Romance, 15

Scandinavian, 18
Semitic, 9, 106, 267

Language index

Serbo-Croatian, 20, 30, 32, 80, 82, 84–87, 91, 92, 108, 109, 136, 185–192, 225, 228, 230
Sierra Miwok, 9, 10, 66–68, 74, 88, 106
sign languages, 12, 21, 22, 29
Songhay, 202

Tiene, 35, 41–43, 66–68, 88, 106, 131, 142, 150, 154–158, 160–166, 168, 184, 221, 222, 225, 227, 228, 230, 266

Tlingit, 15, 58
Turkish, 69–71, 73, 85, 90, 91, 106–109, 111–113, 157, 168, 182, 184, 191, 214, 217, 219, 227, 230, 264, 265

Udi, 181, 271

Yiddish, 175–177

Term index

ad hoc, 31, 79
adjacency, 37, 146–148, 152, 165
adjunct, 172, 173, 277
adposition, 14, 73
    postposition, 73, 200, 267
    preposition, 60, 73, 186, 213, 267
affix, 12, 13, 15, 24, 28, 29, 36, 37, 40–42,
    55–58, 106, 110, 111, 113, 119, 123, 139,
    155, 158–160, 165, 174, 212, 229, 268,
    278
    infix, 42, 43, 113, 120, 181, 212
    mobile, 24, 40, 267
    prefix, 2, 15, 24, 28, 29, 40, 41, 44, 58, 80,
        110, 111, 113–117, 123, 125, 172, 173,
        210, 225, 229, 230, 267, 272
    suffix, 10, 13, 14, 24, 28, 29, 59, 63, 64, 70,
        71, 79, 80, 89, 106, 107, 110–112, 123,
        125, 130, 132–136, 139–144, 146–148,
        150–152, 154, 157–160, 166, 167, 170,
        171, 212, 213, 225, 267, 270, 278
agreement, 12, 112, 118, 178
allomorphy, 70, 71, 160, 166
analogical change, 271
antipassive, 200
applicative, 14, 63–65, 68, 80–85, 89,
    133–135, 140, 142–156, 158, 159, 163,
    166, 167, 225, 230
arch, 49, 76, 77, 80, 82, 84, 93, 99, 115, 139,
    160, 162–164, 188, 197, 200–202, 205,
    207, 212, 217, 244, 247, 249, 252, 253,
    256, 257, 262, 264, 269, 277, 282
areal factors, 104, 199, 261
argument, 37, 40, 41, 76, 130, 177, 179,
    192–195, 199–201, 203, 208, 212, 270,
    277
associate, 58, 126, 164, 205, 210, 280, 281
Atlas of Pidgin and Creole Structures, 102
attribute-value matrices, 62, 95
AUTOTYP, 48, 97, 98, 259
auxiliary, *see* verb, auxiliary

biology, 220, 233, 254
bridging context, 165, 166

Canonical Typology, *see* typology, Canonical
causative, 14, 42, 63, 67, 68, 80–85, 89,
    132–137, 139–152, 154, 155, 158, 159,
    163, 166, 167, 225, 230
chemistry, 220
chimeric, 40, 41, 44, 268
clause, 15, 18, 19, 32, 41, 46, 48, 53, 59, 73,
    75, 91, 92, 96, 126, 169, 170, 173, 174,
    176–180, 185, 187–189, 191, 194–197,
    199, 200, 203, 205, 207, 208, 210, 211,
    217, 227, 230, 243, 251, 260, 261, 274
clause chaining, 170, 171, 179, 277
clitic, 15, 20, 28, 31, 38, 56, 91, 119, 169, 172,
    174, 180, 181, 185–189, 278
    enclitic, 40, 44, 169–172, 183, 278
    endoclitic, 43, 181, 271
    second-position, 20, 30, 32, 43, 91, 92, 183,
        185–190, 204, 225, 228, 230
clitic cluster, 15, 185, 186
coding, 45, 52, 58, 78, 88, 90, 104, 111, 115,
    117, 126, 147, 151, 163–165, 174, 189,
    190, 211, 216, 253, 259, 262–265
coherence, 55, 56, 62, 208, 273, 275, 281
comparative concept, 45, 47, 50, 184
comparison, 3, 4, 39, 43, 45–48, 51, 52, 54,
    56, 59, 63, 65, 66, 85, 90–92, 94–96, 98,
    100, 103, 105, 114, 118, 119, 121, 141,
    164, 168, 175, 180, 216, 217, 220, 221,
    223, 224, 227, 228, 230, 232–234, 240,
    250, 257, 258, 263, 277
    algorithmic, 221, 227, 230
component, 8, 44, 47, 50–65, 68, 76–78, 80,
    82, 87, 91–94, 108, 114, 115, 117, 121,
    129, 136, 139, 141, 142, 146–149, 160,
    163–165, 167, 168, 182, 183, 188–190,
    197, 200–202, 205, 208, 210, 212, 213,
    217, 225–227, 230, 231, 235, 236, 242,

Term index 319

244, 247, 249, 250, 263, 264, 269, 270, 273–282
compound, 71, 77, 172
computer science, 220
conditioning, 48, 51, 65–69, 78, 98, 107, 114, 146, 154, 169, 183, 212, 250, 252, 254–257, 273, 274, 276, 277, 281
  constructional, 68, 114, 126, 197, 213, 255, 256, 273
  lexico-constructional, 68, 80, 130, 146, 147, 170, 183, 184, 212, 244, 273, 278, 281
  morphosyntactic, 67, 273
  phonological, 274
  prosodic, 68, 256, 274
consonant, 9, 10, 23, 35, 42, 67, 74, 110, 131, 157–160, 163, 164, 277
conspiracies, 150
constituent, 1, 7, 9, 19, 20, 22, 30, 41, 47, 51, 57, 66, 68, 74, 77, 78, 82, 85, 89, 90, 106, 139, 172, 190, 191, 193, 204, 210, 250, 252, 254–256, 265, 269, 274, 279–281
  morphological, 1, 88, 126, 274
  morphosyntactic, 126, 274
  phonological, 25, 274
  prosodic, 20, 35, 46, 77, 82, 84, 85, 109–111, 114, 117, 180–184, 187, 191, 274, 278
  syntactic, 41, 57, 256, 274
constraint, 6, 8–10, 12, 14, 16–18, 21, 22, 28, 34, 37, 66, 67, 69, 70, 74, 78–80, 82, 87–89, 92, 93, 107, 112–114, 120, 131, 134, 135, 139, 140, 142, 146–148, 152, 155, 156, 158–160, 164, 166, 167, 173, 174, 181, 185, 186, 190, 191, 199, 200, 262, 265
  repeated morph, 174
Construction Grammar, 20, 21
coronal, 42, 67, 155, 157, 159, 160, 163, 277

dependency, 40, 56, 58, 59, 62, 69, 108, 129, 134, 136, 141, 142, 146, 147, 162, 164, 165, 167, 188, 196, 197, 205, 210, 211, 280, 282
  discontinuous, 57, 60, 129, 204, 205
derivation, 36–38, 155, 159, 167
description language, 3, 45–55, 60, 62, 65, 67, 75, 76, 78, 87, 89, 92, 94, 97, 98, 102–107, 114, 125, 129, 130, 141, 147, 149, 151, 154, 168, 183, 185, 186, 188, 190, 204, 205, 211, 215–217, 220, 221, 238, 240, 242, 259, 260, 263, 264, 268–270
desmeme, 23, 44, 45, 49–51, 65, 66, 77–79, 82, 85, 88, 92, 95, 99, 109, 188, 190,

211–214, 225, 242, 244, 249, 250, 265, 267, 270, 276
diachrony, *see* language change

edges, 100, 117, 221, 233, 243
elasticity, 54, 57, 62, 236, 269, 273, 274, 281
exceptionality, 50, 51, 69, 71, 72, 152, 197, 254, 255, 275, 280, 281
expletive, 78, 79, 178, 194
Extended Projection Principle, 79

feature structure, 44, 48, 52, 62–64, 80, 82, 93–96, 100, 103, 217, 227, 247, 257
  typed, 48, 53, 59, 60, 92–94, 96, 97, 101
filledness, 54–56, 62, 64, 115, 117, 236, 273, 275, 276, 281
filler, 14, 51, 56, 59, 64, 68, 80, 87, 92, 121, 146–148, 183, 188–190, 202, 275
flagging, 105, 143, 196, 200, 212
focus, 170, 176, 193–196, 204, 205, 277
foot, 17, 77, 114
formal linguistics, 4
foundation, 44, 47, 65, 66, 73–78, 80, 82, 84, 85, 93–95, 99, 114, 126, 127, 160, 163, 188, 200, 207, 221, 223, 224, 235, 236, 242, 247, 249, 250, 254–257, 262, 264, 269, 276, 277, 279, 282

genealogical factors, 104, 168, 260, 261
General Ontology for Linguistic Description, *see* ontology
generative linguistics, 4, 9, 11, 15–17, 19, 25, 30–33, 37, 79, 97, 119, 176, 193, 268
grammatical relations, 76, 196
graph, 45, 59–61, 63, 64, 82–84, 86, 94, 95, 100–103, 114, 116, 165, 219–225, 227, 228, 230, 233–236, 238, 240, 242, 243, 245–251, 253, 257, 263, 264
  directed, 94, 101, 221
  pairwise, 234–240, 244, 247
  rendering, 238
  split, 229, 232
graph comparison, *see* comparison

harmony, 160, 163, 165, 269
  length, 269
  nasal, 157, 163, 164
  vowel, 132, 143, 156, 159, 160
head, 30, 40, 41, 47, 76, 77, 99, 115, 119, 256
Head-driven Phrase Structure Grammar, 16, 18, 19, 44, 48, 52, 80, 93–96
homophony, 126, 252, 279
HPSG, *see* Head-driven Phrase Structure Grammar

320 Term index

idiom, 55
implementation, 90, 95, 100, 101, 167, 227, 234, 254
ineffability, 69, 70, 106, 107, 265
infinitive, *see* verb, infinitive
infinity symbol, 62, 108
inflection, 9, 72, 132, 140, 212
information theory, 253–256
insertion, *see* repair, insertion
Item-and-Arrangement model, 45
Item-and-Process model, 45

keystone, 47, 76–78, 80, 82, 93, 99, 114, 115, 117, 126, 139, 141, 160, 163, 164, 188, 197, 200, 202, 205, 207, 208, 210–212, 217, 247, 256, 262–264, 269, 277, 282

labial, 42
language change, 11, 23, 131, 136, 150, 154, 165, 166, 170, 172, 176, 181, 227, 270, 271
lexical phonology, *see* phonology, lexical
Lexical-Functional Grammar, 93
lexicalization, 57, 135, 136, 144
liaison, 276, 278, 282
linear order, 1, 8, 13, 17, 18, 23, 24, 29, 32, 40, 44, 89, 100, 113, 196, 203, 276
lineate, 44, 87, 183, 212, 276
Linked Data, 101, 102
lookahead, 37, 146, 147

mathematics, 28, 95, 100, 101, 217, 220
maximal size restriction, 108, 140, 150, 157, 184
middlefield, 18, 57, 60, 92, 207, 208
minimal size restriction, 70, 72–74, 78, 90, 106–109, 139, 140, 150, 157, 158, 184, 219, 227, 265
Minimalism, 79
Mirror Principle, 29, 63, 143, 150, 151
mora, 1, 11, 74, 157, 159, 252, 274, 277
morpheme order, 14, 63, 110, 112, 117, 118, 143, 150, 270
morphology, 5, 6, 8, 9, 12–14, 21, 28, 36–38, 40, 91, 99, 118, 148, 150, 151, 155, 164, 165, 168, 174, 178, 181, 261, 268, 271
    layered, 13, 15, 36–38
    prosodic, 11, 17, 34–36, 88, 107, 181, 266
    slot-filler, 12, 22, 24, 54, 57, 89, 194
movement, 31, 32, 57, 267

NeighborNet, 227
neural network, 240
nickname, 1, 2
no lookahead, *see* lookahead

noun, 36, 44, 46, 55, 57, 67, 70, 71, 90, 91, 106–108, 113, 164, 178, 186, 200, 212, 219, 227

object, 1, 19, 25–27, 31, 37, 79, 172, 173, 177, 178, 192, 194, 199, 200, 202, 233, 277
    cognate, 174, 177, 178
    direct, 41, 212, 213, 277
    indirect, 41, 212, 213, 277
oblique, 204, 205, 278
ontology, 56, 79, 103, 223, 225, 256, 272, 276, 277
Optimality Theory, 69

parameters, 25, 26, 30
passive, 71, 89, 91, 106, 107, 130, 135, 140
Perl, 103, 234
person, 15, 55, 127, 278
phenogrammar, 40
phonological phrase, *see* constituent, prosodic
phonological word, *see* constituent, prosodic
phonology, 5–9, 11, 25, 34, 140, 165, 184, 268, 271
    lexical, 36, 119
    prosodic, 74
phonotactic, 23, 155
polysynthetic, 99
position class, 12, 14, 18, 37, 59, 60, 74, 89, 118–124, 126, 128
predicate cleft, 176, 177
prosodic hierarchy, 25
Prosodic Morphology Hypothesis, *see* morphology, prosodic
Protégé, 103
Python, 103

R, 103, 254
rara, 27, 34, 113, 157, 269
RDFLib, 103
reciprocal, 46, 89, 135, 148, 151–155, 225
recursion, 150
reduplication, 11, 266
relations, taxonomic, *see* taxonomic relation
repair, 50, 65, 69, 71–73, 90, 91, 107, 109, 114, 126, 140, 152, 157, 164, 184, 191, 197, 252, 254, 255, 265, 279, 280, 282
    insertion, 71, 72, 152, 184, 197, 252, 279
repeated morph constraint, *see* constraint, repeated morph
Resource Description Framework, 102, 103
restkomponente, 47, 76, 77, 126–129, 136, 141, 146, 148, 164, 197, 202, 205, 208, 210, 276, 279, 282
Role and Reference Grammar, 21

Term index

root, 11, 14, 36, 38, 40, 57, 70, 72, 80, 106, 111, 112, 114, 118, 119, 124–126, 130, 133, 135, 136, 139–141, 143, 144, 146, 158–160, 177

sampling, 5, 53, 79, 97, 98, 100, 104, 215, 230, 254, 257, 259–261, 268
Satzklammer, 208
segment, 2, 10, 16, 23, 24, 29, 44, 45, 65, 70, 74, 88, 119, 124, 140, 156, 159–165, 227, 228, 252, 266, 274, 276
Semantic Web, 101, 102
semantics, 14, 70, 72, 80, 121, 142–144, 150–152, 173, 174, 177, 178, 186, 194
shadings, 62
significative absence, 36, 37, 121, 125
similarity flooding, 233, 234, 238, 240, 241, 243, 247, 250, 251
simUI, 223, 224, 233, 234
span, 76, 77, 84, 85, 93, 99, 107, 126, 139, 162–164, 168, 188, 202, 235, 236, 244, 252, 253, 256, 257, 262, 269, 277
SplitsTree4, 227
stability, 54, 58, 62, 236, 260, 273, 279, 282
stem, 2, 10, 37, 40–42, 58, 59, 67–74, 80, 82, 88, 90, 106, 107, 111, 113, 118–121, 131–134, 139, 140, 142, 150, 154–168, 172, 175, 212, 217, 221, 222, 225, 227, 277
stricture, 44, 47, 51, 52, 65, 66, 73–75, 78, 84, 94, 99, 107, 114, 115, 142, 182, 183, 185, 190, 221, 224, 230, 250, 254–257, 262, 264, 269, 276, 280–282
string, 6, 268
subcategorization, 20
subject, 17–19, 37, 41, 46, 79, 178, 192–195, 197, 199, 200, 202, 203, 233, 277
suppletion, 28, 160, 175
support, 68, 75–78, 80, 82, 84, 93, 108, 114, 115, 117, 127, 128, 141, 142, 144, 146, 149, 160, 164, 183, 184, 188, 189, 197, 202, 205, 208, 211–213, 236, 242, 247, 262, 276, 277, 282
syllable, 12, 16, 17, 23, 35, 43, 54, 55, 69–72, 74, 77, 90, 106–111, 114, 120, 140, 180, 181, 219, 227, 252, 256, 269, 274, 277
syntax, 5–8, 17–21, 25, 28–30, 32, 34, 40, 41, 47, 59, 91, 99, 118, 151, 168, 173, 181, 203, 261, 268, 271

tagmemic, 12, 18
taxonomic relation, 93, 126, 279, 280, 282
taxonomy, 93, 94, 208, 276
tectogrammar, 40

template, 1–14, 16, 17, 19–24, 26–35, 38, 39, 41–44, 46–48, 50, 52–57, 60, 62–96, 98, 99, 101, 103–109, 113–122, 125–127, 129–131, 135–139, 141, 142, 144–154, 156–170, 172, 174, 180–193, 196, 197, 200, 202–205, 207, 208, 210–212, 214, 216, 217, 219–222, 224, 226–232, 234, 235, 242–253, 255–257, 259–271, 273–282
   clausal, 79, 196–209, 211, 217, 218, 225, 228, 230, 247
   constructional, 21, 22, 170, 183, 278, 281
   length, 70, 74, 79, 82, 84, 88, 99, 157, 159, 168, 191, 229, 256, 269
   morphological, 7, 151, 168
   morphophonological, 9–11, 13, 15, 20, 25, 29, 30, 35, 41, 73, 88, 162, 168, 182
   morphosyntactic, 12–16, 20, 22, 23, 34, 36, 44, 66, 118, 120
   nominal, 191
   order, 74, 75, 79, 87, 126, 157, 160, 187, 197, 256, 282
   phonological, 16, 17
   phonosyntactic, 20, 182, 187
   semantic, 19
   syntactic, 3, 17–20, 169, 271
   verbal, 2, 120, 126–129, 191, 225, 230
templatic, 1, 3, 4, 6–9, 11–17, 19, 20, 22, 24–40, 43–49, 51–60, 62–76, 78, 79, 82, 85, 87–94, 97, 99, 100, 103–107, 109–111, 113–115, 117, 118, 120, 121, 126, 130–132, 134, 136, 140–142, 144, 146–148, 150–152, 154–157, 162, 163, 165–168, 170, 173, 174, 178–183, 185, 186, 188–191, 193–195, 197, 200, 203, 204, 206–208, 210, 211, 214–217, 219, 220, 223, 225, 227–229, 232, 233, 235, 242, 243, 250, 254, 255, 259–271, 273–276, 279, 281, 282
tense, 2, 10, 12, 41, 55, 118, 121, 170, 186, 197, 210, 269, 277
terminology, 23, 40, 43, 47, 76, 77, 96, 114, 124, 139, 267
tone, 23, 72, 176, 180, 181, 183, 193
topic, 190, 203–205, 278
topicalization, 80, 82, 84–87, 108, 109, 136, 174–177, 190–192, 225, 278
triple, 102
typological, 2–5, 11, 25–27, 30–35, 37–39, 44, 46–48, 51–54, 56, 59, 64–67, 74–76, 85, 88–91, 93–98, 100–106, 111, 114, 115, 119, 125, 126, 129, 130, 139, 141, 147, 150, 151, 154, 160, 163–165, 167, 169, 178, 183–185, 188, 189, 199, 203, 207, 217, 219, 221, 232–234, 243, 250, 251,

322 Term index

253, 254, 256, 257, 259, 262–264, 268, 272, 277
typology, 1, 4, 5, 28, 35, 46, 96, 97, 105, 216, 217, 243, 257, 258, 260, 262, 271
  Canonical, 48, 52, 160
  constructional, 46
  descriptive, 35, 216
  quantitative, 103, 238, 251, 257, 264

unaccusative, 175, 178, 179
unergative, 175, 178, 179
universal grammar, 4
universals, 4, 43, 216, 219, 220, 253
  implicational, 88, 253, 254, 257
  statistical, 217, 221, 251, 257, 259

verb, 1, 9, 13, 14, 18, 19, 25, 30, 35, 36, 41–43, 57, 58, 60, 63, 66–68, 70–75, 80, 82, 90, 91, 94, 105–107, 109, 111, 114, 117–136, 139–144, 148, 150–152, 155–167, 169–181, 183, 184, 191–197, 199–205, 207, 208, 210–212, 221, 222, 227, 228, 230, 233, 260, 261, 265–267, 269–271, 277
  auxiliary, 41, 185, 186, 195–197, 199–202, 210, 278

finite, 18, 19, 60, 170, 171, 179, 210, 261, 277
infinitive, 42, 67, 172, 175, 178, 179, 210
verb phrase, 19, 105, 169–174, 180–184, 193, 212, 214, 225, 228
verb-second, 18, 33, 40, 60, 91, 92, 159, 185, 187–190, 199, 207, 208, 210
violability, 65, 69, 72, 73, 94, 107, 114, 142, 150–152, 162, 164, 184, 197, 221, 250, 254, 255, 276, 280, 282
voussoir, 76, 77, 80, 82, 114, 115, 117, 136, 141, 142, 144, 146, 148, 160, 164, 197, 202, 205, 208, 211–213, 262, 264, 277, 282
vowel, 9, 10, 23, 74, 157, 162, 165, 269

well-formedness, 16
word order, 5, 20, 24–26, 30, 34, 41, 43, 44, 52, 53, 73, 185, 189, 193, 194, 199, 216, 262, 265, 267
Word-and-Paradigm model, 45
World Atlas of Language Structures, 102
World Loanword Database, 102

zero morphemes, *see* significative absence

CPSIA information can be obtained
at www.ICGtesting.com
Printed in the USA
LVHW011711030619
619993LV00016B/428/P